Class and Merit in the American High School

D1248508

Educational Policy, Planning, and Theory

Series Editor: Don Adams, University of Pittsburgh

Class and Merit in the American High School

AN ASSESSMENT OF THE REVISIONIST AND MERITOCRATIC ARGUMENTS

Richard A. Rehberg
State University of New York at Binghamton

Evelyn R. Rosenthal
State University of New York at Binghamton

Longman

New York and London

Class and Merit in the American High School: An Assessment
of the Revisionist and Meritocratic Arguments

Longman Inc., New York

Associated companies, branches, and
representatives throughout the world.

COPYRIGHT © 1978 BY Longman Inc.

All rights reserved. No part of this publication may be
reproduced, stored in a retrieval system, or transmitted
in any form or by any means, electronic, mechanical,
photocopying, recording, or otherwise, without the prior
permission of the publisher.

Developmental Editor: Nicole Benevento
Design: Pencils Portfolio, Inc.
Manufacturing and Production Supervisor: Louis Gaber
Composition: Maryland Linotype
Printing and Binding: The Maple Press Company

Library of Congress Cataloging in Publication Data

Rehberg, Richard A
  Class and merit in the American high school.

  (Educational policy, planning, and theory)
  Includes index.
    1. High schools—United States.   2. Academic
achievement.   2.   Ability grouping in education.
I.   Rosenthal, Evelyn R.   II.   Title.
LB2822.R44   373.73   77-17656
ISBN 0-582-28013-3

MANUFACTURED IN THE UNITED STATES OF AMERICA

To my colleague Walter E. Schafer, and to my wife Pat, from whom I have learned that social science must be made relevant to the plight of humankind.

—R.A.R.

With love to Bernie, Dan, Laura, and Helen.

—E.R.R.

B+T 3/13/79 $ 8.95

CONTENTS

PREFACE

Social and economic inequality has been a dominant concern of social science throughout the 1960s and '70s. Much of this concern focuses on schooling as economists and sociologists seek to reach a better understanding of how the educational process can mitigate inequality.

The research in this book is about schooling and inequality. The use of schooling as a vehicle by which an individual can move from his or her social class of origin into a higher social class of destination necessitates, at minimum, that progress through school as well as the number of school years ultimately attained be as free as possible from social-class restrictions. Equality of educational opportunity requires that merit rather than social class primarily determine success in school. A student's grades, curriculum location, and entry into college must be influenced more by scholastic ability, educational ambition, and academic achievement than by the occupational and educational characteristics of his parents. This is the main issue around which we have constructed our text. What we assess is the degree to which both social-class origin and individual merit influence the individual's progress through school.

Two groups of scholars have guided our thinking about this issue. The first group are those investigators who have pioneered and refined the method and substance of what has come to be known as research on the process of status attainment or socioeconomic achievement. No enumeration of these scholars would be complete without mention of Peter Blau and Otis Dudley Duncan, of William Sewell, Robert M. Hauser, David Featherman, Archibald Haller, Duane Alwin, and Michael Carter, and of Karl Alexander and Bruce Eckland. The second group of scholars consists of critical theorists, individuals who raise fundamental questions about, and seek to revise, the basic social and economic structures of the U.S. capitalistic system and the role that schooling plays in it. Important in this regard are Herbert Gintis, Samuel Bowles, Martin Carnoy, and Michael Katz.

No significant change in our conception of social and economic inequality in American society as a whole emerges from our inquiry. Our research was not designed to address an issue of such broad scope and consequence. Moreover, as such scholars as Raymond Boudon advance our understanding of the relationship between inequality of educational opportunity and inequality of social opportunity, we come reluctantly but inevitably to the conclusion that inequalities in the larger social and economic system may well persist even as inequalities in the smaller and better-defined educational system decline.

What does emerge from our inquiry is a somewhat altered conception of our schools and colleges. At least at the level of the individual student, we find little evidence that is consistent with the critical theorists' view of the schools as institutions of strong social-class bias. Pat Sexton's proposition that "if you know a child's class status, you can quite accurately predict what will happen to him in school" is simply without empirical foundation.

Contributions to the research project around which this book is written have been made by many individuals. We express our appreciation to all of them and regret that we can name but a few. Obviously, a debt of gratitude is due to all 2,788 persons who had the courtesy and patience to complete our questionnaires not just once, but two, three, and four times. And, our gratitude to the school superintendents, principals, teachers, and guidance counselors who cooperated with us, year after year, in administering the survey questionnaires and helping us locate so many of these individuals after they left high school.

On a more personal note, our deepest appreciation is extended to Judy Sinclair, Maria Romanowski, and Mary C. Conklin, our research assistants, who gave unstintingly of their time, talent, and efforts in the coding of the data, in the computer management and analysis of the data, and in the execution of the highly successful postsecondary mail survey, which succeeded in reaching almost 90 percent of the original sample.

Thanks, too, to those students who, as undergraduates and graduates, excited the principal investigator to continue with the project and who received their first extensive introduction to the sociology of education through their work with this project. Ivan

Charner and Michael Cohen, both now with the National Institute
of Education, are most memorable in this regard.

Funds for the project have come from several agencies of the
federal government. Our thanks to the National Science Foundation,
to the National Institute of Mental Health, and to the National
Institute of Education for their continued support of this project.

Finally, our thanks to the continued efforts and interest of
William MacArthur, who did much of the computer programming
for the project, and to Ms. Judy Gaumer, who typed the manuscript.

Class and Merit in the American High School

1. THE ISSUES:
The Revisionist and
Meritocratic Arguments

We are concerned, in this inquiry, more with schools than with education and more with the role of society within the schools than with the role of schools in society. Our unit of analysis is the individual student, and our objective is to assess empirically the truth value of two contradictory arguments that have been advanced with regard to the determinants of student progress within the schools. One argument, the *revisionist* argument as we refer to it, asserts that the predominant influence on an individual's progress in school is the social class of his or her family. The other argument, the *meritocratic* argument as we refer to it, asserts that while social class may influence the progress of a student, merit, in the form of ability, ambition, and achievement, plays a role that may equal or even exceed that of social class.

THE CONTEXT OF THE INQUIRY

Ever since the birth of this nation more than two hundred years ago, Americans have cherished the belief that an individual's life chances are determined more by ability, ambition, achievement, and personal desire than by social-class origin. Merit, not social class, determines one's success.

For more than a century after the founding of the nation, whether the life chances of the individual were determined more by merit than by social class was an issue that could be argued virtually without reference to the schools. Economic enterprises were large in number and small in size. Economic and social success were responsive to an individual's entrepreneurial spirit and ability, and whether one succeeded was almost independent of whether one was schooled.

With the rise of large industrial and commercial entities toward

1

the turn of the present century, the opportunity for individual entre-
preneurship diminished; those opportunities that remained became
ever more dependent upon access to large amounts of venture capital.
Moreover, as the size of enterprises expanded, occupational tasks
became more routinized and specialized, and access to jobs, especially
the more prestigious jobs, increasingly required the ability to manipu-
late symbols and people rather than things. Formal schooling began
to replace entrepreneurial activity as the route to success for many,
if not most, people. From the 1900s onward, any discussion of whether
life chances were determined more by class than by merit was an
issue that could be argued only if reference was made to the schools.[1]

Our inquiry is about schools and about the absolute and relative
influences that class and merit play in an individual's schooling experience. Our concerns are with such issues as these: Is it the social
class of the student's family or the scholastic ability of the student
that has more to do with his being located in the college-preparatory
curriculum in the ninth or tenth grade? Is it family social class more
than student scholastic ability and educational influence from parents
and friends that determines the student's level of ambition for education beyond high school? Is it family class or student ability and
ambition that influences the guidance counselor to encourage the
student to enter college rather than the job market? Is it class or
ability plus ambition that determines the student's level of academic
achievement? And is it the social position of the family or the
ability, educational ambition, and academic achievement of the
student that influence the student's decision as a twelfth grader and
his actual behavior one year later vis-à-vis entry into a four-year
college, a two-year college, or the job market?

Thus our inquiry is more about the school than about education.
Our chief concern is with the social and psychological processes
that operate on the student within the institution that organizes
teaching and learning, not with how much of what is learned and
under what kind of teacher and classroom conditions.

We have also said that our inquiry is more about the role of
society within the schools than it is about the role of schools within
society. Much has been written about the role of schools in the larger
society, particularly about school as an agency through which
government might seek to reduce existing social inequality.[2] Our
concern is not with the broad issue of the school as an instrument of

egalitarian social policies.[3] Certainly that is an issue of consummate importance, but it has been considered in great detail by other social commentators and is beyond the more limited scope of our inquiry. Our focal point is the extent to which the social inequalities of the larger society intrude into the school, i.e., the extent to which the experience of the student *within* the school is determined by the social position of his family in the unequal social system *outside* of the school.

We accept, for purposes of this inquiry, that inequalities of access to power, political influence, health care, legal services, and the like exist in U.S. society; this is a proposition whose truth can be taken for granted.[4] Similarly we accept that the social system of the school mirrors, in many respects, that of the larger society.[5] But while these two propositions give rise to the hypothesis that the social inequalities that organize experiences among people in the larger society also organize the experiences of students within the school, such an hypothesis is subject to empirical verification. This inquiry plans to test that hypothesis with empirical data. The primary source of those data is from a longitudinal study conducted by Richard Rehberg between 1967 and 1971. Some 2,788 young people participated in that study. Initial data were gathered from individuals with a survey questionnaire in 1967 when they were ninth-grade students in a number of school systems in the southern tier of New York State. Subsequent surveys were conducted when the students were in tenth grade, when they were in twelfth grade, and in 1971 when the over-whelming majority had completed their secondary education. Throughout our inquiry we supplement and compare the results of analyses of our own sample with the published findings of a number of other investigators. Some of those other inquiries used regional samples of youth in the U.S., as we did; others employed national samples of American youth. One study used a large sample of youth from one of the provinces of Canada.

THE ARGUMENTS: MERITOCRATIC AND REVISIONIST

Two sets of arguments have been advanced over the past decade or so, primarily but not exclusively by social scientists, regarding the respective roles of social class and merit within the school. One group of social scientists, composed almost entirely of sociologists, is sensitive to the role of social class within the school but regards that role as limited. Many of these individuals have conducted empirical research using data from the school systems of North America from the mid-1950s to the present. The general framework for much of that research has been the study of intergenerational social mobility— the extent to which the ultimate social class of individual adults differs from their social class of birth. The object of that research has been to account for such mobility in terms of specific social and psychological variables. Most of the data necessary to explain social mobility have been gathered from individual respondents, often from the time when they were in high school. As we have noted already, throughout the twentieth century schooling has been viewed as a critical element in social mobility, and the nation's high schools have provided researchers with large numbers of literate individuals in a semicaptive setting; many of them have been willing to complete survey questionnaires about their home and school experiences that may help to account for their intergenerational social mobility. Data obtained from these questionnaires have usually been supplemented with such information from official school records as scholastic ability and academic performance. Other information has often been gathered from the individual at one or more points in time following graduation from high school.

From their analyses social scientists of this first group have developed estimates of the extent to which social-class origin affects progress through school and entry into college. They have detected social-class effects that, although not large in size, have brought forth expressions of professional and personal concern. William Sewell, one of the most prominent investigators of the role of schooling in social mobility, reported at the 1971 Annual Meeting of the American Sociological Association:

> With occupational selection, training, and certification carried out mainly through the schools, and particularly in post-secondary institutions, life chances will not be equal until opportunities for advanced education are equal. The extent to which opportunities for higher education are contingent on characteristics of social origin that are not relevant to learning—most notably sex, socioeconomic origins, race and ethnic background—is a matter of great importance to the study of social stratification and a pressing problem to a society that stresses equality of opportunity as a national goal.[6]

While professionals are concerned about the existence of *any* class effect in the school process, few social scientists in this first group regard the existence of class-based inequalities in schooling as endemic to the larger social system, necessary for its continued functioning, or impervious to enlightened social policies. Moreover, few, if any, of these social scientists magnify the size of the class effect on individual school experience. Seldom do they refer to that effect as "large," "strong," or "powerful." They realize that almost any measure of social class leaves about two-thirds of the variance in school-related criteria *un*accounted for, so they feel that strong adjectives are unwarranted. Finally, many of these social scientists recognize the existence of determinants of the individual's schooling experience other than social class. Prominent among such other determinants are scholastic ability, ambition for formal education beyond high school, and academic achievement. When these social scientists compare the effects of class and merit on the individual's schooling experience they tend to conclude that both class *and* merit influence how well an individual does in school and how far he goes in school, and that class is not dominant over merit in the nation's educational system. Based on his analysis of the mobility experience of a large number of American males, sociologist Otis Dudley Duncan appraised the respective roles of class and merit, indicated only by ability, in U.S. society this way:

> The American ideal of equal educational opportunity is realized in the white population to the extent that progress through the grades of the school system is influenced at least as much by how bright you are as by "who" you are; that the latter, indexed by measures of family size and status, does make a substantial difference in educational outcome apart from its correlation with intelligence, is an indication that the ideal is far from being completely realized at this time.[7]

For lack of a better term, we refer to the thesis that we believe best characterizes the research produced by this first group of scholars as the *meritocratic* thesis. Sociologist David Goslin perhaps captures the essence of this thesis when he writes:

> From the standpoint of the school in general, the trend appears to be toward a greater degree of social differentiation and structure, along

the lines of ability and achievement, as opposed to the traditional bases of social class, race, or religious group affiliation. . . . The school affords individuals from all racial, ethnic, and class backgrounds an opportunity to continue their education and eventually to get a job that is commensurate with their abilities and training.[8]

Opposed in many respects to those who regard the individual's school experience as shaped by both class and merit is a second group of scholars, composed of sociologists, educators, psychologists, historians, and political economists.

An early warning about class effects in the schools was sounded in the mid-1940s by sociologist W. Lloyd Warner. After studying the schools of Yankee City, he wrote:

The evidence is clear that the class system of Yankee City definitely exercises a control over the pupil's choices of curricula. . . . The children of the two upper and the upper-middle classes, in overwhelming percentages, were learning and being taught a way of life which would fit them into higher statuses. On the other hand, the lower-middle and the lower-class children, in their studies in the high school, were learning a way of life which would help adjust them to the rank in which they were born.[9]

More recently, psychologist Kenneth Clark has charged that "American public schools have become significant instruments in the blocking of economic mobility and in the intensification of class distinctions." [10] An even bolder claim has been advanced by sociologist Patricia Cayo Sexton, who has asserted that "if you know a child's class status . . . you can quite accurately predict what will happen to him in school and how successful he will be." [11]

Amid the disenchantment with American institutions that arose in the 1960s, a group of young scholars emerged whose perceptive and articulate critical commentaries on the schools began to give a sense of theoretical cohesion to what had appeared to be informed but ideologically disparate criticisms of schools as class-biased institutions.

Social class, many of these younger critics argued, exercises a strong and perhaps dominant influence over the student's school experience. As one proponent of this point of view, Martin Carnoy, argues, the pervasive and marked effect that a student's class background has on his school experience is deliberate and necessary for the continued existence of the larger social system. It is also necessary that people be beguiled into believing that within the schools students are not discriminated against on the basis of class origins but, rather, on the basis of their ability to perform academically.

> Who gets this schooling? . . . In capitalist economies (and in many postrevolutionary state capitalist economies as well), schooling goes to those children whose parents are wealthy, have high education, or high social status. The school system is ostensibly a meritocracy— grades, not parental background, determine who goes to the higher levels—yet factors outside the school are so important in influencing children's school performance, aspiration, and motivation, that social class is still the most important variable in predicting *how far* a person gets in school. This is no accident. The school system is structured, through its tests, reward system, and required behavior patterns, to allow children of an urban bourgeoisie to do well, and to filter out children of the poor, who are not socialized to function in the highest echelons of a capitalist economy and bourgeois culture. The school system is therefore a mechanism to maintain class structure in a capitalist society. It is a legitimate institution, accepted by all classes in the society (on the belief that it *is* genuinely meritocratic), for passing social position from generation to generation.[12]

Only through a revision of educational history, assert members of this second group of scholars, will the true functions of schools in a capitalist society come to be understood. Such a revision would show, as the revisionist educational historian Michael Katz has written, that schooling has not been the "great engine for identifying talent and matching it with opportunity," but that it has treated "children as units to be processed into particular shapes and dropped into slots roughly congruent with the status of their parents."[13] This second group of scholars we shall refer to as the *revisionists*. We now take a closer look at each of these theses.

The Meritocratic Thesis

Prior to the turn of the century, secondary schools in the United States were relatively few in number. The adolescents who did attend high school, about 10 percent of all adolescents, received a classical education; more than 80 percent then proceeded to college.[14] This was the era of elite education for children of the elite. With the origin of these students mostly upper and middle class and their destination mostly college and the professions, there was little need for the secondary school to serve as an agency of selection and certification, that is, as an organization that sorted, channeled, and credentialed its clients into streams destined for college and the professions, for clerical and office work, or for factory and industrial employment.

Around 1900 however, the manpower needs of the nation began to change. Industrialization and urbanization were creating a demand for large numbers of persons with less than a college degree but with more than an elementary certificate. Large-scale immigration, the enactment of child-labor laws, and the increasing concentration of the population in urban areas provided the supply to meet this demand—contingent only upon the transformation of the system of secondary education from college preparation for the few to mass training for the many.[15] In this phase of American secondary education, the student body was no longer homogeneous.

> Many of the new students in school were in school unwillingly, in obedience to the new or more stringent state compulsory education laws; many came from poor, culturally impoverished homes and had modest vocational goals; many of these were the sons and daughters of recent immigrants, and seemed to observers very much in need of "Americanization." These new students posed new problems for secondary education; and these problems, and the answers which they engendered, transformed public secondary education, its philosophy, and its curriculum.[16]

Changing manpower needs coupled with the changing composition of the American population had thrust upon the schools, and especially upon the secondary schools, the new responsibility of producing individuals with a variety of specialized skills from a population that itself was of greater and greater ethnic and social-class diversity. To discharge this new responsibility, procedures had to be developed for selecting and allocating students in accord with their talents and interests. As Goslin has written of this function:

Not only do individuals differ significantly in their ability to benefit from various kinds of educational experiences, but in addition, the society must ensure a sufficient supply of trained manpower to fill each of the diverse positions necessary to its smooth functioning. Consequently, some means of differentiating among potential candidates for medical schools, college, vocational school, and an unlimited number of other more or less specialized educational opportunities is necessary. In addition to serving as a manpower proving and training ground, therefore, the school also fulfills an important function in screening individuals according to their abilities and occupational inclinations at various stages in their intellectual and physical development.[17]

In the meritocratic view, many of the new jobs created in the rapidly industrializing society were too complex and required too long a preparation time to be filled by individuals selected and allocated in accord primarily with their class or ethnic characteristics. Such criteria were also judged to be wasteful of human talent in that they tended to screen "in" incompetent persons who were from the more favored social classes and ethnic groups, while screening "out" competent persons of less favored class or ethnic origin.

What was needed was a procedure that would identify talent that was predictive both of educational and occupational success. The newly emerging testing movement within psychology provided a procedure: the intelligence test. We can picture, wrote a Michigan educator in 1921,

> . . . the educational system as having a very important function as a selecting agency, a means of selecting the men of the best intelligence from the deficient and mediocre. All are poured into the system at the bottom; the incapable are soon rejected or drop out after repeating various grades and pass into the ranks of unskilled labor. . . . The more intelligent who are to be clerical workers pass into the high school; the most intelligent enter the universities, whence they are selected for the professions.[18]

Schoolmen found evidence of the predictive power of IQ tests for purposes of occupational preparation soon after World War I with the publication of the results of the U.S. Army ability testing program. The results showed a definite association between intelligence and the occupational attainment of those who had served in the war. The association of intelligence with occupational attainment furthered the belief that the society was meritocratic, allocating jobs on the basis of intellectual competence. The credibility of this understanding was strengthened in the 1920s with the advent of the Barr scale, a listing of more than a hundred representative occupations, each of which was rated in accord with the amount of intelligence it was thought to demand. Recently, Duncan compared the intelligence ranking of occupations on the Barr scale with two measures of social status. Using his own socioeconomic index (derived from 1950 census data on the income and educational attainments of people in an extensive range of occupations) and a scale of occupations arrayed in order of the prestige attributed them by a sample of the American public, he found a close correspondence between "intelligence-demands" and "status-prestige" rankings of occupations. His interpretation of this close correspondence is meritocratic in implication:

> [T]he psychologist's concept of the "intelligence demands" of an occupation is very much like the general public's concept of the prestige or "social standing" of an occupation. Both are closely related to the independent measures of the aggregate social and economic status of the persons pursuing an occupation. In short, we suggest . . . that "intelligence" is a socially defined quality and this social defini- tion is not essentially different from that of achievement or status in the occupational sphere. . . . If, as sociologists believe, the occupational role is a central element in the structure of a differentiated society, the abilities required for satisfactory performance of that role must be fairly directly involved in the achievement of occupational status.[19]

From the 1930s to the early 1960s, the use of standardized ability tests grew almost continuously. Goslin, who studied the expansion of these testing procedures, attributed their widespread use to

> . . . the urgency that is felt to make sure that no child fails to receive educational opportunities commensurate with his talents. The roots of this sentiment are both utilitarian and equalitarian; utilitarian in the sense that educators and the public alike are aware of the im-

portance of making maximum use of available talent . . . and equalitar-
ian in the sense that there is a consciousness of the national ideal of
equal opportunity for all.[20]

A second measure used by schoolmen to identify and select students
for one course of study or another was (and is) academic performance
or academic achievement. One advantage of academic performance
over and above intelligence testing alone is that a student's performance reflects not only some of the ability component tapped
by IQ tests, but a scholastic motivation component as well, which is
not fully measured by IQ tests. Indeed, in part this two-dimensional
structure of academic performance gives it a second advantage over
IQ tests alone: its superiority as a predictor of success in college,
precisely because it captures both ability and motivation.[21]
A third advantage of academic performance as a criterion for
talent selection is that most individuals—teachers, students and their
parents, members of the community—regard it as a legitimate yard-
stick with which to judge students. As sociologist Talcott Parsons observed in the 1950s there is a sense of equity about the use of academic
achievement as a criterion with which to differentiate students that
includes, above all,

> . . . recognition that it is fair to give differential rewards for different
> levels of achievement, so long as there has been fair access to oppor-
> tunity, and fair that these rewards lead on to higher-order oppor-
> tunities for the successful.[22]

And, continues Parsons, it is this aura of equity surrounding academic
performance as a criterion of talent selection that

> . . . performs a critical integrative function for the system. Differentia-
> tion of the [school] class along the achievement axis is inevitably a
> source of strain, because it confers higher rewards and privileges on one
> contingent than on another within the same system. This common
> valuation helps make possible the acceptance of the crucial differentia-
> tion, especially by the losers in the competition. The fact is crucial
> that the distribution of abilities, though correlated with family
> status, clearly does not coincide with it. There can then be a genuine
> selective process within a set of "rules of the game." [23]

Both scholastic ability and academic performance are quantitative criteria. Despite the motivational component in academic performance, neither ability nor performance allows for the explicit recognition of another and more qualitative element that Americans have long considered to be a part of the success ethos: *ambition*. In the context of a relatively open society, ambition is usually understood as a desire for social mobility, "a desire to abandon one social position and attain another." [24] Within the micro-environment of the secondary school, ambition usually assumes a more specific form—a desire to continue one's education beyond high school either to maintain one's advantaged social position or to achieve a social position superior to that into which one was born. It is within the school context that we use the term ambition, and by it we mean the educational ambition of the student: his intention or expectation to enroll in college after high school.

Only with the close of World War II did college become a symbol of ambition that extended beyond the elite minority for whom the university had always been a way of life. Thus, in the postwar period the era of terminal secondary education for the masses ended and the era of mass secondary preparation for college began.[25] A pent-up demand for college among those who had served the nation between 1941 and 1945, an expanding and increasingly complex economy, and the flow of substantial sums of money into higher education, in part through the "GI Bill," all contributed to what Trow has termed the second transformation of the high school—the conversion of that institution from terminal to college-preparatory education. In the period from 1940 to 1954, the percentage of 18–21 year olds in higher education doubled from 15 to 30 percent, and by 1960 it had risen by another 8 percentage points.

Driven by internal social and economic forces having their origins in the period immediately following the war and by such external factors as the launching of the Soviet Sputnik in 1957—an event that was interpreted as a "threat" to the scientific and technological preeminence of the United States—college-going during the 1950s and '60s became a source of pride to students and parents, teachers and counselors, school administrators and boards, and the nation itself. In and of itself, going to college symbolized talent, and the school system that managed to send a large portion of its graduating class to college each year was (and is) judged as an institution that maximizes the use of the nation's most precious resource: its talented youth. As Cicourel and Kitsuse observed in the high school they studied in the late 1950s, "The major criterion of the effectiveness of the high school's program for the development of talent is the proportion of its graduates who are admitted to colleges." [26]

In such an environment, the student who wanted to go to college (or could be persuaded to do so) was (and is) judged to be *ambitious* in a way that advanced the effectiveness of the organization and supported the personal values of teachers and counselors. Many school officials, after all, had come from families with above-average educational credentials,[27] had themselves used college as a vehicle to maintain or improve their station in life, and held to the belief that education was of great personal and national benefit.

Although not a criterion of the same genre as scholastic ability or academic performance, the educational ambition of the student assumed a degree of validity by virtue of its association with these two more established criteria. For, as counselors and teachers could easily observe, brighter students tended to be more likely to go to college just as did those with above-average academic performance.

Beyond the fact that the educational ambition of the student is related to his scholastic ability and to his academic performance, there is some evidence to suggest that a student's educational ambition is both a consequence of his ability and an antecedent of his academic performance. Sewell and Hauser[28] and Alexander and Eckland[29] have reported that brighter individuals are more likely than their less able counterparts to go to college, regardless of their social class. Boocock has interpreted several studies as indicating that, regardless of social class, the academic performance of students who plan on college is better than that of students who do not plan on college.[30] And Boyle has interpreted data from his study of high school youth as suggesting that students with college ambitions learn at a faster rate than those without such ambitions, again regardless of social class.[31] Goslin provides some understanding of this independent and positive effect of a college ambition on test scores for the *early school* years:

> [F]rom the standpoint of the child *who has any hopes or expectations of going on to college*, it is becoming increasingly important that he do well during the elementary grades, both on standardized tests and in

the classroom, in order to maximize his opportunities to receive special instruction, to be placed in an advanced group (if one exists), and to be permitted to enroll in college preparatory courses in junior high school and high school. His test scores are especially important if he wishes to be categorized as potential college material by his teachers, counselors, and principal—both current and future—since his record will follow him throughout his primary and secondary school experience.[32]

For the *later or secondary school years*, Cicourel and Kitsuse comment that the college or noncollege decision of students and their differentiation into academic and nonacademic curricula define

> . . . the standards of performance by which they are evaluated by the school personnel and by which [they] are urged to evaluate themselves. It is the college-going student more than his non-college going peer who is continually reminded by his teachers, counselors, parents, and peers of the decisive importance of academic achievement to the realization of his ambitions and who becomes progressively committed to this singular standard of self-evaluation.[33]

And Parsons, addressing himself specifically to the peer group of those who are headed for college writes:

> [T]hose clearly headed for college belong to peer groups which, while often depreciative of intensive concern with studies, also take for granted and reinforce a level of scholastic attainment which is necessary for admission to a good college. Pressure will be put on the individual who tends to fall below such a standard.[34]

Proponents of the meritocratic thesis, then, argue that progress in school proceeds along axes of both merit and class, the former often defined by the student's scholastic ability, educational ambition, and academic performance; the latter defined by the occupational and educational attainments of his parents. But class is not, they argue, the more powerful of those axes. A reasonable amount of scholastic ability, some ambition for higher education, and a record of above-average academic achievement can and does "compensate" for the lack of social-class privilege. As Goslin phrases the meritocratic case:

We conclude that education is the chief means by which the lower class individual . . . may improve his social position. In our achievement-oriented society, although ascribed characteristics of individuals [such as social class] still make a difference in one's chances for success, the school provides an important mechanism that allows high ability and motivation to find its own level in the occupational structure of the society.[35]

With such a representation of the schools and of schooling, proponents of the revisionist thesis take issue.

The Revisionist Thesis

In American society, the revisionists argue, schools

. . . produce and reinforce those values, attitudes, and affective capacities which allow individuals to move smoothly into an alienated and class-stratified society. That is, schooling reproduces the social relations of the larger society from generation to generation.[36]

Integrally linked with the other institutions of a capitalist society dependent upon exploitation, the schools have

functioned to control social change (to maintain order), to produce better labor inputs for more material output, and to transform individuals into competitive men and women who function well and believe in the capitalist system.[37]

Schools reproduce the social division of labor of the larger society from generation to generation because (1) it is within the capacity of the upper (ruling) class to preserve and legitimate an existing social order that serves their interests and (2) it is within the capacity of this class "to control the basic principles of school finance, pupil evaluation, and educational objectives." [38]

Inequalities in the quantity and quality of schooling available to the nation's youth are consequences of this contol. What generates these inequalities is the class structure and the class subculture typical of a capitalist society.

> Unequal education has its roots in the very class structure which it
> serves to legitimize and reproduce. Inequalities in education are a
> part of the web of capitalist society, and are likely to persist as long
> as capitalism survives.[39]

Quantitative inequality, say the revisionists, takes the form of
differences in years of formal schooling rooted in corresponding
social class differences.

> Children whose parents occupy positions at the top of the occupational
> hierarchy receive more years of schooling than working-class children.
> If we define social-class standing by income, occupation, and educa-
> tional level of the parents, a child from the 90th percentile in the
> class distribution may expect on the average to receive over four
> and a half more years of schooling than a child from the 10th
> percentile.[40]

Qualitative inequality occurs in the form of class-based differences
in the internal authority structure of the schools and in the content
of the curriculum. Inequalities in schooling, observes Bowles, "are
not simply a matter of differences in years of schooling attained or in
resources devoted to each student per year of schooling." Bowles
continues:

> Note the wide range of choice over curriculum, life style, and alloca-
> tion of time afforded to college students compared with the obedience
> and respect for authority expected in high school. Differentiation
> also occurs within each level of schooling. One needs only to compare
> the social relations of a junior college with those of an elite four-year
> college, or those of a working-class high school with those of a wealthy
> suburban high school, for verification of this point.[41]

Moreover, the manner in which teachers and school officials socialize students corresponds closely to the social-class composition
of the school, or so the revisionist theorists argue. The roots of such
socialization differences, suggests Bowles, are to be found in the fact
that the educational objectives and expectations

of both parents and teachers, and the responsiveness of students to various patterns of teaching and control, differ from students of different social classes. . . . [T]he financial conditions in poorly supported working-class schools militate against small intimate classes, against a multiplicity of elective courses and specialized teachers, . . . and preclude the amounts of free time for the teachers and free space required for a more open, flexible educational environment.[42]

Revisionist theorists, then, argue that the class-based social inequalities of the larger society, inequalities that are endemic to the capitalist system and necessary for its survival, intrude into the social system of the school with such force that social class becomes a primary axis defining both the content of the curriculum and the relationships among students, among officials, and between students and school officials.

Within the school, continue the revisionists, a number of mechanisms operate by which students are differentiated in accord with their social class of origin. They are taught, graded, and socialized accordingly, and passed on to the next level of schooling or to the job market with appropriate class-linked attitudes and behaviors and with the belief that they have received their due and just reward meted out legitimately as prescribed by the rules of the game. Four such mechanisms receive the attention of the revisionists: (1) the "hidden" curriculum, (2) tracking or curriculum location, (3) guidance counseling, and (4) grading and evaluation.

What is learned in the school that is of real importance to the student's future, asserts revisionist economist Herbert Gintis, is learned not from the manifest curriculum, which stresses *cognitive* skills, but from the "hidden" or latent curriculum, which stresses *affective* skills. Research shows, writes Gintis,

that the type of personal development produced through schooling and relevant to the individual's productivity as a worker in a capitalist enterprise is primarily *non-cognitive*. That is, profit-maximizing firms find it remunerative to hire more highly educated workers at higher pay, essentially *irrespective* of differences among individuals in cognitive abilities or attainments. . . . [T]he education-related

worker attributes that employers willingly pay for must be pre-
dominantly *affective* characteristics—personality traits, attitudes,
modes of self-presentation and motivation.[43]

By virtue of the structure of the social relations of the organization,
Gintis argues, schools teach and reinforce precisely those affective
attributes required by employers. Leverage for such reinforcement is
achieved through the coin of evaluation and certification. The hierarchical structure of schooling itself mirrors the social relations of
industrial production.

> [S]tudents cede control over their learning activities to teachers in
> the classroom. Just as workers are alienated from both the process
> and the product of their work activities, and must be motivated by
> the external reward of pay and hierarchical status, so the students
> learn to operate efficiently through the external rewards of grades
> and promotion, affectively alienated from the process of education
> (learning) and its product (knowledge).[44]

Differentiation of students into various programs of study is a
second mechanism by which, according to the revisionists, the schools
help to perpetuate the social-class inequalities of the larger social
system. Some students, usually those from middle-class backgrounds,
are placed in an academic program where they are prepared for
entry into college and thus into the ranks of professionals, managers,
and executives. Other students, usually those from working-class
backgrounds, are placed in nonacademic programs where they are
prepared, usually inadequately, for employment immediately after
leaving high school.

Addressing himself to the dilemma faced by the ruling classes in
an industrial society as to how both to provide greater quantities of
schooling for the ever expanding numbers of persons in an age of
technological growth and educational inflation while remaining able
to use schooling as the vehicle through which to pass privilege from
generation to generation, Carnoy observes that an historic solution
has been the use of a "dual" school system—private and exclusive
for the privileged, public and common for others. But, Carnoy
notes, the same purpose can be served with a single school system:

A vocational track parallel to an academic track serves the same purpose. The lower-social class children, because of their poorer grades, end up in the vocational track, thus being guaranteed an occupation as a factory worker or technician. Wealthier children enter the academic track, which gives them access to white-collar roles or to a university and the professions.[45]

Differential expectations by school personnel constitute yet a third mechanism by which schools help to ensure the continuation of class-based inequalities. Whether a *student* expects to enter college or the labor market, the revisionists believe, is strongly related to his class of origin. Middle-class students expect to enter college, working-class students expect to enter the job market. Whether a *teacher* or a *guidance counselor* expects a student to enter college or the labor market is strongly related to their perception of the student's social class of origin. Writes Bowles:

Schools reinforce other aspects of family socialization as well. The aspirations and expectations of students and parents concerning both the type and the amount of schooling are strongly related to social class. The expectations of teachers, guidance counselors, and school administrators ordinarily reinforce those of the students and the parents.[46]

Class stratification is thus achieved within the schools

. . . through tracking . . . and in the attitudes of teachers and guidance personnel who expect working-class children to do poorly, to terminate schooling early, and to end up in jobs similar to those of their parents.[47]

Between the teacher and the counselor, it is the counselor whom the revisionists would indict for their complicity in the Pygmalion-like self-fulfilling prophecy. The "growth of the guidance counseling profession," observes Bowles, has "allowed much of the channeling to proceed from the student's own well-counseled choices, thus adding an apparent element of voluntarism to the system." [48]

Finally, the grading system of the school functions not only to perpetuate *within* the school the class-based social inequalities of the larger society, but to legitimize those inequalities in the minds of students and parents as well, to induce them into accepting the social system as fair and just.

Excellence in the schools, according to Bowles, is defined "in terms by which upper class children tend to excel," and that, says Bowles, is "scholastic achievement." [49] Scholastic achievement, in turn, depends on mental or cognitive ability. And, cognitive ability depends on social class, or so writes Carnoy. "Cognitive ability," he argues, "is highly correlated with an individual's social class. . . ." [50] Consequently, deduces Bowles, defining excellence in terms by which upper-class children tend to excel, i.e., scholastic achievement,

> yields inegalitarian outcomes (e.g., unequal access to higher educa-
> tion) while maintaining the principle of fair treatment. Thus the
> principle of rewarding excellence serves to legitimize the unequal
> consequences of schooling by associating success with competence.[51]

All of this has the effect of allowing the larger social system to operate with a minimum of social disruption because, writes Carnoy: "If a person is convinced that he is *not able to do well*, he is less likely to rise up against the social system than if the person believes that the system is unfair and based on class." [52]

Thus is the argument joined between the meritocratic and revisionist theorists of schooling. We propose to examine this argument in some detail in the following chapters of this book. We shall not examine, because we do not have the necessary data, the "hidden curriculum" component of the revisionist perspective. In one sense, the omission of this component is a serious deficiency. In another sense, our inability to examine that particular aspect of the revisionist thesis would not seem to impair our efforts seriously. For, in our discussion of the revisionist thesis, we have attempted to show that an important and practical vehicle by which the schools ostensibly select which students are to be the objects of which socialization efforts is that of social class origin. Fundamental to the revisionist thesis, then, is the proposition that social class defines how well and how far a student will proceed and in what set of schooling experiences he will do so.

A SET OF SCHOOL-RELATED VARIABLES
COMMON TO BOTH THESES

Despite the basic difference between these two theses over the potency of social class in the schooling process, both perspectives define a more or less common set of variables that each has come to regard as pertinent to an understanding of the schooling process. Both meritocratic and revisionist theorists posit that the choice of *curriculum* has important ramifications for the student. *Peer influence* or friendship networks has been the object of considerable inquiry by meritocratic if not by revisionist scholars. *Guidance and counseling* has received the attention of researchers and commentators from each perspective. And, while the *educational ambition* or expectation of the student has been the subject of a number of extensive inquiries by meritocratic scholars, revisionist writers also seem to regard this as a potentially significant variable in the schooling process. Finally, *academic performance* occupies a position of import in both theses.

Given a set of such individual-level school-process variables common to the theoretical perspectives of both sets of scholars, it is possible to proceed to an assessment of the relative truth values of the two perspectives. That assessment requires, *at minimum*:

1. An estimate of the magnitude of the total causal effect of class background on the school-process variables.
2. An estimate of the magnitude of the total causal effect of scholastic ability and other indicators of merit on the school-process variables.

Inasmuch as the revisionist thesis posits that the effect of class background on student progress through school is strong, pervasive, and greater than that of any other variable, unequivocal empirical support for the tenability of the revisionist argument would seem to require finding:

1. The total causal effect of class background is strong or powerful—in an absolute sense.
2. The total causal effect of class background is greater than that of any other explanatory variable in the model.

Less unequivocal but still persuasive support for the revisionist argument would require that the total causal effect of class origin, while not necessarily strong or powerful in any absolute sense, still exceeds the total causal effect of any other explanatory variable.

The meritocratic thesis, as noted, does not deny that class origin influences the student's progress through school. But it does deny that the influence of class is strong or powerful in the absolute sense. The meritocratic thesis would also seem to deny the possibility that the total causal effect of class exceeds that of any other explanatory variable, although class itself may not generate an effect that is strong in the absolute sense. What the meritocratic thesis affirms is the importance of ability, ambition, and achievement on student progress. Seldom, if ever, do advocates of this thesis freely speculate about the magnitude of the effects they would accord to these indicators of merit. Unequivocal empirical support for the meritocratic conception of schooling, then, would require finding:

1. The total causal effects of the indicators of merit are at least moderate in absolute magnitude.
2. The total causal effect of one or more of the indicators of merit exceed by a reasonable margin the total causal effect of class origin.

Less unequivocal but still persuasive support for the meritocratic thesis would require that the total causal effect of one or more of the indicators of merit be at least somewhat greater than that of class origin.

DATA AND MODEL FOR THE ANALYSIS

As we observed, the primary data source for our assessment of the magnitudes of the effects of class background and merit in the schooling process is Rehberg's longitudinal study of 2,788 youth who, in 1967, were ninth-grade students in seven urban and suburban, public and parochial school systems in the southern tier of New York State. In the spring of 1967, in the spring of 1968, and again in the spring of 1970, printed questionnaires requiring approximately one hour to complete were administered, in school, to this cohort of students. In 1970–71, some six to nine months subsequent to the completion of high school, a mail survey was administered to the cohort to ascertain the postsecondary educational, occupational, military, and marital statuses of the respondents. Replies were received from 88 percent of the individuals who had participated in the first panel of the study in 1967.

To estimate the absolute and relative effects that social class and merit have on the progress of the student through high school and one year beyond into college or employment, we have constructed a fourteen-variable model that we believe to be an adequate representation of the schooling process from grade nine to the year following grade twelve.

In the chapters that follow, after a section describing the design and procedure of this inquiry, we analyze the effects that social class and merit have on the schooling experience of students more or less sequentially through high school and for the first post-high school year.

Our first efforts focus on the ninth grade, which we regard as a *year of exploration*, a period during which students seek and test various alternatives for their educational and occupational futures. The outcome of such exploration is a level of educational ambition—a realistic goal to enter a four-year college, a two-year college, or the labor market. That particular level of ambition is subject to effects from class origin and from scholastic ability. More middle-class and scholastically able students express college-level ambitions at the end of the ninth grade than do working-class students or the scholastically weak. We also see ambition as subject to effects from other variables that impinge upon the student during ninth grade. One set of such variables has its locus in the student's perception of parents' efforts to influence him to continue his education beyond high school. Students who perceive those efforts as strong are more likely than those who perceive them as moderate or weak to express an ambition to go to college. Moreover, the perception of such efforts itself is related to social class and scholastic ability: stronger parental educational influence is more characteristic of students from middle-class homes and of students who are above average in scholastic ability.

A second set of effects on ambition we locate in the student's curriculum. Those in the academic program are more likely than others to express a college-level ambition. And curriculum location itself is seen as affected by social class and scholastic ability: middle-class or scholastically able students are usually placed in the academic program. Similarly, parental educational influence has an effect on curriculum location. Students whose parents want them to go to college are more likely to be in the academic program than those who report little parental influence. Finally, the educational ambition level of the student at the end of ninth grade is subject to effects from close friends, i.e., from peers. Students with several peers who intend to go to college are more likely to have an ambition for college than students with few or no peers having college intentions. The number of friends the student has who intend to go to college itself is greater for students in the academic program, for students who report much educational influence from parents, for students from the middle class, and for students whose scholastic ability is above average.

Class and merit, as should be apparent from our description of the ninth-grade component of our model, operate in complex ways on the student. For example, each may affect a student's level of educational ambition *directly*, i.e., "straight through to ambition," and also *indirectly*, as when ability affects ambition by way of curriculum. That is, some of the relationship between ability and ambition may reflect the tendency for scholastically more able students to be in the academic program and for students in the academic program to have higher educational ambitions than those in the nonacademic program. Our model and the statistical method we employ permit us to capture some of that complexity. Thus we are able to estimate not only whether social class or merit affect the student more, but also *how* social class and merit affect the student.

Grade ten is the next phase of our analysis. By the end of tenth grade most students have a rather firm idea about what they will do after they leave high school. Those who intend to enter college, especially a four-year college, must choose courses that will prepare them for admission to the institution of their choice. They must, in other words, commit themselves to a given plan of action by the end of the tenth grade. We thus regard tenth grade as a year of *commitment*. Two variables receive our attention here: curriculum location and counselor educational encouragement. Both are subject to effects from all the variables described as operative in ninth grade. We concentrate our analysis, however, on selected determinants of these two measures. For tenth-grade curriculum location, we focus on the effects that ninth grade curriculum location, social class, scholastic ability, and educational ambition exert. For counselor educational encouragement, we focus on the effects of social class, scholastic ability, and educational ambition. We estimate the extent to which the educational encouragement that students report receiving from the counselor during the tenth grade is determined by social class, as the revisionists suggest, or by scholastic ability and educational ambition, as proponents of the meritocratic thesis say.

Academic achievement, measured as the student's cumulative grade-point average from grades nine, ten, and eleven, is the next object of our attention. Although we consider the effects that all the ninth- and tenth-grade variables have on this crucial criterion, our focus is once again on social class and merit. Do the grades that students receive depend more on social-class origins, as the revisionists assert, or on scholastic ability and educational ambition, as proponents of the meritocratic thesis would suggest?

The decision to enter college, a decision we regard as having been made by most students by the end of the twelfth grade, and actual entry into college, reported to us through a mailed questionnaire administered during the first year after high school, are the criterion measures whose determinants we analyze in the last two chapters. Again, although each of these measures is subject to effects from all the variables specified as operative earlier in the model, the priority of our analysis is the extent to which the decision to enter college and the actual entry into college is determined by social class or by scholastic ability, educational ambition, and academic achievement.

SEX: DOES IT MAKE A DIFFERENCE IN THE SCHOOLING PROCESS?

Most studies of schooling and social mobility have been inquiries into the determinants of the socioeconomic achievements of *males*. Alexander and Eckland's investigation, *Effects of Education on the Social Mobility of High School Sophomores Fifteen Years Later (1955–1970)*, is one of the more notable exceptions.[53]

Although we have not mentioned gender as a variable in our analysis, it indeed is. Throughout most of the text, we execute our analyses separately for males and for females. We note what we consider important within-sex differences in the rank-ordering of the determinants of the particular dependent variable under consideration. The analysis of gender differences, however, and their explanation and implications, are topics of sufficient complexity and importance that we have elected to dedicate an entire chapter to them. Social class may well be a variable from the larger social system that intrudes *less* into the social system of the school than does gender.

NOTES

1. An insightful discussion of the relationship of schooling to the economy is provided in Henry J. Perkinson, *The Imperfect Panacea: American Faith in Education, 1865–1965* (New York: Random House, 1968), esp. chapter 4, "Economic Opportunity and the Schools."

2. Perhaps the most influential and provocative work on the issue of schools and inequality in the twentieth century has been that by Christopher Jencks et al., *Inequality: A Reassessment of the Effect of Family and Schooling in America* (New York: Basic Books, 1972). A very readable account of the cost-effectiveness of education as an instrument with which to reduce poverty has been provided by Thomas I. Ribich in his *Education and Poverty* (Washington, D.C.: Brookings Institution, 1968). One of the most comprehensive assessments of the effectiveness of schooling as a policy tool for use against societal "ills," most often against the various forms of inequality, is the Rand educational policy study by Harvey A. Averch et al., *How Effective Is Schooling?* (Englewood Cliffs, N.J.: Educational Technology Publications, 1974).

3. A comprehensive overview of some of the issues associated with the use of schooling as an instrument of egalitarian social policy may be found in the collected papers of the Seminar on Education, Inequality, and Life Chances sponsored by the Organization for Economic Co-Operation and Development. See *Education, Inequality and Life Chances*, vols. 1 and 2 (Paris: Organization for Economic Co-operation and Development, 1975). A good collection of papers having to do with some of the economic, sociological, and philosophical dimensions of the broad issue of schooling and social inequality may be found in Donald M. Levine and Mary Jo Bane, eds., *The "Inequality" Controversy: Schooling and Distributive Justice* (New York: Basic Books, 1975).

4. For a perspective on social inequality and social stratification, see Edward O. Laumann, Paul M. Siegel, and Robert W. Hodge, *The Logic of Social Hierarchies* (Chicago: Markham, 1970).

5. The Norwegian scholar Johan Galtung sketches a number of similarities between the structure of the larger society and that of

28   CLASS AND MERIT IN THE AMERICAN HIGH SCHOOL

the schools in his essay "Schooling and Future Society," *School Review* 83 (August 1975): 533–68. A somewhat different and more elaborate approach to the issue of correspondence between the larger society and the schools may be found in Samuel Bowles and Herbert Gintis, *Schooling in Capitalist America* (New York: Basic Books, 1976).

6. William H. Sewell, "Inequality of Opportunity for Higher Education," *American Sociological Review* 36 (October 1971): 794.

7. Otis Dudley Duncan, "Ability and Achievement," *Eugenics Quarterly* 15 (March 1968): 8.

8. David A. Goslin, *The School in Contemporary Society* (Glenview, Ill.: Scott, Foresman, 1965), p. 113.

9. W. Lloyd Warner, Robert J. Havighurst, and Martin B. Loeb, *Who Shall Be Educated?* (New York: Harper & Brothers, 1944), p. 61.

10. Kenneth B. Clark, "Alternative Public School Systems," *Harvard Educational Review* 38 (Winter 1968): 101.

11. Patricia Cayo Sexton, *Education and Income* (New York: Viking, 1961), p. 42.

12. Martin Carnoy, *Education as Cultural Imperialism* (New York: McKay, 1974), pp. 323–24.

13. Michael B. Katz, *Class, Bureaucracy, and Schools* (New York: Praeger, 1971), p. xviii.

14. Martin Trow, "The Second Transformation of American Education," in *The School in Society*, ed. Sam D. Sieber and David E. Wilder (New York: Free Press, 1973), pp. 45–61.

15. Trow, "Second Transformation."

16. Ibid., p. 47.

17. Goslin, *School in Contemporary Society*, p. 108.

18. W. B. Pillsbury, "Selection—An Unnoticed Function of Education," *Scientific Monthly* 12 (January 1921): 71.

19. Otis Dudley Duncan, David L. Featherman, and Beverly Duncan, *Socioeconomic Background and Occupational Achievement: Extensions of a Basic Model* (Washington, D.C.: U.S. Office of Educa-

tion, Bureau of Research, Final Report, Project No. 5-0074 (EO-191), Contract No. OE-5-85-072, 1968).

20. Goslin, *School in Contemporary Society*, p. 110.

21. David E. Lavin, *The Prediction of Academic Performance* (New York: Russell Sage Foundation, 1965).

22. Talcott Parsons, "The School Class as a Social System: Some of Its Functions in American Society," reprinted in *Socialization and Schools* (Cambridge, Mass.: Harvard Educational Review, 1968), p. 81.

23. Ibid., pp. 82–83.

24. Ralph Turner, *The Social Context of Ambition* (San Francisco: Chandler, 1964), p. 3.

25. Trow, "Second Transformation."

26. Aaron V. Cicourel and John I. Kitsuse, *The Educational Decision Makers* (Indianapolis: Bobbs-Merrill, 1963), p. 144.

27. Dan C. Lortie, *Schoolteacher* (Chicago: University of Chicago Press, 1975).

28. William H. Sewell and Robert M. Hauser, *Education, Occupation, and Earnings: Achievement in the Early Career* (Madison: University of Wisconsin, Department of Sociology, 1974). A final report of research carried out under Grant No. 314, Social and Rehabilitation Service, Social Security Administration, U.S. Department of Health, Education, and Welfare.

29. Karl Alexander and Bruce K. Eckland, *Effects of Education on the Social Mobility of High School Sophomores Fifteen Years Later (1955–1970)* (Chapel Hill: Institute for Research in Social Science, 1973). Final Report, Project No. 10202, Grant No. OEG-4-71-0037. National Institute of Education, U.S. Department of Health, Education, and Welfare.

30. Sarane S. Boocock, *An Introduction to the Sociology of Learning*, (Boston: Houghton Mifflin, 1972), p. 61.

31. Richard P. Boyle, "Functional Dilemmas in the Development of Learning," *Sociology of Education* 42 (Winter 1969): 71–90.

32.   Goslin, *School in Contemporary Society*, p. 113. Italics added.

33.   Cicourel and Kitsuse, *Educational Decision Makers*, p. 146.

34.   Parsons, "School Class," p. 88.

35.   Goslin, *School in Contemporary Society*, pp. 125–26.

36.   Herbert Gintis, "Towards a Political Economy of Education: A Radical Critique of Ivan Illich's *Deschooling Society*," *Harvard Educational Review* 42 (February 1972): 86.

37.   Carnoy, *Education as Cultural Imperialism*, p. 5.

38.   Samuel Bowles, "Unequal Education and the Reproduction of the Social Division of Labor," in *Schooling in a Corporate Society*, ed. Martin Carnoy (New York: McKay, 1972), p. 56.

39.   Ibid., p. 37.

40.   Ibid., p. 46.

41.   Ibid., p. 49.

42.   Ibid., p. 50.

43.   Gintis, "*Towards a Political Economy*," p. 87.

44.   Ibid.

45.   Carnoy, *Education as Cultural Imperialism*, p. 324.

46.   Bowles, "Unequal Education," p. 58.

47.   Ibid., p. 50.

48.   Samuel Bowles and Herbert Gintis, "I.Q. in the U.S. Class Structure," *Social Policy* (November/December 1972 and January/February 1973): 80.

49.   Bowles, "Unequal Education," p. 60.

50.   Carnoy, *Education as Cultural Imperialism*, p. 364.

51.   Bowles, "Unequal Education," p. 60.

52.   Carnoy, *Education as Cultural Imperialism*, p. 253.

53.   Alexander and Eckland, "Effects of Education."

2. Design and Procedure

In the preceding chapter we discussed the *what* and the *why* of our inquiry. This chapter describes *how* we conducted our inquiry and is divided into four sections. First we describe the geographic, social, economic, and demographic characteristics of the region within which the students of our study lived and attended school. In the second section we discuss our reasons for selecting certain schools to participate in our inquiry and then detail the procedure used to administer the survey questionnaires in those school systems. We also note how many students participated in each of the four measurement panels and attempt to assess what consequences their nonparticipation may have had for the inquiry.

The third section of this chapter discusses each variable used in our study of social class, ability, ambition, and achievement in the American high school. Each variable is defined conceptually, i.e., in words, and operationally, i.e., in terms of the procedures used to measure that variable. We also note the percentage of students who did not give a response to that measure, the adjustments we made for "no responses," and then assess the consequences of those adjustments for the inquiry.

Finally, in the fourth section we describe the statistical tools chosen to analyze our data. Though this section may be somewhat technical, we consider it necessary reading for the individual who wishes to understand and to criticize the substance of our inquiry.

LOCATION OF PARTICIPATING SCHOOLS[1]

All seven school systems that participated in this study from its inception in 1967 are located in the urban and suburban area of Broome County, New York. In 1970 these seven systems served a population of 170,000, four-fifths that of the total county population of 222,000.

Geographically, these schools are located on the Allegheny Plateau, 181 miles northwest of New York City, 78 miles south of Syracuse, New York, and 55 miles north of Scranton, Pennsylvania. The schools are located in two river valleys: the minor valley is that of the southward flowing Chenango River which, at the City of Binghamton, empties into the major valley, defined by the southward flow of the Susquehanna River.

Culturally and historically, the county has a diverse, although predominantly Caucasian, population. There is a strong cultural legacy from eastern and southeastern Europeans who immigrated to the area prior to and around the turn of this century to seek work, mainly in the shoe factories of the Endicott-Johnson Company. The pre-1940 economic base of the county gave the area a distinctly blue-collar character. The post-World War II expansion of major scientific-technical companies such as IBM, General Electric, and General Precision, coupled with the growth of government services including the State University of New York at Binghamton, has transformed the region. Fifty-three percent of the county labor force is now classified as white-collar, 5 percent more than the 1970 census report for the entire United States.

The seven schools of our study reflect the rich sociocultural diversity of the area. Three of the public systems, as well as the one Roman Catholic private system, are located in the older urban areas of the county along the Susquehanna River—Binghamton, Endicott, and Johnson City—from which the region acquired the name "Triple Cities." Although none of the urban school systems suffers the dire problems so characteristic of many large inner-city schools, each serves a body of students that differs from those of the suburban districts by virtue of the somewhat higher proportion of blue-collar households in the urban districts.

The remaining three districts serve suburban communities, mostly of post-World War II construction. One district spans the urban-suburban continuum, drawing students whose backgrounds range from distinctly rural to split-level, low-density suburban to garden-apartment fringe urban. The two other districts are truly suburban communities of middle- and upper-middle-class managers and technocrats. One of these two communities is older and more sedate, with a somewhat larger percentage of private entrepreneurs and small businessmen; the other is newer, and many of its white-collar residents are employed by the technical-scientific corporations in the area.

Employment, Income, and Educational Characteristics

In 1970 about 91,000 persons were employed in the county. Manufacturing provided the largest number of jobs, about 36,000. One-fourth of these were with the area's largest employer, IBM. General Precision, designer of avionics simulation systems; Endicott-Johnson, producers of footwear; General Aniline and Film Corporation, makers of photographic supplies; and General Electric were other major private employers. Government provided some 17,000 individuals with employment at the federal, state, and local levels. Important components in this sector were the State University of New York at Binghamton and Broome Community College. Retail trade provided jobs for almost 12,000 persons, and the "service and miscellaneous" sector employed some 9,200 individuals.

Median family income for the county in 1969 was $10,338, ranking it sixteenth among the fifty-seven counties in the state.[2] As of 1970 almost 60 percent of the county population age 25 and over had graduated from high school, while 22 percent of that segment of the population had at least some college experience; 15 percent of the males and 8 percent of the females age 25 and over were graduates of four-year colleges or universities. Almost one in five employed persons was engaged in an occupation classified by the census as "professional, technical or kindred," with another 8 percent classified as "managers and administrators." Clerical and sales employees accounted for almost a fourth of all employed persons. Another quarter of the work force was categorized by the census in 1970 as in either "craftsmen, foremen and kindred" or "operative" occupations.

The Student Population

Of the 2,788 students who participated in the first panel survey as ninth graders in 1967, 99 percent classified themselves as white. This corresponds with the racial composition of the county, where only 1 percent of the population is nonwhite. More than nine students in ten reported that both their parents were alive, and 87 percent indicated that they lived with both parents. Of those living with only one parent, the majority reported living with their mother.

Somewhat more than half of the students come from middle-class or white-collar homes, to judge from their responses to questions about the occupational and educational attainments of the parents and the subsequent coding of those responses with the Hollingshead Two Factor Index of Social Position.[3]

Scholastically, the median and the mean intelligence quotients of the students are 109 and 110, respectively, about ten points higher than the national average of 100, but probably not atypical of schools outside the central city where students with serious intellectual impairments are segregated and provided with special courses of instruction.

As ninth graders, more than half the students reported that they were in an academic or college-preparatory curriculum. Almost two-thirds reported that in their homes it had been just about "taken for granted" that they would continue their education beyond high school. Four-fifths said that they realistically expected to continue their education beyond high school either to a two-year college (32 percent) or to a four-year college (48 percent). Four years later, during the first post-high school year, when 88 percent of these 2,788 individuals responded to our mailed questionnaire, 63 percent were engaged in some form of postsecondary schooling, with 33 percent enrolled in a two-year college and 30 percent in a four-year college.

For a large portion of the students, high school was viewed as necessary for the future if sometimes requiring almost robotlike compliance with the norms of the institution. Still, it was not entirely lacking in qualities that made the high school experience at least tolerable. By way of illustration, in response to a series of questions asked only in sophomore year, 92 percent of the students agreed that "what we do in school is essentially preparation for what will come later, the payoff will be in college or on the job"; 62 percent agreed that "the main reason for going to high school is to get the diploma, it is your passport to a good job or college." Nevertheless, 48 percent of these tenth graders agreed that "although I usually know what to do in school, I frequently don't know why I am supposed to do it," and 46 percent thought that "it's not important

what you really know, just look alert and give the right answers."
Also, 42 percent agreed that "too much of the work here is meaningless." Nevertheless, 83 percent felt of their respective schools that
they were "proud to be a student here," and 82 percent believed
that "the teachers and administrators here are working in my best
interests."

The County and the Nation

No claim is made for the generalizeability of our data beyond the
seven school systems in which the research took place. Nevertheless,
table 2.1 illustrates that the composition of the county population
does not differ dramatically from that of the nation, with two exceptions: the almost exclusively white population of the county and
the somewhat higher median income of that population. We have
no reason, therefore, to believe that our study population is atypical
except in its racial composition and its slightly higher median income.

**TABLE 2.1. Descriptive Profiles: Characteristics of Populations of
United States, Broome County, and This Study**

Characteristic	U.S. 1970	Broome Co. 1970	This Study 1967[a]
Population	203,184,772	221,815	2,788[b]
Percent change, 1960–70	13.3	4.3	
Residence, urban (in percent)	73.7	73.1	N.A.
Age (in percent):			
Under 15	28.5	28.2	N.A.
15–64	61.6	61.2	N.A.
65+	9.9	10.6	N.A.
Nonwhite Percent	25.6	1.4	1.0
Percentage Native-born:			
Native parents	82.1	80.4	N.A.
Foreign or mixed parents	13.0	15.0	N.A.
Percentage 14 and Over in Labor Force:			
Male	72.9	76.0	N.A.
Female	39.6	42.1	N.A.

TABLE 2.1.   (continued)

Characteristic	U.S. 1970	Broome Co. 1970	This Study 1967[a]
Percentage Civilian Labor Force Employed:			
Male	96.0	96.7	N.A.
Female	94.6	95.8	N.A.
Employment Status of Those 14 and Over:			
White collar	48.2	53.1	57.7[c]
Blue collar (including service)	48.7	46.2	42.3
Farm	3.1	.8	
Education of Those 25 and Over:			
Male:—Twelve years or less	75.9	73.2	62.7
Some college	11.7	11.2	12.8
Completed college or more	10.9	14.7	24.5
Female—Twelve years or less	81.3	81.2	70.9
Some college	11.3	10.6	17.0
Completed college or more	6.9	8.2	12.0
Median Income of Families, 1969	$9,590	$10,338	
School Enrollment (Ages 3–14) K–12:			
Public school	88.7	90.3	85.6
Private school	11.3	9.7	14.4

[a] Data are from questionnaire data, first panel, 1967.
[b] Population of 2,788 refers to the total number of students providing usable questionnaires in the first panel, 1967.
[c] Employment status derived from the Hollingshead seven-level occupational scale. White collar includes levels 1–4; blue-collar levels 5–7. Data computed for fathers only.

SELECTION OF SCHOOLS AND SURVEY PROCEDURE

In the fall of 1966 we contacted the superintendents of seven school districts in the Southern Tier area asking for their cooperation with a study of "adolescent career plans." As the dimensions of the study were explained to each superintendent, we emphasized our intention to monitor the "class of 1970" from its freshman year in 1967 through its senior year in 1970 and, possibly, beyond high school. Each of the superintendents agreed to participate, at least for the first-year phase of 1967. With the benefit of eight years' experience, we are able to say that cooperation has been forthcoming from each system, not only for the four-year period during which the students were actually in school, but also for the four years following their graduation, as occasions have arisen when there has been a need to gain access to students' records for additional data.

Selection of the school districts was guided by two criteria. First, we knew that a longitudinal study would require frequent communication with the participating schools. A modest research budget would permit such liaison only if the participating schools were located in proximity to our research office. Consequently, the districts selected were all within a forty-five-minute drive from the research office at the university. Second, within this locational constraint, we sought to maximize the between-system demographic diversity of the seven student bodies. Three of the systems thus selected served primarily the urban populations of the "Triple Cities." Largely, but not exclusively, urban were two Roman Catholic secondary schools. Essentially suburban in character, but also serving the rural fringe, were three systems on the periphery of the "Triple Cities," although each was well within the boundaries of the Standard Metropolitan Statistical Area.

Administration of Survey Questionnaires: 1967-71

During the winter of 1967 we arranged with the seven school systems for an April–May administration to all freshmen students of a 60-minute, 15-page questionnaire (see Appendix A for copy). Within any given school building, either in a classroom, the auditorium, or the cafeteria, questionnaires were administered to all students within the same hour to avoid the possible contamination of data by virtue of students' discussing the morning questionnaire experience with students who were scheduled to complete the questionnaire in the afternoon. Some 2,788 individuals, about 95 percent of all registered ninth-grade students, completed the questionnaire.

With few exceptions, Rehberg was present for each questionnaire administration and, with research assistants, circulated among the student respondents for the full hour, answering questions and attempting to maintain an acceptable testing environment.

At the end of the hour, questionnaires were collected and returned to the university for editing, coding, and keypunching. Also in the freshman year we obtained intelligence scores from the participating schools for about 85 percent of the freshman class. These scores were from tests administered by the schools, usually in grade eight or nine.

During the winter of 1968 we planned a similar procedure for the administration of the sophomore year April–May survey. As arrangements were being made for this administration, several schools requested that we provide more information and a fuller explanation of the project to the administration and teaching staff prior to the day on which the survey was to occur. One system in particular requested this; following the administration of the first survey, a number of students and their parents (and a few teachers as well) had taken exception to some of the questions, particularly those which requested information on religious affiliation, church attendance, and degree of biblical literalism. We responded positively to these requests, met with interested faculty and administrators, and provided further information on the project. This was time well spent. In those districts where we did meet with the teaching and administrative staff there was a detectable, if not measurable, improvement in the "testing atmosphere" on the day of the survey. Teachers were more attentive to their students and more cooperative with us and our staff.

No survey was done during the students' junior year. This decision was rooted in the belief that neither the schools nor the students desired a third year of survey questionnaires, three years running. Concomitantly, of course, we were able to avoid the substantial amount of time required to prepare and administer questionnaires to some 3,000 individuals spread across seven districts. This was a welcome respite.

Again during the winter of 1970 we made arrangements with all schools for the administration of the senior-year instrument. Heartened by the benefits that had accrued from a more adequately informed teaching and administrative staff in the sophomore year, we sought meetings with the staff of all seven school systems in preparation for the senior-year survey. Most superintendents were responsive, although a few thought such meetings unnecessarily time-consuming and nonproductive. It again seemed, however, that a more favorable testing environment characterized those schools in which we were able to meet with the staff prior to the day of the survey.

Several months prior to June 1970, we decided to launch a follow-up survey of the cohort during the first postsecondary year of 1970–71. While the primary sampling frame was that of all 2,788 students who had participated in the freshman year survey of 1967, the majority of whom were now in their senior year, a quid pro quo with the participating schools necessitated that mailings also be made to seniors who had not participated in the original survey in 1967.

In return for a descriptive profile of their respective graduating classes of 1970 based on data from the T_4 follow-up, each school agreed to distribute to its seniors a mimeographed IBM-size card on which the student was asked to place his name, home address, and for the year beginning September 1970, an address at which he could be reached if that address were different from his June home address. For individuals for whom no card was available, primarily those who had moved away or dropped out of school, a trace procedure was instituted using address location data from the schools, the postal and telephone services, and several cooperative public agencies. By October 1970 viable addresses had been located for almost all of the 2,788 individuals identified in the freshman-year sampling frame. Because of their interest in the descriptive profile of their graduating seniors, two school systems not among the original seven in the longitudinal study were added for the T_4 mail survey. This addition increased the number of initial mailings by about 350 names.

On December 26, 1970, the first of what was ultimately to be five waves of survey mailing began. Mailings one and two were regular first-class postings. Mailings three, four, and five were *certified* first-class postage. By design, the follow-up was intended to secure information *directly* from the respondent. Only in a limited number of cases did we knowingly attempt to secure information from a parent.

Participation Rates

In the spring of 1967 survey questionnaires were administered to all *ninth*-grade students in attendance at the participating schools.

Completed instruments were collected from 2,788 persons, repre-senting about 95 percent of all students officially registered as ninth graders in those schools. In the spring of 1968 survey questionnaires were administered to all *tenth*-grade students in attendance. Completed instruments were collected from 2,696 persons. Of the 2,788 individ-uals who had completed a ninth-grade questionnaire, 2,318, or 83 percent, also completed a tenth-grade questionnaire. In the spring of 1970 survey questionnaires were administered to all *twelfth*-grade students. Completed instruments were collected from 2,447 persons. Of the 2,788 individuals who had completed a ninth-grade ques-tionnaire, 2,055, or 74 percent, also completed a twelfth-grade ques-tionnaire. Of the 2,696 individuals who completed a tenth-grade questionnaire, 2,052, or 76 percent, also completed a twelfth-grade questionnaire. Of the 2,788 individuals who completed a ninth-grade questionnaire, 1,853, or 66 percent, completed *both* the tenth- and twelfth-grade questionnaires.

In the winter and spring of 1970–71, mailed questionnaires were addressed to all 2,788 individuals who had first participated in the study in 1967. Completed instruments were received from 2,463 individuals, or 88 percent of the initial ninth-grade panel. Of the original panel of 2,788 students, 2,107, or 76 percent, completed both a tenth-grade and a post-high school follow-up survey; 1,195, or 69 percent, completed both a twelfth-grade and a post-high school follow-up survey; and 1,734, or 62 percent, completed not only a tenth-grade questionnaire, but a twelfth-grade questionnaire *and* a post-high school follow-up questionnaire.

On single-variable measures of central tendency such as per-centages and arithmetic means, the impact of a respondent loss or attrition is noticeable but not severe. As we can see from table 2.2, that impact is truly minimal on such ascriptive measures as the occu-pation of the father or the scholastic ability of the student. For example, of the 2,788 students who participated in the freshman, or T_1, survey, 58 percent had fathers whose occupations were subse-quently classified "white-collar." That percentage rises only one point when we examine the occupational classification of the fathers of the 2,055 students who participated in both the freshman and senior surveys. Similarly, the mean level of the scholastic ability of all respondents who participated in the T_1 panel was 109.8. The mean level of scholastic ability of those 2,463 individuals who par-

TABLE 2.2. Measures of Central Tendency for Specified Sets of Surveys

Variable Name	Grade 9 T_1	Grade 9 Grade 10 T_1-T_2	Grade 9 Grade 12 T_1-T_3	Grade 9 Grade 10 Grade 12 $T_1-T_2-T_3$	Grade 9 Grade 10 Grade 12 Post H.S. T_1-T_4
			Specified Survey Set		
Occupation of Father (percent white collar)	58	58	59	59	59
Education of Father (percent some college)	34	33	34	34	34
Education of Mother (percent some college)	27	27	29	29	28
Curriculum Location Grade Nine (percent academic program)	60	63	65	66	64
Education Beyond High School Taken for Granted by Parents (percent saying yes)	63	63	65	66	63
Ambition to Pursue Four-Year College Education	48	51	53	54	50
Scholastic Ability:					
Percent above median	50	52	53	54	52
Mean level of ability	109.8	110.2	110.6	110.8	110.3
Number of Respondents	2,788	2,318	2,055	1,853	2,463

ticipated in both the freshman panel and the post-high school follow-up was less than one point higher, 110.3. On school-related measures the effect of respondent attrition is a bit more pronounced than it was on the ascriptive measures. College ambitions were reported by 48 percent of the 2,788 persons who participated in the freshman-year panel, but among the 2,055 persons who also participated in the senior-year panel, the percentage who had reported college ambitions in the ninth grade was five points higher. Similarly, 60 percent of the entire ninth-grade panel reported that they were located in the academic program. But among the 2,463 persons who participated in both the ninth-grade panel and the post-high school follow-up, the percentage who as ninth graders were in the academic program was 64.

Sewell and Hauser[4] and Alexander and Eckland[5] have shown that bivariate measures of degree of association are less sensitive to sample attrition than are measures of central tendency. For these measures we have adopted the procedure of pair-wise case deletion to minimize the effect of attrition on the basic measure of association used in our inquiry, the Pearsonian product moment correlation coefficient. By way of illustration, if a given respondent was present for the ninth-grade (T_1) and twelfth-grade (T_3) panels but not for the tenth-grade (T_2) or postsecondary follow-up (T_4) surveys, his data would be used for those correlations that involved variables either totally *within* the T_1 survey (e.g., the correlation between ability and ninth-grade curriculum location), totally *within* the T_3 survey (e.g., the correlation between counselor encouragement and educational decision), or between the T_1 and T_3 surveys (e.g., the correlation between ninth-grade curriculum location and twelfth-grade educational decision). This respondent's data would not be used, i.e., his "case" would be deleted, for computations of correlations that involved variables from the ninth- and tenth-grade $(T_1$ and $T_2)$ panels, the ninth-grade and postsecondary panels $(T_1$ and $T_4)$, the tenth-grade and postsecondary panels $(T_2$ and $T_4)$, or the twelfth-grade and postsecondary panels $(T_3$ and $T_4)$. Pair-wise deletion thus utilizes the maximum amount of information both *within* any given panel and *between* all pairs of panels.

VARIABLES

Fourteen variables define our model of the secondary school experience:

X_1: Social class
X_2: Scholastic ability
X_3: Parental educational stress
X_4: Does the student regard his continued education beyond high school as "taken for granted" by his parents?
X_5: Curriculum location in ninth grade
X_6: Peer college influence in ninth grade
X_7: Educational ambition
X_8: Curriculum location in tenth grade
X_9: Counselor educational encouragement in tenth grade
X_{10}: Academic achievement, cumulative over grades nine, ten, and eleven
X_{11}: Peer college influence in twelfth grade
X_{12}: Counselor educational encouragement in twelfth grade
X_{13}: Educational decision
X_{14}: Educational enrollment level during first postsecondary year.

A discussion of each variable follows. Included are the conceptual and operational definitions of the variable, rates of nonresponse, and any adjustments that have been made to the variable.

X_1: *Social class.*[6] Conceptually, the social class of a family refers to the location of the family within the hierarchical ordering of a society in accord with the deference, prestige, and power that the family can claim as a result of the occupational and educational attainments of its adult members. Operationally, as we explain in detail in the next section of this chapter, we did not measure social class. We employed multiple indicators and multiple effects of the unobservable variable social class to derive the association of the unmeasured variable with measured variables in our analysis. Our indicators of social class were occupation of father, education of father, education of mother. Each indicator was scaled following the occupation or education metric from the Hollingshead Two Factor Index of Social Position.[7] We obtained data for these indicators from the students during the ninth-grade survey. Rates of nonresponse were: occupation, 3.4 percent; father's education, 11.0 percent; mother's education, 8.2 percent. To ensure the maximum number of usable cases the arithmetic mean of the respective indicator was substituted wherever a student failed to provide the necessary information. Appendix B displays the percentage and frequency distributions for each indicator and the arithmetic means and standard deviations both before and after adjusting for missing data by substituting the arithmetic mean.

X_2:   *Scholastic ability.* Scores from the Otis Quick Scoring Mental Ability Test or the California Test of Mental Maturity provide the measure of scholastic ability. These tests were administered during grades eight or nine by the participating schools as part of their normal testing program. Scores were made available to the authors on a confidential basis. Because of its length, we do not present the distribution of this variable. Data were missing for 12 percent of the 2,788 ninth-grade respondents. The range of the distribution was from a low of 68 to a high of 149. The unadjusted mean was 109.77, and the adjusted mean 109.79. The unadjusted standard deviation was 11.55, and the adjusted standard deviation 10.85.

X_3:   *Parental educational stress.* To measure the intensity with which students perceived each parent as stressing continued education beyond high school, each respondent was asked in the ninth-grade survey:[8]

> During the last few years or so, has your [FATHER, MOTHER] wanted you to continue your education beyond high school, that is, to go to a trade or a business school, to college, etc.?
> 1.   (   ) Yes, [HE, SHE] has stressed it a lot
> 2.   (   ) Yes, [HE, SHE] has stressed it somewhat
> 3.   (   ) Yes, but [HE, SHE] has seldom mentioned it
> 4.   (   ) [HE, SHE] hasn't said one way or the other
> 5.   (   ) No, [HE, SHE] would rather that I did not go beyond high school

We constructed an index of parental educational stress, one of our two indicators of the extent to which students perceive their parents as attempting to influence them to continue education beyond high school, by adding the ordinal levels of each parent-specific indicator. The resulting parent-combined index ranged from 1 (the highest level of intensity) to 9 (the lowest level of intensity). The mean was substituted for 74 nonresponses to the item for the father and 18 nonresponses to the item for the mother. Appendix B displays the distribution of the index variable.

X_4:   *Continued education beyond high school taken for granted?* Our second indicator of the extent to which students perceived parents as attempting to influence their educational career is from a measure also secured during the ninth-grade survey. Each student was asked:

> Would you say that in your home it has been just about taken for granted that you will continue your education after you get out of high school?
> 1.   (   ) Yes
> 2.   (   ) No
> 3.   (   ) Do not know

Since an analysis of this variable revealed no predictive differences in either educational ambitions or actual postsecondary educational enrollment level between students who had responded "No" and those who had responded "Do not know," these two categories have been collapsed into one. The resultant variable is thus a dichotomy and has been coded as a "dummy" variable; a score of 0 indicates that the student regards his continued education as taken for granted, a score of 1 indicates that he does not. Slightly less than 5 percent of all ninth graders did not respond to this question. Appendix B contains the distribution of this dummy variable.

X_5:   *Curriculum in ninth grade.* Schools that participated in this study offered a variety of programs at the high school level, some providing college preparation, others not. During the ninth-grade survey, each student was asked:

> What kind of program are you taking in school?
> 1.   (   ) Academic or college-preparatory
> 2.   (   ) Science
> 3.   (   ) General
> 4.   (   ) Commercial or business
> 5.   (   ) Vocational agriculture
> 6.   (   ) Vocational industrial arts
> 7.   (   ) Other, please specify: ————————

Our coding of this variable reflects the primary division between students in high school: college preparatory, levels 1 and 2; non-college preparatory, levels 3–7. A dummy variable code was assigned to this measure with 0 indicating the college-preparatory program and 1 indicating a noncollege program. Nonresponse to this item totaled 2.1 percent. Appendix B presents the frequency and percentage of distribution for the dummy version of the curriculum measure.

X_6:   *Peer college influence in ninth grade.* The degree to which the student is subject to influence from friends to continue his education beyond high school has been indexed for this study as a simple function of the number of close friends the respondent has who themselves plan on going to college. In the ninth grade, each student was asked separately for each of the student's three close friends: "How far does [HE, SHE] actually expect to go in school?"

The fixed alternative response categories for this probe were coded into the education metric of the Hollingshead Two Factor Index of Social Position, and the appropriate additive operations were performed to generate a score range from 0 (for no close friends college-bound) to 3 (all three close friends college-bound). Rates of nonresponse were: for friend #1, 7.5 percent; for friend #2, 9.2 percent; for friend #3, 10.5 percent. The respective arithmetic means were substituted for each nonresponse prior to the construction of the additive index. It is probable that the higher than average rate of nonresponse is due to the positioning of the peer items toward the end of the questionnaire, a section to which some of the slower students never got. The distribution for the index of peer influence appears in Appendix B.

X_7:   *Educational ambition.* Within the context of social mobility and following the conceptual lead of Turner,[9] we define an educational ambition as the extent to which the individual plans to use educational attainment as a means toward the end of either preserving or enhancing an already favored social position, if the class of origin is one of privilege, or of improving social position, if the class of origin is less than one of privilege. Educational ambition, then, is a motivational construct. In the ninth grade we measured the educational ambition of our students by asking:

CONSIDERING your abilities, grades, financial resources, etc., how far do you *actually* EXPECT TO go in school?

1. ( ) 10th or 11th grade
2. ( ) Graduate from high school
3. ( ) Trade or technical school
4. ( ) Two-year business school
5. ( ) Nursing school
6. ( ) Two years of college
7. ( ) Four years of college
8. ( ) Graduate or professional school

Responses were coded following the Hollingshead education metric. Less than one percent of all ninth-grade students failed to respond to this query. For them the mean of the item was substituted. The distribution of the item appears in Appendix B.

X_8: *Curriculum in tenth grade.* All students at the end of the tenth grade were asked to designate their curriculum location in a manner similar to that used in ninth grade. Less than one percent of all students did not respond to this item. The distribution is in Appendix B.

X_9: *Counselor educational encouragement in tenth grade.* During the tenth-grade survey, each student was asked to indicate what level of education he or she was advised or encouraged to pursue by the guidance counselor. The question was worded so as to restrict the counselor-student encounter to those conversations having to do specifically with career issues, thereby avoiding extraneous material concerning deportment or psychological issues. The item itself read:

When you talk with your guidance counselor, what does he suggest or encourage you to do?

1. ( ) Go on to a four-year college
2. ( ) Go on to a two-year college
3. ( ) Go for technical or advanced job training
4. ( ) Go for business or commercial training
5. ( ) Go into the armed services
6. ( ) Get a job after I get out of high school
7. ( ) Other: ―――――

Two aspects of the response scale for this item required adjustment before we could use this measure in our analysis. The first was that the responses do not constitute an ordered metric. Going into the armed services does not necessarily imply more or less schooling than getting a job right after high school. A more ordered metric was thus formed by leaving the first level, "four-year college," intact; leaving the second level, "two-year college," intact; combining the third and fourth levels into a third level, "occupational training"; and combining the fifth and sixth levels into a fourth level, "no schooling beyond high school."

The second aspect of the response levels that required attention was the "Other" category. This was particularly so for the twelfth-grade measurement of counselor encouragement, i.e., for variable X_{12}. In the twelfth grade, 14 percent of the students checked "Other"; in the tenth grade, 4.5 percent of the students checked that category. So that we could assign the category a score and place it in a more ordered metric, we constructed a listing of all students who had checked "Other" during the twelfth-grade survey and drew a 50 percent sample. Among the more than 75 percent of those in the sample who provided a written response to the "Other" category, three classes of comments were discernible: (1) the counselor tells me to do what I want to do; (2) the counselor essentially tells me nothing *or* I haven't talked with the counselor; and (3) responses that were too general or vague to classify. Inasmuch as those who had written that "the counselor tells me to do what I want to do" had educational goal scores in that same survey with a mean indicating two years of college, and since that was also the approximate mean for the entire scale, we proceeded to assign to the "Other" category the arithmetic mean of the scale. To assess how these adjustments may have affected the counselor variable, we performed an identical set of operations on a similar item we had asked for teachers, an item we have chosen not to include in our model in order to refrain from making an already complex model even more complex. We then compared the correlations of our teacher encouragement variable with those reported by Sewell and Hauser[10] for their twelfth-grade measure of teacher encouragement. The unavailability of similar data from another study for the counselor required that the comparison be limited to the teacher. We find a marked degree of similarity between the correlations published by Sewell and Hauser and those from our own data set. Thus, teacher educational encouragement correlates with intelligence .35 for Sewell and .33 for us; with actual educational attainment it correlates .41 for Sewell while with enrollment level during the first postsecondary year it correlates .47 for us; with academic performance, teacher encouragement correlates .42 for Sewell and .38 for us. And with the separate occupational and educational indicators of social class, Sewell and Hauser's correlations are similar to ours, although ours tend to be a bit higher. Assuming, then, some degree of comparability between measures of educational encouragement from the counselor and from the teacher, we would infer that the adjustments we have made to our measure of counselor encouragement have not seriously distorted that variable. Appendix B presents the distributions of the counselor encouragement scale.

X_{10}: *Academic performance.* Each participating school was asked in 1969–70 to provide for their senior class the grade-point averages on which they compute initial rank in graduating class. This rank, rather than the one computed at the end of the senior year for graduation purposes, tends to be the one reported on high school and employment transcripts when requested. Comparability of grades from different school systems using different grading systems was achieved by converting all grades into stanine scores.[11] The mean stanine, 5 by definition, was substituted for the 43 seniors for whom original raw-score grades were not available. The distribution of cumulative grade-point averages, based on course marks from grades nine, ten, and eleven, are displayed in Appendix B.

X_{11}: *Peer college influence in twelfth grade.* Conceptually, this measure is similar to that used for ninth grade. Operationally, however, it differs in two respects: (1) while the ninth-grade measure was a composite index based on the sum of three separate items, the twelfth-grade measure used a single-item format asking the respondent to indicate whether none, one, two, or three close friends had decided to go on to college; (2) while the ninth-grade measure distinguished between four and two years of college, the twelfth-grade measure made no such distinction. Appendix B displays the frequency distribution for this item.

X_{12}: *Counselor educational encouragement in twelfth grade.* Conceptually and operationally, this measure is identical to that used in tenth grade. Appendix B contains the frequency distribution for this twelfth-grade measure.

X_{13}: *Educational decision.* With Granovetter,[12] we agree that by the last month or so of twelfth grade, most high school students know whether they will be going to college. Indeed, the vast majority of students who are going to college should know also the name of that institution. Most institutions of higher education send acceptance notices to applicants prior to mid-April or May of the senior year. Consequently, we concur with Granovetter, who is critical of the term "aspiration" or "expectation" as applied to the educational orientations of high school seniors, and prefer the concept of "decision." By the last month or so of twelfth grade most students have decided what their educational activity, if any, is to be the following fall. To measure what educational decision had been made by each of our students, we asked a question essentially the same as that used in the ninth grade:

CONSIDERING your abilities, grades, financial resources, etc., how far do you *actually* EXPECT TO go in school?
1. ( ) Graduate or professional school
2. ( ) Four years of college
3. ( ) Two years of college
4. ( ) Nursing school
5. ( ) Two-year business school
6. ( ) Trade or technical school
7. ( ) Graduate from high school
8. ( ) Twelfth grade but not graduate from high school

Less than 3 percent of the twelfth-grade class failed to respond to this item. Responses were coded according to the educational metric of the Hollingshead Two Factor Index of Social Position. Appendix B presents the distribution of this variable.

X_{14}: *Educational enrollment level, first postsecondary year.* In the survey addressed to all 2,788 students who had participated in the ninth-grade survey and mailed during the winter and spring of 1971, two questions were asked from which we have derived the level of schooling the person was engaged in one year subsequent to June 1970:

1. What is the highest grade you COMPLETED in high school?
   1. ( ) Ninth grade
   2. ( ) Tenth grade
   3. ( ) Eleventh grade
   4. ( ) Twelfth grade

2. Are you currently a student in any type of educational institution or school?
   1. ( ) NO: GO TO QUESTION ————
   2. ( ) YES: a technical or trade school
   3. ( ) YES: a business school
   4. ( ) YES: a nursing school
   5. ( ) YES: a two-year community college
   6. ( ) YES: a four-year college
   7. ( ) YES: any other type of educational institution or school

Responses to these two items were combined and scaled in the metric of the educational measure from the Hollingshead Index. Only one individual of the 2,463 who returned a T_4 questionnaire failed to respond to these two items. The distribution for this variable is reproduced in Appendix B.

Consequences of Adjustment for Missing Data

Two considerations informed our decision to substitute the arithmetic mean for missing data rather than make no such adjustment and use pair-wise deletion to cope with absent information. First, at the time we began this text, we contemplated a series of complex or high-order cross-tabulations and sought to avoid the severe attrition of cases that inevitably results from missing data even with a rate of nonresponse per variable seldom exceeding 8 percent. Second, we wished to have a data set that could be compatible with several computer programs we anticipated using, none of which had provisions for missing data. Again, even without very modest rates of nonresponse, this restriction would have resulted in a severe attrition of cases with a consequent biasing of the data.

The one identifiable impact that the substitution of the mean for the missing observation had was to reduce by a hundredth or two the average intercorrelation of those variables vis-à-vis what those correlations are when the technique of pair-wise case deletion is used. Table 2.3 illustrates that effect. Nevertheless, we do not judge this attenuation to be serious. As the reader will observe in subsequent chapters, the correlations from our data set do not differ markedly from those reported for similar variables by other investigators, despite differences in the operationalization of variables, sample composition, and year and region of the country when the study was conducted. A second basis for our confidence in our data appears in table 2.4 where we display the unstandardized and standardized regression coefficients for a rather simple model in which postsecondary enrollment level is posited as dependent upon academic performance, both enrollment and performance as dependent upon educational ambition, and all three variables as dependent upon the occupation of the father and the education of the father and the mother. The same two missing-data procedures described above were used to generate these two sets of coefficients. Use of these two procedures results in differences of a relatively minor and generally unsystematic nature.

On these grounds, then, i.e., the comparability of our correlations with those from other studies and the comparability of the standardized regression coefficients regardless of the procedure used to cope with missing data, we proceed with our analysis with measured confidence.

CAUSAL MODELING OF THE EDUCATIONAL ATTAINMENT PROCESS

In the chapters that follow we explicate the process of educational attainment through the use of causal models. This section presents an overview of the premises, promise, and limitations of causal modeling, followed by a detailed examination of the particular causal models we develop for the educational attainment process. The reader who is unfamiliar with the use of causal models in social research will find in the overview a guide to the logic of the analyses presented in subsequent chapters. More experienced readers may wish to pursue the detailed exposition of the problems we perceived and the solutions we chose in developing our models. We detail the

TABLE 2.3. Correlations Between Specified Educational Attainment Variables Computed with Arithmetic Means Substituted for Missing Data (above diagonal) or with Missing Data Cases Deleted (below diagonal) (decimals omitted)

Variable Names	X_1	X_2	X_3	X_4	X_5	X_6	X_7	X_8	X_9	X_{10}
Occupation of father	X_1	599	372	216	362	237	184	259	312	298
Education of father	635	X_2	457	231	376	244	194	259	308	299
Education of mother	394	486	X_3	211	292	209	135	175	243	259
Scholastic ability	236	259	234	X_4	399	422	556	426	434	416
Educational ambition	369	396	305	429	X_5	491	387	442	583	496
Counselor educ. enc. grade ten	255	268	226	464	518	X_6	402	521	471	455
Academic performance	192	210	162	587	395	391	X_7	473	470	523
Counselor educ. enc. grade twelve	273	288	169	456	455	572	453	X_8	579	544
Educational decision	319	320	252	461	591	499	475	591	X_9	645
Postsecondary educ. enroll. level	302	313	268	444	497	478	526	553	652	X_{10}

Variables

TABLE 2.4. Regression Coefficients in Unstandardized and Standardized Form for a Simple Model of the Educational Attainment Process with Computations Based on Two Methods for Coping with Missing Data

Dependent Variable—Independent Variables	UNSTANDARDIZED COEFFICIENT		STANDARDIZED COEFFICIENT	
	Missing Data Method: Substitute Mean	Missing Data Method: Delete Case	Missing Data Method: Substitute Mean	Missing Data Method: Delete Case
Educ. Enroll. Level—Acad. Performance	.191*	.177*	.333*	.306*
Educ. Ambition	.312*	.331*	.273*	.289*
Schol. Ability	.012*	.011*	.109*	.113*
Educ. of Mother	.058*	.065*	.059*	.063*
Educ. of Father	.013	.017	.017	.022
Occup. of Father	.051*	.052*	.076*	.076*
R^2	.421	.404		
Academic Performance—Educ. Ambition	.461*	.481*	.231*	.242*
Schol. Ability	.081*	.078*	.498*	.454*
Educ. of Mother	.004	.010	.003	.005
Educ. of Father	.029	.032	.022	.024
Occup. of Father	.008	.001	.006	.001
R^2	.404	.359		

TABLE 2.4. (continued)

Dependent Variable—Independent Variables	UNSTANDARDIZED COEFFICIENT Missing Data Method:		STANDARDIZED COEFFICIENT Missing Data Method:	
	Substitute Mean	Delete Case	Substitute Mean	Delete Case
Educational Ambition—Schol. Ability	.026*	.026*	.319*	.296*
Educ. of Mother	.077*	.083*	.090*	.093*
Educ. of Father	.098*	.100*	.147*	.146*
Occup. of Father	.128*	.134*	.218*	.224*
R^2	.289	.289		

* Designates a coefficient that is at least 1.96 times its standard error.

problems of model construction and parameter estimation specific to this study, and our choice of solutions to those problems, in order to encourage critical assessment, revision, and extension of our procedures and the conclusions that follow them.

Causal models are constructed from theory and data and permit us to work out the consequences for the modeled system of the causal processes we have assumed. Our assumptions about causal processes, derived from experimental evidence, nonexperimental observations, and current social theory, are abstracted from social reality to form the causal models that state relations among variables. Causal models display these relations as structural equations. Solutions to sets of structural equations are then estimated with empirical data. Modifications of substantive theory follow when the model solution reveals inconsistent or otherwise unrealistic outcomes.

Plausibility of the estimated solution does not demonstrate the "truth" of the model's explicit assumptions about causal processes, however; the data employed to estimate the solution very likely will yield consistent results when applied to alternative models of reality as well. A causal model cannot provide us with the one best theory of a social process. Causal models are tentative and always incorporate more or less arbitrary simplifying assumptions. The virtue of the causal model is that it makes explicit all the researcher's assumptions and the consequences that flow from them. We use causal models here for modifying or eliminating inadequate theoretical assumptions, assessing the relative strength of specified causes contributing to the same effect, estimating the persistence of effects of specified causes over time, and testing the strength of links in a hypothesized causal chain.

The value of constructing causal models of social processes is limited to substantive areas where theory is well developed and reliable measures for relevant variables exist. The vast amount of theoretical, speculative, and empirical work bearing on the educational attainment process guides the choice of variables we have included in our models. We derived the causal relations among variables from propositions that have been tested in past research or suggested by current theory. For our analysis, whose main thrust is to trace the implications of two conflicting views of the educational attainment process, the choice of variables to include in our causal models raises few problems because both theories, by and large, specify identical sets of relevant factors. Assumed causal relations among the variables, however, are somewhat different for the two views.

For purposes of demonstrating the construction and use of causal models, let us entertain a somewhat oversimplified example. Theorist R sees the educational system as transmitting, reinforcing, and legitimizing existing class distinctions in U.S. society. From this view, Theorist R hypothesizes the role of the guidance counselor in the educational attainment process as encouraging children of privileged backgrounds to aspire to college and, conversely, discouraging such ambition in children from less privileged homes. Theorist M sees the same educational system as the great equalizer of opportunity for social advancement, where rewards are distributed on the basis of demonstrated ability. Theorist M then hypothesizes the guidance counselor's role as a reinforcer of distinctions based on merit: the guidance counselor encourages the ambitions of children with demonstrated scholastic ability regardless of class background.

Theorist R and Theorist M start with different assumptions and hypothesize different effects, but there is some general agreement between them. For some reason they both think the guidance counselor has an important role in the educational attainment process; the encouragement of the counselor affects children's attitudes and, by implication, their subsequent behavior. It is important to note that a host of other theorists may hypothesize the effect of the guidance counselor's encouragement on the educational attainment process to be essentially zero. Theorist M and Theorist R also agree that the guidance counselor is a link between some aspect of the child's past and the child's educational future and, therefore, the counselor must have knowledge of the child's past: the student's demonstrated ability in the case of Theorist M and the student's social-class background in the case of Theorist R.

Four variables are specified in these theories: social-class background (X_1), scholastic ability (X_2), counselor's encouragement (X_9), and the student's educational ambition (X_7). Model R represents the relations among variables suggested by Theorist R; Model M represents the relations among variables suggested by Theorist M. In Model R social class is completely determined by factors not made explicit in the model. No causal assumptions are made in Model R about social class or in Model M about scholastic ability. Equations

$$Model\ R \qquad\qquad Model\ M$$

(1) $X_1 = p_{1a}X_a$ (4) $X_2 = p_{2a}X_a$

(2) $X_9 = p_{91}X_1 + p_{9b}X_b$ (5) $X_9 = p_{92}X_2 + p_{9b}X_b$

(3) $X_7 = p_{71}X_1 + p_{79}X_9 + p_{7c}X_c$ (6) $X_7 = p_{72}X_2 + p_{79}X_9 + p_{7c}X_c$

NOTE: X_a, X_b, X_c represent all unmeasured causal influences not included in the model. Unmeasured causes, or residuals, are assumed to be independent of all causes made explicit in the same equation.

(1) and (4) may be omitted from the respective models with no loss of information since the models do not attempt to explain either X_1 or X_2. In models of this type that require an unequivocal time ordering among variables, the researcher may choose to examine a segment of the temporal process without having to explain prior or subsequent developments.

We may combine these two models to derive specific predictions about direct and indirect effects on X_9 and X_7. These predictions can then be compared to the solution of the model to test the validity of causal relations among variables assumed by Theorist M and Theorist R. The combined assumptions of both theorists are represented in Model C and the predictions implied by the hypotheses are indicated along with the structural equations.

$$Model\ C$$

(7) $X_9 = p_{91}X_1 + p_{92}X_2 + p_{9a}X_a$

(8) $X_7 = p_{71}X_1 + p_{72}X_2 + p_{79}X_9 + p_{7b}X_b$

Predictions implied by Theorist R: $p_{92} = 0$ and $p_{72} = 0$

Predictions implied by Theorist M: $p_{91} = 0$ and $p_{71} = 0$

Granted, this example depicts Theorist M and Theorist R as caricatures of current views. We have dressed them up as strawpersons here in order to highlight the capabilities and limitations of causal models for theory building. A less exaggerated form of the opposing views would perhaps yield less precise predictions for parameter values: a more temperate Theorist R would predict $p_{92} < p_{91}$ and $p_{72} < p_{71}$ and Theorist M might be better served by predicting $p_{91} < p_{92}$ and $p_{71} < p_{72}$.

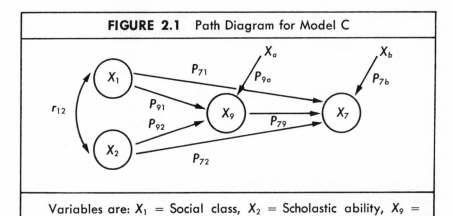

FIGURE 2.1 Path Diagram for Model C

Variables are: X_1 = Social class, X_2 = Scholastic ability, X_9 = Counselor educational encouragement, X_7 = Educational ambition

All causal models constructed for our analyses are of the general type of Model C. These linear, additive, recursive path models may be alternatively represented by path diagrams that are isomorphic with the structural equations. Figure 2.1 illustrates the path diagram equivalent to the equations of Model C. The curved, double-headed arrow connecting X_1 and X_2 indicates that no causal assumptions are made in the model to explain their association, r_{12}. The one-way arrows, or paths, lead from each causal variable to each variable directly dependent upon it. The path coefficients p_{ij} represent the direct effect of variable j on variable i and may be interpreted as the proportion of the standard deviation of variable i explained directly by variable j, with all other variables determining variable i statistically controlled. Endogenous variables X_9 and X_7 are completely determined within the model, and all unmeasured causes of these variables are represented by the literally subscripted residual variables X_a and X_b. A residual variable is defined to be independent of all variables specified as determining variables in the same equation. Thus, there is no double-headed arrow connecting X_a with either X_1 or X_2, or connecting X_b with either X_1 or X_2 or X_9.

By tracing compound paths from effects back to causes, the path diagram makes it easy to see that the model assumes that X_1 directly determines X_7 (path p_{71}) and also that X_1 determines X_7 indirectly through X_9 (compound path $p_{79}p_{91}$). To estimate the causal impact or *total effect* of social-class background on educational ambition we may partition their correlation r_{17} into causal and noncausal com-

TABLE 2.5. **A Path Analysis of the Association Between Social Class and Ambition Following the Assumptions of Model C**

---

r_{17} = total association = $\underbrace{p_{71} + p_{79}p_{91}}_{\text{causal}} + \underbrace{p_{72}r_{12} + p_{79}p_{92}r_{12}}_{\text{noncausal}}$

Causal Component q_{71}
p_{71} = direct effect
$s_{71} = p_{79}p_{91}$ = sum of indirect effects
$q_{71} = p_{71} + p_{79}p_{91}$ = total effect
Noncausal Component $r_{71} - q_{71}$
$p_{72}r_{12}$ = association directly due to unanalyzed correlation r_{12}
$p_{79}p_{92}r_{12}$ = association indirectly due to unanalyzed correlation r_{12}

---

ponents. A noncausal component is that portion of the total association r_{ij} due to common causes of i and j, correlations among common causes or the unanalyzed correlation between exogenous variables. Here, the total effect q_{71} is the sum of the direct effect p_{71} and one (in this case) indirect effect through X_9, the compound path $p_{79}p_{91}$. Table 2.5 summarizes the path analysis that accounts for all the covariation of X_1 and X_7.

By estimating direct effects, indirect effects, and total effects on the endogenous variables X_9 and X_7 we may evaluate the implications of the theoretical assumptions built into the causal model. However, we cannot calculate these estimates without placing some additional restrictions on the model because Model C is a system of two equations in seven unknowns. If we further assume that reliable interval-scale measures of the exogenous variables X_1 and X_2 and endogenous variables X_7 and X_9 have been collected from some relevant population, that the two unmeasured variables X_a and X_b are uncorrelated with each other ($r_{ab} = 0$), and that all measures have been converted to standard scores, then the parameters p_{ij} may be estimated with Ordinary Least-Squares regression techniques. Systematic presentation of parameter estimation methods for causal models of this form are readily available to the interested reader; see, for example the development of path analysis in Land[13] or Blalock.[14] We shall not develop here the solution for Model C; standardized partial regres-

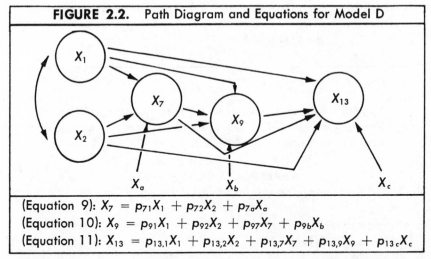

FIGURE 2.2. Path Diagram and Equations for Model D

(Equation 9): $X_7 = p_{71}X_1 + p_{72}X_2 + p_{7a}X_a$
(Equation 10): $X_9 = p_{91}X_1 + p_{92}X_2 + p_{97}X_7 + p_{9b}X_b$
(Equation 11): $X_{13} = p_{13,1}X_1 + p_{13,2}X_2 + p_{13,7}X_7 + p_{13,9}X_9 + p_{13c}X_c$

Variables are: X_1 = Social class, X_2 = Scholastic ability, X_7 = Educational ambition, X_9 = Counselor educational encouragement, X_{13} = Educational decision, X_a–X_c = residuals.

sion coefficients from OLS regression analysis applied sequentially to equations (7) and (8) will yield unbiased and efficient estimators of the p_{ij} in this straightforward case.

The theorists we have conjured to aid our explanation of causal modeling may object to our formalization of their views in Model C. After all, Model C does not take into account the educational ambition of the student before the student ever saw a guidance counselor. We cannot tell from Model C if the counselor is actually encouraging or discouraging a student unless we incorporate into the model some knowledge of what the student's educational ambition was at some earlier time. The model becomes more complex when this objection is taken into account. We need two measures of the student's educational ambition, one before the intervention of the counselor and one after. Model D includes this added complication. The structural equations and equivalent path diagram for Model D are shown in figure 2.2. The parameters p_{ij} are not named explicitly on the path diagram because of the clutter such inclusion entails; conventionally the parameter estimates for already cluttered path diagrams are reported in an accompanying table. Table 2.6 shows a path analysis of the association between social class and ambition for Model D.

TABLE 2.6.   A Path Analysis of the Association Between Social Class and Educational Decision Following the Assumptions of Model D

TOTAL ASSOCIATION:

Symbol for the total association is the correlation coefficient r_{ij}. For the total association between social class and educational decision, the correlation coefficient is $r_{13,1}$.

$$r_{13,1} = p_{13,1} + p_{13,7}p_{7,1} + p_{13,9}p_{9,1} + p_{13,9}p_{9,7}p_{7,1} +$$
$$- - - - - - \textit{Causal Component} - - - - - -$$
$$p_{13,2}r_{2,1} + p_{13,7}p_{7,2}r_{2,1} + p_{13,9}p_{9,2}r_{2,1} + p_{13,9}p_{9,7}p_{7,2}r_{2,1}$$
$$- - - - - - - - \textit{Noncausal Component} - - - - - - - - - - -$$

CAUSAL COMPONENT

Symbol for causal component is q_{ij}. Causal component may consist of a *direct* effect, symbolized by p_{ij} and an *indirect* effect, symbolized by s_{ij}.

$$q_{13,1} = p_{13,1} + s_{13,1}; \text{ where } s_{13,1} = (p_{13,7}p_{7,1} + p_{13,9}p_{9,1}$$
$$+ p_{13,9}p_{9,7}p_{7,1})$$

NONCAUSAL COMPONENT

For the relationship between social class and educational decision, the noncausal component consists of those associations directly due to the unanalyzed correlation between social class and scholastic ability, $r_{1,2}$. That component is:

Noncausal component of $r_{13,1} = (p_{13,2}r_{2,1} + p_{13,9}p_{9,2}r_{2,1}$
$$+ p_{13,9}p_{9,7}p_{7,2}r_{2,1})$$

By including one additional variable, Model D permits us to make several additional predictions. All those who theorize the impotence of the guidance counselor as a cause of student educational decisions may hypothesize $p_{13,9} = 0$ or, equivalently, $q_{13,9} = 0$. This hypothesis represents the view that all the association between what the counselor advises and what the student decides is noncausal and may be explained as "spurious" correlation due to common causes and correlations between common causes and unanalyzed correlations. Theorist M may now predict $p_{13,9}p_{92} > p_{13,9}p_{91}$ or perhaps $q_{13,2} > q_{13,1}$ in addition to earlier predictions. Theorist R would hypothesize the reverse, and most likely maintain that the earlier prediction of a sizable positive value for p_{91} will persist as a continuing direct effect of social class on the counselor despite the student's early ambition.

By including only one more variable in the causal model we have added a great deal to its explanatory possibilities, but the cost is high and the new problems are great. We now need panel data to solve the model and this necessity brings with it all the complications of panel attrition discussed earlier in this chapter. We may employ straightforward Ordinary Least-Squares regression estimators only if we are still willing to make the assumption that the correlations among all three residual variables X_a, X_b, and X_c are identically zero. Since X_a summarizes all unmeasured causes of educational ambition and X_c summarizes all unmeasured causes of the same variable measured at a later time, we must be quite certain that any common cause of both X_7 and X_{13} is specified in the model. If not, the assumption $r_{ac} = 0$ will be extremely unrealistic and Ordinary Least-Squares estimators will be biased.

How can we be sure that social class and ability are the only common causes of X_7 and X_{13}? In nonexperimental research we cannot even pretend to have controlled for all relevant causes. Short of abandoning nonexperimental research on humans, we may evaluate several other options. We may continue our analysis with Model D as it stands, quite certain that the results will be biased. We may search for additional variables to include. We may abandon the assumption $r_{ac} = 0$ and seek other estimation methods that do not demand this restriction.

For models in the following chapters we have followed the second option and included additional variables suggested by our search of current theory and past research. We have followed the third option as well and abandoned Ordinary Least-Squares estimation methods. And, in line with option 1, we are still quite certain that our results remain somewhat biased; causal models are always tentative and at least in the social sciences we do not expect definitive models for quite a while. In the remaining pages of this chapter we present an outline of the decisions we made to cope with the complexities introduced into our analysis as we attempted to construct causal models that reflect social reality with less distortion than the models used here as illustrations of the modeling process.

The causal models presented and analyzed in the following chap-

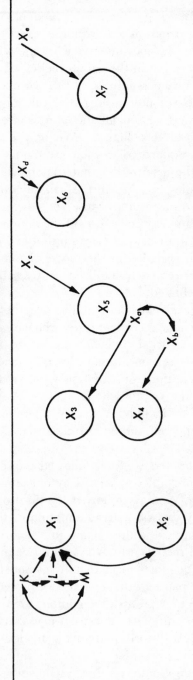

FIGURE 2.3. Path Diagram (Simplified*), Structural Equations, and Variable Names for Model of the Educational Process in Grade Nine

(Equation 12): $X_1 = p_{1k}K + p_{12}L + p_{1m}M$
(Equation 13): $X_3 = p_{31}X_1 + p_{32}X_2 + p_{3a}X_a$
(Equation 14): $X_4 = p_{41}X_1 + p_{42}X_2 + p_{4b}X_b$
(Equation 15): $X_5 = p_{51}X_1 + p_{52}X_2 + p_{53}X_3 + p_{54}X_4 + p_{5c}X_c$
(Equation 16): $X_6 = p_{61}X_1 + p_{62}X_2 + p_{63}X_3 + p_{64}X_4 + p_{65}X_5 + p_{6d}X_d$
(Equation 17): $X_7 = p_{71}X_1 + p_{72}X_2 + p_{73}X_3 + p_{74}X_4 + p_{75}X_5 + p_{76}X_6 + p_{7e}X_e$

Variables are: X_1 = Social class, X_2 = Scholastic ability, X_3 = Parental educational stress, X_4 = "Taken for granted," X_5 = Curriculum location, grade nine, X_6 = Peer college influence, grade nine, X_7 = Educational ambition, K = Education of mother, L = Education of father, M = Occupation of father, X_a–X_e = residuals

* This and all succeeding path diagrams in the text are "simplified" because we have elected to omit the unidirectional arrows usually used to indicate causal connections, direct causal connections, or "paths" between variables. We have elected to omit these arrows to reduce the considerable "clutter" that would otherwise result from their inclusion in a many-variable model.

ters are similar to Model C and Model D in that all are linear, additive, recursive models. However, the estimation method most appropriate for Model C will not yield unbiased and efficient estimators for our models because in all cases at least one of the further assumptions about explicit variables, residual variables, and the relations among them cannot be made. The first complicating factor, mentioned earlier in our description of the conceptualization and measurement of variables, is that we have no measure of social-class background.

A large part of the accumulated empirical research in sociology attests to the difficulty of developing a universally, or even specifically, satisfactory measure of social class. The best efforts of social researchers have focused on identifying objectively measured indicators of social class and validating the indicators against subjective evaluations. For males in advanced industrialized societies, a ranking of their jobs by the average education and earnings of all male incumbents provides one index of social class, and this procedure yields similar hierarchies when compared with subjective evaluations.[15] In this study our youthful subjects cannot be ranked by this measurable indicator or by their own subjective rankings. Nevertheless, we may employ parental education and occupation as reported by the student as indicators of the social class of the family of orientation of the student. We were unable to obtain any data on family income for our subjects.

We have chosen to use student reports of mother's education, father's education, and father's occupation (see note 7) as our three indicators of social-class background. There are two reasons for this decision. First, for many research purposes parental education and occupation serve as indicators of family class position. Second, it is our view that the main representative of the family unit to the school system is the student. During the secondary school years the primary source of information about a student's social-class background for school officials is the student.

We rejected the option of including both mother's occupation and father's occupation as indicators of social class because, for this population, about half the students from two-parent homes reported that their mothers were not employed outside the home. We could not devise a satisfactory scheme to represent adequately and objectively a nonemployed mother's contribution to a child's social-class background, except for her educational attainment. To include in our analysis a measure of mother's occupation that left us with missing data for about 60 percent of our subjects would distort our results too seriously to make up for the added information on the remaining 40 percent.[16]

Having decided on father's occupation, mother's education, and father's education as our indicators of social class, our next problem was to choose a method for combining the three indicators to best represent the unobserved variable. Social-class background is a key variable in our analysis and is the major explanatory variable in the revisionist view of the educational attainment process. Since our biases run counter to revisionist hypotheses, we selected a solution to the problem of combining these multiple indicators that in our estimation favors the role of social class as a causal influence on educational attainment.

Rather than assign arbitrary weights to the three indicators to construct an index of social-class background, we chose weights for each indicator from the results of a canonical correlation analysis carried out separately for each model. This procedure estimates the linear combination of one set of variables and the linear combination of a second set of variables such that the correlation between the two linear combinations is maximized. For each model we estimated the linear combination of mother's education, father's education, and father's occupation most highly correlated with a second estimated linear combination consisting of all endogenous variables in the particular model. The causal model for the ninth grade is presented in figure 2.3. In subsequent chapters the indicators of social class are omitted from the presentation of the causal models in the interests of simplicity, but the estimation procedures for those more complex models follow the procedure employed on the ninth grade model illustrated here.

Inspection of figure 2.3 and equations (12) through (17) reveals several features that preclude the use of the straightforward OLS estimation procedures appropriate for Model C. The unobserved variable, social-class background, is assumed to be completely determined by its indicators, K, L, and M. No restriction is placed on the correlation of the residual variables X_a and X_b and variables X_3 and X_4 are assumed to operate simultaneously and to be causally independent of each other. Scholastic ability X_2 is modeled as antecedent to all endogenous variables and the association between X_1 and X_2 remains unanalyzed.

Our procedure for estimating the solution to the model in figure 2.3 (and subsequent models as well) follows closely the method of Modified Generalized Least Squares outlined in Hauser and Goldberger[17] and Hauser.[18] From the zero-order correlations calculated from the data on all measured variables, we calculated a matrix of first-order partial correlation coefficient $r_{ij.2}$, controlling for X_2 throughout. Then a canonical correlation analysis between the indicator variables K, L, and M and the effect variables X_3 through X_7 yielded constrained partial correlations between these two sets of variables, one canonical variate in the set of indicators and path coefficients between the indicators and the canonical variate. The constrained partial correlations were then substituted back into the equations for zero-order correlations to give us a matrix of partly constrained correlations among all measured variables and the unmeasured canonical variate X_1. The remaining parameters p_{ij} were then estimated from the constrained matrix using Ordinary Least-Squares applied sequentially to equations (13) through (17). The method of Generalized Least Squares yields minimum-variance unbiased linear estimators in overidentified models that allow auto-correlated residuals. The results of the Modified Generalized Least-Squares canonical correlation procedure in this case give efficient parameter estimates that are unbiased to the extent that all relevant variables have been measured without error in the population under study.

We recognize many, but certainly not all, the unrealistic assumptions imposed on our analysis by the limitations of the data, the statistical tools available to us, and our interpretation of the assumptions of current social theories. We have discussed in this chapter most of our assumptions about data and estimation; our interpretation of theory is presented informally in chapter 1 and formally in the causal models of the chapters that follow. Throughout, our choices among alternative assumptions have been made with the primary objective of best assessing the process of educational attainment experienced by most high schoolers; we make no attempt to single out the experiences of a highly favored or highly disfavored minority. Secondarily, we chose assumptions that, in our estimation, enhanced the explanatory power of social-class background as a determinant of educational outcomes.

NOTES

1. Demographic, social, and economic data for this section are from a number of sources: A. G. Holtman, T. J. Parliament, and J. A. Raffa, *Consolidation of the School Districts of Broome County* (Binghamton: State University of New York at Binghamton, Center for Urban Studies, Economic Growth Institute, Consolidation Report No. 7, 1974); Olaf G. Larson, *The People of New York State Counties* (Ithaca: New York State College of Agriculture and Life Sciences, a Statutory College of the State University, Cornell University, 1974); U.S. Bureau of the Census, *Census of the Population: 1970. General Social and Economic Characteristics* (Washington, D.C.: Government Printing Office, 1973), Final Report PC(1)-C1; and U.S. Bureau of the Census, *Census of the Population: 1970. Detailed Characteristics* (Washington, D.C.: Government Printing Office, 1973), Final Report PC(1)-D1

2. These 57 counties *do not* include the five counties of New York City. These five counties were excluded in the compilation of the data by Larson, *People of New York State Counties.*

3. August B. Hollingshead, "The Two Factor Index of Social Position" (New Haven: Yale University, 1957). Mimeographed.

4. William H. Sewell and Robert M. Hauser, *Education, Occupation, and Earnings: Achievement in the Early Career* (Madison: University of Wisconsin, Department of Sociology, 1974). A final report of research carried out under Grant No. 314, Social and Rehabilitation Service, Social Security Administration, Department of Health, Education, and Welfare, Washington, D.C.

5. Karl Alexander and Bruce K. Eckland, *Effects of Education on the Social Mobility of High School Sophomores Fifteen Years Later (1955–1970)* (Chapel Hill: Institute for Research in Social Science, the University of North Carolina, 1973). A final report of research carried out under Grant No. OEG-4-71-0037, National Institute of Education, U.S. Department of Health, Education, and Welfare, Washington, D.C.

6. Within the context of a Marxist orientation, we are sensitive to the issue of operationalizing a Marxian definition of "social class."

Advocates of the revisionist thesis may well view social class in Marxian terms, i.e., as the relationship of the unit (family) to the means of production. Such an understanding is usually regarded as implying two classes: those who own (or control) and those who do not own (or control) the means of production. However, as numerous writers have noted, Marx neither adhered consistently to one definition of social class nor to a strict dichotomous conception of social class. None of the proponents of the revisionist thesis, to the knowledge of the present authors, has ever executed and published a study of schooling and social class using the Marxian dichotomous conception and measure of social class. Rather, their indicators of social class are usually similar to those we employ in our study, namely, educational, occupational, or income attainment. See, for example, Samuel Bowles and Herbert Gintis, "I.Q. in the U.S. Class Structure," *Social Policy*, November/December 1972 and January/February 1973, 65–96. See also Samuel Bowles and Herbert Gintis, *Schooling in Capitalist America* (New York: Basic Books, 1975).

7.   Hollingshead, *Two Factor Index of Social Position*. We asked the students living in single-parent homes to recall father's occupation and used this recalled statement as the measure of father's occupation for these students. For students who did not recall father's occupation, we coded the variable in the Hollingshead metric according to regression estimates generated from knowledge of parental education. Only for cases with no data on parental education or occupation was the mean Hollingshead score substituted. Hence a student who recalled father's occupation was classified according to that occupation whether or not the father was present in the home at the time of the survey.

8.   The measure of parental educational stress is from a study by David Bordua, "Education Aspirations and Parental Stress on College," *Social Forces*, March 1960, 262–69.

9.   Ralph Turner, *The Social Context of Ambition* (San Francisco: Chandler, 1964), p. 3.

10.   Sewell and Hauser, *Education, Occupation, and Earnings*.

11.   For a discussion of stanine scores, see J. P. Guilford, *Fundamental Statistics in Psychology and Education* (4th ed.; New York: McGraw-Hill, 1956), pp. 528–29.

12.   Mark Granovetter, review of William H. Sewell and Robert M. Hauser, *Education, Occupation, and Earnings: Achievement in the Early Career* (New York: Academic Press, 1975), in the *Harvard Educational Review*, February 1976, pp. 123–27.

13.   Kenneth C. Land, "Principles of Path Analysis," in *Sociological Methodology*, ed. E. F. Borgatta (San Francisco: Jossey-Bass, 1969), pp. 3–37.

14.   Hubert M. Blalock, Jr., *Social Statistics* (2nd ed.; New York: McGraw-Hill, 1972).

15.   Albert J. Reiss, Jr., *Occupations and Social Status* (New York: Free Press, 1961).

16.   Joan Acker, "Women and Social Stratification: A Case of Intellectual Sexism," *American Journal of Sociology* 78 (January 1973): 936–45.

17.   R. M. Hauser and A. S. Goldberger, "The Treatment of Unobservable Variables in Path Analysis" in *Sociological Methodology*, ed. H. L. Costner (San Francisco: Jossey-Bass, 1971), pp. 81–117.

18.   R. M. Hauser, "Disaggregating a Social-Psychological Model of Educational Attainment" in *Structural Equation Models in the Social Sciences*, ed. Arthur S. Goldberger and Otis D. Duncan (New York: Seminar Press, 1973), chap. 12.

3. Grade Nine: The Year of Exploration

The student's ninth-grade experience reflects the confrontation of individual uncertainty of goals with school organization demands for choices among alternative opportunities. The differentiated curricula of the first year of high school stand in contrast to the single curriculum pursued by most students through the eighth grade. The students in our study are offered some small choice of courses in the fine and practical arts prior to ninth grade, but the primary alternative offered them to the standard pattern and sequence of academic offering is to begin some ninth-grade courses a year earlier. By the end of ninth grade, a student must have chosen, however tentatively, among college preparatory, general, commercial, and vocational curricula. By that time, about 60 percent of our students have chosen a college-preparatory program.

Curriculum choice is an important correlate of a student's eventual educational attainment, and as such it is justified as a main focus of this analysis. In addition, other school outcomes are related to the ninth-grade curriculum decision: the physical and social segregation of students that results from curriculum differentiation also conditions friendship choices in high school. *Peer influence*, then, is a second outcome of the ninth-grade experience that shapes the student's subsequent educational decisions. Both curriculum location and peer influence play a part in shaping the student's *educational ambitions*, our third ninth-grade outcome. This chapter traces the effects of class and ability on these three outcomes of ninth grade: curriculum choice; whether the student has several, few, or no close friends with college ambitions; and the educational ambition of the student himself at the end of ninth grade.

By tracing the effects of socioeconomic-class background and scholastic ability on the student's early educational ambition, we may begin to assess the validity of the two competing theses discussed

71

in chapter 1. For the meritocrats, ability plus ambition equals success. In the context of the high school years, ability means scholastic ability and ambition is the amount of formal schooling the student expects to complete. Ambition is shaped in part by interpersonal influences from parents, peers, and educators. The meritocratic thesis predicts that any effect of class background on success is limited and probably mediated by those interpersonal influences. For the revisionists, by contrast, the effect of class background on success is strong and largely direct. In the revisionist view, ability plays a lesser role, and the structure of the school ensures that curriculum location will depend strongly on class background and in turn influence ambition.

Evidence from the ninth grade alone cannot fully test these ideas, since the ultimate measure of success in this context, college enrollment, is still in the future. But evidence from the ninth grade does allow a partial testing. Both viewpoints posit a similar sequence of events; their basic difference lies in the theoretical importance attributed to the events. Figure 3.1 is a graphic representation of the sequence of events through the end of ninth grade. The model depicted by figure 3.1 is made explicit in equations 1 to 5 (but see note 7):

Eq. 1: $X_3 = p_{31}X_1 + p_{32}X_2 + p_{3a}X_a$

Eq. 2: $X_4 = p_{41}X_1 + p_{42}X_2 + p_{4b}X_b$

Eq. 3: $X_5 = p_{51}X_1 + p_{52}X_2 + p_{53}X_3 + p_{54}X_4 + p_{5c}X_c$

Eq. 4: $X_6 = p_{61}X_1 + p_{62}X_2 + p_{63}X_3 + p_{64}X_4 + p_{65}X_5 + p_{6d}X_d$

Eq. 5: $X_7 = p_{71}X_1 + p_{72}X_2 + p_{73}X_3 + p_{74}X_4 + p_{75}X_5 + p_{76}X_6$
$+ p_{7e}X_e$

Social class (X_1) and scholastic ability (X_2) are exogenous to the ninth-grade schooling process, and their interrelationship is not explained in the model. Parental influence to continue education beyond high school $(X_3$ and $X_4)$ is taken to be a function of both social class and scholastic ability. Curriculum location (X_5) is the result of social class, scholastic ability, and parental influence. The number of friendship choices that the student makes among his age mates who intend to go to college (X_6) is posited as a result of class, ability, parental influence, and curriculum location. The final outcome of the ninth-grade school experience, educational ambition (X_7), depends upon all six preceding variables. The error terms $(X_a$ through

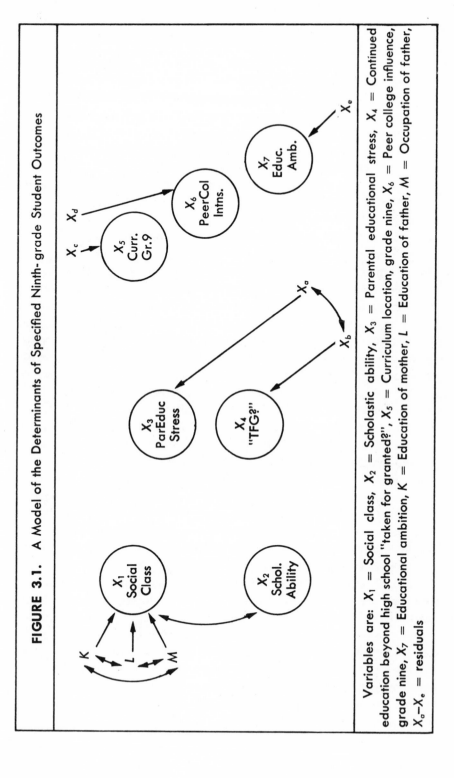

FIGURE 3.1. A Model of the Determinants of Specified Ninth- grade Student Outcomes

Variables are: X_1 = Social class, X_2 = Scholastic ability, X_3 = Parental educational stress, X_4 = Continued education beyond high school "taken for granted?", X_5 = Curriculum location, grade nine, X_6 = Peer college influence, grade nine, X_7 = Educational ambition, K = Education of mother, L = Education of father, M = Occupation of father, X_a–X_e = residuals

X_e) indicate the influence of factors not included in the model plus measurement error.

We discuss in detail below each outcome of interest in the ninth-grade model, i.e., curriculum location, peer college intentions, and educational ambition. Given the specification of the model, the parameter estimates, p_{ij}, derived from the data do not provide unequivocal evidence for accepting one theoretical view in preference to the other. Since the meritocratic and revisionist theses were stated in a form that emphasizes the contrasts between them, it is not too surprising that the actual experiences of ninth-grade students turn out to have a more complex explanation than either view provides.

The major determinant of curriculum location is ability, not class background. Nevertheless, scholastic ability alone or in combination with class background leaves much to be explained in the curriculum location of ninth graders. For predicting the college intentions of friendship choices, the reverse situation holds: social class has the stronger influence. As for educational ambition, social class has a stronger effect compared to ability for boys only, and exerts a direct effect on ambition for both boys and girls. As with much social research, the empirical evidence here is less definitive than are the pronouncements of the theorists. We shall therefore have to defer conclusive judgment as to the empirical tenability of the revisionist and meritocratic theses until we have analyzed data that pertain to student experiences in the later years of high school.

Viewing just the results of the ninth-grade experience, however, the meritocrats may claim victory in that ability is a strong determinant of curriculum location. Yet one-quarter of the highest-ability students are not in a college-preparatory program, and about half the low-ability students are. The revisionist argument is supported by the strongly persistent direct effects of class on ambition, regardless of ability and parental influence. Yet about a third of the ninth graders from blue-collar homes expect to go to college, and about two-fifths from white-collar backgrounds have no college ambitions.

Because the decisions made in ninth grade may be tentative does not imply that they are unimportant for the future; much of the student's subsequent high school experience is conditional on these early outcomes. We focus on each of these outcomes in turn, assessing our results for their implications for the two views of the educational process.

CURRICULUM LOCATION: EFFECTS OF CLASS, ABILITY, AND PARENTAL INFLUENCE

The social heterogeneity of today's high schools provides educators with a justification and a rationale for differentiating the secondary school curriculum into college-preparatory and noncollege-preparatory programs. This rationale persists from the turn of the century when the American high school became a democratized institution serving students from all class backgrounds rather than primarily those of the upper and middle classes.

In his historical account of the transformation of the American secondary school, Trow has written that the increasing diversity of the student body at the turn of the century provided the impetus for the development of the differentiated curriculum.[1] And, as Kerckhoff has observed, the differentiation of the curriculum does little to overcome the diverse character of the student body; students of similar backgrounds and interests tend to be attracted or placed into similar courses of study. Once in those programs, they tend to form intimate relationships with one another and to separate themselves from others who are in different programs within the same school.[2]

Differentiation is one of the defining characteristics of the secondary years, and curriculum is a major organizational instrument for that differentiation. Furthermore, curriculum differentiation is an organizational instrument that has potentially powerful consequences for the student. One such consequence, probably the most obvious, is that location in the academic or college-preparatory program tends to preserve the student's options to pursue education beyond high school or to seek immediate entry into the job market after high school. Location in a nonacademic program tends to impair the student's chances for future college entry, unless, of course, he is prepared to do remedial and compensatory academic work. The longer a student remains in the nonacademic program beyond ninth grade, the greater will be his cumulative deficit of college-entry requirements.

There is another, more subtle consequence of curriculum location. Differentiation of students into college and noncollege programs, write Cicourel and Kitsuse, places those individuals in microenvironments in which there develop

... standards of performance by which [the students] are evaluated by the school personnel and by which students are urged to evaluate themselves. It is the college-going student more than his non-college-going counterpart who is continually reminded by his teachers, parents, and peers of the decisive importance of academic achievement to the realization of his ambitions. . . .[3]

Now, students do not come into the college-preparatory program on a random, helter-skelter basis. There are systematic differences between those who are and those who are not in the college-preparatory program. Advocates of the revisionist thesis argue that social-class origin is a major source of such systematic differences between the two groups. Advocates of the meritocratic thesis would not deny the presence of systematic class differences between students in different curricula. They would assert, however, that the magnitude of those differences is not large and that the systematic differences due to scholastic ability are as great, or greater than, those attributable to class origin.

Social class and scholastic ability affect a student's chances of being in the college-preparatory program, as figure 3.2 illustrates. Among boys with above-average ability, 71 percent are in the academic program in comparison with 53 percent of their less-able counterparts. And, 70 percent of all boys from white-collar families are in the college-preparatory program in contrast with 53 percent of those from blue-collar homes. Among girls, the respective percentages for location in the college-preparatory program are 75 and 43 by ability and 69 and 50 by father's occupation as the indicator of social class. While these percentages do not permit a sound inference as to whether ability or class is the *stronger* influence on curriculum, they do enable us to state with certainty that social class is *not* a *strong* determinant of who is in what curriculum in the ninth grade. There is no evidence of an overwhelming tendency for most middle-class students to be in the academic program and working-class students not to be. For while it is true that almost three of every four middle-class students are in the college-preparatory course sequence, it is also true that about two of every four working-class students are in the same course sequence.

To assess which of these two variables—social class or scholastic

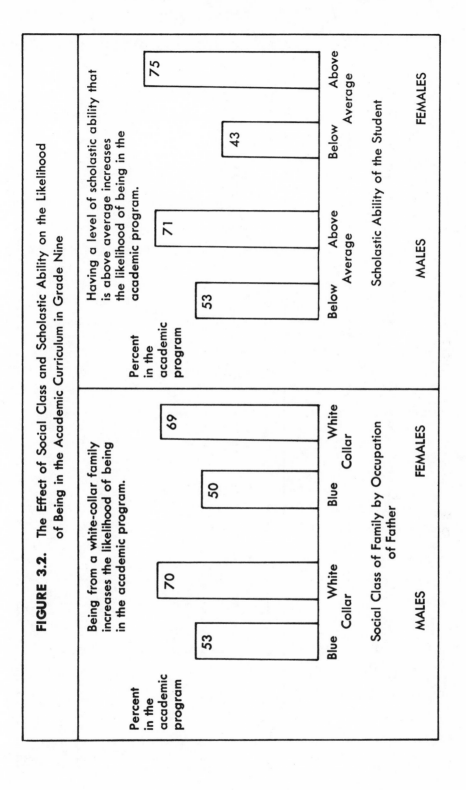

FIGURE 3.2. The Effect of Social Class and Scholastic Ability on the Likelihood of Being in the Academic Curriculum in Grade Nine

Being from a white-collar family increases the likelihood of being in the academic program.

Percent in the academic program

MALES

Blue Collar — 53	White Collar — 70

FEMALES

Blue Collar — 50	White Collar — 69

Social Class of Family by Occupation of Father

Having a level of scholastic ability that is above average increases the likelihood of being in the academic program.

Percent in the academic program

MALES

Below Average — 53
Above Average — 71

FEMALES

Below Average — 43
Above Average — 75

Scholastic Ability of the Student

TABLE 3.1. The Impact on Curriculum Location of Specified Variables: Correlations (Total Associations) from Various Studies

Identification of the Study	Description of Study Sample	Gender of Student	Correlations of Curriculum With:[d]				
			Indicators of Class[a]			Class[b] Comp.	Scholastic Ability
			POPOC	POPED	MOMED		
Williams	Sample from panel survey begun 1959–60 with almost all students in Ontario, Canada, and continued each subsequent year to grade 13.	Male	.27	.23	.21	N.A.[c]	.44
		Female	.27	.27	.25	N.A.	.41
Douglas	Panel study of 5,362 males born in Britain during first week of March 1946	Male	.33	.31	N.A.	N.A.	.48
Heyns	Selected sample of 15,384 12th graders from the Coleman et al. 1965 Equality of Educational Opportunity Survey	Male and Female	.24	.26	N.A.	N.A.	.49
Alexander and Eckland	National probability sample, panel design, of 2,077 males first surveyed as 10th graders in 1955	Male	.27	.34	.27	N.A.	.35

Median Correction[e]		.27	.29	.25	N.A.	.46
This study	See chapter 2					
	Male	.21	.20	.17	.24	.29
	Female	.25	.27	.22	.31	.41

Sources: Trevor Williams, "Educational Aspirations: Longitudinal Evidence on Their Development in Canadian Youth," *Sociology of Education* 45 (Spring 1972): 107–33. Data also provided in personal communication from Professor Williams. J. W. B Douglas, J. M. Ross, and H. R. Simpson, *All Our Future* (London: Davies, 1968), in Alan C. Kerckhoff, "Patterns of Educational Attainment in Great Britain," *American Journal of Sociology* 80 (May 1975): 1428–37; Barbara Heyns, "Social Selection and Stratification within Schools," *American Journal of Sociology* 79 (May 1974): 1434–51; Karl Alexander and Bruce K. Eckland, *Effects of Education on the Social Mobility of High School Sophomores Fifteen Years Later (1955–1970)* (Chapel Hill: Institute for Research in Social Science, University of North Carolina, 1973), Final Report, project no. 10202, OECG-71-0037, Department of Health, Education, and Welfare, National Institute of Education. Mimeographed.

a POPOC = occupation of father; POPED, MOMED = education of each parent. See original study for complete definition of how these variables were measured.

b "Class Comp." is a composite measure of social class, combining two or more of the separate indicators. See original study for complete definition and procedure.

c N.A. = coefficient not calculated for the particular study cited.

d Curriculum defined in these studies as a dichotomy: college-preparatory or other.

e In computing the median correlations, the gender-specific coefficients for the Williams' study were first combined by estimating the median coefficient between genders, inasmuch as both genders are from the same sample. Where rounding has been necessary, the coefficient has been rounded upward.

ability—has the stronger total association with curriculum, we refer to the correlation coefficients in tables 3.1 and 3.2. Unlike estimates of the strength of a relationship that are based on percentages and on the differences between percentages, estimates based on correlations are much less subject to variations and error that result from more or less arbitrary decisions as to where to "cut" or "divide" the several levels of a variable for the purpose of analysis (see, for example, Blalock[4]). Furthermore, the use of correlation rather than percentages frees us from the severe constraint that percentages impose on multivariate analysis—the limitation of the number of variables that can be controlled at the same time, a limitation that results from the rapid loss of observations as more and more predictor variables are brought under control.

Table 3.1 enables the reader to compare the correlations or total associations of class and ability with curriculum from this study with those reported in four other studies: (1) Alexander and Eckland's national longitudinal survey of 2,077 boys who were high school sophomores in 1955; (2) Douglas' study of more than 5,000 British men born in the first week of March 1946; (3) Heyns' analysis of data from more than 15,000 boys and girls who participated in the 1965 national Equality of Educational Opportunity Survey conducted by James Coleman and colleagues; and (4) Williams' analysis of data from a 1959–60 longitudinal survey of Ontario, Canada, youth.

The inference from table 3.1 is unequivocal. *Curriculum is more strongly associated with scholastic ability than with social class.* Coefficients for the ability-curriculum relationship have a median value of .46, almost twice that of the median value for the class-curriculum relationship of .25–.29 when class is defined by the component elements of father's occupation, father's or mother's education. Even when all three elements of class are combined via canonical correlation into one summary construct, the total association of class with curriculum is still less than that of ability. From our own data, also displayed in table 3.1, we observe that the correlation of our class construct with curriculum for boys is .24 while that of ability with curriculum is .29. For girls, the respective correlations are .31 and .41. With these simple correlations, the evidence is convincing: neither ability nor class is a powerful determinant of curriculum, but ability has more to do than does social class with whether the student, as a ninth grader, is in a college-preparatory program.

It is difficult to know precisely just how social class and scholastic ability affect the curriculum location of the student. From the perspective of the school, it is reasonable to assume that counselors and teachers who evaluate a student as being of above-average scholastic ability, as being from a middle-class home, or as being from a family where the parents have high educational ambitions for their child are more likely to want to see that student located in the academic program. From the perspective of the home, it is equally reasonable to assume that parents, particularly those of the middle class or those with scholastically able offspring, express directly to the school counselor or teacher their desire that their son or daughter be placed in the academic program. Either as a supplement to or in lieu of such a direct approach, parents, particularly those from the middle class or those with scholastically able offspring, may attempt to influence the curriculum preference of their son or daughter by trying to raise the educational ambition of their offspring. Perceiving such parental influence, the son or daughter may convey those ambitions to the counselor or teacher either by overtly requesting to be placed in the academic program or by displaying those academic behaviors and attitudes that make such placement more likely.

Such parental efforts to influence the educational ambition of their children have been noted by several investigators, the first of whom was Joseph Kahl. Those efforts he referred to as "parental pressure," that is, any "clear and overt attempt by either or both parents to influence their son to go to college." [5] Other investigators, using somewhat similar constructs, have referred to this parental behavior as "urgings," or "stress." Generically, we shall subsume all such labels under the rubric of "parental educational influence." Each of these investigators also has reported a tendency for such influence to vary with the social class of the parent and with the scholastic ability of the student. [6] The higher the social class of the parents or the brighter the adolescent, the more probable it is that the student will report efforts by his mother and father to influence him to continue his education beyond high school.

What we propose is thus an indirect linkage between social class and scholastic ability, on the one hand, and curriculum on the other. The class of the parents and their evaluation of the adolescent's ability affect the intensity of their efforts to influence the educational ambition of the adolescent, and those efforts in turn affect the curriculum location of the adolescent.

From each of our students we secured two measures of their perceptions of the extent to which their parents were attempting to influence them to be educationally ambitious, that is, to continue their education beyond high school. Each student was asked to indicate: (1) the degree to which each parent had stressed that the student continue his education beyond high school; and (2) whether, in point of fact, the student had come to regard continued education as "taken for granted" by his parents.

Each measure, as figure 3.3 illustrates, is positively associated with the social class and scholastic ability of the student. High stress on continued education is reported by 45 percent of the boys from white-collar homes compared with 32 percent from blue-collar homes. Having one's education beyond high school "taken for granted" characterized 71 percent of the girls whose fathers had white-collar jobs in contrast with 50 percent of those girls whose fathers had jobs classified as blue-collar. Thirty-five percent of the scholastically more able girls reported that their parents placed high stress on postsecondary education, a level of influence equaled by only 22 percent of the scholastically less able girls. Almost three in four boys with above-average ability said that their continued education was "taken for granted," an assertion made by only about two in four boys with below-average ability.

And, as figure 3.4 illustrates, curriculum is associated with each of the two measures of parental influence. Of those male students who indicated a high level of parental educational stress (PES), 77 percent are located in the academic program in contrast with 44 percent of those who reported a low level of stress. For girls, having their continued education "taken for granted" (TFG) boosted their chances of being in the academic program to 76 times out of 100, double the 37 times out of 100 characteristic of girls whose continued education was not "taken for granted."

Table 3.2 presents correlations of parental influence with social class and scholastic ability from several other studies. Included in that table are coefficients from the Alexander and Eckland and the Williams' studies described earlier as well as from the Sewell and Hauser analysis of 1,789 men who graduated in 1957 from Wisconsin high schools and who in 1964 were employed in the civilian labor

FIGURE 3.3. The Effect of Social Class and Scholastic Ability on Two Indicators of Parental Educational Influence

Students from white-collar homes are more likely to report high parental stress on continued education beyond high school.

Percent reporting high educ. stress

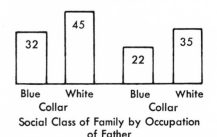

Social Class of Family by Occupation of Father

MALES   FEMALES

The more scholastically able a student, the more likely is that individual to report high parental educational stress on continued education.

Percent reporting high educ. stress

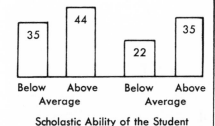

Scholastic Ability of the Student

MALES   FEMALES

White-collar students are more likely to report that their continued education beyond high school has been "taken for granted."

Percent reporting continued educ. "taken for granted"

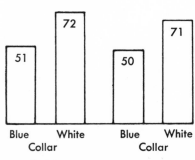

Social Class of Family by Occupation of Father

MALES   FEMALES

Scholastically more able students are more likely to report that their continued education beyond high school has been "taken for granted."

Percent reporting continued educ. "taken for granted"

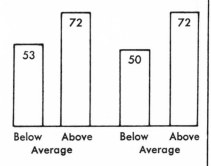

Scholastic Ability of the Student

MALES   FEMALES

FIGURE 3.4. The Effect of Parental Educational Influence on the Likelihood of Being in the Academic Program

Having parents who place much stress on continued education increases the likelihood of being in the academic program.

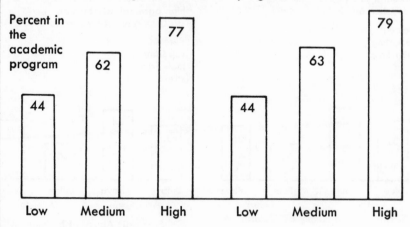

Percent in the academic program

Intensity of Parental Educational Stress

MALES   FEMALES

Having one's education beyond high school "taken for granted" increases the likelihood of being in the academic program.

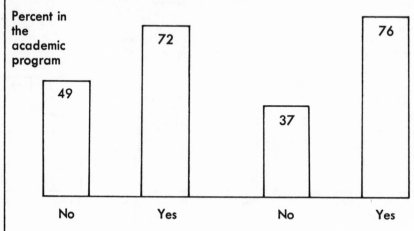

Percent in the academic program

Continued Education Beyond High School "Taken for Granted?"

MALES   FEMALES

force. Parental influence, it would seem, correlates about the same with social class as it does with scholastic ability. All total associations fall within the range of .20 to .30.

From our own data in table 3.3, we can see that curriculum correlates with parental educational stress r_{53}, .31 for boys and .33 for girls, while with "taken for granted" curriculum correlates r_{54}, .24 for boys and .39 for girls. The average curriculum-influence relationship is thus in the mid-30s while the average influence-class and ability relationship is in the mid-20s. Curriculum, then, has a stronger association with the efforts of parents to influence the future educational career of their children than do those efforts with the social class of the family or with the scholastic ability of the children.

Location in one curriculum or another in ninth grade thus is affected by the more proximate variable of parental educational influence, by the more distal variables of social class and scholastic ability, and it is probably through the more proximate variable of parental influence that the more distal variables of family class and student ability come to affect whether, as a ninth grader, the student is in the academic or nonacademic program.

Revisionist and meritocratic perspectives on the school provide some testable propositions regarding what we may expect in the way of total associations, direct and indirect effects from the four determinants of curriculum we have specified in our model. The revisionist position posits a strong class effect on curriculum with much of that effect being the result of class discrimination by the school in favor of placing middle-class students in the academic program. Thus the revisionist argument suggests a large total association between class and curriculum, larger than that between ability and curriculum, and a strong direct effect from class to curriculum, stronger than that between ability and curriculum. Furthermore, since much of the total class association should be direct, a reflection of class discrimination by the school, not much of that association should be mediated through the educational influence of the parents.

The meritocratic argument, on the other hand, posits a stronger total association of ability with curriculum than of class with curriculum. And, we might venture the proposition that if the school places students into one program or another mostly on the basis of "objective" measures of academic potential, then much of that total association between ability and curriculum should be direct, unmediated

TABLE 3.2. The Impact on Measures of Parental Educational Influence of Specified Variables: Correlations (Total Associations) from Various Studies

Identification of the Study	Description of Study Sample	Gender of Student	Correlations of Parental Influence With:[a]				
			Indicators of Class			Class Comp.	Scholastic Ability
			POPOC	POPED	MOMED		
Williams	Canadian students	Male	.24	N.A.	N.A.	N.A.	.23
		Female	.23	N.A.	N.A.	N.A.	.27
Alexander and Eckland	National U.S. sample	Male	.21	.29	.24	N.A.	.26
Sewell and Hauser	Subset of male high school[b] seniors, state of Wisconsin, surveyed initially in 1957 and subsequently	Male	.26	.25	.23	N.A.	.35
Median Correlation[c]			.24	.27	.24	N.A.	.26
This Study	See chapter 2 Measure is *Parental Ed. Str.*[d]	Male	.22	.20	.16	.24	.20
		Female	.21	.24	.19	.26	.22
	Measure is *"Taken for Gntd."*	Male	.27	.25	.21	.30	.26
		Female	.26	.29	.23	.33	.30

Sources: For Williams and for Alexander and Eckland, see source reference in table 3.1. Sewell and Hauser source is William H. Sewell and Robert M. Hauser, *Education, Occupation, and Earnings: Achievement in the Early Career* (Madison: Department of Sociology, University of Wisconsin, 1974). Final report of research carried out under Grant Nr. 314, Social and Rehabilitation Service, Social Security Administration, Department of Health, Education, and Welfare, Washington, D.C.

[a] Parental influence measures are: Williams, tenth-graders' estimates of what parents want them to do educationally, scaled in a seven-level measure; Alexander and Eckland, tenth-graders' reports of the extent to which they discussed with parents or guardian going on to college; Sewell and Hauser, twelfth-graders' reports of extent to which their parents wanted them to go to college.

[b] This subset consists of 1,789 men who in 1964 "were employed in the civilian labor force but were not in school and for whom information on 1965–67 Social Security earnings and for all the other variables in the [Sewell and Hauser] model was available."

[c] In computing the median correlations, the gender-specific coefficients for the Williams' study were first combined by estimating the median coefficient between genders, inasmuch as both genders are from the same sample. Where rounding has been necessary, the coefficient has been rounded upward.

[d] See the text and chapter 2 for definition of these two measures.

TABLE 3.3. The Total Associations with Ninth-grade Curriculum Location of Specified Independent Variables and Their Total, Direct, and Indirect Effects

Independent Variables		Male Students				Female Students			
		Total Assoc. r_{ij}	Direct p_{ij}	Effect: Indir. s_{ij}	Total q_{ij}	Total Assoc. r_{ij}	Direct p_{ij}	Effect: Indir. s_{ij}	Total q_{ij}
Social class	X_1	.241	.133	.052	.185	.306	.118	.085	.203
Scholastic ability	X_2	.287	.206	.036	.242	.413	.287	.067	.354
Parental ed. stress	X_3	.312	.238	.000	.238	.325	.141	.000	.141
Taken for granted	X_4	.237	.000	.000	.000	.393	.208	.000	.208
Proportion of Variance Accounted for: R^2		.166				.282			

by the efforts of the parents to influence the educational ambition of their child.

Table 3.3 contains the information necessary to assess the tenability of these propositions.[7] Contrary to the revisionist position, class does not have a strong total association with curriculum. Its correlation with curriculum, r_{51}, is .24 for boys and .31 for girls. In fact, class has the second smallest total association with curriculum among boys and the smallest among girls. Class also does *not* have a strong direct effect on curriculum. For boys its path (p_{51}) is .13, ranking it third and last ("taken for granted" has no effect once class, ability, and parental educational stress are taken into account). For girls, the direct effect of class (p_{51}) is .12, also ranking it last. Finally, between one-fourth and one-half the total effect that class has on curriculum is indirect, mediated by parental educational influence.

Consistent with the meritocratic position, ability has a total association with curriculum that is larger than that of class: $r_{52} = .29$ for boys and .41 for girls. The direct effect that ability has on curriculum also is larger than that of class: $p_{52} = .21$ for boys and .29 for girls. Finally, parental educational influence mediates a smaller portion of the ability-curriculum causal relationship than it does of the class-curriculum causal relationship. No more than one-fifth of the total effect that ability has on curriculum is mediated by the parents.

With respect to the causal impact that parental educational influence has on curriculum, it is noteworthy that for both boys and girls such influence equals or exceeds that of social class. For boys, the total effect from parental educational stress to curriculum, r_{53}, is .24, .05 units higher than the total effect of class. For girls, the total effect from "taken for granted," r_{54}, is .21, about equal to the total effect from class, r_{51}, of .20.

Contrary to the revisionist thesis, but consistent with the meritocratic thesis, merit is more important than privilege of birth in determining who will be placed in the academic program to prepare for college and subsequent occupational and income attainments.

PEER COLLEGE INTENTIONS: ANALYSIS OF THE DETERMINANTS OF FRIENDSHIP CHOICE

Proponents of the revisionist thesis have not paid much attention to the process by which the educational progress of the student is influenced by close friends, i.e., by the peer group. Mainstream sociologists, however, have studied carefully and at length this process of interpersonal influence. The neglect of this process by the revisionist is ironic for, as we show below, the social-class origin of the student is the strongest single causal determinant of whether he has three, two, one, or no close friends who are college-bound. The number of such friends the student has is itself one of the strongest determinants of that individual's educational ambition. The peer group is thus one social instrumentality by which the social-class origin of the individual comes to be associated with his educational ambition at the end of ninth grade.

Peers, of course, play an important role in the socialization of the individual, particularly in the critical period between childhood and adulthood. S. N. Eisenstadt has written that in modern industrial societies the family can no longer provide the adolescent with an environment sufficient for him to develop a sense of full identity and complete maturity. To a degree this void has been filled by the peer group. Among his age mates, the adolescent can seek "some framework for the development and crystallization of his identity, for the attainment of personal autonomy, and for his effective transition into the adult world." [8]

In modern industrial societies, where on a daily basis almost all youth under the age of majority are physically segregated from the rest of society with their age mates to be "educated," the school tends to be the setting where many friendships form. From their study of youth in both the United States and Denmark, Kandel and Lesser found that "the majority of adolescents, approximately 60 percent of the boys and 70 percent of the girls, report that their very best friend is in the same school." [9] Within the school, the formation of friendships tends to be facilitated by social similarities among students and, as Kerchoff has observed, by the continued physical and social proximity that results from individuals sharing common courses of study in one program or another. [10]

While we have information on some social characteristics of our students, we lack comparable information for each of the individuals they named as their close friends. Nevertheless, the attribute of the peer group that we have measured is the same attribute we measured for the individual student: level of educational ambition. It is plausible to assume that the social characteristics that produce a given level of ambition in the student are also the social characteristics that produce a given level of ambition in the student's close friends. Consequently, if the social class of the student is positively related to his educational ambition (as we shall see it is in the concluding section of this chapter), then the social class of each friend is positively related to the friend's own educational ambition. If similarities in social class are a basis for the formation of friendships, then middle-class students are more likely to associate with middle-class friends, and, hence, middle-class students are more likely to have several rather than few friends with college ambitions. Similar reasoning leads us to predict a positive association between the scholastic ability of the student and the number of his friends who are college-bound and between the amount of parental educational influence perceived by the student and the number of his friends who are college-bound.

Finally, since one consequence of the differentiated curriculum is to place students of similar social and academic characteristics together in their respective college-preparatory or noncollege-preparatory programs, it is likely that students will tend to form friendships *within* rather than between those programs. Thus, students in the academic program are more likely to associate with several college-bound peers, and those in the nonacademic program with few college-bound peers.

Of the four determinants of peer choice specified in our model, the total associations displayed in table 3.4 reveal social class to be the largest determinant of whether the individual has three, two, one, or no college-bound friends.[11] For boys, the total association of class with that peer attribute, r_{61}, is .33, of which 82 percent is causal. For girls, the total association of class with that peer attribute, r_{61}, is .35, of which 84 percent is causal. Illustrated with percentages, as in figure 3.5, we can see that 38 percent of all boys from white-collar homes reported all three friends as having college intentions, twice the percentage for those boys from blue-collar homes.

Ability is also an important determinant of this attribute of the peer relationship. Among boys, the total association of ability with the number of college-bound friends, r_{62}, is .30, of which 78 percent is causal; among girls the total association, r_{62}, is .28, and 70 percent of that is causal. As figure 3.5 illustrates, all three close friends were

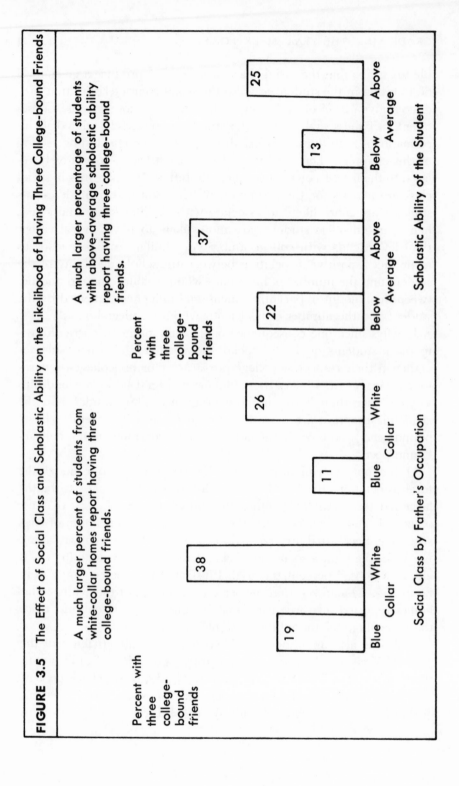

FIGURE 3.5 The Effect of Social Class and Scholastic Ability on the Likelihood of Having Three College-bound Friends

TABLE 3.4. Total Associations with Ninth-grade Peer College Intentions of Specified Independent Variables and Their Total, Direct, and Indirect Effects

Independent Variables		Male Students				Female Students			
		Total Assoc. r_{ij}	Direct p_{ij}	Effect: Indir. s_{ij}	Total q_{ij}	Total Assoc. r_{ij}	Direct p_{ij}	Effect: Indir. s_{ij}	Total q_{ij}
Social class	X_1	.327	.181	.088	.269	.353	.225	.070	.295
Scholastic ability	X_2	.303	.154	.083	.237	.284	.114	.084	.198
Parental ed. stress	X_3	.297	.132	.037	.169	.235	.055	.021	.076
Taken for granted	X_4	.302	.127	.000	.127	.301	.113	.000	.113
Curriculum gr. 9	X_5	.315	.156	.000	.156	.322	.144	.000	.144
Proportion of Variance Accounted for: R^2		.233				.205			

reported as having college ambitions by 25 percent of girls with above-average scholastic ability but by only 13 percent of girls with below-average scholastic ability.

Parental educational influence also affects whether the student is friendly with college-going peers. The more the student perceives his parents as stressing his own education beyond high school or the more the student believes that his parents take such education for granted, the more likely he is to report several rather than few friends who themselves are college-bound. Figure 3.6 illustrates this relationship. Of those boys who have come to regard their continued education as "taken for granted," 38 percent have all three peers with college ambitions. Only 18 percent of those boys who do not regard their own education as "taken for granted" claim such a peer group. Parental influence has less of an impact on this attribute of the peer group than does either class or ability. The total effects of "stress' and of "taken for granted" on the number of college-bound peers are $r_{63} = .17$ and $r_{64} = .13$, respectively for boys; $r_{63} = .08$ and $r_{64} = .11$, respectively, for girls. It is noteworthy that at least in this sphere of adolescent activity, both parents and peers are somewhat mutually supportive.

Lastly, we observe that the likelihood of the student having several rather than few college-bound friends is higher if the student is in the college-preparatory program (see figure 3.7). For boys and for girls, the total association between curriculum and the number of peers with college ambitions, r_{65}, is .32. About half of that total association, 50 percent for boys, 55 percent for girls, is *noncausal*. This noncausal component is a consequence of the fact that both the curriculum location of the student and the educational ambitions of his friends are products of a common set of antecedents, a set specified in our model as consisting of social class, scholastic ability, and parental educational stress. Nevertheless, even when the effects of these common antecedents are statistically removed, location in the academic program still makes it more likely that the individual student will have several rather than few or no friends who are college-bound. Curriculum affects the number of college-bound friends directly with a path of $p_{65} = .16$ for boys and .14 for girls.

With the student's own social class, scholastic ability, parental educational influence, and curriculum location affecting whether he associates with three, two, one, or no friends who themselves have

FIGURE 3.6. How Parental Educational Influence Affects One's Choice of Close Friends

Students who regard their continued education beyond high school as "taken for granted" are more likely to have all three of their close friends "college-bound."

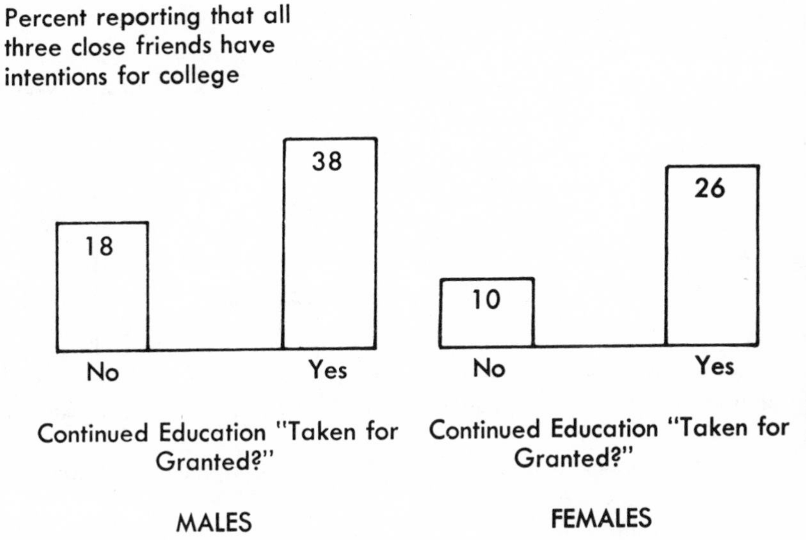

Percent reporting that all three close friends have intentions for college

MALES

18 — No
38 — Yes

Continued Education "Taken for Granted?"

FEMALES

10 — No
26 — Yes

Continued Education "Taken for Granted?"

ambitions for college, and with those same four variables affecting whether the student himself has an ambition for college, the question that arises is what proportion, if any, of the total association between the college ambition of the student and those of the student's peers is causal? We answer that question as we turn now to an analysis of the determinants of the final ninth-grade outcome—the student's own level of educational ambition.

EDUCATIONAL AMBITION: ANALYSIS OF ITS DETERMINANTS

In the first chapter, we ventured two propositions about educational ambition, that is, about the intention to abandon a lower-level social position inherited from one's parents in order to attain a higher-level position for oneself, or to maintain or enhance an inherited middle- or upper-level social position.[12] Those propositions

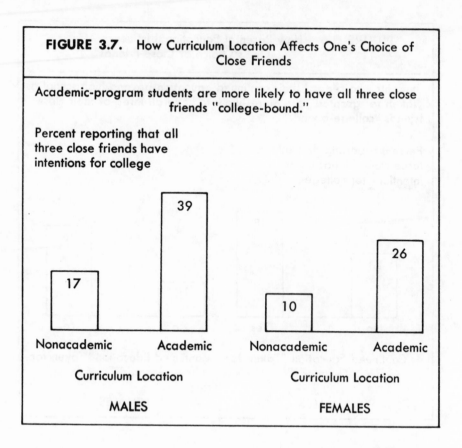

FIGURE 3.7. How Curriculum Location Affects One's Choice of Close Friends

Academic-program students are more likely to have all three close friends "college-bound."

Percent reporting that all three close friends have intentions for college

39

26

17

10

| Nonacademic | Academic | Nonacademic | Academic |

Curriculum Location   Curriculum Location

MALES   FEMALES

were that:

1. The ultimate educational attainment of the individual and his progress through school are rather strongly determined by the level of educational ambition which that individual brings with him to high school.

2. A significant portion of the effect that the individual's social class of origin has on his ultimate educational attainment and his progress through school is mediated through the level of ambition that he brings with him to high school.

In succeeding chapters, we analyze educational ambition as an *independent* and as an *intervening* variable. That is, we estimate just how much of an independent effect the ambition of the student, measured during ninth grade, has on his progress through grades ten, eleven, and twelve. And we estimate just what proportion of the effects from social class are mediated through that ambition, as an inter-vening variable, to such indicators of school progress as curriculum location, counselor encouragement, and academic achievement. But our concern here is with educational ambition as a *dependent* variable, as a product of the individual's class and ability, the efforts of his parents to influence his educational future, and his curriculum loca-tion and peer group. Figure 3.1 graphically represents our theoretical understanding of the causal structure of educational ambition. But before we pursue that multivariate mode of analysis, we shall place our own data in comparative perspective by reviewing the correla-tions published by several other investigators as estimates of the total associations between an educational ambition (or similar measure) and the various determinants specified in our model.

The Total Associations of an Educational Ambition with Its Specified Determinants

A remarkable consistency characterizes the correlations from various studies that are presented in table 3.5. In this table, we have added to those studies described earlier in this chapter the inquiry of Bachman based on panel data from a national probability sample of some 2,200 tenth graders first surveyed in 1968 and a project by Kerckhoff that involved students in Fort Wayne, Indiana, schools, with the correlations shown in table 3.5 being those for some 320 ninth-grade boys. From these correlations in table 3.5, we would conclude that the educational ambitions of ninth- or tenth-grade students have their highest total association with interpersonal influence from parents (median $r = .79$); followed by that from peers (median $r = .51$). With a median correlation of .45, curriculum is almost as strongly associated with ambition as is peer influence. Scholastic ability and social class are remarkably similar in their total associations with educational ambition, both having correla-tions averaging in the middle to lower 30s.

For our own sample of students, table 3.6 displays the various correlation coefficients estimating the size of the total associations between the ambition level of the student as a ninth grader and the social class, scholastic ability, parent and peer educational influence, and curriculum location of that student. The rank order of those co-efficients, and their sizes parallel closely if not completely the rank

TABLE 3.5. The Impact on Educational Ambition of Specified Variables: Correlations (Total Associations) from Various Studies

Identification of the Study	Description of Study Sample	Gender of Student	Correlations of Educational Ambition With[a]							
			Class Indicators			Class Comp.	Schol. Ability	Curriculum	Par. Infl.	Peer Infl.
			POPOC	POPED	MOMED					
Williams	Canadian students	Male	.20	.18	.20	N.A.	.25	.40	.78	.45
		Female	.25	.28	.22	N.A.	.32	.49	.80	.40
Alexander and Eckland	National U.S. sample	Male	.36	.36	.31	N.A.	.36	.45	.51	.53
Bachman	National U.S. panel study of 2,200 tenth-grade students first surveyed in 1968	Male	N.A.	N.A.	N.A.	.29	.27	N.A.	N.A.	N.A.
Kerckhoff	Survey of students from Fort Wayne, Indiana, schools, 320 ninth graders surveyed in 1969	Male	.46	.45	.44	N.A.	.49	N.A.	.78	.51
Median Correlation[b]			.36	.36	.31	.29	.33	.45	.79	.51

This Study	See chapter 2							
Male	.40	.38	.31	.46	.39	.42	.48[c]	.51
Female	.32	.36	.29	.40	.41	.48	.47	.44

Sources: Jerald G. Bachman, *Youth in Transition*, vol. 2 (Ann Arbor: Institute for Social Research, 1970); Alan C. Kerckhoff, *Ambition and Attainment* (Washington, D.C.: American Sociological Association, 1974), tables 6.3, 7.4.

[a] Ambition measures are: Williams, tenth-graders' indication of educational plans ranging over seven levels from "leave school as soon as possible" to "complete secondary school and then enter university." All correlations are from data provided to authors in personal correspondence except for parent and peer influence, which are from Williams (1972) as referenced in table 3.1; Alexander and Eckland, tenth-grade students asked to indicate on an eight-level scale what they would be doing when they finished high school; Bachman, tenth-grade measure, dichotomy, plan to go to college or not; Kerckhoff, measure of ambition is the educational expectations of ninth-grade students.

[b] Median r between genders used for the Williams' sample. Coefficients rounded upward where necessary.

[c] Measure of parental influence is that of "taken for granted."

TABLE 3.6. The Total Associations with Educational Ambition of Specified Independent Variables and Their Total, Direct, and Indirect Effects

Independent Variables		Male Students				Female Students			
		Total Assoc. r_{ij}	Direct p_{ij}	Effect: Indir. s_{ij}	Total q_{ij}	Total Assoc. r_{ij}	Direct p_{ij}	Effect: Indir. s_{ij}	Total q_{ij}
Social class	X_1	.455	.201	.183	.384	.399	.121	.183	.304
Scholastic ability	X_2	.389	.131	.164	.295	.407	.144	.174	.318
Parental ed. stress	X_3	.402	.127	.081	.208	.453	.210	.041	.251
Taken for granted	X_4	.483	.233	.030	.263	.472	.163	.069	.232
Curriculum gr. 9	X_5	.421	.162	.039	.201	.482	.189	.030	.219
Peer col. int. gr. 9	X_6	.513	.249	.000	.249	.442	.199	.000	.200
Proportion of Variance Accounted for: R^2		.502				.458			

order and sizes of those coefficients from the studies reviewed in table 3.5. That is, table 3.6 indicates that in the ninth grade, a student is most likely to report that his realistic educational ambition is to a four-year college if that student is:

1. *Subject to efforts by parents or peers to influence him to continue his education beyond high school.* Between parental educational stress and educational ambition, for example, the total association, r_{73}, for boys is .40 with 68 percent of those who report a high level of parental stress expecting to go on to a four-year college in comparison with only 31 percent of those who report a low level of parental educational stress (see figure 3.8). For girls, there is a total peer influence-educational ambition association, r_{76}, of .44 with 75 percent of those girls with all three friends college-bound themselves planning on a four-year college, a stark contrast to the 19 percent who plan on a four-year college when none of their friends is college-bound (see figure 3.9).

2. *In the college-preparatory program.* Curriculum location correlates with ambition, r_{75}, .42 for boys and .48 for girls. More than two-thirds of the boys in the academic program have an ambition to four years of college. Less than a third of the boys in the nonacademic program have that ambition (see figure 3.10).

3. *From a middle-class or white-collar home.* Class has a total association with ambition, r_{71}, of .46 for boys and .40 for girls. About two-thirds of the boys from white-collar families have an ambition for a four-year college; less than one-third of the boys from blue-collar families have that ambition (see figure 3.11).

4. *Scholastically more able.* Scholastic ability correlates with ambition, r_{72}, .39 for boys and .42 for girls. Almost six of every ten girls with above-average ability have a college ambition but fewer than three in every ten with below-average ability do (see figure 3.11).

When all six determinants are taken together in a multiple-regression equation to predict the level of a student's educational ambition as a ninth grader, the explanatory power of that prediction is rather good. Together, these six variables account for about half of all individual differences or "variance" in the ambition levels of ninth-grade boys, $R^2 = .501$. For girls, those six variables account

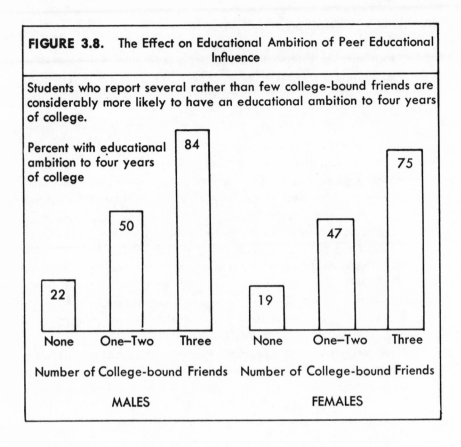

FIGURE 3.8. The Effect on Educational Ambition of Peer Educational Influence

Students who report several rather than few college-bound friends are considerably more likely to have an educational ambition to four years of college.

Percent with educational ambition to four years of college

MALES

None	One–Two	Three
22	50	84

Number of College-bound Friends

FEMALES

None	One–Two	Three
19	47	75

Number of College-bound Friends

for something less than half of all individual differences in an ambition level, $R^2 = .457$. At this point, we shall look more closely at the multivariate causal structure of educational ambition among ninth-grade students.

A Causal Analysis of the Determinants of Educational Ambitions of Ninth Graders

Total associations or correlations, of course, enable us to estimate only the upper limits of the relationships that a dependent variable such as educational ambition has with various independent variables such as social class, scholastic ability, parent and peer influence, and curriculum location. The understanding of these relationships, that is, their decomposition into noncausal, causal direct, and causal indirect components, requires a model that specifies the causal structure among those variables. Figure 3.1 provides a sight-image of the

FIGURE 3.9. The Effect of Parental Educational Influence on Level of Educational Ambition

The more the parents stress continued education beyond high school, the more likely it is that the student will have a college-level ambition.

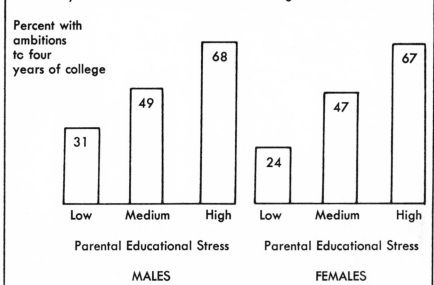

Percent with ambitions to four years of college

MALES

Low 31 Medium 49 High 68

Parental Educational Stress

FEMALES

Low 24 Medium 47 High 67

Parental Educational Stress

Students who regard their continued education beyond high school as "taken for granted" are more likely to have a college-level ambition.

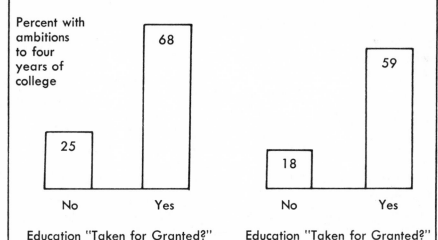

Percent with ambitions to four years of college

MALES

No 25 Yes 68

Education "Taken for Granted?"

FEMALES

No 18 Yes 59

Education "Taken for Granted?"

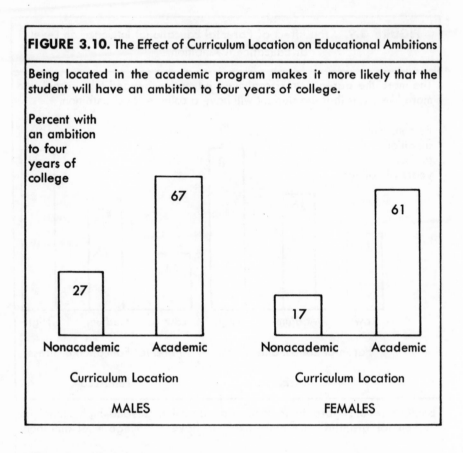

FIGURE 3.10. The Effect of Curriculum Location on Educational Ambitions

Being located in the academic program makes it more likely that the student will have an ambition to four years of college.

Percent with an ambition to four years of college

MALES

Nonacademic	Academic
27	67

Curriculum Location

FEMALES

Nonacademic	Academic
17	61

Curriculum Location

theoretical structure of causality for ambition level, and table 3.6 presents the results of the path analytic estimation procedure applied to that causal structure.[13]

Our understanding of how the average ninth-grade student comes to have a given level of educational ambition is rather straightforward. Peers exert the most immediate influence on the ambition level of the student—the greater the number of college-bound friends, the more likely it is that the student has such an ambition for himself. This is a very simple *direct* effect (p_{76}) since there are no variables specified in the model as intervening between peer influence and student ambition. Location in the college-preparatory program may contribute causally in two ways to the educational ambition of the student: *directly* (p_{75}), and *indirectly*, by making it more likely that the individual will have several rather than few or no college-bound peers ($p_{76}p_{65}$).

Having a college ambition may also be affected causally by parents

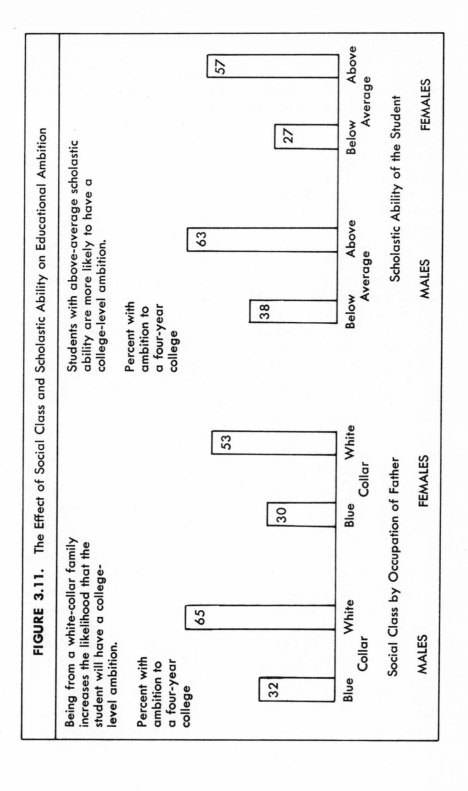

FIGURE 3.11. The Effect of Social Class and Scholastic Ability on Educational Ambition

Being from a white-collar family increases the likelihood that the student will have a college-level ambition.

Percent with ambition to a four-year college

Students with above-average scholastic ability are more likely to have a college-level ambition.

Percent with ambition to a four-year college

32   65   30   53

Blue   White   Blue   White
Collar Collar   Collar Collar

MALES   FEMALES

Social Class by Occupation of Father

38   63   27   57

Below   Above   Below   Above
Average Average   Average Average

MALES   FEMALES

Scholastic Ability of the Student

who try to influence whether the student continues his education
beyond high school. That influence may be *direct*, either from "stress"
(p_{73}) or from "taken for granted" (p_{74}); or it may be *indirect*. That is,
having parents who try to influence one's educational future may
make it more likely that the student will be in the college-preparatory
program ($p_{75}p_{54}$ or $p_{75}p_{53}$); it may make it more likely that the student
will have several rather than few college-bound peers ($p_{76}p_{64}$ or $p_{76}p_{63}$);
or the educational influence of the parents may affect the ambition
level of the student because such influence affects *both* the student's
likelihood of being in the college-preparatory program and his
chances of having several college-bound friends ($p_{76}p_{65}p_{54}$ or $p_{76}p_{65}p_{53}$).

Finally, a student may be more likely to have a college ambition
if he is from a middle-class family or if he is of above-average scholastic ability. Either class or ability may causally affect the ambition
of a student *directly* (p_{51} or p_{52}) or *indirectly* through a series of one,
two, and three-step compound paths. Table 3.7 summarizes the
various routes by which the social class or scholastic ability of the
student may affect causally the student's level of educational ambition.

Reference to the total associations and to the total direct and indirect effects in table 3.7 indicates that the educational ambitions of
students at the end of the ninth grade are indeed the product of
social class, scholastic ability, parental and peer influence, and curriculum location.

Peer educational influence is a decided force in the formation or
maintenance of the student's educational ambition. While slightly
more than half the total association between peer college influence
and ambition is noncausal, almost half is causal and direct. For boys,
that direct effect, p_{76}, is .25 and for girls .20. Thus, even though those
who have ambitions for college and whose friends have ambitions
for college are more likely to be predisposed to college by virtue of
their being middle-class, more scholastically able, having parents
who attempt to influence them to continue their education beyond
high school, and being in the academic program, having several
rather than few or no college-bound friends adds to the likelihood
that the student will seek to continue his education beyond high
school.

Curriculum location is also a causal factor in the educational ambitions of ninth graders. As with the relationship between peer influence
and ambition, so too with the relationship between curriculum loca-

TABLE 3.7. The Routes by Which Social Class and Scholastic Ability May Affect Educational Ambition

The Effect Is: Sentence Description of the Route	Symbolic Expression for:	
	X_1 Social Class	X_2 Scholastic Ability
Direct:		
From/CLASS/ABILITY/to ambition	p_{71}	p_{72}
Indirect:		
From/CLASS/ABILITY/to parental educational stress to ambition	$p_{73}p_{31}$	$p_{73}p_{32}$
From/CLASS/ABILITY/to "taken for granted" to ambition	$p_{74}p_{41}$	$p_{74}p_{42}$
From/CLASS/ABILITY/to curriculum to ambition	$p_{75}p_{51}$	$p_{75}p_{52}$
From/CLASS/ABILITY/to peer influence to ambition	$p_{76}p_{61}$	$p_{76}p_{62}$
From/CLASS/ABILITY/to parental educational stress to curriculum to ambition	$p_{75}p_{53}p_{31}$	$p_{75}p_{53}p_{32}$
From/CLASS/ABILITY/to "taken for granted" to curriculum to ambition	$p_{75}p_{54}p_{41}$	$p_{75}p_{54}p_{42}$
From/CLASS/ABILITY/to parental educational stress to peer influence to ambition	$p_{76}p_{63}p_{31}$	$p_{76}p_{63}p_{32}$
From/CLASS/ABILITY/to "taken for granted" to peer influence to ambition	$p_{76}p_{64}p_{41}$	$p_{76}p_{64}p_{42}$
From/CLASS/ABILITY/to curriculum to peer influence to ambition	$p_{76}p_{65}p_{51}$	$p_{76}p_{65}p_{52}$
From/CLASS/ABILITY/to parental educational stress to curriculum to peer influence to ambition	$p_{76}p_{65}p_{53}p_{31}$	$p_{76}p_{65}p_{53}p_{32}$
From/CLASS/ABILITY/to "taken for granted" to curriculum to peer influence to ambition	$p_{76}p_{65}p_{51}p_{41}$	$p_{76}p_{65}p_{54}p_{42}$

tion and ambition: slightly more than half the total association between curriculum and ambition is noncausal, due to the tendency
for those who are in the academic program and who have college
ambitions to be also from the middle class, of above-average scholastic ability, and with parents who attempt to influence them to continue their education beyond high school. Yet curriculum location
has a total effect, q_{75}, of .20 for boys and .22 for girls, most of which
is direct, $p_{75} = .16$ for boys and .19 for girls, some of which is indirect because those in an academic program tend to have more
friends who are college-bound, which in turn increases the likelihood
that the student has a college ambition. Just being in the academic
program as a ninth grader, then, regardless of class origin, scholastic
ability, or parental influence, increases the likelihood that the
student has an educational ambition for college.

Parental educational influence too is a causative factor in the development of educational ambitions. For boys and girls, the total effect
of one or both indicators of parental influence exceeds those from
either curriculum or peer influence. For boys, $q_{73} = .21$ and $q_{74} = .26$;
for girls, $q_{73} = .25$ and $q_{74} = .23$. Expressed as a portion of the total
association between each indicator of parental influence and ambition, those total effects average out to slightly more than 50 percent.
Major portions of those total effects are direct from the indicators of
parental influence to the ambition of the student. Some of those
effects are indirect, i.e., the more likely the student is to perceive
parental influence, the more likely he is to be in the academic program or have several peers with college intentions. And those in the
academic program or with peers who have college intentions are
themselves more likely to intend to continue their education beyond
high school.

Social class and scholastic ability are, of course, both associated with
educational ambition: $r_{71} = .46$ for boys and .40 for girls; $r_{72} = .39$
for boys and .42 for girls. Three-quarters or more of those total
associations are causal: $q_{71} = .38$ for boys and .30 for girls; $q_{72} = .30$
for boys and .32 for girls. The remaining quarter or so of those total
associations is due to the causally unanalyzed association between
class and ability, i.e., to the tendency for middle-class students to
be scholastically more able. Causally, both class and ability have
impacts on ambition that exceed those from the other four determinants.

Between 40 and 50 percent of the total effects that class and ability have on student educational ambition is direct, unmediated by parent or peer influence or by curriculum location: $p_{71} = .20$ for boys and .12 for girls; $p_{72} = .13$ for boys and .14 for girls. The privileges of an advantaged class position and of a superior intellect thus are translated into ambitions for higher education either in ways that have to do with class and ability per se, or in ways that involve mechanisms not specified in our model. However, the privileges of an advantaged class position and of a superior intellect are also translated into an ambition for higher education through some of the mechanisms that we have specified in our model. To a degree, higher levels of class and ability result in higher levels of ambition because middle-class students and those who are more scholastically able are more likely to be located in an academic program, which in turn is conducive to a college ambition. Curriculum mediates some 7 or 8 percent of the total effect of social class and some 14 to 20 percent, depending on gender, of that from ability. Obviously, curriculum plays but a minor part in translating the advantages of a middle-class position into a college-level ambition.

Peers play a role in the causal chain that links the social class and the scholastic ability of the student to his educational ambitions. Depending on gender, between 7 and 15 percent of the total class or ability effect on ambition is due to the tendency for middle-class or scholastically more able students to have several college-bound friends and for that network of peers to heighten the student's own level of educational ambition.

Parents, however, play the major role in transforming class origin and scholastic ability into an educational ambition. About one-third of the total effect that class or ability has on student ambition results from the tendency for middle-class parents or for parents of scholastically more able students to stress the importance of their children continuing their education beyond high school or to their conveying the understanding that such continued education is taken for granted in that family and to the effects that such influence has on the ambition of the student.

Of these six determinants, which exerts the largest total effect on ambition? For boys the source of the largest total effect is social class: $q_{71} = .38$, followed by scholastic ability, $q_{72} = .30$. For girls, the total effect from ability, $q_{72} = .32$, is just slightly greater than that from social class, q_{71} = .30. There can be no question, then, that while neither class nor ability overwhelmingly determines the educational ambition of students, class origin is about as much a factor as is scholastic ability in determining whether a ninth-grade student has the drive to continue his education beyond high school.

Summary: Determinants of Ambition

We have defined an educational ambition as the realistic expectation of the individual to use formal school attainment as an instrument either to maintain an already privileged class position or to increase his chances for entering a social class higher than the one into which he was born. The higher the level of the individual's expected educational attainment, the higher is his level of ambition.

As a construct, ambition has been all but ignored by revisionist writers, perhaps because they prefer structural concepts such as social class to attitudinal constructs such as ambition. It is ironic that a variable ignored by the revisionists has as one of its largest determinants the social-class position of the individual's family. For boys, the total effect of class exceeds that of ability, the second largest causal determinant. For girls, class exerts a causal effect on ambition about equal to that from ability.

Yet the predisposition of an individual toward college, at least in ninth grade, is not *strongly* determined either by class or by ability. Of more modest but still substantial consequence as determinants of an educational ambition are the interpersonal process measures of parent and peer educational influence and the school organization measure of curriculum. Even though class and ability affect interpersonal influence and curriculum and, through these measures, the ambition level of the student, interpersonal influence and curriculum affect the student's ambition *independently* of class origin and scholastic ability. Lacking privileged class position and above-average ability, a ninth-grade student may still express an ambition for college. Having parents who try to influence one's educational future, numbering among one's friends several who have ambitions for college, and taking one's sequence of courses in the academic program separately and severally increase the likelihood that the individual will realistically expect to attend college, independently of class origin or scholastic ability.

CONCLUSIONS

Our initial testing ground for propositions rooted in either the meritocratic or the revisionist thesis of schooling is the ninth grade. Our conception of ninth grade is that of a year of transition and exploration. As such it is a time of decision for the student, but of tentative and provisional rather than firm and irrevocable decision. One such decision whose determinants we have sought to analyze is that of curriculum—whether to pursue an academic program with its enduring option for college after high school or a nonacademic program with its more limited possibilities for college or perhaps even for successful entry into the labor market. The second decision whose determinants we have sought to analyze is that of an educational goal or expectation, a decision we take to indicate the student's level of educational ambition, his intention to use formal school attainment as an instrument of social mobility.

Both curriculum location and educational ambition have been discussed in the literature on schooling and social class by proponents of the revisionist thesis and by those who have a more meritocratic conception of schooling in an industrial, market-oriented society. Revisionist theorists are unequivocal in their causal attribution to social class: both the curriculum location and the educational ambition of the student are seen as depending *strongly* on the social class of the individual.

Meritocratic theorists are more cautious in their causal attributions. Their writings suggest that class is less important than ability in the curriculum decision, and that class is important but more indirectly than directly in the ambition decision.

Our own analyses of the ninth-grade experience of 2,788 students conclusively confirms neither perspective. For our sample, location in the academic program depends more on the ability of the student than on class background. Curriculum location, however, is not strongly associated with either ability or with social class. In our model, as in the models of many previous investigators, social class, scholastic ability, and interpersonal influence leave more variance in curriculum unexplained than they collectively explain. We have little evidence, then, to suggest that the differentiated curriculum of the high school is currently used as a mechanism for the segregation of students along the lines of their social-class origins.

The decision to set one's sights on continued education beyond high school does depend more on social class than on scholastic ability if the student is a male, and about equally on class and ability if the student is a female. But for neither gender can those dependencies be described as "strong." Indeed, class and ability are not the only variables to exert sizable effects on the ambition level of the student. Independent of those two background attributes, the ambition level of the student is affected by interpersonal influence from his parents and his peers and by his location in the school curriculum.

Finally, even though we were able to explain much more of the variance in ambition (about 50 percent) than we were in curriculum (about 20 percent), the fact that half the variance in ambition was not accounted for by class, ability, interpersonal influence, and curriculum suggests that such a decision is far from fixed, particularly by the relatively immutable ascriptive attributes of social class and scholastic ability. Nevertheless, the role of social class in the determination of an ambition level is a sizable one. And if, as we have hypothesized, the role of a student's ambition as a determinant of his progress through high school is also sizable, then it may well be that it is through the individual's ambition that class of origin comes to exercise a good portion of whatever causal effect it does have upon the student as he makes his way from ninth to twelfth grade. This is a possibility that we explore in some detail in the following chapters.

NOTES

1. Martin Trow, "The Second Transformation of American Secondary Education," in *The School in Society*, ed. Sam D. Sieber and David E. Wilder (New York: Free Press, 1973), pp. 45–61.

2. Alan C. Kerckhoff, *Socialization and Social Class* (Englewood Cliffs, N.J.: Prentice-Hall, 1972).

3. Aaron V. Cicourel and John I. Kitsuse, *The Educational Decision Makers* (Indianapolis: Bobbs-Merrill, 1963), p. 146.

4. Hubert M. Blalock, Jr., *Causal Inferences in Nonexperimental Research* (Chapel Hill: University of North Carolina Press, 1961), pp. 119–24.

5. Joseph A. Kahl, "Educational and Occupational Aspirations of 'Common Man' Boys," in *Education, Economy, and Society*, ed. A. H. Halsey, Jean Floud, and C. Arnold Anderson (New York: Free Press, 1961), pp. 348–66.

6. See, for example, William H. Sewell and Vimah P. Shah, "Social Class, Parental Encouragement, and Educational Aspirations," *American Journal of Sociology* 73 (March 1968): 559–72.

7. Estimates of direct and indirect effects shown in the tables of this text are values computed after our general understanding or "theory" of the schooling process was refined or "trimmed" in accord with the procedure first suggested by David R. Heise, "Problems in Path Analysis and Causal Inference," in *Sociological Methodology 1969*, ed. Edgar F. Borgatta (San Francisco: Jossey-Bass, 1969). Path coefficients were first computed by regressing the particular dependent variable on all predictors, inasmuch as there were no theoretically compelling reasons to eliminate any predictor prior to the first set of estimates. The resulting coefficients were then examined. When a coefficient was not approximately twice its standard error we inferred that there probably was no *direct* causal linkage between the respective independent and dependent variables, although, of course, there could be indirect causal linkages. A second set of coefficients was then computed using only those independent variables from the first run that had generated path coefficients approximately equal

to or greater than twice their respective standard errors. For variable X_5, curriculum location in ninth grade, this procedure resulted in the elimination of X_4, "taken for granted" from the male model as a source of direct causal effect. Both before and after the elimination of X_4, 17 percent of the variance in the curriculum location of males in ninth grade was accounted for. The equations for the trimmed model of curriculum location, grade nine, males, are:

Eq. 1.: $X_3 = p_{31}X_1 + p_{32}X_2 + p_{3a}X_a$

Eq. 2.: $X_4 = p_{41}X_1 + p_{42}X_2 + p_{4b}X_b$

Eq. 3.: $X_5 = p_{51}X_1 + p_{52}X_2 + p_{53}X_3 + p_{5c}X_c$

8. S. N. Eisenstadt, "Archetypal Patterns of Youth" in *Youth: Change and Challenge*, ed. Eric H. Erickson (New York: Basic Books, 1963), p. 32.

9. Denise B. Kandel and Gerald S. Lesser, *Youth in Two Worlds* (San Francisco: Jossey-Bass, 1972), p. 58.

10. Kerckhoff, *Socialization and Social Class*, p. 84.

11. With peer college intentions, X_6, as the dependent variable, there were significant paths or direct effects from all five predictor or independent variables. The equations that define the model thus are: (1) for males, equations 1, 2, and 3 as above in note 7, plus Eq. 5, which is $X_6 = p_{61}X_1 + p_{62}X_2 + p_{63}X_3 + p_{64}X_4 + p_{65}X_5 + p_{6d}X_d$; (2) for females, equations 1 and 2 as in note 7 for males, plus Eq. 3, which is $X_5 = p_{51}X_1 + p_{52}X_2 + p_{53}X_3 + p_{54}X_4 + p_{5c}X_c$, and Eq. 4, which is $X_6 = p_{61}X_1 + p_{62}X_2 + p_{63}X_3 + p_{64}X_4 + p_{65}X_5 + p_{6d}X_d$.

12. Ralph Turner, *The Social Context of Ambition* (San Francisco: Chandler, 1964), p. 3.

13. The model for the determination of educational ambition is defined by these equations which, with the exception of Eq. 3, are identical for males and females:

Eq. 1.: $X_3 = p_{31}X_1 + p_{32}X_2 + p_{3a}X_a$

Eq. 2.: $X_4 = p_{41}X_1 + p_{42}X_2 + p_{4b}X_b$

Eq. 3.: $X_5 = p_{51}X_1 + p_{52}X_2 + p_{53}X_3 + p_{54}X_4 + p_{5c}X_c$
      (with $p_{54}X_4$ deleted for males)

Eq. 4.: $X_6 = p_{61}X_1 + p_{62}X_2 + p_{63}X_3 + p_{64}X_4 + p_{65}X_5$
      $+ p_{6d}X_d$

Eq. 5.: $X_7 = p_{71}X_1 + p_{72}X_2 + p_{73}X_3 + p_{74}X_4 + p_{75}X_5$
      $+ p_{76}X_6 + p_{7e}X_e$

4. Grade Ten: The Year of Commitment

As a ninth grader, the student had relative freedom to explore the various educational options of the comprehensive high school. The latitude for such freedom diminishes in tenth grade. College entry requires certain course content and sequence; by the end of tenth grade the student should be in the academic program if he plans to attend college. Grade ten is a year of commitment for the student, one in which he encounters institutional forces that progressively constrain opportunities for vascillation, equivocation, and trial-and-error experimentation. Erving Goffman's analysis of institutional forces and their consequences for the individual describes well the context of commitment faced by the tenth grader. He

> becomes commited to something when, because of the fixed and interdependent character of many institutional arrangements, his doing or being this something irrevocably conditions other important possibilities in his life, forcing him to take courses of action, causing other persons to build up their activity on the basis of his continuing his current undertakings, and rendering him vulnerable to unanticipated consequences of these undertakings.[1]

This chapter explores an institutional arrangement of the school that commits the student to one course of action or another: curriculum location. We explore, too, an "activity of another person," to paraphrase Goffman, which, affected by past undertakings of the student, also affects his future. That activity is the educational guidance function, and the person is the school guidance counselor.

Both the institutional arrangement of alternative curriculum tracks and the organizationally mandated function of the guidance counselor as sorter and selector set the context for the student's educational experience as a tenth grader. In the pages that follow we trace the factors that determine whether, at the end of tenth grade, the student is committed to a path of college-preparatory work in the academic program or to a path of employment in the nonacademic program. We trace also the factors that determine whether, during tenth grade, the student reports that the counselor has encouraged him to continue his education beyond high school or prepare for entry into the job market.

To anticipate briefly the results of our analysis, we find that neither social class nor peer influence noticeably affects these two tenth-grade outcomes. We find that curriculum location at the end of grade ten follows closely curriculum location at the end of grade nine. The modest amount of movement between programs is more "upward," i.e., into the academic program, than "downward." Independently contributing both to the prediction of curriculum location at the end of grade ten and to the pattern of movement between grades nine and ten are scholastic ability and educational ambition. Ability actually is a stronger determinant of curriculum location at the end of tenth grade than it was at the end of ninth grade. Social class tends to decline in strength as a predictor of curriculum location. To the extent that class affects curriculum location by the end of tenth grade, it does so indirectly. These patterns are more descriptive for boys, however, than for girls.

Counselor educational encouragement conforms closely to student curriculum location. Those in the academic program are much more likely to report being encouraged to continue their education beyond high school than are those in the nonacademic program. But encouragement is also responsive to the scholastic ability and educational ambition of the student. Counselors encourage students on to college because, as school officials, they judge them able to perform scholastically and because they consider them sufficiently ambitious. No direct class effect on the counselor was detected. To the modest extent that class influences the counselor, it does so indirectly, largely because middle-class students are more educationally ambitious than their lower-class counterparts.

The pattern of our findings from tenth grade are somewhat more definitive with respect to the tenability of the revisionist and meritocratic theses than was true from ninth grade. The results clearly support the meritocratic role of the high school. We conclude that the operation of the high school, at least as indicated through the curriculum location process and counseling function, supports the student's ambitions and responds to evidence of the student's scholastic ability. Ambition, ability, and earlier choice behaviors are the primary determinants of institutional response. Compared with these factors, the effect of social class is very modest and even gives some evidence of a decline.

CURRICULUM LOCATION IN TENTH GRADE

In the model constructed to represent the ninth-grade experience of the student, location in an academic rather than nonacademic program was hypothesized to be more likely for individuals from middle- rather than working-class families, for individuals with above- rather than below-average scholastic ability, and for students who perceived their parents as attempting to influence them to continue their education beyond high school. In the model constructed to represent the tenth-grade experience of the student (see figure 4.1), location in the academic rather than nonacademic program continues to depend on the variables that determined curriculum location in ninth grade, i.e., social class, scholastic ability, and parental educational influence. In addition, the model specifies that as a tenth grader, being in the academic program depends on at least three measurable aspects of experience as a ninth grader. That is, in addition to class, ability, and parental influence affecting the curriculum location of a tenth grader, being in the academic program in grade ten is more likely for individuals who, as ninth graders: (1) were already in the academic program, (2) had several college-bound friends, and (3) had educational ambitions for college.

Curriculum location in tenth grade is indeed related to each of these seven antecedents at the simple, two-variable, level of analysis, as an inspection of the *total associations* in table 4.1 indicates. When, however, we consider the interrelationships among these seven antecedents, several do not generate *direct* effects to the curriculum location of tenth graders, i.e., the paths from those variables are essentially zero. Thus, whether a tenth-grade boy is in the academic or nonacademic program does not depend directly upon either our "taken for granted" indicator of parental educational influence or upon peer educational influence. Neither does it depend directly

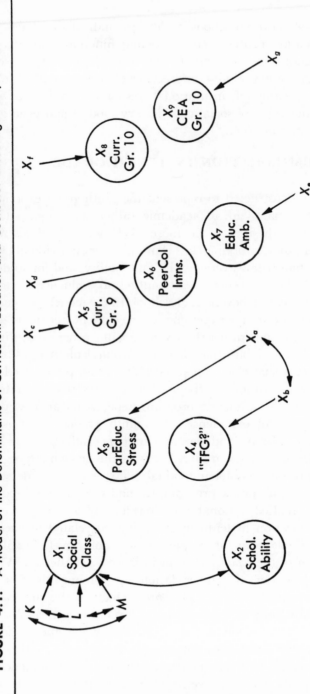

FIGURE 4.1. A Model of the Determinants of Curriculum Location and Counselor Encouragement, Grade Ten

Variables are: X_1 = Social class, X_2 = Scholastic ability, X_3 = Parental educational stress, X_4 = Continued education beyond high school "taken for granted?", X_5 = Curriculum location, grade nine, X_6 = Peer college influence, grade nine, X_7 = Educational ambition, X_8 = Curriculum location, grade ten, X_9 = Counselor educational encouragement, grade ten, K = Education of father, M = Occupation of father, X_a–X_g = residuals

TABLE 4.1. The Total Associations with Tenth-grade Curriculum Location of Specified Independent Variables and Their Total, Direct, and Indirect Effects

Independent Variables		Male Students				Female Students			
		Total Assoc. r_{ij}	Direct p_{ij}	Effect: Indir. s_{ij}	Total q_{ij}	Total Assoc. r_{ij}	Direct p_{ij}	Effect: Indir. s_{ij}	Total q_{ij}
Social class	X_1	.251	.000	.175	.175	.358	.079	.163	.242
Scholastic ability	X_2	.352	.133	.176	.309	.470	.172	.228	.400
Parental ed. stress	X_3	.338	.100	.153	.253	.339	.000	.208	.208
Taken for granted	X_4	.270	.000	.097	.097	.406	.073	.120	.193
Curriculum gr. 9	X_5	.569	.413	.041	.454	.649	.440	.037	.477
Peer col. int. gr. 9	X_6	.317	.000	.065	.065	.341	.000	.062	.062
Educational ambition	X_7	.473	.208	.000	.208	.525	.177	.000	.177
Proportion of Variance Accounted for: R^2		.413				.517			

upon social class. Whether a tenth-grade girl is in the academic or nonacademic program does not depend directly upon either our "stress" measure of parental influence or upon peer influence. While none of these variables generates *direct* effects to tenth-grade curriculum, they may and do generate indirect effects to that dependent variable. In accord with the procedure described earlier, these paths, i.e., p_{86}, p_{84}, and p_{81} for boys and p_{86} and p_{83} for girls, were set to zero and the coefficients for the remaining paths recalculated. Formally, the equations that define the trimmed model are:

For both boys and girls

Eq. 1: $X_3 = p_{31}X_1 + p_{32}X_2 + p_{3a}X_a$

Eq. 2: $X_4 = p_{41}X_1 + p_{42}X_2 + p_{4b}X_b$

For boys only

Eq. 3: $X_5 = p_{51}X_1 + p_{52}X_2 + p_{53}X_3 + p_{5c}X_c$

Eq. 4: $X_6 = p_{61}X_1 + p_{62}X_2 + p_{63}X_3 + p_{64}X_4 + p_{65}X_5$
$\qquad\quad + p_{6d}X_d$

Eq. 5: $X_7 = p_{71}X_1 + p_{72}X_2 + p_{73}X_3 + p_{74}X_4 + p_{75}X_5$
$\qquad\quad + p_{76}X_6 + p_{7e}X_e$

Eq. 6: $X_8 = p_{82}X_2 + p_{83}X_3 + p_{85}X_5 + p_{87}X_7 + p_{8f}X_f$

For girls only

Eq. 3: $X_5 = p_{51}X_1 + p_{52}X_2 + p_{53}X_3 + p_{54}X_4 + p_{5c}X_c$

Eq. 4: $X_6 = p_{61}X_1 + p_{62}X_2 + p_{63}X_3 + p_{64}X_4 + p_{65}X_5$
$\qquad\quad p_{6d}X_d$

Eq. 5: $X_7 = p_{71}X_1 + p_{72}X_2 + p_{73}X_3 + p_{74}X_4 + p_{75}X_5$
$\qquad\quad + p_{76}X_6 + p_{7e}X_e$

Eq. 6: $X_8 = p_{81}X_1 + p_{82}X_2 + p_{84}X_4 + p_{85}X_5 + p_{87}X_7$
$\qquad\quad + p_{8f}X_f$

Both prior to and following the trimming of the model, we were able to account for 41 percent of the variance in the tenth-grade curriculum location of boys and 52 percent of the variance in the tenth-grade curriculum location of girls.

Interpersonal Influence and the Curriculum Location of Tenth Graders

Interpersonal influence causally affects the curriculum of the student in tenth grade as it did in ninth grade. For boys the total causal effect from parental educational stress, q_{83}, is .25, while that from "taken for granted," q_{84}, is .10. For girls, both "stress" and "taken for granted" exert total causal effects of similar magnitude, i.e., q_{83} = .21 and q_{84} = .19, respectively. In contrast to the causal effects from the educational influence of *parents*, that from the students *peers* is minimal, i.e., q_{86} is .07 for boys and .06 for girls. Students who perceive their parents as attempting to influence them to continue their education beyond high school and students who associate with several friends who themselves are college-bound are more likely to be in an academic program as high school sophomores, regardless of their class origins, scholastic ability, or curriculum location and educational ambition as high school freshmen.

Social Class: Its Effect on Tenth-grade Curriculum

In tenth grade as in ninth, students from more privileged class origins are more likely to be in the academic program preparing for college than are those from less privileged class origins. Thus, in figure 4.2 we can observe that 73 percent of the boys from white-collar homes are in the college-preparatory program, while only 56 percent of those from blue-collar homes are similarly located.

With tenth-grade curriculum, as with ninth-grade curriculum, both *total association* and *total effect* of social class are less than that of ability. From table 4.1 we can see that the total association of class with the curriculum location of the student in the tenth grade is r_{81} = .25 for boys, some .10 standard units *less* than that of ability, while for girls r_{81} = .36, a total association some .11 standard units below that of ability.

Causally, the *total effect* that family class origin exerts on the curriculum location of tenth-grade students, q_{81}, is .18 for boys and .24 for girls. For boys, all that effect is indirect. Slightly more than a third of that total effect is attributable to the somewhat greater tendency for boys of the middle class to be in an academic program in ninth grade and for boys in that program to remain there throughout tenth grade. Almost one-quarter more of that total effect can be traced to the higher educational ambitions of middle-class students in ninth grade and to the greater likelihood that those who had college-level ambitions in ninth grade will be in the college-preparatory program in tenth grade. For girls, almost one-third of the total

FIGURE 4.2. Effect on the Likelihood of Being in the Academic Program, Grade Ten, of Social Class, Scholastic Ability, and Educational Ambition

Being from a white-collar family increases the likelihood of being in the academic program in tenth grade.

Having a level of scholastic ability which is above average increases the likelihood of being in the academic program in tenth grade.

Percent in the academic program.

Percent in the academic program

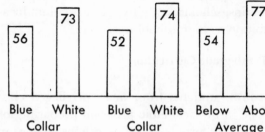

Blue Collar   White   Blue Collar   White

Social Class of Family by Occupation of Father

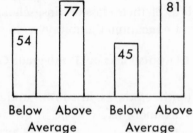

Below Average   Above   Below Average   Above

Scholastic Ability of the Student

Having an educational ambition to college increases the likelihood of being in the academic program in tenth grade.

Percent in the academic program

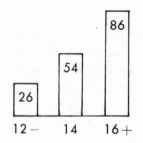

12 −   14   16 +

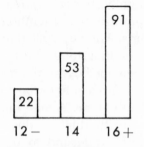

12 −   14   16 +

Educational Ambition in Years of Formal Schooling

MALES   FEMALES

effect that their class background has on their curriculum location as tenth graders is direct, p_{81} = .08. Quite possibly, the existence of such a direct effect for girls, but not for boys, indicates that school officials may be influenced more by the occupational and educational attainments of the parents in placing girls in the academic program in the tenth grade. For girls, as for boys, curriculum location in ninth grade also serves to link class origins with curriculum location in tenth grade—about one-quarter of the total effect that a girl's class origin has on her curriculum location as a sophomore is indirect by way of her curriculum location as a freshman. Ambition, which accounted for about a fourth of the total effect that class had on the tenth-grade curriculum location of boys, accounts for less than a tenth of the total effect that class has on the tenth-grade curriculum location of girls. Since ambition has about the same effect on the curriculum location of girls as it does for boys, but since class has less of an effect on the ambition of girls than for boys, the educational ambitions of high school girls are apparently less an extension of their parents' occupational and educational attainments than are the ambitions of boys.

Scholastic Ability: Its Effect on Tenth-grade Curriculum

Considerable leverage is available to the student with above-average scholastic ability in gaining access to the academic curriculum in tenth grade. As figure 4.2 illustrates, almost eight of every ten students with above-average abilities are in college-preparatory programs as sophomores, in contrast with about five in ten of those with below-average abilities.

Ability causally affects the curriculum location of a tenth grader with notable strength: q_{82} = .31 for boys and .40 for girls. And it does so both directly, with p_{82} = .13 for boys and .17 for girls; and indirectly, with s_{82} = .18 for boys and .23 for girls. This direct-effect component could well reflect the use by numerous school officials of standardized ability and achievement test scores in deciding who is given preference for access to the college-preparatory program in the sophomore year. For both boys and girls this direct effect accounts for more than four-tenths of the total ability effect. Another third of that total effect is due to the tendency for more able students to be in an academic program in ninth grade and to remain in that curriculum throughout ninth and tenth grades. Some of the ability effect can also be attributed to the higher educational ambitions that characterize the scholastically more able; the proportion of the total effect so accounted for is not impressive, however: slightly less than a tenth for boys and slightly more than a twentieth for girls.

When compared with social class, ability clearly emerges as the dominant determinant of whether a tenth grader is in the academic program preparing for entry to college or not. In its total effect on tenth-grade curriculum, ability is 1.77 times larger than social class for boys and 1.65 times larger than social class for girls. Moreover, for boys, although not for girls, when the correlations of grade-ten curriculum with ability and social class are compared with those of grade-nine curriculum, we find that the role of ability has increased while that of social class has remained about the same. Thus, the total association between ability and curriculum rose from $r_{52} = .29$ in ninth grade to $r_{82} = .35$ in tenth grade, while the total association between class and curriculum stood still at $r_{51} = .24$ in ninth grade and $r_{81} = .25$ in tenth grade. For girls, there was a rise in the correlation of ability with curriculum from .41 in grade nine to .47 in grade ten, but there was also a slight rise in the correlation of class with curriculum, from .31 in grade nine to .35 in grade ten. We return to the issue of changes in the roles of class and ability during the high school years in a subsequent chapter.

Educational Ambition: Its Effect on Tenth-grade Curriculum

Admissions requirements to most colleges and universities make it advisable if not mandatory that students pursue an academic program in high school. Thus, as figure 4.2 illustrates, while more than eight of every ten students whose ambition as a ninth grader was to go to a four-year college are in the academic program as tenth graders, only five of every ten whose ninth-grade ambition was to go to a two-year college are in that program as tenth graders, and fewer than three of every ten whose ninth-grade ambition was only to complete high school are in that program in tenth grade.

Between the ambition of the student as a ninth grader and his curriculum as a tenth grader, there is a relatively strong association: $r_{87} = .47$ for boys and .53 for girls. A good portion of this association, however, does not represent the causal effect of ambition on curriculum. Rather, 56 percent of that association for males and 66 percent for females reflects the operation of variables antecedent to both ambition and curriculum. Between one-half and two-thirds of the total association between a student's ambition as a ninth grader and his or her curriculum location as a tenth grader merely reflects the fact that ninth graders with college-level ambitions who become tenth graders pursuing an academic program are already predisposed toward that level of ambition and curriculum by virtue of: (1) a more privileged class background, (2) a higher level of scholastic ability, (3) greater exposure to parent and peer educational influence, and (4) an existing position in the academic program. Nevertheless, a sizable causal effect runs from grade-nine ambition to grade-ten curriculum: $p_{87} = .21$ for boys and .18 for girls. For boys, the magnitude of that causal effect ranks ambition below ability but above social class as a determinant of the sophomore-year curriculum location. For girls, however, the rank order of ambition is below that of both ability and social class, suggesting that educational ambition per se is less of a driving force in the high school experience of girls than of boys.

Ninth-grade Curriculum: Its Effect on Tenth-grade Curriculum

Stability, rather than change, describes the curriculum location of students during grades nine and ten. Overall, at least eight in every ten students were in the same curriculum, freshman and sophomore years. Stability, however, as figure 4.3 illustrates, is more characteristic of those in the academic program: 86 percent of the boys and 88 percent of the girls who were in the academic program as ninth graders were also in that program as tenth graders. By comparison, persistence in the nonacademic program characterizes only 67 percent of the boys and 75 percent of the girls.

Between these two grade-level measures of curriculum location is a rather high total association: $r_{85} = .57$ for boys and .65 for girls. And, much of this association is causal: 80 percent for boys and 74 percent for girls. Regardless of class of origin, scholastic ability, or educational influence from parents, one's curriculum location in ninth grade is the largest single net determinant of one's curriculum location in tenth grade. For boys, the total causal effect from ninth-grade curriculum, q_{85}, is .45, 90 percent of which is direct, not mediated by either peer influence or educational ambition, i.e., $p_{85} = .41$. For girls, the total causal effect, q_{85}, is .48, of which 92 percent is direct, i.e., $p_{85} = .44$.

Continuity is the hallmark of student curriculum location from the year of exploration through the year of commitment. Ability and parental influence, as we have seen in the preceding chapter, more than social class, determine whether a ninth grader comes to be located in an academic or nonacademic program. Once located in a program, however, that student tends to remain in the same program throughout both grades nine and ten. Yet students do change programs, and such change tends to be patterned. As we shall see, the direction of that change is "upward," i.e., more from the nonacademic to the academic than vice versa, and social class, scholastic ability, and educational ambition are some determinants of that change.

Observe from figure 4.3 that in tenth grade almost twice as many students are in academic as in nonacademic programs (the ratio is 1.93 to 1), that the ratio for tenth grade is higher than that for ninth grade (1.78 to 1), and that, as noted, continuity from ninth to tenth grade is higher for students in the academic program. Students, it would appear, strive to preserve the option of seeking entry either to college or to the labor market upon completion of high school either by gaining access to the academic program in ninth grade or shifting to that program in tenth grade. Continuity in the academic program and the propensity to shift into that program, grade nine to grade ten, are both associated with student social class, scholastic ability, and educational ambition. As figure 4.4 reveals, persistence in the academic program is slightly more characteristic of boys from white- than from blue-collar homes—88 vs. 82 percent, respectively. For girls the pattern is similar: 92 and 82 percent, white- and blue-collar, respectively. Persistence in the academic program is somewhat more characteristic of scholastically more able students than it is for the scholastically less able: 90 and 78 percent, respectively, for boys; and 93 and 77 percent, respectively, for girls. Persistence in the academic program is definitely more characteristic of those students who had ambitions to four years of college than for those with ambitions to two years of college. Persistence was lowest for those whose ambitions were to enter the labor market upon completion of high school. Almost all students who, as ninth graders,

FIGURE 4.3. Curriculum Stability, Grades Nine and Ten, and Numbers of Students in Each Curriculum Location, Grades Nine and Ten

Stability is higher among students in the academic than in the nonacademic program during grades nine and ten.

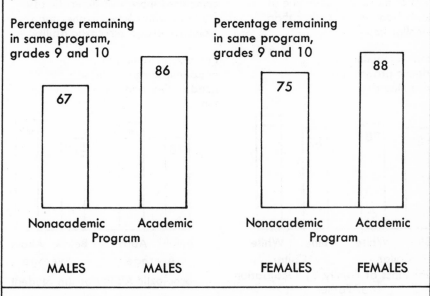

The ratio of the number of academic- to nonacademic-program students is higher in tenth than in ninth grade.

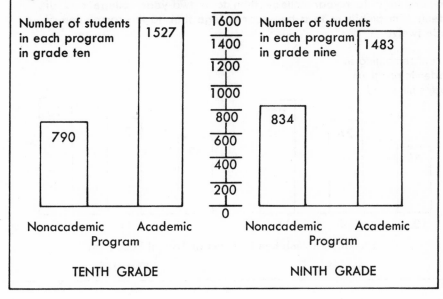

FIGURE 4.4. The Effect on Curriculum Location Stability of Social Class, Scholastic Ability, and Educational Ambition on Stability in the Academic Program, Grades Nine and Ten

Persistence in the academic program is somewhat more characteristic of students from white- rather than blue-collar homes.

Percent remaining in academic program in grades nine and ten

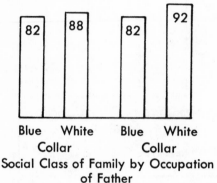

Social Class of Family by Occupation of Father

Persistence in the academic program is somewhat more characteristic of students with above- rather than below-average scholastic ability.

Percent remaining in academic program in grades nine and ten

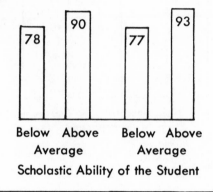

Scholastic Ability of the Student

Persistence in the academic program is more characteristic of students with ambitions to a four-year college than to a two-year college and of students with ambitions to a two-year college than to the completion of grade twelve.

Percent remaining in academic program in grades nine and ten

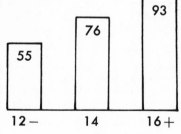

MALES

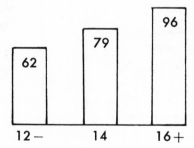

Educational Ambition in Years of Formal Education

FEMALES

expressed a four-year college ambition and who were in the academic program, 93 percent of the boys and 96 percent of the girls, remained there through tenth grade. Such persistence characterized 76 percent of the boys and 79 percent of the girls with ambitions to a community college. Among those whose ambition did not include any formal education beyond high school, only 55 percent of the boys and 62 percent of the girls remained in the academic program during grades nine and ten.

A shift "up" from the nonacademic program in ninth grade to the academic program in tenth grade is associated somewhat with class origin, a bit more so with scholastic ability, and definitely so with educational ambition. Figure 4.5 illustrates how the shift from the nonacademic program in grade nine to the academic program in grade ten is affected by class, ability, and ambition. With data from the girls to illustrate, we can see that among those girls from white-collar homes who were not in the academic program in ninth grade, 33 percent shifted into an academic program in tenth grade. Only 18 percent of the girls from blue-collar homes shifted in a similar manner. Scholastically more able girls who were not in the academic program in ninth grade showed a greater tendency to shift into that program by the end of tenth grade (39 percent) than did their scholastically less able counterparts (18 percent). But the greatest tendency to move into the academic program characterizes those girls who as ninth graders had a four-year college ambition but were not in the college-preparatory program. Sixty-four percent of those girls shifted their program upward by the end of tenth grade. Such an upward shift was made by only 23 percent of the girls whose ambition was a community college and by only 10 percent of the girls who planned to enter the labor market as soon as they completed high school.

Summary

Given the cumulative and sequential character of course work in an academic program, designed as it is to prepare students for college, it is highly unlikely that there will be much movement from one program to another after tenth grade, save perhaps for those few students who seek release from the heavier demands of the academic track by shifting into a nonacademic curriculum.

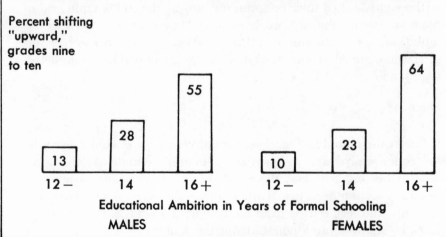

FIGURE 4.5. The Effect on the Likelihood of an Upward Shift from the Nonacademic to the Academic Program, Grade Nine to Grade Ten, of Social Class, Scholastic Ability, and Educational Ambition

Students from white-collar homes are more likely to shift from the nonacademic to the academic program than are those from blue-collar homes.

Percent shifting "upward," grades nine to ten

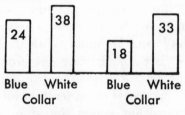

Blue Collar   White Collar   Blue Collar   White Collar

24   38   18   33

Social Class of the Family by Father's Occupation

MALES   FEMALES

Students who are more scholastically able are more likely to shift from the nonacademic to the academic program than are those who are less scholastically able.

Percent shifting "upward," grades nine to ten

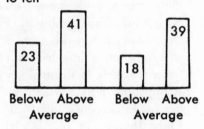

Below Average   Above Average   Below Average   Above Average

23   41   18   39

Scholastic Ability of the Student

MALES   FEMALES

Students with ambitions to four years of college are more likely to shift from the nonacademic to the academic program than are students with ambitions to two years of college, who are, in turn, more likely to shift upward than are students whose ambitions are just to complete high school.

Percent shifting "upward," grades nine to ten

13   28   55   10   23   64

12–   14   16+   12–   14   16+

Educational Ambition in Years of Formal Schooling

MALES   FEMALES

If we are correct in assuming curriculum stability from tenth grade on, then whatever curriculum arrangement the student has made by the end of the sophomore year represents, for that individual, a firm commitment. On the preceding pages we have sought to develop some understanding of the determinants of that commitment.

The curriculum location of the student in ninth grade and the scholastic ability of the student are two determinants distinguished by the magnitudes of their total effects on the curriculum location of the student in tenth grade. Even as early as the period from ninth to tenth grade we are able to observe a rather high degree of curriculum stability. And much of the limited amount of change takes place among students who, as ninth graders, were in the nonacademic program where the tendency was to shift into an academic program by the end of tenth grade. This upward shift was seen to be somewhat more likely for middle- than working-class students; even more likely for scholastically able students, and most likely for students whose educational ambition was to a four-year college rather than mere completion of high school.

Ranked a close second to ninth-grade curriculum as a determinant of tenth-grade curriculum location was the scholastic ability of the student: the more scholastically able the student, the more likely it is that he will be in the college-preparatory program by the end of tenth grade.

Interpersonal educational influence from parents, far more than from peers, also had a notable effect on program location by the end of sophomore year. Students who perceived their parents as attempting to influence them to continue their education beyond high school were more likely than those lacking such a perception to be in the college-preparatory program by the end of tenth grade.

Ambition and class are the remaining determinants of curriculum location, grade ten, specified in our model. For boys, the realistic educational ambition of entering a four-year college on completion of high school had more to do than did a privileged social-class background with whether they would be in the academic program by the end of tenth grade. For girls, however, curriculum was somewhat more dependent upon class of origin than upon educational ambition.

Thus we conclude that access to the academic program, *either in ninth or tenth grade*, and, by extension, access to college and ultimately to the professions, depends more upon the student's own scholastic ability and perception of parental interest in and concern about his continued education than it does upon his social class. Once in a program as a ninth grader, the student tends to remain in that same program as a tenth grader. Moreover, for boys if not for girls, personal volition in the form of an educational ambition exercises more of a causal role than does social class in determining whether, by the end of the sophomore year, the individual is to be committed to an academic course of study with its open-career horizon or to a non-academic course of study with its more limited set of educational and occupational opportunities.

COUNSELOR EDUCATIONAL ENCOURAGEMENT IN TENTH GRADE

Curriculum differentiation, as noted, can be understood as a response by the schools to the ever increasing differentiation of the labor force in a society experiencing rapid industrialization and urbanization.

From the turn of the century on, the industrialization and urbanization of the nation meant that secondary school could no longer continue almost exclusively as a preparatory institution for children of privileged parentage on their way to the university. Expansion of the secondary (production) and tertiary (business, commerce, and service) sectors of the economy increased the demand for labor with more than an elementary school certificate but with less than a college degree. Changes in the structure of the nation's economy triggered changes in the structure of the nation's schools, especially its high school. A more complex and differentiated economy necessitated a more complex and differentiated system of secondary education. No longer could the nation's secondary schools produce a homogeneous product—the college-bound. What was needed was a heterogeneous product—part of which would go on to college, part of which would enter business offices, and part of which would go into the mines and factories of the industrializing nation.

The American high school, then, was to become a selector and an allocator of manpower. Initially, this task was to be left to teachers. But, as Charles W. Eliott, president of Harvard, phrased the issue in his 1908 address to the National Society for the Promotion of

Industrial Education, the sorting of students "by their evident or probable destinies" was far too important a responsibility to be left to teachers.[2] What was necessary was a "professional selector," a guidance counselor, of whom there were soon sufficient numbers that by 1910 a national conference was held in Boston, followed three years later by the creation of the National Guidance Association.[3]

In a very important sense, then, the guidance counselor became, as Carnoy has phrased it, "an intermediary between corporate needs and students. In that role he classified students for the labor force."[4]

But—on which criteria did the counselor classify students for the postsecondary educational or occupational market? What the revisionist theorists allege is that such sorting and allocation was done in accord with class origins. Samuel Bowles indicts both counselor and teacher as agents through which schools maintain the class structure of society when, in discussing how schools perpetuate the class structure of the larger society, he cites "the attitudes of teachers and guidance personnel who expect working-class children to do poorly, to terminate schooling early, and to end up in jobs similar to those of their parents.[5] In a somewhat more elaborate description, Carnoy concedes the use of ability and achievement tests by counselors in placement activities but considers such tests little more than "objective" surrogates of the student's social class.

> The schools prepared children for future work roles defined by class-biased "ability" tests and by the vocational guidance counselor. The tests and guidance served to "objectify" selection processes in a way that made people think that they were being gives the fairest deal possible within their own limitations.[6]

Proponents of a meritocratic perspective on the schools are by no stretch of the imagination either champions of or apologists for the guidance counselor. Indeed, the posture of these scholars tends, as often as not, to be critical of the counselor, questioning both the professional orientation and the effectiveness of the "professional selector."[7] Nevertheless, advocates of the meritocratic perspective tend *not* to regard class origin as an overriding determinant of whether the counselor encourages the student to enter college or the labor market upon completion of high school. More important as sources of influence on the counselor are the ability of the student, independent of his social class; his curriculum; and his own plans for postsecondary education. Thus, in her analysis of the determinants of the student's perception of whether, during the senior year, the guidance counselor provided encouragement to college, Heyns failed to detect a strong class-origin effect. What effect there was

> seemed quite small when intervening variables are considered. . . . To the extent that counseling represents a service or resource allocated within schools, the student's curriculum placement is a more important determinant of the differential allocation than either grades or ability level.[8]

In our present analysis of counselor encouragement in tenth grade, we examine in some detail for their total associations, their direct and indirect effects, four antecedents of special theoretical interest: (1) social class, (2) scholastic ability, (3) educational ambition, and (4) curriculum location in tenth grade.

An Overview of the Variables

During tenth grade, as figure 4.6 reveals, 53 percent of the boys and 46 percent of the girls reported being encouraged by the counselor to pursue a four-year college education. Thirty-one percent of the boys and 31 percent of the girls reported that they were encouraged to pursue some form of education beyond high school *other than* that of a four-year college. And, among the boys, 3 percent indicated that they had been advised by the counselor to enter the labor market after the completion of high school; 3 percent of the girls reported a similar lack of counselor encouragement for education beyond high school.

From the total associations and the total causal effects presented in table 4.2 we can see that in deciding whether to encourage a student to continue his or her education beyond high school, counselors are affected by cues from many sources. Not all these sources affect the counselor *directly*, however. The educational encouragement a boy receives as a sophomore is not affected directly by his social class, the degree to which his parents stressed his continued education beyond high school, or his curriculum location as a ninth grader.

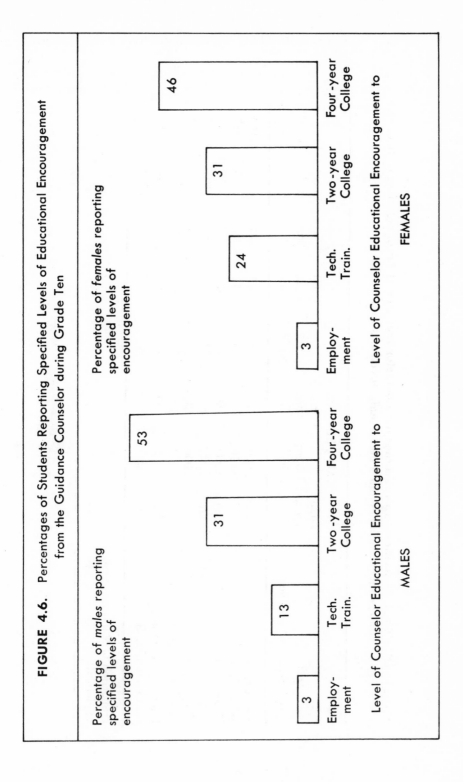

FIGURE 4.6. Percentages of Students Reporting Specified Levels of Educational Encouragement from the Guidance Counselor during Grade Ten

TABLE 4.2. Total Associations with Tenth-grade Counselor Educational Encouragement of Specified Independent Variables and Their Total, Direct, and Indirect Effects

Independent Variables		Male Students				Female Students			
		Total Assoc. r_{ij}	Direct p_{ij}	Effect: Indir. s_{ij}	Total q_{ij}	Total Assoc. r_{ij}	Direct p_{ij}	Effect: Indir. s_{ij}	Total q_{ij}
Social class	X_1	.260	.000	.174	.174	.312	.000	.199	.199
Scholastic ability	X_2	.395	.176	.177	.353	.445	.142	.245	.387
Parental ed. stress	X_3	.284	.000	.186	.186	.320	.053	.150	.203
Taken for granted	X_4	.328	.089	.084	.173	.336	.000	.124	.124
Curriculum gr. 9	X_5	.347	.000	.183	.183	.479	.000	.278	.278
Peer col. int. gr. 9	X_6	.356	.093	.057	.150	.342	.070	.052	.122
Educational ambition	X_7	.478	.197	.039	.236	.499	.152	.063	.215
Curriculum gr. 10	X_8	.467	.259	.000	.259	.635	.447	.000	.447
Proportion of Variance Explained: R^2		.346				.464			

Similarly, class has no direct effect on the encouragement reported by girls as tenth graders. Neither does the fact that their parents have or have not taken for granted her continued education or whether, as a ninth grader, she had several or no college-bound peers. In accord with the procedure described earlier, we set those paths to zero and recomputed the coefficients for the remaining determinants. Both before and after trimming the model, we were able to account for 35 percent of the variance in the encouragement of the counselor to boys and 46 percent in that to girls. The equations that make our model explicit are:

For both boys and girls

Eq. 1: $X_3 = p_{31}X_1 + p_{32}X_3 + p_{3a}X_a$

Eq. 2: $X_4 = p_{41}X_4 + p_{42}X_2 + p_{4b}X_b$

For boys only

Eq. 3: $X_5 = p_{51}X_1 + p_{52}X_2 + p_{53}X_3 + p_{5c}X_c$

Eq. 4: $X_6 = p_{61}X_1 + p_{62}X_2 + p_{63}X_3 + p_{64}X_4 + p_{65}X_5$
$+ p_{6d}X_d$

Eq. 5: $X_7 = p_{71}X_1 + p_{72}X_2 + p_{73}X_3 + p_{74}X_4 + p_{75}X_5$
$+ p_{76}X_6 + p_{7e}X_e$

Eq. 6: $X_8 = p_{82}X_2 + p_{83}X_3 + p_{85}X_5 + p_{87}X_7 + p_{8f}X_f$

Eq. 7: $X_9 = p_{92}X_2 + p_{94}X_4 + p_{96}X_6 + p_{97}X_7 + p_{98}X_8$
$+ p_{9g}X_g$

For girls only

Eq. 3: $X_5 = p_{51}X_1 + p_{52}X_2 + p_{53}X_3 + p_{54}X_4 + p_{5c}X_c$

Eq. 4: $X_6 = p_{61}X_1 + p_{62}X_2 + p_{63}X_3 + p_{64}X_4 + p_{65}X_5$
$+ p_{6d}X_d$

Eq. 5: $X_7 = p_{71}X_1 + p_{72}X_2 + p_{73}X_3 + p_{74}X_4 + p_{75}X_5$
$+ p_{76}X_6 + p_{7e}X_e$

Eq. 6: $X_8 = p_{81}X_1 + p_{82}X_2 + p_{84}X_4 + p_{85}X_5 + p_{87}X_7$
$+ p_{f}X_f$

Eq. 7: $X_9 = p_{92}X_2 + p_{93}X_3 + p_{96}X_6 + p_{97}X_7 + p_{98}X_8$
$+ p_{9g}X_g$

Returning to our description of the total associations and total effects that each of the eight antecedents of counselor encouragement has on that variable, we can see that either from personal knowledge or from inferences about the student's parents, counselors are more

likely to encourage the student to continue education beyond high
school if they believe that the parents themselves want him to enter
a community college or a four-year college. Total causal effects
from our indicators of parental influence range from a q_{94} of .12 for
"taken for granted" for girls to a q_{94} and a q_{93} of .18 for both "taken
for granted" and parental educational stress for boys, to a q_{93} of .20
for parental stress for girls. Similarly, the data suggest that when it
comes to giving educational encouragement, counselors are not
oblivious to the peer group with which the student associates.
Whether, as a ninth grader, the student had several, few, or no
college-bound friends generates a total effect to counselor encouragement, q_{96} = .15 for boys and .12 for girls.

And, as we would expect, the likelihood of the student reporting
college encouragement from the counselor in tenth grade is facilitated by more privileged class origin, by higher scholastic ability,
by location in the academic program, and by having a high level of
educational ambition. Since these are our variables of key interest, we
turn now to a detailed analysis of their effects on the counselor.

A Detailed Analysis of the Major Determinants
of Counselor Educational Encouragement

Curriculum Location. Being in the academic program in grade ten
means, for a boy, that he is more than two-and-one-half times as
likely as his nonacademic counterpart to be encouraged to go to a
four-year college by his counselor. The odds that favor the girls in
the academic program are even greater: she is six-and-a-half times
as likely to be counseled to college than her nonacademic peer (see
figure 4.7).

Curriculum, Heyns has written, has more to do with whether the
counselor encourages the student on to college than does either social
class or scholastic ability. Heyns made that inference on the basis of
a comparison of *direct* effects. We would make the same inference
from table 4.2 were we to rank-order those three variables solely on
the basis of their *direct* effects. To do so, however, would be to ignore
a second component: *indirect* effects. Class, which has no direct effect
on counselor encouragement, does have a sizable indirect effect:
s_{91} = .17 for boys and .20 for girls. Ability affects the counselor in-

FIGURE 4.7. The Effect on the Likelihood of Being Encouraged to Enter a Four-year College by the Counselor of Tenth-grade Curriculum, Educational Ambition, Scholastic Ability, and Social Class

Being in the academic program increases the likelihood of college encouragement from the counselor.

Percent reporting four-year college encouragement

Being educationally ambitious increases the likelihood of college encouragement from the counselor.

Percent reporting four-year college encouragement

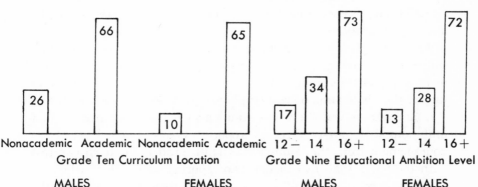

26	66	10	65
Nonacademic	Academic	Nonacademic	Academic

Grade Ten Curriculum Location

MALES   FEMALES

17	34	73	13	28	72
12—	14	16+	12—	14	16+

Grade Nine Educational Ambition Level

MALES   FEMALES

Scholastically more able students are more likely to report four-year encouragement from the counselor.

Percent reporting four-year college encouragement

37	64	27	60
Below	Above	Below	Above
Average		Average	

Scholastic Ability

Students from white-collar families are more likely to report four-year encouragement from the counselor.

Percent reporting four-year college encouragement

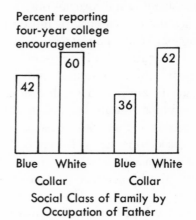

42	60	36	62
Blue	White	Blue	White
Collar		Collar	

Social Class of Family by Occupation of Father

directly about as much as it does directly, producing total causal effects on encouragement of $q_{92} = .35$ for boys and .39 for girls. Curriculum, grade ten, the variable that immediately precedes the encouragement of the counselor, can affect that encouragement only directly: $p_{98} = .26$ for boys and .45 for girls. In terms of *total causal effects*, then, curriculum affects the counselor's encouragement of boys *less* than does ability but more than class; for girls, however, curriculum location affects the counselor's encouragement more so than does ability or social class. Location in the organizational structure of the high school more than class origin thus determines whether a tenth grader is encouraged by the counselor to think seriously about a college education.

Educational Ambition. Anecdotal evidence from guidance counselors suggests that they give more than passing attention to the students' own plans and ambitions before encouraging or advising them to further their education or seek employment. As we can see from figure 4.7, more than seven of every ten students who, as ninth graders, had ambitions to a four-year college reported precisely that level of encouragement from the counselor as tenth graders, a sharp contrast with the fewer than two in ten who reported such advice when, as ninth graders, their ambition was to finish their schooling with the high school diploma.

Between the ambition of the student in ninth grade and the student's report of counselor encouragement in tenth grade there are rather sizable total associations: $r_{97} = .48$ for boys and .50 for girls. But are those relationships more appearance than substance? Or do counselors really pay attention to the ambitions of students before giving educational advice, regardless of the student's class of origin, scholastic ability, parental and peer educational support, and curriculum location as a ninth grader? Our best estimate is that these relationships contain important components of substance. For while 51 percent of that total association for boys and 57 percent of that total association for girls can be "explained away" by reference to the more privileged class origins, the greater amounts of scholastic ability, the higher levels of parental and peer educational support, and the curriculum advantages that characterize students who have college-level ambitions, it is also true that the complement of those percentages represents the substantive causal impact that a student's ambition has on the encouragement he or she receives from the counselor during the sophomore year. For boys that total causal effect, q_{97}, is .24 and for girls .22, most of which is direct with the remainder being indirect by way of the student's curriculum location as a tenth grader. The magnitude of these causal effects places ambition below ability but above class and interpersonal influence as a determinant of the educational encouragement that students report receiving from their counselor as high school sophomores.

Scholastic Ability. Almost two out of every three students with above-average scholastic ability reported that they were encouraged as sophomores to seek entry to a four-year college. Only one in three with below-average ability reported that they were so encouraged (see figure 4.7). Moderately strong total associations characterize the relationship between these two variables: r_{92} = .40 for boys and .45 for girls.

Advocates of both revisionist and meritocratic theses agree on the *existence* of a relationship between ability and counselor encouragement. What they do not agree upon is the *meaning* of that relationship. To some revisionists, ability is so highly correlated with social class that the use of ability by the counselor in deciding who to encourage to enter college and who to encourage to enter the job market is tantamount to the use of social class. The use of "ability" is seen by these critics as "objectifying" and therefore "legitimating" the sorting process. As Carnoy has written of measuring merit with objective tests, counseling, and social class:

> With the advent of vocational courses, testing, and guidance, the efficiency of selecting the greatly expanded number of enrollees for the various courses increased. The schools' methods of measuring merit were therefore seriously biased by inherited status and culture. . . . The definition of democracy had changed from rule by the people to rule by the intelligent. The intelligent, as defined by the designers of tests and vocational guidance counselors, were those of higher social classes, who were at the same time "moral" and had the characteristics necessary for leadership in America.[9]

Proponents of the meritocratic view, failing to find much empirical evidence of anything other than a weak association between a child's social class and his ability, believe that the ability of the student has a sizable impact on the counselor independent of any association that exists between ability and social class.

Ability does have an impact on the counselor. That impact is largely independent of social class. Almost 90 percent of the total association between student ability and counselor encouragement is causal and thus not attributable to the causally unanalyzed association between ability and class. Moreover, between a third and a half of the total effect that ability has on the encouragement of the counselor is *direct*: $q_{92} = .18$ for boys and .14 for girls. Before deciding whether to encourage a student to continue his education beyond high school, counselors probably review the ability and achievement test scores of the individual and are guided in their decision directly by those scores.

Student ability affects counselor encouragement *indirectly* also. For all students, such indirect effects are considerable. Almost half the total ability effect is indirect for boys and about two-thirds is indirect for girls. Basic indirect effects from ability to encouragement by way of the student's educational ambition in ninth grade account for about a tenth of the total ability effect for both boys and girls. The basic indirect effect that ability has on the counselor via the curriculum location of the student as a tenth grader accounts for another tenth or so of that total effect, for boys; for girls, their curriculum location in tenth grade accounts for twice that proportion, or about two-tenths of the total ability effect.

Of the total effect that student ability has on the educational encouragement of the guidance counselor, we are thus able to account for almost two-thirds. For both boys and girls, the major portion of that total effect is direct, indicating counselor reliance on standardized test scores when deciding whether to encourage a student on to college. Some of that total effect is indirect. For boys, our analysis suggests that scholastic ability is "legitimated" to the counselor as much by what the student wants to *do* after high school, i.e., his educational ambition, as by what the student's curriculum location *is* during high school. The ability of girls, however, is "legitimated" to the counselor less by what she wants to *do* after high school and more by what her curriculum location *is* during high school. As a mediator of the effects of ability, personal educational ambition counts for more with the counselor when the student is a male than when the student is a female.

Social Class. A student's social class simply has less to do than does his ability, educational ambition, or curriculum location with whether the counselor offers encouragement to college or not. On our measure of counselor encouragement, for boys, the total effect of ambition is 1.4 times larger than that of social class, while the total effect of ability is more than twice as large as that of social class.

Class does, of course, affect the likelihood that the student will report being encouraged by the counselor to enter college. As we can see from figure 4.7, the chances of a girl reporting college encouragement are more than six in ten if she is from a white-collar home, less than four in ten if she is from a blue-collar home. Two-thirds of the very modest total association between class and counselor encouragement, $r_{91} = .26$ for boys and .31 for girls, is causal, with $q_{92} = .17$ for boys and .20 for girls. None of that total effect, however, is direct! Apparently, counselors do not rely on the occupational or educational attainments of a student's parents when deciding whether to encourage the student on to college.

Curriculum location in sophomore year does not serve to link a boy's social class to his report of counselor encouragement. It does, however, link a girl's social class to her report of counselor encouragement. Although a boy's curriculum as a tenth grader directly affects the encouragement he reports from the counselor, $p_{98} = .26$, his social class of origin does not directly affect his curriculum location, $p_{81} = 0$. Thus, there is no simple causal chain connecting his social class to the encouragement of the counselor through his curriculum location as a sophomore. For girls, grade-ten curriculum is directly associated with counselor encouragement, $p_{98} = .45$; and social class is directly associated with grade-ten curriculum, $p_{81} = .08$. Therefore, about one-fifth of the total effect that a girl's class has on the counselor is indirect by way of her curriculum location in tenth grade.

Educational ambition also serves to link class of origin with encouragement from the guidance counselor. The tendency for middle-class students to be more educationally ambitious and for counselors to encourage the more educationally ambitious on to college accounts for more than a quarter of the total class effect on the counselor for boys and for about a seventh of the total class effect on the counselor for girls.

Summary

As we shall see in subsequent chapters, counseling for postsecondary educational career choices is a school function that definitely affects the behavior of the student both during and subsequent to high school. Since counseling is a consequential function of the school, an understanding of the determinants of that activity is useful in helping us to assess the extent to which the school tends either to constrain the student into a future class position not markedly different from his class of origin, or to free the individual from his class of origin so that his future class position may be more commensurate with his abilities and ambitions.

Our analysis indicates persuasively that merit, not social class, more strongly determines whether the "professional selector" encourages a student to seek entry to college or employment in the labor market. In deciding on what to encourage the student to do with his or her educational future, counselors are influenced more by the student's scholastic ability, educational ambition, and presumed degree of parental educational interest than they are by the occupational and educational attainments of the student's parents. Furthermore, the student's curriculum location as a sophomore, that institutional arrangement by which the student becomes committed either to a demanding course of study in preparation for college or to a less intellectually rigorous program of study in anticipation of employment, also has an impact on the counselor that is larger than the impact of social class.

Significantly, none of the effect that class does have on the level of counselor educational encouragement is direct. Unlike ability, where a direct effect of some magnitude led us to infer that counselors are influenced by scores, per se, from standardized tests, the absence of any direct effect from class led us to speculate that social class, as such, plays no apparent role in the educational counseling process. Class affects the encouragement level of the counselor indirectly, of course. Middle-class males are more likely than working-class males to report being encouraged to enter college because they are more likely to be educationally ambitious and counselors tend to encourage the educationally ambitious on to college. Middle-class females are more likely than working-class females to report being encouraged to enter college in part because of higher educational ambitions and in part because they are more likely to be in the academic program as tenth graders.

CONCLUSION

To the extent that high schools channel students into various post-secondary careers, the content and the structure of course work most likely require that the student commit himself no later than the end of tenth grade either to a program designed to prepare him for some form of postsecondary education or for some kind of employment. In this chapter, we have analyzed the determinants of two variables that define that commitment: the curriculum location of the student and the educational encouragement which the student reports he has received from the guidance counselor.

So defined, commitment is seen by revisionist theorists as occurring primarily along social-class lines. Students who come to be located in the college-preparatory program and who find themselves the recipients of counselor encouragement to enter college are pre-dominantly those from the middle class. Those from the working class are likely to find themselves shunted into the noncollege pro-gram and encouraged to enter the labor, not the educational, market.

Proponents of the meritocratic thesis do not view commitment as occurring primarily along social-class lines. Rather, they argue that the school is an arena in which the disadvantages or advantages of social class become gradually submerged, while ability, ambition, and achievement come to the fore as determinants of the educational experience of the student.

Commitment, our analysis has shown, is determined more by merit than by social class. The likelihood that the student is in a college-preparatory program at the end of ninth grade and the likelihood that he is in a college-preparatory program at the end of tenth grade depend more on ability and parental educational influ-ence than on social class. Moreover, regardless of curriculum location at the end of ninth grade, being in the college-preparatory program at the end of tenth grade is more a function of scholastic ability and ambition than of social class, although for girls social class is somewhat stronger a determinant than ambition. Similarly, whether the student reports the counselor as encouraging him to continue his education beyond high school or to enter the labor market depends more on his scholastic ability, curriculum location as a tenth grader, and educational ambition than it does on his class origins. Indeed, to the very modest degree that social class causally affects either curriculum location or educational encouragement in tenth grade, it does so almost all indirectly. The absence of a direct class effect suggests the absence of overt discrimination against working-class students or for middle-class students on the basis of the occupational or educational attainments of their parents. In fact, significant portions of the indirect-class effect on either curriculum location or counselor encouragement were found to be indirect by way of educational ambition, especially for boys. This finding indicates that the higher educational ambitions of middle-class students are in large part responsible for the overrepresentation of middle-class students among those who become committed to college by virtue of their location in the academic program or the college encouragement they receive from the guidance counselor.

NOTES

1. Erving Goffman, *Encounters* (Indianapolis: Bobbs-Merrill, 1961), pp. 88–89.

2. Cited from Henry J. Perkinson, *The Imperfect Panacea: American Faith in Education, 1865–1965* (New York: Random House, 1968), p. 145.

3. Ibid., p. 147.

4. Martin Carnoy, *Education as Cultural Imperialism* (New York: McKay, 1974), p. 251.

5. Samuel Bowles, "Unequal Education and the Reproduction of the Social Division of Labor," in *Schooling in a Corporate Society*, ed. Martin Carnoy (New York: McKay, 1972), p. 50.

6. Carnoy, *Education as Cultural Imperialism*, p. 253.

7. See, for example, the rather critical appraisal of the guidance profession and its practitioners in Aaron V. Cicourel and John I. Kitsuse, *The Educational Decision Makers* (Indianapolis: Bobbs-Merrill, 1963).

8. Barbara Heyns, "Social Selection and Stratification within Schools," *American Journal of Sociology* 79 (May 1974): 1447.

9. Carnoy, *Education as Cultural Imperialism*, p. 253.

5. Academic Achievement

Access to prestigious and high-income occupations depends strongly and directly on access to postsecondary education.[1] Access to postsecondary education depends strongly and directly on academic achievement in high school,[2] a fact we shall confirm in a subsequent chapter.

Precisely because academic achievement is a direct determinant of access to postsecondary education and, via that access, an indirect determinant of occupational attainment, it is a variable both theoretically and empirically consequential to an understanding of individual intergenerational social mobility and the role that schooling plays in that process. In a subsequent chapter, we investigate academic achievement as an *independent* variable, that is, we estimate the extent to which academic achievement causally affects the level of postsecondary educational enrollment. In this chapter, our concern is with academic achievement as a *dependent* variable, that is, as an effect of those variables that our model (see figure 5.1) specifies as antecedent to student cumulative grade-point average, our measure of academic achievement. Specifically, what we investigate here is the extent to which academic achievement can be attributed causally to the ascriptive construct of social class, to the merit constructs of scholastic ability and early educational expectation or ambition, and to the school-process constructs of curriculum location and counselor educational encouragement.

A strong causal effect of social class on academic achievement, particularly if found along with a moderate or weak causal effect from ability and ambition, would provide added support for the revisionist thesis that schools are class-biased institutions. Strong causal effects from ability and ambition, especially if detected in

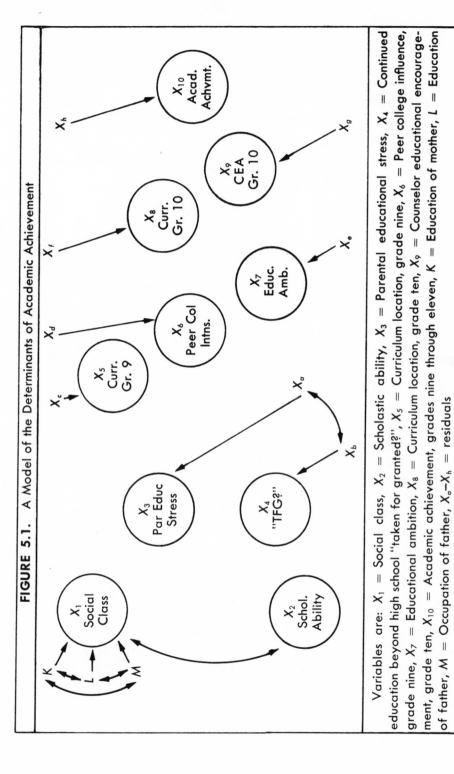

FIGURE 5.1. A Model of the Determinants of Academic Achievement

Variables are: X_1 = Social class, X_2 = Scholastic ability, X_3 = Parental educational stress, X_4 = Continued education beyond high school "taken for granted?", X_5 = Curriculum location, grade nine, X_6 = Peer college influence, grade nine, X_7 = Educational ambition, X_8 = Curriculum location, grade ten, X_9 = Counselor educational encouragement, grade ten, X_{10} = Academic achievement, grades nine through eleven, X_a–X_h = residuals of father, M = Occupation of father, K = Education of mother, L = Education the context of a weak causal effect from social class, would provide further empirical confirmation for the meritocratic perspective on schooling.

Prior to our discussion of the data, however, we describe the structure of academic achievement in the typical secondary school, consider the relationship of that structure to achievement in the larger society, and review the perspectives of the revisionist and meritocratic protagonists on academic achievement.

THE STRUCTURE OF ACADEMIC ACHIEVEMENT IN THE HIGH SCHOOL

Despite their differences on other aspects of schooling, revisionist and meritocratic theorists tend to agree that in most secondary schools the structure of academic achievement is: (1) relational; (2) competitive; and (3) isomorphic with competition in the larger society, i.e., competition for occupational prestige and for income.

The Relational Character of Academic Achievement

Grades that students receive for their schoolwork are best thought of as symbols that result from a bargaining relationship between teacher and student. Most often, that bargaining is subtle, occurring even below the level of consciousness. Thus grades are not totally "objective" tokens clinically dispensed by value-free teachers to students exclusively in recognition of performance in the cognitive domain. Subjective conditions enter into the grading process. While cognitive performance may provide the dominant cues for teacher grading, affective stimuli including dress, speech, deference, etc., also affect the grading process—a thesis argued strongly by revisionist economist Herbert Gintis.[3] Thus, as Lavin cautions, a "grade should be viewed as a function of the interaction between student and teacher. In short, it is one index of this social relationship."[4]

We do not wish to overemphasize the teacher-student relational character of academic achievement, however. For as Boocock concludes, after noting the personal biases to which teacher grades are subject:

[W]hatever grades measure, they affect one's subsequent educational career and are a good predictor of subsequent educational achievement. Within a given system, they can be used as a means of ranking individual students providing one keeps in mind the possible subjectivity of the graders.[5]

THE COMPETITIVE NATURE OF ACADEMIC ACHIEVEMENT

The comparatively few adults who manage to compete successfully within the system win the scarce tokens of success: prestigious occupations and high incomes. In real life, not everyone can win; indeed, too liberal a distribution of the tokens of success would only debase their value. Furthermore, in real life there is but a finite amount of time during which all may compete. For most, the race for "success" is effectively decided by age forty-five.

For youth, high grades and test scores are the tokens that adults have seen fit to dispense in recognition of academic success to the comparatively few who manage to come out on top in the competition that takes place within that microcosm of the real world—the school. Just as in the adult world, where prestigious jobs and high incomes are scarce and there is but a finite amount of time in which to run the race, so too in the school. *A*s and high percentile scores are scarce and limited. Academic achievement in the school, then, is *normative* and *time-bound*.[6] It is *normative* rather than absolute because the standards by which schools judge achievement are not fixed at some absolute level but vary according to the overall performance of the student body. Courses are not designed with finite amounts of knowledge to be learned and with grades given in direct proportion to the amount learned. A mark of 90 percent in eleventh-grade biology does not mean that the student has learned nine-tenths of all the biology there is to know at eleventh-grade level. Rather, courses and examinations are designed, a priori, to distribute students along a continuum of performance with the *A* given to those few at the top of the continuum, *B*s and *C*s to those in the middle, and *D*s and *F*s to those at the bottom of the grading scale, or "curve." And achievement is *time-bound* rather than open in that, regardless of individual differences in learning ability, students are given the same finite period of time in which to learn a subject, usually the traditional module of the academic year or academic semester. By pitting students against each other in the quest for the scarce rewards of *A*s or high percentile scores, the organization of academic achievement in the typical secondary schools

> reinforces interpersonal differences by applying fixed time limits for performance. . . . This means that the instructional program of the school is typically structured to impose and reinforce interpersonal competition (Coleman, 1965) within fixed time and spatial bounds so that the fastest learners not only learn more within a given amount of time but also are rewarded and selected differentially as well.[7]

The Isomorphism of the Competition for Academic Achievement with the Struggle for Occupational Prestige and Income

Our discussion of the last few paragraphs has drawn a number of parallels between the structure of academic achievement and the structure of occupational and income achievement in the larger society. To a degree neither fully understood nor measured, the allocation of incomes and occupations and grades are all transactional processes; each reflects the influence of nonobjective, interpersonal affective variables. And whether constrained by the forces of the market, as may be the case with occupational prestige and income, or by custom and the statistical characteristics of the normal or "bell" curve, as is the case with school grades, contestants for the symbols of success in the larger society and in the school compete for goods or prizes that are scarce, and they must engage in that competition within fixed, finite periods of time.

Proponents of both the meritocratic and revisionist theses tend to agree on these similarities between the structure of academic achievement and the structure of occupational and income attainment. They even tend to agree on some of the functions that those structures serve.

A calm and reasoned description of the learning system in the schools is provided by sociologist Richard P. Boyle.

> Clearly, one manifest function of the educational system is to bring about learning. . . . [T]he educational system must accomplish not only the production of learning but also its distribution. . . . [T]his means that the educational system must perform the functions of

selecting out those students who can best benefit from further incre-
ments of education, and of *certifying* that certain students have in
fact acquired certain kinds of knowledge and skills. . . . This involves
the assumption that at least within a given school the development
of learning is the individual responsibility of the student, and the
further assumption that the accomplishment of learning can be
measured, through the mechanism of grades. The result, then, is a
competitive process. . . . Furthermore, since at least the material
rewards of a person's life depend very strongly on the level at which
he is "outputted" from the educational system, there is assumed to
be a strong motivation on the part of the students, their families,
and even their schools to attain the highest possible level of output. . . .
In other words, the development of learning is not a discrete system, but one
which is central to the larger society, and grades are the key mechanism in the
functioning of this subsystem.[8]

Samuel Bowles is decidedly less "clinical" in his discussion of the
structure of academic achievement and of its consequences.

The power of the upper class is hypothesized as existing in its capacity
to define and maintain a set of rules of operation or decision criteria—
"rules of the game"—which, though often seemingly innocuous and
sometimes even egalitarian in their ostensible intent, have the effect
of maintaining the unequal system. [One example of this is the princi-
ple] that excellence in schooling should be rewarded. Given the
capacity of the upper class to define excellence in terms in which
upper-class children tend to excell (e.g., scholastic achievement), ad-
herence to this principle yields inegalitarian outcomes (e.g., unequal
access to higher education) while maintaining the appearance of fair
treatment.[9]

Agreement between meritocratic and revisionist scholars about the
nature of academic achievement, however, is limited to a consensus
on the relational, competitive, and isomorphic aspects of the structure.
Disagreement separates these two groups of theorists over the issue
of the equity of that structure. Those who view the schools as ap-
proximating the model of a meritocracy evaluate the structure of
academic achievement as basically fair: ability and ambition, more
than social class, determine who wins. Those of the revisionist per-

suasion evaluate the struggle for grades as inherently unfair. The achievement game, having been established by the establishment in the first place, is rigged in favor of those from the upper and middle classes at the obvious expense of those from the working and lower classes. We turn briefly to a more careful examination of these two positions on the issue of equity.

MERITOCRATIC AND REVISIONIST POSITIONS ON GRADES

David Goslin, a sociologist who has done much work in education, perhaps best expressed the meritocratic view on the inherent equity of academic achievement when he wrote:

> The educational setting provides the first major testing ground for the individual's abilities and energies. One's early academic performance has a lot to do with the opportunities, both educational and occupational, that will be open to him from this point on. The school affords individuals from all racial, ethnic, and class backgrounds an opportunity to show what they can do and thereby earn the chance both to continue their education and eventually to get a job that is commensurate with their abilities and training. . . . We conclude that education is the chief means by which the lower class individual or minority group member may improve his social position. In our achievement-oriented society, although ascribed characteristics of the individuals still make a difference in one's chances for success, the school provides an important mechanism that allows high ability and motivation to find its own level in the occupational structure of the society.[10]

But, while Goslin concludes his statement with the qualification that "the system is not perfect,"[11] Bowles makes such a qualification the very premise of his position

> Not surprisingly, the results of schooling differ greatly for children of different social classes. The differing educational objectives implicit in the social relations of schools attended by children of different social classes has already been mentioned. Less important but more easily measured are differences in scholastic achievement. If we measure

the output of schooling by scores on nationally standardized achievement tests, children whose parents were themselves highly educated outperform children of parents with less education by a wide margin.[12]

Martin Carnoy, also a revisionist economist, carries the assault on achievement even further. Ostensibly, writes Carnoy,

> ...the school system is...a meritocracy—grades, not parental background, determine who goes to the higher levels—yet factors outside the school are so important in influencing children's school performance, aspiration, and motivation that social class is still the most important variable in predicting *how far* a person gets in school. This is no accident. The school system is structured, through its tests, reward system, and required behavior patterns, to allow children of an urban bourgeoisie to do well, and filter out children of the poor, who are not socialized to function in the highest echelons of a capitalist economy and bourgeois culture. The school system is therefore a mechanism to maintain class structure in a capitalist society.[13]

Thus is the argument joined once again. A system of academic achievement seen by advocates of both meritocratic and revisionist theses as competitive and individualized is seen by those of meritocratic persuasion as essentially fair and comparatively free from the bias of social class while viewed by the revisionist as inherently inequitable by virtue of its being rooted in the class system of a capitalist society.

Whether and to what extent the empirical evidence supports one perspective over the other is the issue now before us.

DETERMINANTS OF ACADEMIC ACHIEVEMENT

At the basic, two-variable level of analysis, we can see from the total associations in table 5.1 and from the several illustrations in figure 5.2 that the academic achievement of high school students is related to each of the variables that the model specifies as antecedent to our measure of cumulative grade-point average.

By way of illustration: On the stanine scale where a grade-point average of 1.00 is high, 5.00 is average, and 9.00 is low, among the

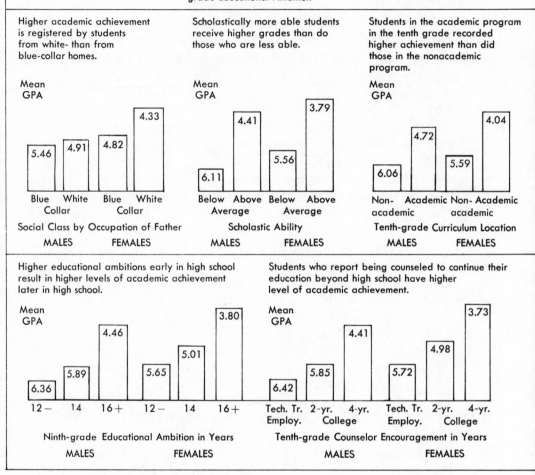

FIGURE 5.2. The Effect on Academic Achievement of Social Class, Scholastic Ability, Tenth-grade Curriculum Location, and Counselor Educational Encouragement and of Ninth-grade Educational Ambition

Higher academic achievement is registered by students from white- than from blue-collar homes.

Mean GPA

5.46 | 4.91 | 4.82 | 4.33

Blue Collar | White | Blue Collar | White

Social Class by Occupation of Father

MALES | FEMALES

Scholastically more able students receive higher grades than do those who are less able.

Mean GPA

6.11 | 4.41 | 5.56 | 3.79

Below Average | Above Average | Below Average | Above Average

Scholastic Ability

MALES | FEMALES

Students in the academic program in the tenth grade recorded higher achievement than did those in the nonacademic program.

Mean GPA

6.06 | 4.72 | 5.59 | 4.04

Non-academic | Academic | Non-academic | Academic

Tenth-grade Curriculum Location

MALES | FEMALES

Higher educational ambitions early in high school result in higher levels of academic achievement later in high school.

Mean GPA

6.36 | 5.89 | 4.46 | 5.65 | 5.01 | 3.80

12 − | 14 | 16+ | 12 − | 14 | 16+

Ninth-grade Educational Ambition in Years

MALES | FEMALES

Students who report being counseled to continue their education beyond high school have higher level of academic achievement.

Mean GPA

6.42 | 5.85 | 4.41 | 5.72 | 4.98 | 3.73

Tech. Tr. Employ. | 2-yr. College | 4-yr. | Tech. Tr. Employ. | 2-yr. College | 4-yr.

Tenth-grade Counselor Encouragement in Years

MALES | FEMALES

TABLE 5.1. Total Associations with Academic Achievement of Specified Independent Variables and Their Total, Direct, and Indirect Effects

Independent Variables		Male Students				Female Students			
		Total Assoc. r_{ij}	Direct p_{ij}	Effect: Indir. s_{ij}	Total q_{ij}	Total Assoc. r_{ij}	Direct p_{ij}	Effect: Indir. s_{ij}	Total q_{ij}
Social class	X_1	.238	.000	.109	.109	.216	.000	.055	.055
Scholastic ability	X_2	.553	.418	.109	.527	.571	.441	.114	.555
Parental ed. stress	X_3	.135	−.090	.092	.002	.158	−.061	.088	.027
Taken for granted	X_4	.256	.000	.102	.102	.233	.000	.058	.058
Curriculum gr. 9	X_5	.238	.000	.065	.065	.339	.000	.110	.110
Peer col. int. gr. 9	X_6	.244	.000	.037	.037	.259	.000	.077	.077
Educational ambition	X_7	.427	.213	.056	.269	.384	.132	.033	.165
Curriculum gr. 10	X_8	.327	.045	.037	.082	.400	.000	.113	.113
Cnslr. enc. gr. 10	X_9	.401	.139	.000	.139	.444	.202	.000	.202
Proportion of Variance Accounted for: R^2		.380				.382			

1,853 individuals present for all three in-school surveys, boys from white-collar families registered a higher level of achievement, 4.91, than did boys from blue-collar homes, whose mean level of achievement was 5.46. Somewhat larger differences in achievement are associated with differences in scholastic ability. Girls with more than the average amount of scholastic ability recorded a cumulative grade-point of 3.79, more than 1.5 scale points higher than did girls with less than the average amount of scholastic ability. Locating in the academic curriculum and having an ambition to enter a four-year college are also associated with higher levels of academic achievement. Boys who were in the academic program in tenth grade had earned a grade average of 4.72 by the end of their junior year, those in the nonacademic program an average of 6.06. Girls with ambitions for college as ninth graders received, by the end of their junior year, grades averaging 3.80, 1.76 scale points above the average of 5.56 registered by girls whose highest educational ambition was to complete high school. Finally, recall our observation in chapter 4 that the educational encouragement efforts of guidance counselors have measurable effects on student behavior, both during and following high school. One of those effects that we have been able to detect is on academic achievement. Among boys who, as tenth graders, reported being encouraged to go on to a four-year college, the cumulative grade-point average is 4.41, a full two scale points above the grade-point average of boys who, as tenth graders, reported being encouraged by their counselors to seek technical training or employment.

Bivariate relationships such as these reveal whether a difference in one variable, such as curriculum, is associated with a difference in another variable, such as cumulative academic achievement. Those same relationships, however, tell us nothing about what portion of that relationship, if any, may be causal. Curriculum and achievement provides a good case study of the necessity to go beyond simple two-variable relationships prior to making any inference about how important one variable may be as a determinant of another. Over grades nine, ten, and eleven, as we noted, students in the college-preparatory program rack up achievement gains more than a full scale point above that registered by students in the noncollege preparatory program. For boys, the total association between their curriculum as tenth graders and their record of academic achievement, $r_{10,8}$, is .33; for girls that total association is even a bit higher, $r_{10,8} = .40$. Certainly, the impression is that being in the academic program results in the student being exposed to social learning experiences that lead to or provide the motivation for superior academic performance. For British schools, Hargreaves[14] provides a vivid description of those kinds of experiences; Schafer and Olexa[15] do about the same for American schools. Yet, although their reference was to standardized test scores rather than to grade-point averages, Jencks et al. were led to conclude: "After an extensive review of previous research and reanalysis of four school surveys, we have concluded that if tracking affects test scores at all, the effect is too small to be pedagogically significant.[16]

Perhaps, then, much of the achievement difference between college-preparatory and noncollege-preparatory students is due, not to the *socialization* or experiential effects of curriculum location, but to the effects of those social and psychological forces that *select* students into one program or the other. If, indeed, much of the curriculum effect really stems from the already established tendency for the academic curriculum to select, disproportionately, students from more advantaged class backgrounds, with higher levels of scholastic ability, more parental support for continued education, higher levels of educational ambition, etc., then our analysis will show much of the total association between curriculum and achievement to be noncausal. We proceed now to that kind of causal analysis.

Sources of Minor Influence

While *all* nine antecedents of achievement specified in the model have total associations with achievement, not all exert a *direct* causal effect on achievement. Accordingly, we have trimmed the model and reestimated the direct causal effects of those antecedents that do exert direct effects on achievement. For boys, no direct effects are generated by social class, "taken for granted," ninth-grade curriculum or ninth-grade peer educational encouragement. For girls, direct effects are absent from social class, "taken for granted," ninth-grade curriculum, ninth-grade peer influence, and tenth-grade curriculum. Four of the nine antecedents thus do not generate direct effects to achievement for boys; five do not generate direct effects to achievement for girls. All antecedents, of course, may generate indirect effects. Both before and after trimming the model, 38 percent of the total variance in academic achievement was explained, regardless of gender. The defining equations for the model, then, are:

For both boys and girls

Eq. 1: $X_3 = p_{31}X_1 + p_{32}X_2 + p_{3a}X_a$

Eq. 2: $X_4 = p_{41}X_1 + p_{42}X_2 + p_{4b}X_b$

For boys only

Eq. 3: $X_5 = p_{51}X_1 + p_{52}X_2 + p_{53}X_3 + p_{5c}X_c$

Eq. 4: $X_6 = p_{61}X_1 + p_{62}X_2 + p_{63}X_3 + p_{64}X_4 + p_{65}X_5$
$+ p_{6d}X_d$

Eq. 5: $X_7 = p_{71}X_1 + p_{72}X_2 + p_{73}X_3 + p_{74}X_4 + p_{75}X_5$
$+ p_{76}X_6 + p_{7e}X_e$

Eq. 6: $X_8 = p_{82}X_2 + p_{83}X_3 + p_{85}X_5 + p_{87}X_7 + p_{8f}X_f$

Eq. 7: $X_9 = p_{92}X_2 + p_{94}X_4 + p_{96}X_6 + p_{97}X_7 + p_{98}X_8$
$+ p_{9g}X_g$

Eq. 8: $X_{10} = p_{10,2}X_2 + p_{10,3}X_3 + p_{10,7}X_7 + p_{10,8}X_8$
$+ p_{10,9}X_9 + p_{10h}X_h$

For girls only

Eq. 3: $X_5 = p_{51}X_1 + p_{52}X_2 + p_{53}X_3 + p_{54}X_4 + p_{5c}X_c$

Eq. 4: $X_6 = p_{61}X_1 + p_{62}X_2 + p_{63}X_3 + p_{64}X_4 + p_{65}X_5$
$+ p_{6d}X_d$

Eq. 5: $X_7 = p_{71}X_1 + p_{72}X_2 + p_{73}X_3 + p_{74}X_4 + p_{75}X_5$
$+ p_{76}X_6 + p_{7e}X_e$

Eq. 6: $X_8 = p_{81}X_1 + p_{82}X_2 + p_{84}X_4 + p_{85}X_5 + p_{87}X_7$
$+ p_{8f}X_f$

Eq. 7: $X_9 = p_{92}X_2 + p_{93}X_3 + p_{96}X_6 + p_{97}X_7 + p_{98}X_8$
$+ p_{9g}X_g$

Eq. 8: $X_{10} = p_{10,2}X_2 + p_{10,3}X_3 + p_{10,7}X_7 + p_{10,9}X_9$
$+ p_{10h}X_h$

If, as a rule of thumb, we regard as substantively trivial any antecedent that does not generate a total effect of .10 or more, then for *both* boys and girls neither the educational stress of their parents nor the educational plans of their own friends have much of an effect on their academic achievement during grades nine, ten, and eleven. Moreover, for boys, curriculum location in grades nine and ten is also inconsequential; for girls, social class and whether their parents "took for granted" their continued education beyond high school are also inconsequential. In fact, since their total effects hover near our .10 minimum threshold, for boys we may regard as inconsequential for academic achievement whether their continued education was "taken for granted," while for girls we may add their curriculum location in ninth and tenth grades to the list of inconsequential variables.

Interpersonal educational influence from either parents or peers thus appears to be of little more than marginal importance to student academic achievement. Perhaps the lack of any sizable effect is due to our measures' referring exclusively to educational career orientations rather than to academic performance. Efforts to influence the educational career of a student may not generalize to the academic achievement of the individual. Yet our counselor measure referred exclusively to educational career orientations, and as we shall see, it has a total effect of some consequence on academic achievement. Or the lack of effect from interpersonal influence may be due to the fact that our measures are from ninth grade while the measure of achievement is inclusive of the ninth, tenth, and eleventh grades. Interpersonal influence may atrophy over time, its effects may decay with the passage of the high school year. Yet, as we shall see in the next chapter, our ninth-grade measures of interpersonal influence extend total effects to the twelfth-grade measure of educational decision. Cautiously, then, we would conclude, that efforts by either parents or peers to influence the educational orientations of high school students have little causal consequence for the academic performance of those individuals.

Curriculum location is every bit as noteworthy as parent and peer influence for its lack of even a modest effect on academic achievement. Certainly, the very positive portraits of the educational experiences students are thought to have in a college-preparatory program, in contrast with the stifling of intellect pictured as occurring in the non-college-preparatory program, would have led us to anticipate a sizable total effect from curriculum location to academic achievement (see Hargraeves[17] and Schafer and Olexa[18] for those word murals of the various secondary curricula or tracks). Apparently, however, that anticipation has little empirical support. Much of whatever achievement differences characterize students in one program from those in another are attributable less to any social learning experi-

ences of academic import in those programs and more to the kinds
of students who go into each program. By way of example, we estimate
that for students of either gender in our sample, more than two-
thirds of the total association between ninth-grade curriculum location and academic achievement is due to the tendency for those in
the academic program to be already predisposed toward high
scholastic performance by virtue of their more privileged class origins,
higher levels of scholastic ability, and educationally supportive
parents. Our conclusion with respect to curriculum and achievement,
then, is the same as reached by Jencks and his associates with respect
to curriculum and performance on standardized tests; namely, that
to the extent that curriculum affects academic achievement at all,
it does so in a way that is too small to be pedagogically significant.

On what, then, does academic achievement depend? If the variables
of social class, parent and peer influence, and curriculum location
are not of major consequence for the academic performance of high
school students, what variables are? And what do such consequential
determinants tell us about the relative tenabilities of the revisionist
and meritocratic arguments?

Sources of Major Influence

Differences in the academic achievement of high school students
during grades nine, ten, and eleven are due chiefly to differences
among students in scholastic ability, educational ambition, and the
educational encouragement students report having received from
their guidance counselors as sophomores. The more scholastically
able the student, the more educationally ambitious the student, or
the more he perceives being encouraged by the counselor to plan on
college, the more likely is that individual to be the recipient of high
course grades.

Scholastic ability dominates the determination of academic achievement. Almost all of its total association with achievement is independent of its relationships with social class. More than 95 percent
of the total ability-achievement association is causal; that is, less
than 5 percent can be attributed to the causally unanalyzed relationship between social class and scholastic ability. On the achievement
of students during grades nine to eleven, ability exerts a total effect,
$q_{10,2}$, of .53 for boys and of .56 for girls. Almost 80 percent of this

total effect is direct to achievement, $p_{10,2} = .42$ for boys and .44 for girls, unmediated by any of the intervening variables in the model. Ability also affects achievement indirectly with those effects, $s_{10,2}$, being .11 for boys and .11 for girls. Two intervening variables, ambition and counselor encouragement, account for half this indirect effect, or about 10 percent of the total effect. Thus, of the rather sizable total effect that scholastic ability has on academic achievement, eight-tenths or so is direct with another tenth indirect. Bright students receive higher grades largely because they are scholastically more capable of doing superior academic work but also because they are educationally more ambitious and are more likely to be urged on to college by the counselor of the school.

Ambition ranks second to ability as a determinant of the educational achievement of boys and third as a determinant of achievement for girls.

Slightly more than one-third of the total ambition-achievement association for boys and somewhat more than one-half of that for girls is noncausal, a result of the operation on the ambition-achievement relationship of variables temporally prior to ambition. That is, some of the tendency for the more educationally ambitious to receive higher grades is attributable *not* to any motivating force of ambition, but to the tendency of those with high educational ambitions to be predisposed toward higher grades by virtue of their higher social origins, superior scholastic ability, perception of parents and peers as strong influences on their educational plans, and location in the academic program.

Nevertheless, ambition generates a notable total causal effect, especially to the achievement of boys, $q_{10,7} = .27$, and even to the achievement of girls, where $q_{10,7} = .17$. For students of both genders, the major portion of that total effect, 80 percent or so, is direct, $p_{10,7} = .21$ for boys and .13 for girls. Indirectly, ambition has an effect, $s_{10,7}$, of .06 on the achievement of boys, half of which is because educationally more ambitious boys are more likely to receive counselor encouragement to college, and students who receive that encouragement are more likely to earn higher grades. The indirect effect of ambition on the achievement of girls, $s_{10,7}$, is .03, all of which is mediated by counselor encouragement.

That college-bound students excel over their noncollege-bound peers in academic achievement is neither surprising nor novel. More than a decade ago, Boyle detected a similar pattern for standardized (Iowa) test scores in his 1965 study of 2,299 tenth-grade boys who were enrolled in 35 Iowa public schools. "Differences in the rate of learning among students are systematically associated with their educational aspirations," concluded Boyle.[19] What is significant about our finding is that even after statistically removing the associated effects of social class, scholastic ability, parent and peer influence, and curriculum location, educational ambition remains a causative force in student academic achievement. Regardless of whether a student is from a middle- or a working-class family, of above- or below-average ability, in the academic or nonacademic program, etc., the more educationally ambitious that student is, the more highly motivated he is to earn superior grades.

Counselor educational encouragement is the third and last consequential determinant of student academic achievement. A large segment of the counselor-achievement total association is noncausal. For boys, two-thirds of that association, and for girls, one-half, can be explained away by virtue of the fact that students who are encouraged to go on to college and who receive good grades tend also to be from more privileged families, be more scholastically able, to have stronger peer educational support, be more ambitious educationally, and be more likely to be in the college-preparatory program. Nevertheless, we find a total effect from counselor to achievement of $q_{10,9} = .14$ for boys and .20 for girls. School officials thus do influence the academic behavior of students. Even though restricted by the wording of the survey questionnaire to encouragement relating specifically to post-secondary career plans, encouragement by the counselor apparently is both sufficiently strong and generalized to affect the academic performance of the individual as well.

Academic achievement, then, depends on comparatively few variables. In our model it has depended primarily upon three: scholastic ability, educational ambition, and counselor encouragement. It has *not* depended, to any comparable degree, upon social class! Not only is the total effect of class on achievement rather small, $q_{10,1} = .11$ for boys and .06 for girls, it is also *all* indirect, thus failing to suggest any overt discrimination whatsoever by teachers against working-class and in favor of middle-class students in the assignment of grades. In fact, a substantial portion of the limited total effect that class does have on student achievement, especially for boys, is indirect by way of educational ambition: two-thirds for boys, one-third for girls. Much of whatever class difference exists in academic achievement is understandable, therefore, as a tendency for higher grades to be earned by more educationally ambitious students and for more educationally ambitious students to be drawn somewhat disproportionately from the middle rather than from the lower class.

Academic achievement, then, is distributed essentially in accord with the principle of merit. High grades are awarded to those students who are scholastically most able and educationally more ambitious.

Are our data atypical? Does social class have more of an impact on student academic achievement in other parts of the United States? The answer is an unequivocal no, as the correlations in table 5.2 demonstrate. In that table are the total associations of academic achievement with social class, scholastic ability, educational ambition, and several other determinants for six different studies ranging from Williams' inquiry based on Canadian high school students, through Heyns' analysis using some 15,000 students from the 1965 Coleman et al. national Equality of Economic Opportunity Survey to Sewell and Hauser's subset of Wisconsin high school students, class of 1957. Achievement correlates most highly with scholastic ability (median $r = .47$); next so with early high school educational ambition (median $r = .47$), and least so with social class (median r, at best, is in the high 20s).

SUMMARY AND CONCLUSION

In the struggle for achievement, grades are to the student what earnings and occupational prestige are to the adult. Despite the difference in the ages of the contestants, the structures of those achievement struggles are remarkably similar. Just as high earnings or prestigious jobs are limited in quantity, so too are high grades. Just as most adults must run their career race in a finite time period that for most is over by age forty, so too must most students complete their efforts for high grades within the hour or so allotted to a given test or within the semester allotted to a given subject. Finally, just as the allocation of earnings and jobs is subject to the vagaries of the personalities of employer and prospective employee, so too is the allocation of grades subject to the interaction between teacher and student.

TABLE 5.2. The Impact on Academic Achievement of Specified Variables: Correlations (Total Associations) from Various Studies

Identification of the Study	Description	Gender of Student	Correlations of Academic Achievement With:[a]									
			Class Indicators:			Class Comp.	Sch. Abil.	Par. Infl.	Curri- culum	Peer Infl.	Educ. Ambit.	Tchr. Infl.
			POPOC	POPED	MOMED							
Williams	Canadian students	Male	.07	.08	.10	N.A.	.23	.16	.07	.19	.17	.19
		Female	.08	.10	.10	N.A.	.32	.24	.01	.13	.14	.24
Alexander and Eckland	National U.S.	Male	.21	.24	.12	N.A.	.49	.36	.29	.30	.49	.23
Bachman	National U.S.	Male	N.A.	N.A.	N.A.	.22	.36	N.A.	N.A.	N.A.	.31	N.A.
Sewell and Hauser	Wisconsin subset	Male	.13	.15	.14	N.A.	.56	.32	N.A.	.31	N.A.	.42
Heyns	National U.S.	Male and Female	.15	.16	N.A.	N.A.	.37	N.A.	N.A.	N.A.	N.A.	N.A.
Kerckhoff	Fort Wayne students	Male	.22	.25	N.A.	N.A.	.57	N.A.	N.A.	N.A.	.50	N.A.
Median Correlation[b]			.15	.16	.12	.22	.47	.32	.07	.30	.40	.23
This Study	See chapter 2	Male	.20	.20	.17	.24	.55	.26[c]	.33[d]	.24	.43	.40[e]
		Female	.18	.18	.16	.22	.57	.23	.40	.26	.38	.44

Sources: Williams, see reference in table 3.1.; all measures except for teacher influence are described in preceding tables. Teacher influence measure is similar to that used by Williams for peer influence. Ambition measure is from grade ten. All correlations from Williams are from personal correspondence except those of parent and peer influence, which are from Williams (1972). Alexander and Eckland, see reference in table 3.1. Bachman, see reference in table 3.1. Kerckhoff, see reference in table 3.5. Sewell and Hauser, see reference in table 3.2. Heyns, see reference in Table 3.1. Kerckhoff, see reference in table 3.5.

[a] Measures of academic achievement are: Williams, grade-point average of the student in all courses, eleventh grade; Alexander and Eckland, self-reported grades, quartile format, tenth grade; Bachman, self-report by tenth-grade students of their performance in ninth grade; Sewell and Hauser, rank in senior class from school records, transformed into approximately normal distribution; Heyns, self-reports from grade twelve; and Kerckhoff, grades in senior year, from school records (synthetic cohort model).

[b] In computing median correlation, gender-specific correlations from Williams' study were first combined by estimating the median coefficient between genders since both subsets are from the same sample.

[c] Parental influence measure is that of "taken for granted."

[d] Curriculum measure is from tenth grade.

[e] For "This Study" the measure is that of "counselor influence," for all other studies it is that of "teacher influence."

Achievement inside the school thus mirrors and anticipates achievement in the real world outside the school. Because of this anticipatory training function and because high school grades have so much to do with access to postsecondary education and hence to jobs and earnings, the analysis of what kinds of students receive which grades can provide some insight into the workings of a society, or at least into the workings of the schools of that society, which in turn may tell us something about the society itself.

Schools, argue the revisionists, are the captives of the ruling classes. As such, the rules of the game within the school are rigged to favor the children of the privileged. Since those children are superior at tasks involving numbers and words, so the argument goes, achievement in the schools will be defined in terms of performance involving numerical and verbal skills. High grades, the tokens dispensed in recognition of superior achievement, will thus be disproportionately *over*distributed to students of the middle and upper classes and disproportionately *under*distributed to students from the working and lower classes. Class origin is thus seen as the primary determinant of grades.

Not so, counter the proponents of the meritocratic thesis. Grades may vary by social class, but not by much. Academic achievement, argue the meritocrats, depends primarily on scholastic ability and ambition or motivation, and only secondarily on social class.

Course grades, our data reveal, are just not strongly affected by student social class. The total association of class with achievement is modest at best; none of it is causally direct, and of the portion that is causally indirect a good part is indirect by way of educational ambition, itself a merit construct.

Ability and ambition are two of the stronger determinants of academic achievement. Both have sizable total associations with achievement. Most of the association between ability and achievement is causal, with much of it being direct and with a good portion of the indirect effect being indirect by way of early educational ambition.

"Ambition" here means the realistic educational expectations of the student as a ninth grader. Despite the fact that a portion of its comparatively strong total association with achievement is noncausal by virtue of a set of common antecedents to both ambition and achievement, ambition nevertheless exerts a *direct* causal effect on the achievement of boys second only in size to that of ability; for girls, that direct effect ranks third behind ability and counselor encouragement.

With respect to curriculum and achievement, our finding does not differ dramatically with the conclusion of Jencks et al. The causal effect that curriculum has on academic achievement is so limited in size as to be of questionable pedagogical significance.

To our surprise, the counselor emerged from the analysis as exerting a fairly sizable direct causal effect on student academic achievement—the third largest such effect for boys, the second largest for girls. Perhaps these "keepers of the career gate" have more influence on students than researchers have been wont to give them credit for. More research is necessary before that distinct possibility becomes a sizable probability.

Contrary to the revisionist penchant for citing curriculum location and the guidance counselor as prime vehicles by which the schools move students along a treadmill from class of origin to class of destination, our inquiry has produced little evidence suggestive of this. The causal link between curriculum and achievement is too weak for this organizational variable to mediate more than a minor portion of any effect that class might have on academic achievement. Similarly, the causal link between class and counselor is too weak for that school official to mediate more than a minor portion of the already very modest effect of class on academic achievement.

To the extent that we can understand why students differ in their academic achievement in terms of specific variables, we can say with reasonable assurance that knowledge of differences in scholastic ability and educational ambition increase that understanding far more than does knowledge of social-class origin. Merit, more than class, is the basis of academic achievement—a position that some revisionists are now coming to acknowledge.[20]

NOTES

1. Peter Blau and Otis Dudley Duncan, *The American Occupational Structure* (New York: Wiley, 1967); see also Otis Dudley Duncan, "Ability and Achievement," *Eugenics Quarterly* 15 (March 1968): 1–11.

2. William H. Sewell and Robert M. Hauser, *Education, Occupation, and Earnings: Achievement in the Early Career* (Madison: University of Wisconsin, Department of Sociology, 1974). A final report of research carried out under Grant. No. 314, Social and Rehabilitation Service, Social Security Administration, U.S. Department of Health, Education, and Welfare; see also David Lavin, *The Prediction of Academic Performance* (New York: Russell Sage Foundation, 1965).

3. Herbert Gintis, "Education and the Characteristics of Worker Productivity," *American Economic Review* 61 (May 1971): 266–79.

4. Lavin, *Prediction of Academic Performance*, p. 21

5. Sarane Spence Boocock, *An Introduction to the Sociology of Learning* (Boston: Houghton Mifflin, 1972), p. 29.

6. William G. Spady, "The Sociological Implications of Mastery Learning," in *Schools, Society, and Mastery Learning*, ed. James H. Block (New York: Holt, Rinehart & Winston, 1974), pp. 89–116.

7. Ibid., p. 10.

8. Richard P. Boyle, "Functional Dilemmas in the Development of Learning," *Sociology of Education* 42 (Winter 1969): 71–72. Italics added.

9. Samuel Bowles, "Unequal Education and the Reproduction of the Social Division of Labor," in *Schooling in a Corporate Society*, ed. Martin Carnoy (New York: McKay, 1972), p. 60.

10. David Goslin, *The School in Contemporary Society* (Glenview, Ill.: Scott, Foresman, 1965), pp. 125–26.

11. Ibid., p. 126.

12. Bowles, "Unequal Education," p. 51.

13. Martin Carnoy, *Education as Cultural Imperialism* (New York: McKay, 1974), pp. 323–24.

14. David H. Hargreaves, *Social Relations in a Secondary School* (London: Routledge & Kegan Paul, 1967).

15. Walter E. Schafer and Carol Olexa, *Tracking and Opportunity: The Locking-Out Process and Beyond* (Scranton, Pa.: Chandler, 1971).

16. Christopher S. Jencks et al., *Inequality: A Reassessment of the Effect of Family and Schooling in America* (New York: Basic Books, 1972), p. 107.

17. Hargreaves, *Social Relations in a Secondary School*.

18. Schafer and Olexa, *Tracking and Opportunity*.

19. Boyle, "Functional Dilemmas in the Development of Learning," p. 90.

20. In a paper published in 1973, two revisionist theorists, Samuel Bowles and Herbert Gintis, acknowledge that "recent studies . . . indeed indicate a lack of social class bias in school grades: given a student's cognitive attainment, his or her grades seem not to be significantly affected by class or racial origins, at least on the high school level." Samuel Bowles and Herbert Gintis, "I.Q. in the U.S. Class Structure," *Social Policy*, November/December 1972 and January/February 1973, pp. 65–96.

6. Grade Twelve: The Year of Educational Decision

For some students, the twelfth grade marks the end of formal schooling and the beginning of the world of work; for others, it does little more than separate the elementary and secondary years from the college years. For all students who progress as far as twelfth grade, however, the year is one of decision. It is a year during which alternative educational and occupational careers must be considered, preferences established or crystallized, decisions made with respect to those preferences, and preparations made for their implementation. The educational dimension of that decision and the forces shaping it constitute the subject matter of this chapter.

Toward the end of grade twelve we asked all students in our sample about their educational decision. In the survey questionnaire, our respondents were requested to indicate if they realistically expected to conclude their formal education with the high school diploma or if they expected to continue on with their education to a community college or a four-year college or university. By the last month or so of grade twelve, most high school students know whether or not they will be continuing their education. We regard our twelfth-grade measure as an indicator of the student's educational *decision*, rather than as an expression of an educational aspiration or expectation, as other investigators have tended to term it.[1]

This chapter explores some determinants of that educational decision, a decision regarded by Sewell and Shah as "perhaps the most critical factor in the process of obtaining higher education." [2] As such, the decision can be construed as one in a sequence of identifiable events that define what Blau and Duncan have referred to as the individual's *socioeconomic* career.[3] An individual's educational decision determines whether he actually enters college. Both decision and college entry are highly correlated with rs ranging from the high 60s to the high 70s.[4] College entry, in turn, determines the individual's ultimate educational attainment. These two measures correlate well into the 80s.[5] And educational attainment explains almost half the variance in occupational attainment, with these two measures characterized by coefficients in the mid-60s.[6] An educational decision is thus a *direct* determinant of college enrollment and, by way of college enrollment, an *indirect* determinant of educational and occupational attainment.

Decisions about education made by students in the twelfth grade are decisions of consequence. Directly and indirectly, the twelfth grader's decision to continue or not to continue education beyond high school affects his social class of destination. And from the relationship of educational decision with class of destination, the question of the relationship between educational decision and class of origin derives its importance. If that decision is affected primarily and strongly by class of origin, then the revisionist's conception of American society and its schools gains credibility. If that decision is affected more by ability, ambition, or achievement than by social-class origin, then the meritocratic conception of American society and its schools becomes more credible.

REVISIONIST AND MERITOCRATIC CONTEXTS OF EDUCATIONAL DECISIONS

Revisionist scholars have virtually ignored the decisions students make about their educational careers. Perhaps this neglect stems from the revisionist preference for structural variables such as social class or for organizational variables such as curriculum rather than for attitudinal variables such as an educational decision or, more generally, an educational goal orientation under which we may subsume the related concepts of aspiration and expectation.[7] Nevertheless, when these theorists have concerned themselves with the determinants of an educational goal orientation, they have alleged, as has, for example, Samuel Bowles, that "the aspirations and expectations of students and parents concerning both the type and the amount of schooling are *strongly* related to social class."[8] We find no indication in Bowles' writing, however, of what constitutes a "strong" relationship or how a "strong" relationship is distinguished from one that is "moderate" or "weak."

If the revisionist critics have tended to ignore educational decisions, nonrevisionist students of schooling and social mobility have tended to be all but preoccupied with the subject. Educational goal orientations, usually termed "aspirations" or "plans," have been the subject of abiding concern to those social scientists who have sought to add a social-psychological dimension to the study of schooling and social mobility. It is a bit ironic, given the resources invested in this pursuit, to find that definitive agreement on the roles of class and merit in the determination of educational goals has proven elusive. "The literature regarding the relative importance of ability and status variables in influencing such orientations is equivocal. Some studies accord primary importance to ability . . . while others emphasize status background and values," wrote Alexander and Eckland recently.[9]

On this particular issue, the result of our inquiry is not equivocal. With "importance" defined by the size of the total effect coefficient, the ability of our students, more than their social class, determines whether, by the end of their senior year, they had decided to continue their education beyond high school. Moreover, their ambition for continued education is more important than their class of origin in determining that decision.

THE DECISION TO ENTER COLLEGE: SOME DETERMINANTS

Figure 6.1 maps the system of variables that we hypothesize as determinants of an educational decision. Sequentially, the decision, X_{13}, depends most immediately on two sources of interpersonal influence: X_{12}, the educational encouragement reported by the student from the guidance counselor during grade twelve, and X_{11}, any educational influence the student may have received from his three close friends by virtue of their own educational goal orientations.

The educational decision, and each of the two sources of twelfth-grade interpersonal influence, in turn, are subject to effects from the student's own cumulative academic achievement, X_{10}; those who achieve higher grades during grades nine, ten, and eleven are more likely in grade twelve to have several friends who intend to go to college, to receive college-level encouragement from the counselor, and to decide to continue their education beyond high school. Aca-

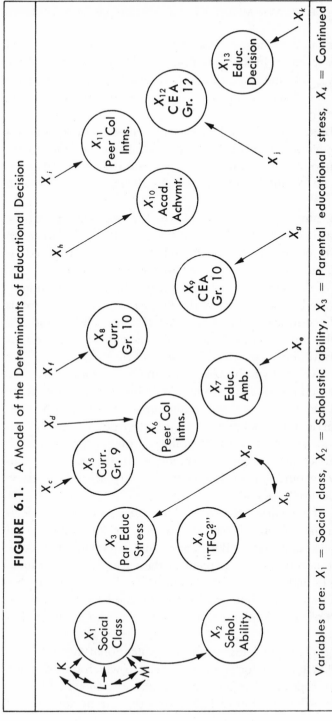

FIGURE 6.1. A Model of the Determinants of Educational Decision

Variables are: X_1 = Social class, X_2 = Scholastic ability, X_3 = Parental educational stress, X_4 = Continued education beyond high school "taken for granted?", X_5 = Curriculum location, grade nine, X_6 = Peer college influence, grade nine, X_7 = Educational ambition, X_8 = Curriculum location, grade ten, X_9 = Counselor educational encouragement, grade ten, X_{10} = Academic achievement, grades nine through eleven, X_{11} = Peer college influence, grade twelve, X_{12} = Counselor educational encouragement, grade twelve, X_{13} = Educational decision, K = Education of mother, L = Education of father, M = Occupation of father, X_a–X_k = residuals.

demic achievement, and the peer, counselor, and decision experiences of the student as a senior, in turn, are linked to two measures from the tenth grade: X_9, whether the student was encouraged to plan on college by the counselor, and X_8, whether the student was in the academic program.

All six variables, from X_{13} to X_8, are represented as depending on three student outcomes measured during ninth grade: X_7, the educational ambition of the individual; X_6, the number of friends who themselves had ambitions for college; and X_5, the curriculum location of the student.

Finally, these nine variables, each of which represents an attitude or behavior that occurred either within the school or was subject to experiences that occurred within the school, are hypothesized as dependent on four measures whose locus is outside the school: X_1, the social class of the family; X_2, the scholastic ability of the student; X_3, the perception by the student of the degree to which the parents have "stressed" continued education beyond high school; and X_4, the perception by the student of whether the parents have "taken for granted" the continuation of education beyond high school.

Among the twelve hypothesized determinants, some have no *direct* effects on educational decision. As table 6.1 reveals, those variables are, for boys: parental educational stress, ninth- and tenth-grade curriculum location, and tenth-grade counselor encouragement; for girls, scholastic ability, "taken for granted," ninth-grade curriculum location, peer college intentions and tenth-grade counselor encouragement. Each variable may affect the decision of the student *indirectly*, of course.

Accordingly, those variables that did not generate direct effects to the criterion have been deleted, and the direct effects for the remaining variables reestimated. Both before and after such trimming, we were able to account for 55 percent of the variance in the educational decisions of males and for 50 percent in the decisions of females. The equations that define our gender-specific model for the educational decisions of our sample are presented in a note at the end of this chapter.[10]

In analyzing the determinants of an educational decision, we proceed topically. First we focus on the extent to which that decision is affected by interpersonal influence from parents, peers, and guidance counselors. What we find is that neither the parent nor the peer

TABLE 6.1. The Total Associations with Educational Decision of Specified Independent Variables and Their Total, Direct, and Indirect Effects

Independent Variables		Male Students				Female Students			
		Total Assoc. r_{ij}	Direct p_{ij}	Effect: Indir. s_{ij}	Total q_{ij}	Total Assoc. r_{ij}	Direct p_{ij}	Effect: Indir. s_{ij}	Total q_{ij}
Social class	X_1	.375	.057	.223	.280	.355	.078	.178	.256
Scholastic ability	X_2	.458	.092	.297	.389	.413	.000	.338	.338
Parental ed. stress	X_3	.289	.000	.155	.155	.338	.070	.148	.218
Taken for granted	X_4	.399	.053	.164	.217	.324	.000	.095	.095
Curriculum gr. 9	X_5	.363	.000	.164	.164	.404	.000	.179	.179
Peer col. int. gr. 9	X_6	.396	.044	.103	.147	.338	.000	.123	.123
Educational ambition	X_7	.617	.297	.094	.391	.534	.205	.098	.303
Curriculum gr. 10	X_8	.410	.000	.071	.071	.479	.070	.111	.181
Cnslr. enc. gr. 10	X_9	.440	.000	.090	.090	.496	.000	.186	.186
Academic achvmt.	X_{10}	.516	.150	.075	.225	.500	.187	.083	.270
Peer col. int. gr. 9	X_{11}	.393	.133	.022	.155	.339	.099	.014	.113
Cnslr. enc. gr. 12	X_{12}	.569	.236	.000	.236	.586	.304	.000	.304
Proportion of Variance Accounted for: R^2		.549				.449			

is as important a factor in that decision as is the guidance counselor. In shaping the educational decisions of twelfth-grade students, the encouragement given them by the counselor during the senior year is about equal to that which can be attributed to the student's record of academic achievement accumulated during the period spanning the ninth, tenth, and eleventh grades. Next we consider the extent to which the educational decisions reached by our students as of the end of twelfth grade are affected by their curriculum locations as of the end of ninth and tenth grades. Once we take into account existing differences between students in the academic and the nonacademic programs in terms of social class, scholastic ability, parent and peer influence, and educational ambition, we find no evidence that students in the nonacademic program are at a severe disadvantage when it comes to the decision to continue education beyond high school vis-à-vis their counterparts in the academic program. In some respects the effect that curriculum location has on educational decision parallels that which curriculum location has on academic achievement: those in the academic program enjoy a moderate edge over those in the nonacademic program and that edge is somewhat more pronounced for females than for males. Finally, we consider the respective impact that social class and merit have on the educational decisions of high school seniors. The decision to enter college, we find, depends less on social class than on merit. Both scholastic ability and educational ambition have more to do with that decision than does class. Academic achievement, however, exerts a smaller effect than does class on the decisions of males; the reverse is true for the decisions of females. There is no evidence that the educational decisions of students are *strongly* associated with their class origins.

Interpersonal Influence

Having parents who place emphasis on one's continued education beyond high school and who "take for granted" one's continued education as early as ninth grade increases the likelihood that the student will decide, by the end of twelfth grade, to enter college. As figure 6.2 illustrates, 71 percent of the males who, as ninth graders, reported that their continued education beyond high school was "taken for granted" reported, by the end of twelfth grade, that they had decided to enter a four-year college. Only 34 percent of those males who reported that their continued education beyond high school was *not* "taken for granted" reported a similar decision. Respective percentages for females are 53 and 23. Although such influence is more characteristic of middle- than of working-class parents and of parents with scholastically above-average rather than scholastically below-average students, table 6.1 suggests that the total effect which both indicators of parental influence have on the decision of males, $q_{13,3} = .16$ and $q_{13,4} = .22$, is more than half the total association between each indicator and educational decision, $r_{13,3} = .29$ and $r_{13,4} = .40$. For females, the impact that parental stress has on educational decision, net of class and ability, is greater than that of "taken for granted." Sixty-five percent of the total association that "stress" has with decision, $r_{13,3} = .34$, is independent of class and ability, for a total effect, $q_{13,3}$, of .22. Only 29 percent of the total association between "taken for granted" and educational decision, $r_{13,4} = .32$, however, is independent of social class and scholastic ability, for a total effect, $q_{13,4}$, of .10. Within reasonable limits, it would appear that without regard to either class or ability, parents reach and maintain an "understanding" about college at an earlier age with their *sons* than with their daughters. The higher correlation between ninth-grade ambition and twelfth-grade decision for males, $r_{13,7} = .62$, than for females, $r_{13,7} = .53$, is consistent with an inference of earlier and more stable goal setting between parents and sons than between parents and daughters.

Having several rather than few or no close friends who themselves plan on college as early as ninth grade or as late as twelfth grade also increases the likelihood that a student will reach the decision to enter college by the end of the senior year. Eighty percent of all ninth-grade males who reported three close friends as having ambitions for college had decided by the end of twelfth grade to enter a four-year college, as figure 6.2 illustrates. Only 38 percent of ninth-grade males who reported no close friends with college ambitions had reached the decision to enter a four-year college by the end of their senior year. Respective percentages for females are 64 and 23.

Peers, our data suggest, have less of an impact than do parents on the educational decisions of students. The difference, however, is small. For males, the total effect from "taken for granted," $q_{13,4} = .22$, exceeds that from peers in either the ninth grade, where the peer effect, $q_{13,6}$, is .15 or in the twelfth grade, where the peer effect,

FIGURE 6.2. The Effect on the Decision to Enter a Four-year College of Specified Sources of Interpersonal Influence

PARENTS: Students are more likely to decide to enter college when they believe that their education beyond high school has been "taken for granted."

Percent having decided on a four-year college

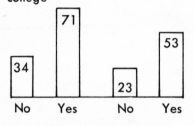

No   Yes   No   Yes

Continued Education
Taken for Granted?

MALES   FEMALES

COUNSELOR: A college decision is more likely when the counselor has given encouragement for college entry.

Percent having decided on a four-year college

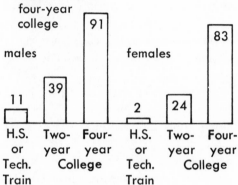

males   females

H.S. Two- Four-   H.S. Two- Four-
or   year year   or   year year
Tech.   College   Tech.   College
Train   Train

Counselor Educational Encouragement

PEERS: The more college-bound friends, the more likely a college decision.

Percent reporting decision to enter a four-year college

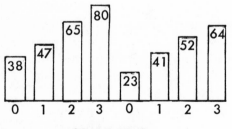

GRADE NINE:
Number of College-bound Peers
MALES   FEMALES

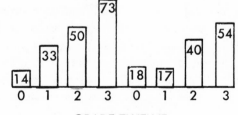

GRADE TWELVE:
Number of College-bound Peers
MALES   FEMALES

$q_{13,11}$, is .16. For females, the total effect from "stress," $q_{13,3}$, is .22, which is larger than that from peers in grade nine, where $q_{13,6} = .12$ or in grade twelve, where $q_{13,11}$ is .11. Finally, while almost two-thirds of the total association between educational decision and peer influence in the *ninth grade* can be attributed to the social class, scholastic ability, and parental educational influence advantages characteristic of students who have several rather than few or no close friends with college ambitions, it is significant that the proportion of the peer-decision total association that is noncausal is no larger for the total association between educational decision and peer influence in *twelfth grade*. The net effect that close friends have on the educational decisions of students remains relatively constant throughout the high school years.

Neither the parent nor the peer, however, emerges as the most influential "significant other" vis-à-vis the educational decisions of our students. It is the guidance counselor. Or, more correctly, it is the student's perception of the educational encouragement received from the guidance counselor during the senior year that enables us to make that inference. Eighty-three percent of all senior females who reported being counseled to enter a four-year college during the senior year also reported a decision to enter a four-year college, as figure 6.2 illustrates. Only 2 percent of those senior females who reported being counseled to seek technical training or employment reported having made the decision to enter a four-year college. Respective percentages for males are 91 and 11. Despite the fact that those who reported college-level encouragement from the counselor as seniors were already highly disposed toward college entry by virtue of their social class, scholastic ability, parents and peers, curriculum location, educational ambition and academic achievement, for males more than 40 percent and for females more than 50 percent of the sizable total association between grade-twelve encouragement and educational decision is causal. Independently of all associated effects from the eleven variables specified in the model as temporally prior to the encouragement of the counselor in the twelfth grade, this school official exerted a total effect, $q_{13,12}$, of .24 on the decisions of male students and .30 on the decisions of female students. For males, a total effect of this size ranks twelfth-grade counselor encouragement equal with that of academic achievement ($q_{13,10} = .23$) and just a bit below that from social class ($q_{13,1} =$

.28); for females it ranks the counselor above both academic achievement ($q_{13,10} = .27$) and social class ($q_{13,1} = .26$).

Moreover, the evidence indicates that in twelfth grade as in tenth grade, the counselor bases educational encouragement more on student merit than on student social class. Ability has a small direct effect, $p_{12,2}$, of .06 on the encouragement reported by senior males and .09 on the encouragement reported by senior females. Ability has larger indirect effects on the encouragement reported by seniors, mostly by way of their academic achievement, $p_{12,10}$, $p_{10,2} = .11$ for males and .10 for females, but also by way of the encouragement given students in tenth grade, encouragement that presumably becomes part of the student's official school record, $p_{12,9}$, $p_{9,2} = .04$ for males and .04 for females. Social class exerts only a very small direct effect on the encouragement reported by high school seniors: $p_{12,1} = .05$ for males and .06 for females. In the absence of a larger direct effect, we are left to conclude that there is an apparent absence of overt class discrimination in the counseling process.

Decisions about college thus are responsive to the influence of significant others. Both parents and peers play a role in the decision process, parents somewhat more than peers, but both parents and peers in a mutually supportive manner. Much more of a role in the educational decisions that students make by the end of their senior year, however, is played by the school guidance counselor. While the counselor may be the official keeper of the educational gate, the data suggest that the decision to open or close the entrance to college is made primarily in accord with merit and not social class.

Curriculum Location

Both educational practice and "common sense" imply that students who have been in the academic program during ninth or tenth grade are considerably more likely than those who have been in the nonacademic program to arrive at the decision to enter college. Among our students, 70 percent of the males who had been in the academic program in ninth grade, as figure 6.3 reveals, made the decision to enter a four-year college by the end of twelfth grade. Only 38 percent of those males who had been in the nonacademic program arrived at that same decision. Respective percentages for females are 55 and 19. The *existence* of a relationship between cur-

FIGURE 6.3. The Effect on Educational Decision of Curriculum Location, Grades Nine and Ten

Students in the academic program in grades nine and ten are more likely than students in the nonacademic program to decide to enter a four-year college by the end of the twelfth grade.

Percent reporting decision to enter a four-year college

GRADE NINE: Curriculum Location

MALES

Nonacademic	Academic
38	70

FEMALES

Nonacademic	Academic
19	55

Percent reporting decision to enter a four-year college

GRADE TEN: Curriculum Location

MALES

Nonacademic	Academic
31	72

FEMALES

Nonacademic	Academic
11	57

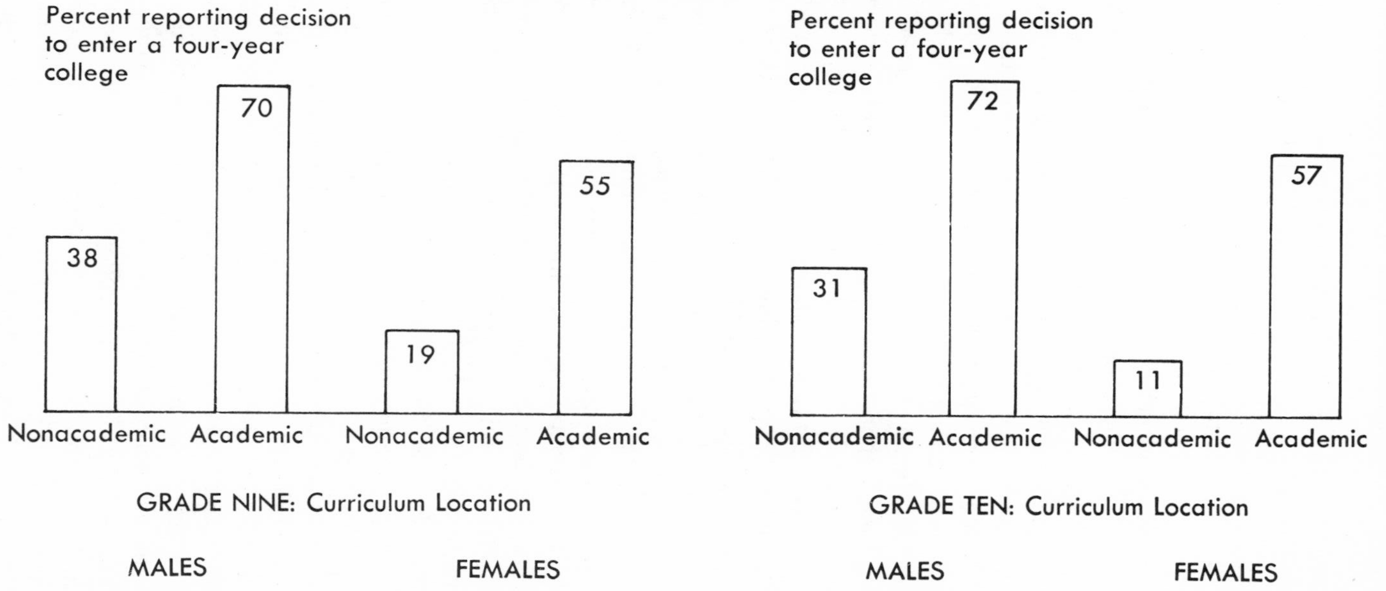

riculum location and educational decision is thus not at issue in this analysis. The *size* of that relationship and the *portion* of that relationship that is *causal* are at issue.

With educational decision, curriculum correlates more highly for females, $r_{13,5} = .40$ and $r_{13,8} = .48$, than for males, $r_{13,5} = .36$ and $r_{13,8} = .41$. This gender difference is thus a continuation of a trend noted earlier, where program location was more highly associated with tenth-grade counselor encouragement of girls than of boys and with the academic achievement of girls than of boys. For students of both sexes, tenth-grade curriculum correlates more highly with educational decision than does ninth-grade curriculum. This is probably an indication that program location is more stable by the end of tenth grade than by the end of ninth grade, i.e., that the organizational apparatus of the school "commits" students to one course of action or another by the end of the sophomore year. Finally, from table 6.2 we can observe that curriculum location is somewhat more highly correlated with educational decision in the Alexander and Eckland national U.S. study of high school students, class of 1957, and in the Williams Canadian study of high school students, class of 1967–68, than it is in our study of students, class of 1970. Understandably, we are cautious about imputing too much substantive meaning to these differences. Nevertheless, we do believe that these coefficients may reveal a decline in the relevance of program location not only on the decision to enter college but on the actual entry into college as well. We return to this conjecture, briefly, below, and at greater length in the following chapter.

What do the moderately sized coefficients between curriculum location and educational decision mean? Do they represent mostly *socialization* effects of program location? Do the college decisions of students in the academic program reflect the "educationally uplifting" experiences so often associated with the college-preparatory program? Are decisions to enter college more prevalent among students in the college-preparatory program because of that program's ostensibly more supportive teachers, more challenging subject matter, more stimulating student-body composition, and the Pygmalion effect whereby college-preparatory students are thought to do better and have higher career goals because that is what is expected of them? Or do the college decisions of students in the academic program reflect the fact that, as we have seen, students who find themselves *selected* for the college-preparatory program are already more likely to decide to enter college by virtue of their class origin, their higher scholastic ability, their greater parental and peer educational support, etc.?

For the relationship between a student's ninth-grade curriculum location and twelfth-grade educational decision, our answer is that for both males and females almost equally, the *socialization* effects of curriculum location account for slightly less than half that relationship, about 45 percent, while the *selection* of students into one program or the other accounts for slightly more than half, about 55 percent, of that relationship. For males, the total effect that ninth-grade location has on twelfth-grade decision, $q_{13,5}$, is .16; for females that effect is .18. For males, the total effect that tenth-grade location has on decision, $q_{12,8} = .07$, is substantially less than that from ninth-grade location and as a portion of the total $r_{12,8}$ association, it is only 17 percent. For females, the total effect that tenth-grade location has on decision is $q_{13,8} = .18$, equal to that of the ninth-grade total effect but somewhat less as a portion of the total association: 38 percent. Curriculum location in tenth grade, of course, is subject to two more "selection" variables than is ninth-grade location: educational ambition and ninth-grade location itself. Finally, the perceptive reader will have noted that a student's curriculum location in ninth grade has more of an effect on his educational decision in twelfth grade than it has on his record of academic performance where $q_{10,5}$ was .07 for males and .11 for females, a reflection, perhaps, of the more "social" nature of an educational decision than of a classroom grade.

Portraits of curriculum location as the organizational asset for the college-bound and as the organizational liability for those headed for the job market thus appear to be somewhat overdrawn. Curriculum location, as Jencks has noted, has but a minimal effect on standardized test scores.[11] Curriculum location, as we have noted, has but a modest effect on student academic achievement. And on educational decision, it has but a modest effect also. Curriculum location, we believe, is no longer *the* dividing line between students that it once may have been. The expansion of two-year community colleges, many with policies of "open admissions," now provides postsecondary educational options to many students who have not followed the usual high school practice of an academic course se-

TABLE 6.2. The Impact on Educational Decisions of Specified Variables: Correlations (Total Associations) from Various Studies

Identification of the Study	Description	Gender of Student	Correlations of Educational Decisions With:[a]										
			Class Indicators:			Class Const	Schl Abil	Par. Infl	Educ Ambit	Curriculum	Acad Achv	Tchr Infl	Peer Infl
			POPOC	POPED	MOMED								
Williams	Canadian students	Male	.21	.19	.20	N.A.	.26	.57[b]	.42[c]	.45[d]	.24[e]	.49[f]	.46[g]
		Female	.27	.28	.27	N.A.	.32	.47	.49	.51	.20	.52	.39
Sewell and Hauser	Wisconsin subset	Male[h]	.27	.27	.26	N.A.	.43	.52	N.A.	N.A.	.45	.45	.49
Sewell and Shah	Wisconsin seniors, class of 1957, one-third sample	Male	N.A.	N.A.	N.A.	.42[i]	.43	N.A.	N.A.	N.A.	N.A.	N.A.	N.A.
		Female	N.A.	N.A.	N.A.	.44	.35	N.A.	N.A.	N.A.	N.A.	N.A.	N.A.
Wilson and Portes	National U.S.	Male	N.A.	N.A.	N.A.	.34[j]	.33	.38	.40[k]	N.A.	.42	N.A.	N.A.
Heyns	National U.S.	Male and Female	.24	.28	N.A.	N.A.	.43	N.A.	N.A.	.56[l]	.30	N.A.	N.A.
Kerckhoff	Fort Wayne students	Male	.42	.44	N.A.	N.A.	.64	N.A.	.69[m]	N.A.	.46[m]	N.A.	N.A.
Median Correlation[n]			.26	.28	.25	.39	.41	.52	.46	.52	.42	.48	.46
This Study	See chapter 2	Male	.33	.31	.26	.37	.46	.40[o]	.62	.41	.52	.57[p]	.39[q]
		Female	.28	.32	.26	.36	.41	.32	.53	.48	.50	.59	.34

Sources: References for Williams, Sewell and Hauser, Heyns, and Kerckhoff are provided in earlier tables. Other references are William H. Sewell and Vimal P. Shah, "Socioeconomic Status, Intelligence, and the Attainment of Higher Education," *Sociology of Education* 40 (Winter 1967): 1–23; Kenneth L. Wilson and Alejandro Portes, "The Educational Attainment Process: Results from a National Sample," *American Journal of Sociology* 81 (September 1975): 343–63. *Note:* The Wilson and Portes study is based on the sample described for the Bachman inquiry.

a All measures of educational decisions are from grade twelve and refer to plans or definite educational intentions for the postsecondary period.

b Measure is of parental educational expectation, reported by the student in grade ten, Williams (1972).

c Measure is of the student's educational ambition in grade ten.

d Measure is of the student's curriculum location in grade ten.

e Measure is of student's course grades in grade eleven.

f Measure is of teacher's educational expectation, reported by the student in grade twelve.

g Measure is of student's report of peers' aspirations in grade twelve, from Williams (1972).

h All Sewell and Hauser measures are from twelfth grade.

i This composite variable of socioeconomic status is based on a weighted combination of father's occupation, father's and mother's education, the student's estimate of the funds the family could provide if the student were to attend college, the degree of sacrifice this would entail for the family, and the approximate wealth and income status of the student's family.

j This composite measure of class is a six-item index composed of father's occupation, father's and mother's education, possessions in the home, number of books in the home, and number of rooms in the home. All components are weighted equally.

k Ambition measure is from tenth grade or 1968 panel survey.

l Curriculum measure is from grade twelve.

m Ambition measure is from junior year, eleventh grade; academic achievement is also from junior year.

n In computing the median correlations, medians were first estimated for the two gender-specific studies, i.e., the Williams and the Sewell and Shah studies. All estimates were rounded upward where rounding was necessary.

o Measure of parental educational influence is that of "taken for granted," from ninth-grade survey.

p Measure here is that of "counselor educational influence," grade twelve.

q Measure of "peer influence" is from grade twelve.

quence in the college track. In the next chapter we look more closely at the actual postsecondary educational behavior of students as a function of their curriculum location during high school.

Class, Ability, Ambition, and Academic Achievement

Given the causal chain that connects the individual's educational decision with his subsequent class of destination, as indicated by educational and occupational achievement, a strong link between class of origin and educational decision would confirm the revisionist proposition that class of origin, however transmitted, is a major determinant of class of destination. Conversely, evidence of no more than a moderate link between class and decision and of larger links between ability, ambition, achievement and decision, would confirm the meritocratic proposition that talent, motivation, and accomplishment can liberate the individual from his class of origin.

Reference to the appropriate coefficients in table 6.1 indicates that merit, more than social class, determines the decisions that students make by the end of senior year with regard to entry into college. Moreover, reference to the coefficients from other inquiries for equivalent variables (see table 6.2) suggests that the dominance of merit over class in the determination of an educational decision is not peculiar to our sample of students.

Figure 6.4 illustrates the total association of *ability* with decision: $r_{13,2} = .46$ for males and .41 for females. Seventy-four percent of scholastically more able males decided on a four-year college by the end of twelfth grade, in contrast with 40 percent of the less able. Among the four variables we are presently considering, ability has the largest total effect on the decisions of females, $q_{13,2} = .34$, and ability is tied with ambition for that effect on the decisions of males, $q_{13,2} = .39$. Eighty-five percent of the ability-decision association is causal for males, and 82 percent is causal for females. The small noncausal component reflects the unanalyzed association between ability and class. Ability thus influences educational decision largely independently of social class. This is a finding that has been repeatedly confirmed by researchers over the past decade or so and it is a finding which tends, as Alexander and Eckland have written,

to strain the assumptions implicit in much of the "anti-testing"—

FIGURE 6.4. The Effect on Educational Decision of Social Class and Merit

College decisions are more likely to be made by students from white- than from blue-collar homes.

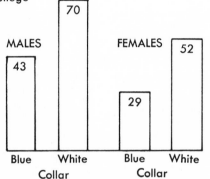

Percent deciding to enter a four-year college

MALES — Blue Collar 43, White Collar 70

FEMALES — Blue Collar 29, White Collar 52

Social Class by Occupation of Father

College decisions are more likely to be made by students with above-average than with below-average scholastic ability.

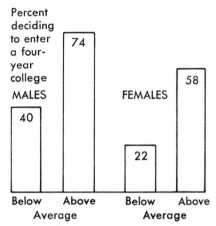

Percent deciding to enter a four-year college

MALES — Below Average 40, Above Average 74

FEMALES — Below Average 22, Above Average 58

Scholastic Ability of Student

Ambitions for college lead to decision to enter college.

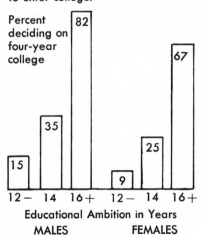

Percent deciding on four-year college

MALES — 12− 15, 14 35, 16+ 82

FEMALES — 12− 9, 14 25, 16+ 67

Educational Ambition in Years
MALES   FEMALES

The higher the grade-point average, the more likely the decision to enter college.

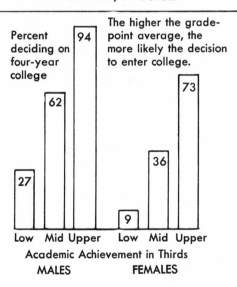

Percent deciding on four-year college

MALES — Low 27, Mid 62, Upper 94

FEMALES — Low 9, Mid 36, Upper 73

Academic Achievement in Thirds
MALES   FEMALES

"anti-certification" literature . . . that "ability" or "intelligence" mainly serves to transmit status advantage and to legitimate and promote the "structural" failure of low status and minority youth.[12]

Much of the causal effect that ability has on educational decision is *indirect*: 76 percent for males and 100 percent for females. Of this indirect effect, about half can be traced to the tendency for more able students to:

1. Receive higher grades and for those who receive higher grades to:
    (a) decide to go to college
    (b) be encouraged by the counselor to go to college, and hence to be more likely to make that decision as a result of that encouragement
2. Have higher educational ambitions and for those with higher ambitions to:
    (a) decide to go to college
    (b) earn higher grades, which in turn makes it more likely that they will decide to go to college

Ambition, like ability, has a total association with, and a total effect on, educational decision that exceed those from social class. For males, $r_{13,7} = .62$, and for females, $r_{13,7} = .53$. College decisions were reported by 67 percent of those females who had college ambitions as ninth graders but by only 9 percent of those who had just high school ambitions as ninth graders (see figure 6.4).

Of the total association that ambition has with decision, about 40 percent (37 percent for males, 44 percent for females) is noncausal. This noncausal component merely reflects the fact that college ambitions in ninth grade and college decisions in twelfth grade are made more by students who are from middle-class homes, are more able scholastically, have stronger parent and peer support for their continued education, and were located in the academic program in ninth grade.

Of the total effect that ambition has on decision, $q_{13,7} = .39$ for males and .30 for females, about two-thirds is direct. Of the remainder, that is, of the indirect effect, about one-half can be traced to the tendency of those who have higher ambitions to:

1. Receive higher grades and for those who receive higher grades

to be more likely to decide on college

2. Be encouraged by their counselors, either in grade ten or grade twelve, to go on to college and for those so encouraged to decide to do just that

3. Earn higher grades, which in turn makes it more likely that they will be encouraged by the counselor to go on to college, and as a result of that encouragement, to do just that

Academic achievement has a larger total association with educational decision, $r_{13,10} = .52$ for males and .50 for females, than does social class. Figure 6.4 illustrates that among males in the upper three stanines of the grade-point distribution, 94 percent decided to enter a four-year college. Among males in the lower three stanines of that distribution, only 27 percent decided to enter a four-year college. Achievement does not have a stronger total effect than class on the decisions of males, however, $q_{13,10} = .23$. For females, the total effect of achievement on decision, $q_{13,10}$, is .27, about equal to that from class. Almost half the association between achievement and decision, therefore, is noncausal. Higher grades are received by, and college decisions are made by, students who are from more privileged class backgrounds, are brighter, have higher educational ambitions, etc. Nevertheless, academic achievement remains a distinct factor in the educational decisions of students, ranked above most indicators of parental influence and above all forms of peer influence and curriculum effects.

Social class has a relationship with educational decision that is larger in size than with any other school-related measure we have examined since educational ambition. With decision, class correlates, $r_{13,1}$, .38 for males and .36 for females. Seventy percent of males from white-collar homes have decided to enter a four-year college. Forty-three percent of the males from blue-collar homes have made that same decision. Almost three-fourths of the total association between class and decision is causal: $q_{13,1} = .28$ for males and .26 for females. As a determinant of educational decision, class ranks above all measures except ability and ambition for males, and above all measures except ability, ambition, achievement, and counselor encouragement for females.

Directly the effect of class on decision is comparatively small, less than 25 percent of its total association for both sexes. For males, that direct effect, $p_{13,1}$ = .06, for females, it is .08. The *indirect* effects of class on decision are diffused throughout the system represented by our model. Class affects decision primarily through complex linkages that involve many of the intervening variables in the model. It is thus not as simple to trace the indirect effects that class has on decision as it was to trace those of ability or ambition. Perhaps the most salient link that connects class to decision is that through ambition. This chain accounts for between a fifth and a third of the indirect effect that class exerts on the decisions that students make by the end of twelfth grade regarding their educational futures.

The modest size of the total association between class and decision thus does not warrant the use of the adjective "strong" to describe the overall relationship between those two variables. Its weak direct effect does not justify an inference of more than a minimal amount of class discrimination on the part of the school in the formation or maintenance of educational goals. And its diffuse indirect effects suggest that, while the influence of social class may be persistent and pervasive, it is also modest and dispersed, particularly when compared with the more specific indirect effects of ability and ambition.

CONCLUSION

Educational decisions reached by students no later than the closing months of the senior year have ramifications that extend outward to ultimate social class of destination. Thus the issue of whether those decisions are determined more by social class than by merit is consequential for the tenability of the revisionist and meritocratic theses.

Our analysis has revealed that the educational decisions reported by high school students toward the end of their senior year are determined more by their own scholastic ability and educational ambition than by their social class of origin. Moreover we found no evidence, either in our study or in those of six other investigators whose findings we reviewed, that would support the revisionist thesis of a *strong* relationship between social class and educational decision.

In addition, with respect to the comparative roles of class and merit in the high school, a comparison of correlation and total-effect coefficients for the relationship of class and ability with educational ambition (see table 3.6) and with educational decision (see table

6.1) indicates that for all students the overall and causal role of social class in the formation and maintenance of educational goal orientations *declines* during the years of secondary school and that, for males, the overall and the causal role of ability *increases* (see McDill and Coleman[13] and Alexander and Eckland[14] for similar findings).

More than social class, merit determines whether an individual will decide to continue his formal education beyond high school. Whether this pattern extends to actual college entry is the major issue we explore in the next chapter.

NOTES

1. As noted in chapter 2, Granovetter has argued that by twelfth grade, most students actually know whether they will enter college the following fall. They have made their applications and have been either accepted or rejected. Thus the term "aspiration" or "expectation" is less appropriate for a measure of student educational goals made during the last month or so of senior year than is the concept of educational "decision." Alexander and Eckland have made similar comments with respect to the use of the term "expectations" or "plans" to refer to a measure secured during the senior year: "Although commonly employed as a motivational indicator . . . such plans have likely undergone considerable reality-testing by the senior year of high school. Many seniors would have already received college entrance test results, guidance counseling, and perhaps even preliminary responses on college applications. These experiences would all operate to transform goal orientations into realistic assessments or outcomes." Karl Alexander and Bruce K. Eckland, "Basic Attainment Processes: A Replication and Extension," *Sociology of Education* 48 (Fall 1975): 460.

2. William H. Sewell and Vimal P. Shah, "Socioeconomic Status, Intelligence, and the Attainment of Higher Education," *Sociology of Education* 40 (Winter 1967): 22.

3. Peter Blau and Otis Dudley Duncan, *The American Occupational Structure* (New York: Wiley, 1967).

4. Sewell and Shah, "Socioeconomic Status," p. 16.

5. Ibid.

6. See, for example, William H. Sewell and Robert M. Hauser, *Education, Occupation, and Earnings: Achievement in the Early Career* (Madison: University of Wisconsin, Department of Sociology, 1974), a final report of research carried out under Grant No. 314, Social and Rehabilitation Service, Social Security Administration, Department of Health, Education, and Welfare, Washington, D.C. See also Otis Dudley Duncan, "Ability and Achievement," *Eugenics Quarterly* 15 (March 1968): 1–11.

7.   For discussions of the concepts of "aspirations" and "expectations," see Archibald O. Haller and Irwin M. Miller, *The Occupational Aspiration Scale: Theory, Structure, and Correlates* (East Lansing: Michigan State University, 1963), Technical Bulletin No. 288, Agricultural Experiment Station. See also Archibald O. Haller, "On the Concept of Aspiration," *Rural Sociology* 33 (December 1968); and Richard A. Rehberg, "Adolescent Career Aspirations and Expectations: Evaluation of Two Contrary Hypotheses," *Pacific Sociological Review*, Fall 1967, pp. 81–90.

8.   Samuel Bowles, "Unequal Education and the Social Division of Labor," in *Schooling in a Corporate Society*, ed. Martin Carnoy (New York: McKay, 1972), p. 58. Italics added.

9.   Alexander and Eckland, "Basic Attainment Processes, p. 482.

10.   Those equations are:

For males and females

Eq. 1: $X_3 = p_{31}X_1 + p_{32}X_2 + p_{3a}X_a$

Eq. 2: $X_4 = p_{41}X_1 + p_{42}X_2 + p_{4b}X_b$

For males only

Eq. 3: $X_5 = p_{51}X_1 + p_{52}X_2 + p_{53}X_3 + p_{5c}X_c$

Eq. 4: $X_6 = p_{61}X_1 + p_{62}X_2 + p_{63}X_3 + p_{64}X_4 + p_{65}X_5$
$+ p_{6d}X_d$

Eq. 5: $X_7 = p_{71}X_1 + p_{72}X_2 + p_{73}X_3 + p_{74}X_4 + p_{75}X_5$
$+ p_{76}X_6 + p_{7e}X_e$

Eq. 6: $X_8 = p_{82}X_2 + p_{83}X_3 + p_{85}X_5 + p_{87}X_7 + p_{8f}X_f$

Eq. 7: $X_9 = p_{92}X_2 + p_{94}X_4 + p_{96}X_6 + p_{97}X_7 + p_{98}X_8 + p_{9g}X_g$

Eq. 8: $X_{10} = p_{10,2}X_2 + p_{10,3}X_3 + p_{10,7}X_7 + p_{10,8}X_8 + p_{10,9}X_9$
$+ p_{10h}X_h$

Eq. 9: $X_{11} = p_{11,1}X_1 + p_{11,4}X_4 + p_{11,5}X_5 + p_{11,6}X_6 + p_{11,8}X_8$
$+ p_{11,9}X_9 + p_{11,10}X_{10} + p_{11i}X_i$

Eq. 10: $X_{12} = p_{12,1}X_1 + p_{12,2}X_2 + p_{12,3}X_3 + p_{12,4}X_4 + p_{12,7}X_7$
$+ p_{12,8}X_8 + p_{12,9}X_9 + p_{12,10}X_{10} + p_{12,11}X_{11}$
$+ p_{12j}X_j$

Eq. 11: $X_{13} = p_{13,1}X_1 + p_{13,2}X_2 + p_{13,4}X_4 + p_{13,6}X_6 + p_{13,7}X_7$
$+ p_{13,10}X_{10} + p_{13,11}X_{11} + p_{13,12}X_{12} + p_{13k}X_k$

For females only

Eq. 3: $X_5 = p_{51}X_1 + p_{52}X_2 + p_{53}X_3 + p_{54}X_4 + p_{5c}X_c$

Eq. 4: $X_6 = p_{61}X_1 + p_{62}X_2 + p_{63}X_3 + p_{64}X_4 + p_{65}X_5 + p_{6d}X_d$

Eq. 5: $X_7 = p_{71}X_1 + p_{72}X_2 + p_{73}X_3 + p_{74}X_4 + p_{75}X_5$
$\qquad\qquad + p_{76}X_6 + p_{7e}X_e$

Eq. 6: $X_8 = p_{81}X_1 + p_{82}X_2 + p_{84}X_4 + p_{85}X_5 + p_{87}X_7 + p_{8f}X_f$

Eq. 7: $X_9 = p_{92}X_2 + p_{93}X_3 + p_{96}X_6 + p_{97}X_7 + p_{98}X_8 + p_{9g}X_g$

Eq. 8: $X_{10} = p_{10,2}X_2 + p_{10,3}X_3 + p_{10,7}X_7 + p_{10,9}X_9$

Eq. 9: $X_{11} = p_{11,2}X_2 + p_{11,3}X_3 + p_{11,6}X_6 + p_{11,8}X_8$
$\qquad\qquad + p_{11,10}X_{10} + p_{11i}X_i$

Eq. 10: $X_{12} = p_{12,1}X_1 + p_{12,2}X_2 + p_{12,7}X_7 + p_{12,8}X_8 + p_{12,9}X_9$
$\qquad\qquad + p_{12,10}X_{10} + p_{12,11}X_{11} + p_{12j}X_j$

Eq. 11: $X_{13} = p_{13,1}X_1 + p_{13,3}X_3 + p_{13,7}X_7 + p_{13,8}X_8$
$\qquad\qquad + p_{13,10}X_{10} + p_{13,11}X_{11} + p_{13,12}X_{12} + p_{13k}X_k$

11.   Christopher Jencks et al., *Inequality* (New York: Basic Books, 1972), p. 107.

12.   Alexander and Eckland, "Basic Attainment Processes," p. 482.

13.   Edward L. McDill and James Coleman, "Family and Peer Influences in College Plans of High School Students," *Sociology of Education* 38 (Winter 1965): 112–26.

14.   Alexander and Eckland, "Basic Attainment Processes."

7. Postsecondary Educational Enrollment Level

In his perceptive paper "Schooling and Future Society" the Norwegian social scientist Johan Galtung draws a series of parallels between the structure of the economy and the structure of schooling in a modern industrial society. Both the economic and the educational systems of that society, suggests Galtung, are vertically or hierarchically structured. Thus, thinking of the *economic system*, it is useful to distinguish between the *primary* sector, which involves those activities that extract raw materials; the *secondary* sector, which involves those activities that process and distribute those materials; and the *tertiary* sector, which involves the administration and management of the entire process. In conceptualizing the *educational system*, Galtung advises, it is useful to distinguish between the *primary* or elementary level, the *secondary* or high school level, and the *tertiary* or college level. Given this similarity of structure, what happens is that

> ... primary school graduates are put into the primary sector doing agriculture and extraction work; secondary school graduates are put into the secondary sector as skilled workers, functionaries; and tertiary graduates are put into the tertiary sector as professionals and administrators.[1]

Access, then, to the professional and administrative occupations that constitute the positions of the tertiary level of the economy tends to be limited to individuals with credentials from postsecondary educational institutions. For example, in the United States in 1973 almost two-thirds of all white men and women employed in "professional, technical and kindred" occupations had completed four

197

years of college. More than half of all men earning $25,000 and more in 1972 had completed at least sixteen years of formal education.[2]

Some form of postsecondary schooling, therefore, is almost a necessary condition for an individual to enter those occupations that afford the opportunity for the creation and control of the dynamics of a modern industrial society. A more comprehensive understanding of the role of schooling in intergenerational social mobility thus requires that we develop some understanding of how social class and merit affect the likelihood that an individual will have access to some form of postsecondary education.

Ideally, of course, our study would have followed the sample of 2,788 students from grade nine all the way through and even beyond the college or university. Our actual reach, however, falls short of that ideal grasp. We have no information on the ultimate educational attainments of our sample. We do have information on the educational activities of the sample during the first postsecondary year, 1970–71, and we have that information for 88 percent of the individuals who participated in our study some five years earlier. Granted that there may be some "slippage" between the educational activity of an individual one year beyond high school and the ultimate educational attainment of that individual some three to six years hence. But that slippage is minimal, if we may judge from the correlations between attainment and activity (or "college attendance") reported by Sewell and Shah for their seven-year follow-up of a random sample of high school seniors in the state of Wisconsin in 1957. Sewell and Shah report that postsecondary educational activity ("college attendance") correlates with ultimate educational attainment .86 for males and .87 for females.[3]

Postsecondary educational entry, i.e., entry into a four-year or two-year college or its equivalent or, alternatively, entry into the labor market, is the focal point of our analysis in this chapter. For ease of reference we shall refer to this criterion variable as *college entry*, distinguishing where necessary between a four- and a two-year institution. In this chapter we seek to develop some ability to explain why different individuals pursued different educational activities beyond high school; that is, why about a third of our sample entered a four-year college, another third entered a two-year college, and another third sought no entry to an institution of higher education.

Hypothetically, each one of the thirteen variables that our model (see figure 7.1) represents as antecedent to college entry affects whether the individual continues his education beyond high school. Indeed, each antecedent has some causal effect on that criterion. For males, however, four of those antecedents generate no *direct* effect to the measure of postsecondary educational activity: (1) scholastic ability, (2) grade-nine curriculum, (3) grade-ten curriculum, and (4) grade-ten counselor encouragement. For females there are no *direct* effects from five antecedents: (1) parental educational stress, (2) "taken for granted," (3) grade-nine curriculum, (4) educational ambition, and (5) grade-ten counselor encouragement. Accordingly, the gender-specific models have been trimmed, and the final equations that define those models are given in a note at the end of this chapter.[4]

POSTSECONDARY EDUCATIONAL ENROLLMENT LEVEL AND THE MERITOCRATIC-REVISIONIST ARGUMENT

In this chapter our primary analytical emphasis is on the extent to which college entry depends upon the class origins of our students or on their "merit," i.e., their scholastic ability, educational ambition, academic achievement, and personal educational decisions.

In a truly meritocratic society access to any educational institution beyond high school would depend exclusively on the individual's academic merit—i.e., on his intellectual ability, educational ambition, and record of academic performance—and on his own decision whether to seek education beyond that certified by the high school diploma. In a truly meritocratic society talent, ambition, and personal choice rather than family position in the social hierarchy would determine "who is to be educated" beyond high school.

Although some Scandinavian countries may now be approaching a truly meritocratic model of educational access, most industrialized nations have some distance to go before access to the tertiary level of schooling becomes completely independent of individual class origin.

Liberal social scientists are acutely aware of the persistence of social class as a determining factor in who goes to college. While they differ among themselves as to the precise extent to which access to college is class dependent, few liberal social scientists would assert that the effect of class is a strong or a powerful one or that class is

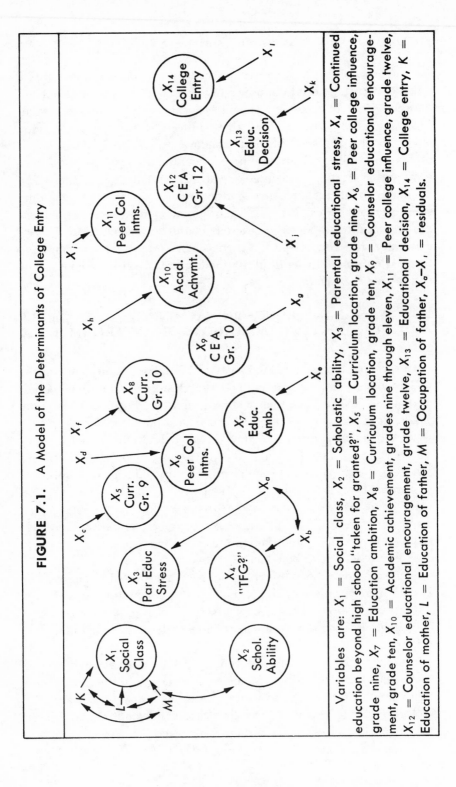

FIGURE 7.1. A Model of the Determinants of College Entry

Variables are: X_1 = Social class, X_2 = Scholastic ability, X_3 = Parental educational stress, X_4 = Continued education beyond high school "taken for granted?", X_5 = Curriculum location, grade nine, X_6 = Peer college influence, grade nine, X_7 = Education ambition, X_8 = Curriculum location, grade ten, X_9 = Counselor educational encouragement, grade ten, X_{10} = Academic achievement, grades nine through eleven, X_{11} = Peer college influence, grade twelve, X_{12} = Counselor educational encouragement, grade twelve, X_{13} = Educational decision, X_{14} = College entry, K = Education of mother, L = Education of father, M = Occupation of father, X_a–X_i = residuals.

the predominant determinant of who goes on to college. Indeed, evidence gathered within the past decade or so from a number of nations has led several social scientists to speculate that class may be a declining influence on who goes to college. Alexander and Eckland have ventured such an inference for the United States,[5] and Busch has reported the presence of such a trend for all member nations of the Organization for Economic Cooperation and Development.[6]

Few liberal social scientists accept with equanimity either the modest nature of the class effect on educational access or its apparent declining influence on that access. As citizens, many of these social scientists regard the existence of any class effect on college entry as morally objectionable,[7] and, as scientists, many regard the class-contingent nature of college entry as inimical to an optimal allocation of human resources. Few of these social scientists, however, see the problem of class-conditioned access to higher education as necessarily endemic to the social system. Rather, they tend to view the problem as a tractable one, amenable to solution given the political will and the economic and social means. In the mid-1940s Warner, Havighurst, and Loeb phrased the issue this way:

There is enough native ability in America to provide the skilled individuals who are needed to solve our problems. It is demonstrable that some of the ills of the present are directly traceable to our failure to use trained people. Because of our status system we have maintained many people of inferior ability and training in responsible jobs who should have been eliminated to permit competent people to rise from lower levels to fill these higher places. We must spread our net wider to find people of talent wherever they exist and we must permit them to compete with everyone for the prized positions. The rewards of talent and hard work must be made more secure and more sure.[8]

Revisionist scholars have a much less sanguine view of the class-contingent nature of access to higher education. To many revisionists, the relationship of college access to individual social-class background is one of great strength ("social class is still the most important variable in predicting *how far* a person gets in school"), and it is a relationship that is both endemic to, and functional for, the capitalist system. In such systems, writes political economist Martin Carnoy:

... schooling goes to those children whose parents are wealthy, have high education, or high social status. The school system is ostensibly a meritocracy—grades, not parental background, determine who goes to the higher levels—yet factors outside the school are so important in influencing children's school performance, aspiration and motivation that social class is still the most important variable in predicting how far a person gets in school. This is no accident. The school system is structured, through its tests, reward system and required behavior patterns, to allow children of an urban bourgeoisie to do well and to filter out children of the poor, who are not socialized to function in the highest echelons of a capitalist economy and bourgeois culture. The school system is therefore a mechanism to maintain class structure in a capitalist society.[9]

Thus is the argument joined once again. Meritocratic scholars agree that social class does indeed condition who gets the chance to continue their education beyond high school, but they aver that the extent to which access to postsecondary education is contingent upon social class is not large and find evidence that over the past generation the extent of that contingency has been declining. Revisionist scholars view the class bias in access to postsecondary education as endemic to the social system of capitalism. They claim that the magnitude of this bias is large, and they see no evidence of its decline over the past twenty years. Our own inquiry is limited to an over-time study of a single cohort of youth. Thus we cannot address the question of whether class has become a weaker determinant of college entry with the passage of time. We can, however, address the basic question raised by Carnoy, a question that is central to the meritocratic-revisionist argument: is social class still the most important variable in predicting how far a person gets in school? We address this question within the context of our model, which posits that entry into college is a product of a number of determinants, of which social class is but one and not necessarily the most dominant one.

THE DETERMINANTS OF POSTSECONDARY EDUCATIONAL ENROLLMENT LEVEL

Collectively, the nine antecedent variables that generate statistically significant direct effects to the postsecondary educational activities of males account for 50.3 percent of the variance in that criterion.[10] This is an explanatory capability that compares favorably with the 54 percent explained variance reported by Sewell and Hauser for their criterion of educational attainment[11] and with the 46 percent explained variance reported by Alexander and Eckland for their criterion of educational attainment.[12] The eight antecedent variables that generate significant direct effects to the postsecondary educational activities of females account for 59 percent of the variance in that criterion measure.[13] By the customary variance-accounted-for standards of social science research, where the individual rather than the group is the unit of analysis, both percentages are rather impressive. Moreover, such explanatory power indicates that the extensive causal modeling of the educational attainment process by social scientists has succeeded in identifying more than just the basic elements of the process.

Our exposition of the determinants of level of postsecondary educational enrollment considers, first, the role of interpersonal influence, then the role of curriculum location, and finally the respective roles of social class and merit.

Interpersonal Influence

Parents and Peers. Much has been made of the role of interpersonal influence in the educational-attainment process, especially by researchers like William Sewell and his associates, who have sought to elaborate the social-psychological dynamics by which a career goal orientation is formed, maintained or altered, and then transformed into an actual achieved reality. Research in this tradition usually identifies three major sources of such interpersonal influence, i.e., three sets of "significant others": parents, peers, and school officials. To judge from the results of previous investigations, it would appear that parents and peers exert more influence over the goal orientations and attainments of the individual than do school officials. As we shall show, the results from our own inquiry are not entirely consistent with that particular conclusion from past research.

At the basic, bivariate level of analysis, interpersonal influence exhibits moderate to sizable correlations in the range of .30 to .60 with measures of college entry (see the data from our inquiry in table 7.1) or with measures of ultimate educational attainment (see the data from other inquiries in table 7.2). Illustratively, as figure 7.2

TABLE 7.1. The Total Associations with College Entry of Specified Independent Variables and Their Total, Direct, and Indirect Effects

Independent Variables		Male Students				Female Students			
		Total Assoc. r_{ij}	Direct p_{ij}	Effect: Indir. s_{ij}	Total q_{ij}	Total Assoc. r_{ij}	Direct p_{ij}	Effect: Indir. s_{ij}	Total q_{ij}
Social class	X_1	.359	.069	.202	.271	.349	.058	.196	.254
Scholastic ability	X_2	.426	.000	.360	.360	.399	−.063	.388	.325
Parental ed. stress	X_3	.285	.047	.113	.160	.276	.000	.153	.153
Taken for granted	X_4	.376	.062	.138	.200	.311	.000	.112	.112
Curriculum gr. 9	X_5	.289	.000	.088	.088	.394	.000	.188	.188
Peer col. int. gr. 9	X_6	.385	.084	.078	.162	.353	.053	.101	.154
Educational ambition	X_7	.521	.050	.205	.255	.467	.000	.210	.210
Curriculum gr. 10	X_8	.371	.000	.097	.097	.481	.081	.150	.231
Cnslr. enc. gr. 10	X_9	.444	.000	.154	.154	.466	.000	.155	.155
Academic achvmt.	X_{10}	.522	.211	.080	.291	.541	.198	.164	.362
Peer col. int. gr. 12	X_{11}	.351	.068	.051	.119	.385	.119	.050	.169
Cnslr. enc. gr. 12	X_{12}	.516	.125	.073	.198	.589	.187	.118	.305
Educational decision	X_{13}	.629	.295	.000	.295	.690	.390	.000	.390
Proportion of Variance Accounted for: R^2		.503				.585			

FIGURE 7.2. The Effect on Entry to a Four-year College of Interpersonal Influence

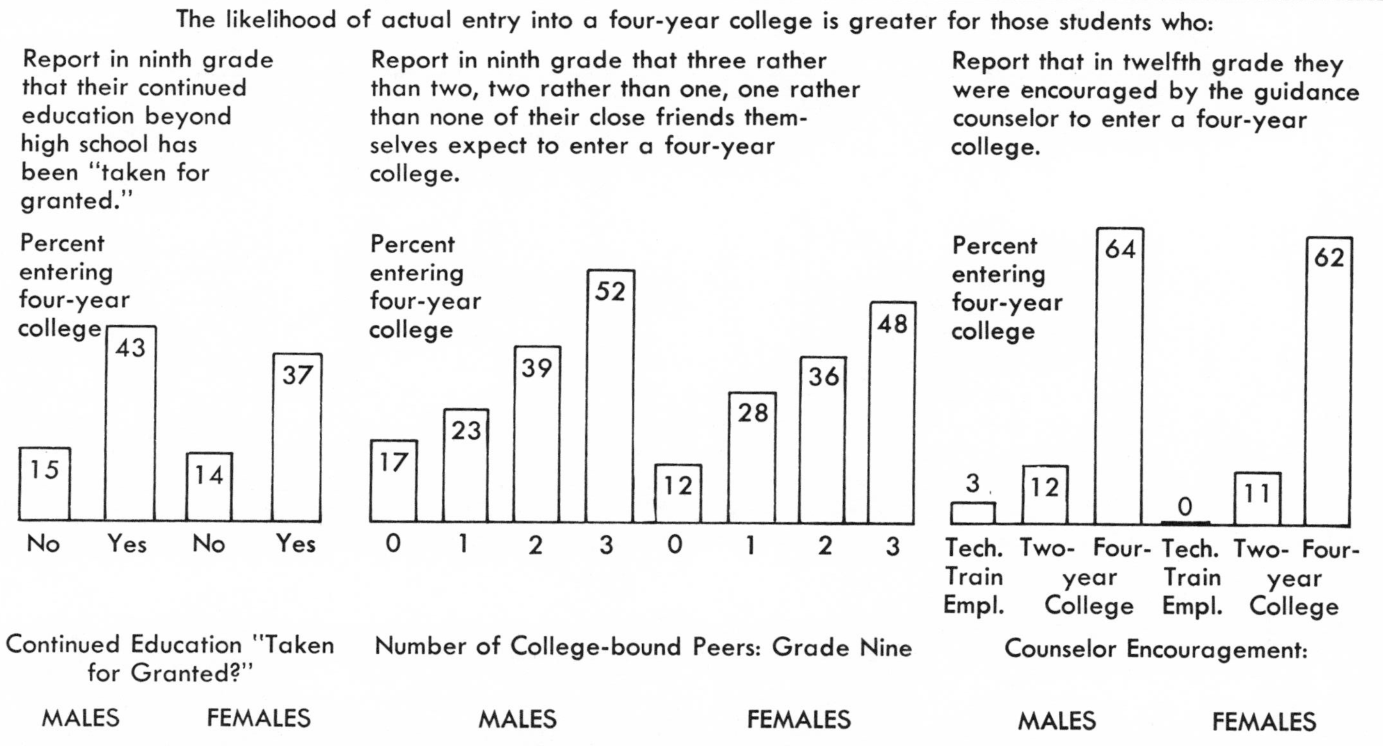
The likelihood of actual entry into a four-year college is greater for those students who:
Report in ninth grade that their continued education beyond high school has been "taken for granted."
Percent entering four-year college
15
43
14
37
No
Yes
No
Yes
Continued Education "Taken for Granted?"
MALES
FEMALES
Report in ninth grade that three rather than two, two rather than one, one rather than none of their close friends themselves expect to enter a four-year college.
Percent entering four-year college
17
23
39
52
12
28
36
48
0
1
2
3
0
1
2
3
Number of College-bound Peers: Grade Nine
MALES
FEMALES
Report that in twelfth grade they were encouraged by the guidance counselor to enter a four-year college.
Percent entering four-year college
3
12
64
0
11
62
Tech. Train Empl.
Two-year College
Four-year College
Tech. Train Empl.
Two-year College
Four-year College
Counselor Encouragement:
MALES
FEMALES

TABLE 7.2. The Impact on Educational Attainment of Specified Variables: Correlations (Total Associations) from Various Studies

Identification of Study	Description of Study	Gender of Student	Correlations of Educational Attainment with:[a]											
			Class Indicts.											
			POP OCC	POP EDU	MOM EDU	Class Comp.	Sch Abl	Par Inf	Edu[b] Amb	Cur	Acd Ach	Tch Inf	Peer Infl	Edu[c] Dec
Sewell and Hauser	Wisconsin subset	Male	.29	.31	.37	N.A.	.45	.47	N.A.	N.A.	.51	.41	.47	.66
Sewell and Shah	Wisconsin seniors, class of 1957	Male	N.A.	N.A.	N.A.	.42	.45	N.A.	N.A.	N.A.	N.A.	N.A.	N.A.	.67
		Female	N.A.	N.A.	N.A.	.45	.35	N.A.	N.A.	N.A.	N.A.	N.A.	N.A.	.78
Alexander and Eckland	National U.S.	Male	.38	.38	.27	N.A.	.48	.37	.49	.45	.49	.20	.44	N.A.
Wilson and Portes	National U.S.	Male	N.A.	N.A.	N.A.	.41	.46	N.A.	N.A.	N.A.	.51	N.A.	N.A.	.49
Kerckhoff	Fort Wayne, synthetic cohort	Male	.41	.38	N.A.	N.A.	.49	N.A.	N.A.	N.A.	.42	N.A.	N.A.	.74
Median Correlation[d]			.38	.38	.32	.43	.46	.42	.49	.45	.49	.31	.46	.67
This Study	See chapter 2	Male	.32	.30	.25	.36	.43	.38[e]	.52	.37	.52	.52[e]	.35	.63
		Female	.28	.31	.25	.35	.40	.31	.47	.48	.54	.59	.39	.69

Sources: References for all studies are provided in earlier tables.

[a] For the Sewell and Hauser, Sewell and Shah, and Alexander and Eckland studies, as well as for Kerckhoff's inquiry, there was an adequate interval of time between high school graduation and the measurement of educational attainment such that, for most purposes, the highest level of education reported by the respondent was the highest level of education he would ever achieve. For the Wilson and Portes study, where the time lapse between high school graduation and the measurement of the criterion variable was less than four years, and for our study, where the time interval was less than one year, the criterion measure is more correctly understood as "attainment in process" or "college entry."

[b] For the variable we have termed "educational ambition," Alexander and Eckland's measure was taken in grade ten, the measure for this study was taken in grade nine.

[c] All measures for the variable we have termed "educational decision" are from grade twelve.

[d] In computing the median correlations, medians were first estimated for Sewell and Shah's gender-specific study. All estimates were rounded upward where rounding was necessary.

[e] Our measure is of counselor educational encouragement, grade twelve, rather than of teacher encouragement; our measure of parental influence is that of "taken for granted."

reveals, entry into a four-year college was reported by 43 percent of our male students who, as ninth graders, regarded their continued education beyond high school as "taken for granted," but by only 15 percent of those who did not so regard their continued education. Similarly, entry into a four-year college characterized 48 percent of those girls who, in the ninth grade, reported that all three of their close friends were college-bound, but such entry characterized only 12 percent of those girls who, in the ninth grade, reported that none of their three close friends was college-bound.

Substantial portions of these total parent/peer-student college-entry associations are causal, with the effects from parental influence being mostly indirect and those from peer influence being about as much indirect as direct. Having parents who, as early as the ninth grade, take for granted the continued education beyond high school of their children generates a total effect to the postsecondary educational activity of the individual equal to a $q_{14,4}$ of .20 for males and .11 for females. Having parents who, as early as ninth grade, place stress or emphasis on the continued education of their children generates a total effect on the postsecondary criterion of $q_{14,3} = .16$ for males and .15 for females.

In a similar vein, the supportive and maintenance roles played by close friends of the student who themselves are college-bound generates a total effect, $q_{14,6}$, of .16 for males and of .15 for females when those friendships were operative in ninth grade and of $q_{14,11} = .12$ for males and .17 for females when those friendships were operative in twelfth grade.

Counselor Influence. For our sample of students, the source of the strongest interpersonal influence on college entry is neither the parent nor the peer. It is the school guidance counselor (twelfth grade). Counselor encouragement during the sophomore year does affect causally that postsecondary activity, but with a magnitude not much different from that of the parent or the peer: $q_{14,9} = .15$ for males and .16 for females. Twelfth-grade counselor educational encouragement generates a total association with the student's educational activity one year later, $r_{14,12}$, equal to .52 for males and .59 for females. Sixty-four percent of all males who reported four-year college encouragement from the guidance counselor during twelfth grade had entered a four-year college one year later. Among those who reported technical training or job-seeking encouragement from the counselor during twelfth grade, only 3 percent had entered a four-year college one year later (see figure 7.2).

For males, some 38 percent of the total association between twelfth grade counselor educational encouragement and college entry is causal, with $q_{14,12} = .20$. Almost two-thirds of that causal effect is direct. One-third or so is indirect, all by way of the student's educational decision. For males, then, the counselor exerts more influence over actual postsecondary educational behavior than do peers and about as much as do parents, when "taken for granted" is used as the indicator of parental educational influence. For females, about 52 percent of the total association between their report of twelfth-grade counselor encouragement and subsequent educational activity is causal, with $q_{14,12}$ equal to .31. Almost two-thirds of that total effect is direct, with the remainder being indirect by way of educational decision. When compared to influence from parents or peers, the counselor emerges as the dominant "significant other" for girls. Indeed, for females, the total effect of this school official on postsecondary enrollment level is larger than that of social class or educational ambition, about equal to that of ability, but somewhat less than that of academic achievement.

Curriculum Location

Before the turn of the century, only a minority of youth enrolled in high school, and of those who did, the majority were of privileged-class origin and sought a secondary education primarily to prepare for entry into college. After the turn of the century, partially in response to the industrialization and urbanization of the nation, larger numbers of youth began to enroll in high school. Many of these newer students were from less privileged backgrounds and their motivation for seeking a high school diploma was less to prepare for entry into college and more to prepare for entry into the labor market. Moreover, inasmuch as upon entry into high school some students were uncertain of their post-high school careers, and because both the public and its educators thought it wasteful of human talent not to encourage a bright student to seek a college education even if he was from a less privileged home, the schools soon found themselves actively participating in the process of curriculum placement. School officials placed students in one program or another on the basis of student intentions, social class (primarily, according to the revision-ists), or scholastic ability (preferably, according to the meritocrats).

For most of the twentieth century, then, curriculum location during high school has been associated with educational careers after high school. That association is reflected in the data from Alexander and Eckland's study of a national sample of students who graduated from high school in 1957 and in our study of a regional sample of students who graduated from high school in 1970. The cor-relation between tenth-grade curriculum location and ultimate *educational attainment* reported by Alexander and Eckland (see table 7.2) for males is .45. The correlation between tenth-grade curriculum location and *college entry* generated from our study is .37 for males (see table 7.1). We shall return to this difference and its possible sources below. Ninth-grade curriculum location and college entry correlates, in our study, .29 for males and .39 for females. Tenth-grade location and college entry, correlates in our study, for females, .48. Illustratively, figure 7.3 shows that among males who were in the college-preparatory program at the end of tenth grade, 43 percent entered a four-year college compared with only 15 percent who were in the noncollege-preparatory program. Respective percentages for females are 40 and 5.

The existence of correlations in the range of .30 to .50 between curriculum location and college entry testifies to the fact that these two variables are indeed associated. It does not, however, reveal the source or meaning of that association. Is college entry more charac-teristic of students who have been in the academic program primarily because of what we have previously referred to as *selection* effects? That is, is the association between curriculum location and college entry largely due to the fact that those who are in the college-prepara-tory program are more likely to enter college by virtue of their more privileged class origins, higher levels of scholastic ability, more edu-cationally supportive parents and peers, and higher educational ambitions? Or is college entry more characteristic of those who have been in the academic program because of the *socialization* experiences encountered in that program, experiences such as "better" teachers, more challenging subjects, more ambitious peers, and the like?

The answer to that question depends somewhat upon the gender of the student. For males, more of the association between curriculum location and college entry is the result of selection than of socializa-

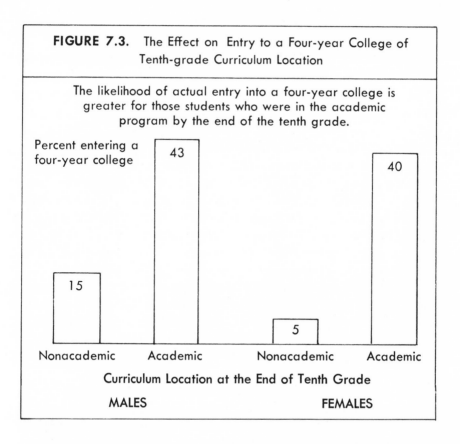

FIGURE 7.3. The Effect on Entry to a Four-year College of Tenth-grade Curriculum Location

The likelihood of actual entry into a four-year college is greater for those students who were in the academic program by the end of the tenth grade.

Percent entering a four-year college

43

40

15

5

Nonacademic   Academic   Nonacademic   Academic

Curriculum Location at the End of Tenth Grade

MALES   FEMALES

tion. Differences between students in terms of class origin, scholastic ability, educational support of parents and peers, and educational ambition account for 69 percent of the total association between ninth-grade curriculum location and college entry and for 73 percent of the relationship between tenth-grade curriculum location and college entry. The minor total effects from curriculum location to college entry, $q_{14,5} = .09$ and $q_{14,8} = .10$, rank curriculum location below all other determinants specified in our model as sources of causal effects on the college entry of males.

For females, almost as much of the association between curriculum location and college entry is the result of socialization as of selection. Existing differences between students that determine both their curriculum and their postsecondary educational behavior account for 51 percent of the relationship between grade-nine program and college entry, and for 52 percent of the grade-ten relationship. The complement of those percentages, however, 49 and 48 percent, respectively, represents the consequences of program location per se on college entry, i.e., $q_{14,5} = .19$, $q_{14,8} = .23$. Compared with the other determinants of college entry, curriculum location plays a somewhat greater role in the college entry chances of females than males, a finding that parallels our earlier observations of curriculum location being more consequential for the academic achievement and the educational decisions of females than of males.

In the introduction to our analysis of curriculum location we noted that the correlation between curriculum location and educational attainment of .45 reported by Alexander and Eckland for males is higher than that of .37 we have reported for our males. Both studies have measured curriculum location in the same grade—the tenth. Both studies have measured the variable in the same way—as a dichotomy between college-preparatory and noncollege-preparatory. Both studies have measured that variable for the same gender of student—males. Where the studies have differed is in the definition of the dependent variable and in the year in which their respective samples were in tenth grade. Alexander and Eckland's dependent variable is *ultimate educational attainment*, and it was measured some fifteen years after their sample of males had been in tenth grade in 1955. Our dependent variable is *college entry*, and we measured it after the passage of only three years beyond tenth grade in 1968. Had Alexander and Eckland measured college entry only three years after their sample had been in the tenth grade, it is our inference that they would have reported an even larger correlation coefficient, inasmuch as the size of a relationship tends to decay as the time interval between the variables measured increases.

Our cautious and speculative inference is that over the past decade or so, the role of curriculum location in determining a student's postsecondary educational career has declined. Much of the diminished role of high school curriculum location in the 1970s, compared with that in the 1960s and 1950s, we speculate, has come about because of two changes in American higher education. One change has been the easing of admission standards to four-year colleges and universities, i.e., the introduction of special admissions programs that have allowed students with somewhat less than adequate high school credentials to matriculate in four-year colleges and universities. Some of these special-admissions students, no doubt, did not pursue their high school work in the college-preparatory program.

The second change, and the change to which we attribute much of the declining role of curriculum location in college entry, has been the rapid expansion of the two-year community college. In 1960, for example, some three years after Alexander and Eckland's students completed their high school education, there were 451,000 students in the nation's two-year colleges—13 percent of all enrollment in higher education. By 1970, the year in which our students completed their high school education, there were 1.6 million students in the nation's two-year colleges—21 percent of all enrollment in higher education.[14] Two-year colleges generally have less stringent admissions standards than do four-year colleges. Many two-year colleges admit students to first-semester status contingent upon only the possession of a high school diploma, without regard to whether the student pursued a college-preparatory program. For our students, who live in a state that has been a leader in the two-year college movement and in a county where the community college is a prominent local institution, the consequence of the availability of the community college and its effect on the relationship between curriculum location and college entry is obvious. The likelihood of one of our students reporting entry into a *two-year college* is only slightly greater if that student had been in the academic program (37 percent of the males, 43 percent of the females) than if that student had been in the nonacademic program (32 percent of the males, 33 percent of the females). Entry into a *four-year college*, as our data suggest, still remains somewhat dependent upon having been in the academic program while in high school. Entry into a two-year college, as our data also suggest, is all but independent of having pursued one curriculum or the other while in high school. The presence of a major postsecondary alternative to the four-year college, an alternative that has much less rigorous standards of admission, thus has weakened the capacity of high school curriculum location to predict who does and who does not continue formal education beyond twelfth grade.

CLASS AND MERIT: WHICH DETERMINES COLLEGE ENTRY MORE?

Social Class and College Entry

Entry into college is *not* strongly determined by an individual's social class of origin. The highest total association of class with either college entry or with ultimate educational attainment of which we are aware is the correlation of .48 reported by Alexander and Eckland from their study of the mobility careers of a national probability sample of males who were high school sophomores in 1955 (see table 7.2). For our sample, the total association between postsecondary enrollment level and social class is .36 for males and .35 for females. Even if we were to regard ability as causally dependent upon class such that *all* the total association of class with postsecondary educational enrollment were causal, i.e., so that $r_{14,1} = q_{14,1}$, the total effect that class would have upon college entry would be equal to that of ability for males, i.e., both would be .36; for females, the total effect of class, .35, would be just slightly greater than that of ability, .33.

In our model, where we regard both class and ability as exogenous variables correlated, but in a causally unanalyzed way, in deference to the still unresolved debate over the extent to which class-related environmental components determine ability, about one-fourth of the total association between class and college entry is attributable to the causally unanalyzed correlation between those two exogenous variables. Given the structure of our model, with both class and ability as correlated exogenous variables, it can be seen from table 7.1 that class does not exert a strong total effect on level of postsecondary enrollment: $q_{14,1} = .27$ for males and .25 for females.

Nevertheless, in a society that continues to adhere to the ideal of equality of educational opportunity, the presence of even a modest class effect on the educational careers of its youth is a matter of social and political concern. For, as the simple two-variable display in figure 7.4 illustrates, the odds that a student will enter a four-year college are about five in ten for males and four in ten for females *if* they are from white-collar families; for students from blue-collar families, those odds drop to less than two in ten.

Confronted with a causal relationship, however modest in size, between social class and level of postsecondary enrollment, there is an obvious temptation to interpret that relationship primarily in economic terms. Working-class parents, so the reasoning might run, are less capable than middle-class parents of financing the direct, out-of-the-pocket costs of higher education. Moreover, some working-class parents may be less able to withstand the financial burden of their offspring's foregone earnings for the period that he is in college.

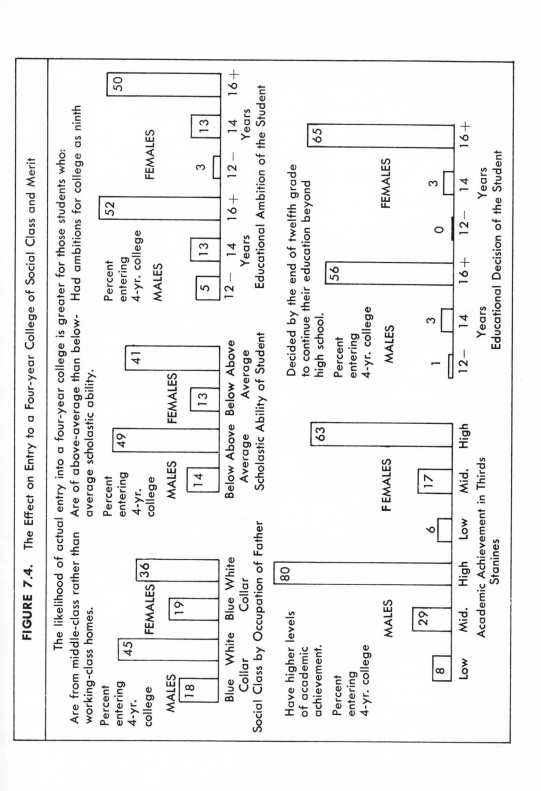

FIGURE 7.4. The Effect on Entry to a Four-year College of Social Class and Merit

The likelihood of actual entry into a four-year college is greater for those students who:

Are from middle-class rather than working-class homes.

Are of above-average than below-average scholastic ability.

Had ambitions for college as ninth

Decided by the end of twelfth grade to continue their education beyond high school.

Have higher levels of academic achievement.

Social Class by Occupation of Father

Scholastic Ability of Student

Educational Ambition of the Student

Educational Decision of the Student

Academic Achievement in Thirds Stanines

Our lack of data on the family incomes of our students prevents us from addressing directly the question of how much of the relationship between social class and college entry among our sample is economic. In lieu of data from our own study we can refer to the work of Sewell and Hauser, who have excellent income data (from Wisconsin state income tax returns), along with good measures of the class components of father's occupation and parents' education. To place into perspective the role of the economic dimension of social class in postsecondary educational enrollment and attainment, we cite here the conclusions reached by Sewell and Hauser:

> The extent to which socio-economic origins reduce the average educational achievement of those from the lower socio-economic strata is impressive. For example, each year of father's or mother's education was worth .08 years of higher education for their son—after controlling for the effects of father's occupation and family income. Consequently, the sons of parents with only grade school education obtained, on the average, one and a quarter fewer years of higher education than the sons of parents who were college graduates—even if their fathers had similar jobs and their families had similar incomes.
>
>   A thousand dollar increase in the annual income of the family, on the average, also yielded .08 years of educational attainment. Thus a shift from the poverty level of $3,000 . . . to the median income at that time, $6,000, increased the average years of education by a quarter of a year when the effects of parents' education and father's occupation were taken into account. A shift from $3,000 to $10,000 in family income led to an increase of more than half an additional year in post-secondary schooling.
>
>   . . . This approximate equality of effects of the four stratification variables suggests that there may be little merit in the efforts of some social scientists to interpret all social inequalities in terms of income differences or any other single status characteristic.[15]

Differential command over financial resources, then, does constitute a portion of the causal association between class and postsecondary level of enrollment. There is no evidence, however, to suggest that this component is the dominant reason why disproportionately more students of middle-class origins continue their education beyond high school than do students of working-class origins.

How else to account for the relationship between class and going to college? Reference to our summary table 7.1 reveals class as having a *direct* effect on postsecondary enrollment that is equal to about a fourth of its total causal effect: $p_{14,1}$ = .07 for males and .06 for females. Part of this direct effect may reflect overt discrimination by college officials against students from working-class origins. Part of it may be the result of class differences in income available to finance a college education. Part of it may be due to class differences in the desirability of higher education. And part of it may represent class differences in knowledge about college and the procedures necessary to enter and finance a college education. Whatever the reason, or reasons, for the existence of this direct effect, it is not a large effect, particularly when compared with the unmediated effects of academic achievement, counselor encouragement in grade twelve, or the educational decision of the student as a high school senior.

Substantially larger than the direct effect that class has on the postsecondary criterion is its *indirect* effect. $s_{14,1}$ = .20 for males and .20 for females! That is, of the total causal effect that class has on level of postsecondary enrollment, fully three-fourths is mediated through those variables represented by our model as intervening between family class background and the criterion. There is no simple, easily identifiable way by which the indirect effects of class can be traced to that criterion. Even educational ambition mediates no more than 20 percent of the total class effect for males, and even less for females—10 percent.

Students from middle-class homes thus do have an advantage over students from working-class homes when it comes to continuing education beyond high school. By any absolute standard, that class advantage is not a large one. No study of which we are aware has produced a correlation coefficient for that relationship larger than .60. Most of those correlations fall within the range of .30 to .50. By relative standards, the advantage in college entry enjoyed by middle-class students over their working-class counterparts is greater than that which accrues to students who have several, rather than few, college-bound peers or who have parents who stress and "take for granted" the continuation of their education beyond high school. Similarly, the class advantage in college entry is greater than that associated with being in the academic rather than the nonacademic program. But, by the same token, the college-entry advantage due to class privilege is *less than* that which can be traced to being above rather than below average in scholastic ability, to being a high academic achiever, or to having made the decision as a senior to continue with one's education beyond high school.

Finally, as we have seen, much of the modest effect that class has upon college entry is indirect. But it is not indirect through just one, two, or even three mediating variables. Rather, the indirect effects of class on that criterion are scattered throughout most of the eleven variables that intervene between that exogenous measure and the ultimate dependent measure. The indirect effects of class are thus pervasive throughout the social systems of the home and the school. No single mediating variable, or any small set of mediating variables, acts as a leverage point available for manipulation to the social engineer who would seek to reduce the extent to which college entry is dependent upon class of origin by altering one or another of the processes within the home or school. The very systemically pervasive nature of these class effects thus requires an equally systemic meliorative effort if the opportunity for entry into educational institutions beyond high school is to be made equal for all, regardless of their social class of origin.

Ambition, Educational Decision, Achievement, and Ability

Merit, as a determinant of college entry, contrasts with social class in two important respects. First, three of the four merit indicators—ability, academic achievement, and educational decision—each have total causal effects on college entry that exceed the effect from social class. Second, two of the four merit indicators—ability and ambition—like social class, affect college entry mostly indirectly. Unlike the indirect effects of social class that are diffused throughout the family and school components of our model, however, the indirect effects of ability and ambition are more specific, mediated to college entry largely through two or three of the more theoretically salient intervening variables of the model.

Educational ambition, among the four indicators of merit, has the smallest total causal effect on college entry: $q_{14,7} = .26$ for males and .21 for females. This is in spite of a rather strong total association of $r_{14,7} = .52$ for males and .47 for females, an association illustrated in figure 7.4, where we can observe that a student who had an ambition for four years of college as a ninth grader was ten times more likely to enroll in a four-year college the year after graduation than a student whose ambition was limited to high school graduation.

The rather marked difference between the total association and the total effect of ambition upon college entry reflects the influence that variables antecedent to ambition have upon both ambition and the criterion. More than half the overall association between those two variables arises because both the actual behavior of continuing one's education beyond high school and the ambition to do just that are more characteristic of students from middle-class homes, of students with parents who stress and "take for granted" continued education, of students who are of above average scholastic ability, and of students who, as ninth graders, were in the academic program and had several, rather than few, college-bound friends.

Ambition causally affects level of college enrollment, mostly indirectly for males and totally indirectly for females. For males 80 percent, and for females 70 percent, of that indirect effect can be accounted for with just three mediating variables: educational decision, counselor encouragement in twelfth grade, and academic achievement. Having college-level ambitions in ninth grade translates into actual entry into college after high school, primarily because the ambition to go to college leads to the decision to enter college, a decision that strongly enhances the likelihood of actual entry. Ambition also is transformed into actual behavior through its effect on academic achievement and on counselor encouragement. Those students who have high educational ambitions receive higher grades and college encouragement from the counselor during the senior year, both of which, in turn, make it very likely that the individual will actually continue his education beyond high school.

Academic achievement has a decided effect on whether the student continues his education beyond high school. Its total association with that criterion, $r_{14,10}$, is a sizable .52 for males and .54 for females. Both coefficients are very similar to those reported for several other inquiries and presented in table 7.2. As figure 7.4 illustrates, 80 percent of the males and 63 percent of the females in the highest three grade-point stanines reported that they had entered a four-year college. But of those with cumulative grade points in the lowest three stanines, such an entry was reported by only 8 percent of the males and 6 percent of the females.

Achievement affects college entry directly and indirectly. Whether or not a male continues his education beyond high school depends on achievement much more directly than indirectly, with a $p_{14,10} = .21$ and with $s_{14,10} = .08$. Whether a female continues her education beyond high school depends on her record of academic performance somewhat more directly than indirectly, with $p_{14,10} = .20$ and $s_{14,10} = .16$. Almost three-fourths of the indirect effect that achievement has on college entry occurs because of the tendency for students with strong academic records to make the decision to go to college while they are seniors, and because those with strong records of academic performance are quite likely to be encouraged by their guidance counselors to continue their education beyond high school.

When both the direct and the indirect effects of achievement on college entry are summed, the total causal effect that academic performance has on the college entry criterion ia a $q_{14,10} = .29$ for males and .36 for females. For all students, regardless of gender, their academic performance during high school is of greater causal consequence to their chances of entering college than are their social-class origins.

Exerting considerable impact on college entry, independently of any and all other variables in our model, is the *educational decision* the student makes about his postsecondary career while in twelfth grade. Among males who, toward the end of their senior year, reported that they had decided to enter a four-year college, 56 percent during the following year reported that they were enrolled in a four-year college. The comparable percentage for females is 65. But among those who reported toward the end of their senior year that their educational decision was to enter a two-year college or discontinue formal education entirely, less than 3 percent were enrolled in a four-year college the year following high school graduation (see figure 7.4). Deciding to enter a four-year college during twelfth grade does not ensure the occurrence of that event in the subsequent year, but not deciding to enter a four-year college during twelfth year all but ensures the nonoccurrence of that event.

Educational decision correlates strongly with college entry: $r_{14,13} = .63$ for males and .69 for females. Both coefficients are very close to those reported by other investigators and shown in table 7.2.

Of the total association between decision and college entry, almost half is causal for males and slightly more than half is causal for females. Directly, decision affects college entry with a $q_{14,13} = .30$ for males and .39 for females, thus making this twelfth-grade variable the second largest causal factor in the postsecondary educational behavior of males and the most important causal factor in that behavior for females. What the presence of such a relatively high causal component in the relationship between decision and college entry suggests is that, within limits, ample latitude remains up to almost the end of twelfth grade for the individual to decide whether or not to continue formal education beyond high school. That is, although the lack of class privilege, superior scholastic ability, parent, peer, or counselor educational support, early educational ambition, location in the academic curriculum, or superior academic achievement may singly and collectively reduce the likelihood that the student will continue his education beyond high school, an adverse position on any one or combination of those variables does not render that likelihood an impossibility. It would appear, then, that the educational system of the high school and the admissions procedures of colleges both have sufficient flexibility to allow the educational volition and initiative of the individual to remain potent even through the final year of secondary school.

Scholastic ability is the last of the four indicators of merit. Its total association with college entry is an $r_{14,2} = .43$ for males and .40 for females, well within the range of the coefficients from other studies shown in table 7.2. Figure 7.4 illustrates the overall relationship of ability to college entry. Forty-nine percent of those scholastically more able male students and 41 percent of the scholastically more able female students entered a four-year college during the year following high school graduation, a behavior characteristic of a considerably smaller percentage of those who were among the less scholastically able: 14 percent of the males and 13 percent of the females.

Much of the association between ability and college entry is causal. The very modest correlation of ability with class, $r_{21} = .25$ for males and .29 for females, limits the noncausal portion of the association between ability and college entry to less than 20 percent. On college entry, ability has a total effect, $q_{14,2} = .36$ for males and .33 for females.

Entry into college for females, as we can note from table 7.1, is directly dependent on ability to a very limited degree, but the sign of that direct dependency is negative: $-.06$. We do not wish to magnify out of proportion the potential import of an effect that is numerically as small as a path of .06, yet the fact that it is negative, and negative for females, tempts us to speculate that in the home, the school, and the society at large, social and psychological forces remain that either fail to encourage bright women to enter college or actively deter them from doing so.

Notwithstanding the presence of this limited negative direct effect of ability on female college entry, the major effect that this merit construct has on the criterion for females is indirect: $s_{14,2} = .39$. The totality of the effect that ability has on the criterion for males is indirect: $s_{14,2} = .36$. Mediating a good portion of the effect that ability has on college entry, and more of that effect than any other single variable, is academic achievement. Somewhat more than 40 percent of the total effect that ability has on male college entry, and somewhat more than 50 percent of that effect for females, is indirect by way of cumulative grade-point average. By and large, the higher rates of college entry that characterize the more scholastically able students result from the strong tendency of intellectually superior individuals to manifest that capability by earning higher than average school grades. Ability, in its raw form, whether as a standardized test score recorded on paper and stored in a file or as the underlying symbol-manipulating capacity of the individual, thus has almost no effect whatsoever on the likelihood that the individual will continue his education beyond high school. For ability to affect the chances for college entry it must be transformed, it must be "legitimized"; and it is transformed and legitimized by the school as academic performance, a form that colleges and universities recognize as highly predictive of academic performance in their own institutions.

In comparison with social class, scholastic ability is 1.33 times more consequential as a determinant of college entry for males and 1.28 times more consequential as a determinant of college entry for females. For males, ability is the strongest determinant of college entry. For females, ability plays a slightly more modest role, falling behind both academic achievement and educational decision as a determinant of who is to be educated beyond high school.

CONCLUSIONS

In this chapter we have sought to develop an understanding of the forces that determine whether an individual continues his or her education beyond high school. Although our measure of that criterion is restricted to the individual's report of educational behavior during only the first post-high school year, the high correlation reported by Sewell and Shah between college attendance and ultimate educational attainment gives us some confidence in the predictive validity of the variable we have tagged as "college entry."

Entry into college during the first year following high school depends, in part, upon the extent to which the student has perceived parents, peers, and school guidance counselors as having encouraged that kind of behavior. Parents, peers, and counselors each play a mutually supportive role in this respect inasmuch as the influence efforts of each are positively associated, one with the other. It is, however, the influence of the guidance counselor, exerted during the senior year, that registers the greatest effect on whether the student actually enters college the year following graduation from high school.

Entry into college is also contingent upon the curriculum location of the student during high school. But this contingency is of modest strength, especially for males. Indeed, for males, much of the association between curriculum location and college entry is spurious, a result of the tendency for males whose class origin, scholastic ability, parent and peer educational influence, and educational ambition already predispose them to enter college at the end of high school to locate in the college-preparatory program at the beginning of high school. Moreover, in our discussion of the effect of curriculum location on the likelihood of college entry for males, we noted that, for their sample high school class of 1957, Alexander and Eckland reported a correlation between curriculum and educational attainment which exceeded that which we have reported for curriculum and college entry, high school class of 1970. Cautiously, we inferred that this over-time decrease in the extent to which curriculum location predicts postsecondary educational behavior may well be due to the rapid expansion of student enrollment in two-year community colleges, institutions of higher education in which entry depends much more on whether an individual completed high school than whether he or she did so as a student in the college-preparatory program.

Finally, we assessed the respective roles of social class and merit in college entry. Matriculation in an institution of higher education during the first year after high school depended more on the student's own scholastic ability, academic achievement, and educational decision than it did on the social class of his or her family. Entry into college, of course, did depend on social class. That dependency is and must continue to remain a source of political and moral concern, particularly so in a nation dedicated to equality of opportunity. But that dependency is not strong. It is not strong among our sample of students, high school class of 1970, from the southern tier of New York. It was not strong among Sewell and Hauser's sample of students, high school class of 1957, from Wisconsin. And it was not strong among Alexander and Eckland's sample of students, high school class of 1957, from the entire United States. Social class is *not* the *most* important determinant of how far a person will go in school. But until social class is the *least* important determinant of how far a person will go in school, the ideals of those who seek a truly meritocratic society will remain unfulfilled, as will the aspirations of countless able, ambitious, and talented individuals born not into privilege but into poverty.

NOTES

1. Johan Galtung, "Schooling and Future Society," *School Review* 83 (August 1975): 549.

2. U.S. Department of Health, Education, and Welfare. National Center for Educational Statistics, *Digest of Educational Statistics: 1974* (Washington, D.C.: Government Printing Office, 1975). "Table 19. Occupation of employed persons 16 years old and over, by sex, color, and years of school completed: United States, March 1973," p. 19; and, "Table 20. Total money income of persons 25 years old and over, by years of school completed, sex, and age: United States, 1972," p. 20.

3. William H. Sewell and Vimal P. Shah, "Socioeconomic Status, Intelligence, and the Attainment of Higher Education," *Sociology of Education* 40 (Winter 1967): 16.

4. The equations that define the trimmed models for each gender are:

For males

Eq. 1: $X_3 = p_{31}X_1 + p_{32}X_2 + p_{3a}X_a$

Eq. 2: $X_4 = p_{41}X_1 + p_{42}X_2 + p_{4b}X_b$

Eq. 3: $X_5 = p_{51}X_1 + p_{52}X_2 + p_{53}X_3 + p_{5c}X_c$

Eq. 4: $X_6 = p_{61}X_1 + p_{62}X_2 + p_{63}X_3 + p_{64}X_4 + p_{65}X_5 + p_{6d}X_d$

Eq. 5: $X_7 = p_{71}X_1 + p_{72}X_2 + p_{73}X_3 + p_{74}X_4 + p_{75}X_5 + p_{76}X_6 + p_{7e}X_e$

Eq. 6: $X_8 = p_{82}X_2 + p_{83}X_3 + p_{85}X_5 + p_{87}X_7 + p_{8f}X_f$

Eq. 7: $X_9 = p_{92}X_2 + p_{94}X_4 + p_{96}X_6 + p_{97}X_7 + p_{98}X_8 + p_{9g}X_g$

Eq. 8: $X_{10} = p_{10,2}X_2 + p_{10,3}X_3 + p_{10,7}X_7 + p_{10,8}X_8 + p_{10,9}X_9 + p_{10h}X_h$

Eq. 9: $X_{11} = p_{11,1}X_1 + p_{11,4}X_4 + p_{11,5}X_5 + p_{11,6}X_6 + p_{11,8}X_8 + p_{11,9}X_9 + p_{11,10}X_{10} + p_{11i}X_i$

Eq. 10: $X_{12} = p_{12,1}X_1 + p_{12,2}X_2 + p_{12,3}X_3 + p_{12,4}X_4 + p_{12,7}X_7 + p_{12,8}X_8 + p_{12,9}X_9 + p_{12,10}X_{10} + p_{12,11}X_{11} + p_{12j}X_j$

Eq. 11: $X_{13} = p_{13,1}X_1 + p_{13,2}X_2 + p_{13,4}X_4 + p_{13,6}X_6 + p_{13,7}X_7 + p_{13,10}X_{10} + p_{13,11}X_{11} + p_{13,12}X_{12} + p_{13k}X_k$

Eq. 12: $X_{14} = p_{14,1}X_1 + p_{14,3}X_3 + p_{14,4}X_4 + p_{14,6}X_6$
$+ p_{14,7}X_7 + p_{14,10}X_{10} + p_{14,11}X_{11} + p_{14,12}X_{12}$
$+ p_{14,13}X_{13} + p_{14l}X_l$

For females

Eq. 1: $X_3 = p_{31}X_1 + p_{32}X_2 + p_{3a}X_a$

Eq. 2: $X_4 = p_{41}X_1 + p_{42}X_2 + p_{4b}X_b$

Eq. 3: $X_5 = p_{51}X_1 + p_{52}X_2 + p_{53}X_3 + p_{54}X_4 + p_{5c}X_c$

Eq. 4: $X_6 = p_{61}X_1 + p_{62}X_2 + p_{63}X_3 + p_{64}X_4 + p_{65}X_5$
$+ p_{6d}X_d$

Eq. 5: $X_7 = p_{71}X_1 + p_{72}X_2 + p_{73}X_3 + p_{74}X_4 + p_{75}X_5$
$+ p_{76}X_6 + p_{7e}X_e$

Eq. 6: $X_8 = p_{81}X_1 + p_{82}X_2 + p_{84}X_4 + p_{85}X_5 + p_{87}X_7$
$+ p_{8f}X_f$

Eq. 7: $X_9 = p_{92}X_2 + p_{93}X_3 + p_{96}X_6 + p_{97}X_7 + p_{98}X_8$
$+ p_{9g}X_g$

Eq. 8: $X_{10} = p_{10,2}X_2 + p_{10,3}X_3 + p_{10,7}X_7 + p_{10,9}X_9$
$+ p_{10h}X_h$

Eq. 9: $X_{11} = p_{11,2}X_2 + p_{11,3}X_3 + p_{11,6}X_6 + p_{11,8}X_8$
$+ p_{11,10}X_{10} + p_{11i}X_i$

Eq. 10: $X_{12} = p_{12,1}X_1 + p_{12,2}X_2 + p_{12,7}X_7 + p_{12,8}X_8$
$+ p_{12,9}X_9 + p_{12,10}X_{10} + p_{12,11}X_{11} + p_{12j}X_j$

Eq. 11: $X_{13} = p_{13,1}X_1 + p_{13,3}X_3 + p_{13,7}X_7 + p_{13,8}X_8$
$+ p_{13,10}X_{10} + p_{13,11}X_{11} + p_{13,12}X_{12} + p_{13k}X_k$

Eq. 12: $X_{14} = p_{14,1}X_1 + p_{14,2}X_2 + p_{14,6}X_6 + p_{14,8}X_8$
$+ p_{14,10}X_{10} + p_{14,11}X_{11} + p_{14,12}X_{12}$
$+ p_{14,13}X_{13} + p_{14l}X_l$

5. Karl L. Alexander and Bruce K. Eckland. *Effects of Education on the Social Mobility of High School Sophomores Fifteen Years Later (1955–1970)*, Final Report, Project No. 10202, Grant No. OEG-71-0037 (Washington, D.C.: National Institute of Education, U.S. Department of Health, Education, and Welfare, 1973), p. 113.

6. Georg Busch, "Inequality of Educational Opportunity by Social Origin in Higher Education," in *Education, Inequality, and Life Chances* (Paris: OECD, 1975), 1:159.

7. See, for example, the Presidential Address by William H. Sewell to the 66th Annual Meeting of the American Sociological Association, 30 August 1971, as reprinted, "Inequality of Opportunity for

Higher Education," *American Sociological Review* 36 (October 1971): 793–809.

8. W. Lloyd Warner, Robert J. Havighurst, and Martin B. Loeb, *Who Shall Be Educated?* (New York: Harper & Brothers, 1944), p. 142.

9. Martin Carnoy, *Education as Cultural Imperialism* (New York: McKay, 1974), pp. 323–24.

10. Prior to trimming the model, 50.5 percent of the variance was accounted for.

11. William H. Sewell and Robert M. Hauser, *Education, Occupation, and Earnings*: *Achievement in the Early Career* (Madison: University of Wisconsin, Department of Sociology, 1974). A final report of research carried out under Grant No. 314, Social and Rehabilitation Service, Social Security Administration, U.S. Department of Health, Education, and Welfare, p. 4.

12. Alexander and Eckland, *Effects of Education*, p. 166.

13. This is the same percentage of variance accounted for with all thirteen predictor variables.

14. U.S. Department of Health, Education, and Welfare, Office of Education, National Center for Educational Statistics, *Projections of Educational Statistics to 1980–81*, 1971 edition, tables 6, 7, and 8.

15. Sewell and Hauser, *Education, Occupation, and Earnings*, pp. 133–34.

8. Gender and
School Outcomes

The effects of class and merit on school outcomes are not identical for male and female students. In previous chapters we analyzed school outcomes separately for each sex in order to highlight the role of class and merit as determinants of the school experience. Here our aim is to highlight the role of sex as a determinant of school outcomes, to assess its causal strength relative to class and merit, and to examine the interaction of sex with school-process variables during the high school years.

A student's gender is unrelated to class background and scholastic ability, both theoretically and empirically. For this population, the empirical correlations of sex of student with social-class background and ability are virtually nil, $-.028$ and $-.003$ respectively (the negative sign indicates a minuscule "disadvantage" to females). Persistent effects of sex on school outcomes may therefore be interpreted directly as evidence contrary to a meritocratic interpretation of the schooling process. Such effects would also weaken arguments of a class-based analysis of schooling, but conform to a view of schooling that includes class and sex as two examples of the ascribed criteria that underly the stratification process in the United States. Unless definitions of class and merit are broadened to the point of absurdity, the existence of sex effects on the educational attainment process calls for revision or specification of current theoretical stances.

We would be extremely surprised to find no sex effects on the schooling process because such effects pervade social life. Studies of male and female job opportunities and earnings find strong sex effects.[1] Sex differences in family roles and allocation of resources have been so thoroughly documented in recent years that proponents of the thesis of the egalitarian family have disappeared.[2] How unrealistic it appears for investigators to assume that the schooling process and its outcomes are unique in not being conditioned by gender differences. Yet this assumption is implicit in recent studies of school populations that do not include sex as a variable in the analysis, and also in studies of all-male populations.[3] We believe that educational outcomes for high school students are not as strongly conditioned by gender as are many individuals' experiences as family members or labor-force participants. Nevertheless, sex effects exist and have implications for our assessment of the relative influence of class background and scholastic ability on the educational attainment process.

Two recent studies of the effects of sex on the schooling process conclude that social-class effects are stronger relative to scholastic ability for girls and that the reverse is true for boys.[4] Both are longitudinal studies that measure the educational plans and attainment of individuals who were in high school in the 1950s. Alexander and Eckland confirm with a national sample the primacy for educational outcomes of ability for boys and socioeconomic background for girls noted in the regional sample reported by Sewell and Shah. Sewell and Shah conclude from their analysis that "female attainments appear to be more closely tied to the ascribed criterion of family background status; while those of males are more strongly related to the presumably functional criterion of academic ability."[5]

Do these same relationships hold for our sample, class of 1970? If they do, we must conclude that the consistently meritocratic outcomes reported in our earlier review of the findings from several previous studies would have been modified had all investigators assessed outcomes for females along with males. Table 8.1 juxtaposes our results with those of Alexander and Eckland and Sewell and Shah. Comparing total effects on educational goals within categories of sex, we see that in our recent sample ability shows stronger effects than class for both males and females. The effects of ability on the attainment of those goals also exceed those of social class for both sexes. Our data do not conform to earlier results shown in table 8.1, and this may be due to real changes in the schooling process since the 1950s. We cannot dismiss the possibility that the different results reflect differences in the measures used for the four variables, however, especially the measure of educational behavior. Both earlier studies measure such behavior as actual educational attainment several years after high school graduation when most people have completed all the schooling they will ever get. Our measure is college entry one

TABLE 8.1. Comparisons of Sex Differences in Strength of Total Effects of Social Class (X_1) and Scholastic Ability (X_2) on Selected School Outcomes

	Outcomes							
	College Plans				Educational Attainment			
	Sex				Sex			
	Female		Male		Female		Male	
	Predictor		Predictor		Predictor		Predictor	
Identification of Study	Class	Ability	Class	Ability	Class	Ability	Class	Ability
This Study[a]	.26	.34	.28	.39	.25	.33	.27	.36
Sewell and Shah[b]	.37	.23	.32	.34	.38	.23	.31	.36
Alexander and Eckland[c]	.48	.08	.37	.21	.40	.23	.30	.37

Sources: W. H. Sewell and V. P. Shah, "Socioeconomic Status, Intelligence and the Attainment of Higher Education," *Sociology of Education* 40 (Winter 1967): 1–23; K. Alexander and B. K. Eckland, "Sex Differences in the Educational Attainment Process," *American Sociological Review* 39, no. 5 (1974): 668–82.

[a] In this study, "college plans" are the educational decisions of high school seniors; "educational attainment" is college entry, or the educational enrollment of the student one year after the senior year.

[b] In the Sewell and Shah's study, "college plans" are the educational decisions of high school seniors; "educational attainment" is the total amount of schooling completed by the individual ten years after the senior year.

[c] In Alexander and Eckland's study, "college plans" are the educational ambitions of high school sophomores; "educational attainment" is the total amount of schooling completed by the individual fifteen years after the sophomore year.

year after high school graduation. A future measure of educational goal attainment for our sample may yield different observed relationships by sex.

The inclusion of table 8.1 may seem somewhat repetitious here; most of the same data are reported in the analyses of the two preceding chapters. We repeat the findings not only to highlight the implications of this study for the merit and class views of schooling once sex is taken into account, but also to point out the limitations of separate analyses by sex employing path coefficients and standardized total effects for our purposes in this chapter. Separate analyses by sex control for the effects of sex as an independent determinant of school outcomes and therefore obscure the main effect of sex on the process. We may validly make comparisons of the relative effects of ability and class within gender subsamples from table 8.1 but we cannot come to any valid conclusions about cross-sex comparisons of effects, or about the independent role of sex as a determinant of the two dependent variables of college plans and educational attainment. For example, in our study as shown in table 8.1, the total-effect coefficients on college plans for males and females are much more alike than the corresponding total-effect coefficients from Alexander and Eckland, and an invalid comparison might lead to the erroneous conclusion that the sexes are much more alike in their educational goals in our study than in Alexander and Eckland's study. In fact, the main effect of sex on college plans in the earlier study is $-.017$, not significant by any conventional criterion.[6] In contrast, the main effect of sex on twelfth-grade educational decision in our study is a highly significant and substantively important $-.13$ (see table 8.2). Here again, and throughout this chapter, a negative sign indicates an advantage for boys, and a positive sign indicates an advantage for girls.

In order to expose the strength and direction of any main effects of sex on educational outcomes, we will introduce sex as an additional exogenous variable in the causal model and estimate effects with data from the entire sample, a strategy equivalent to the analysis of covariance.

Comparisons across sexes from total-effect coefficients q_{ij} or path coefficients p_{ij} may also be misleading when there are differences by sex in the dispersion of relevant variables. Although differences by sex in variances are minimal in our study, we shall present unstand-

TABLE 8.2 Main Effects of Sex, Class, and Ability on School Process Variables: Total Associations, Total Effects, and Direct Effects

Dependent Variables		Sex			Predetermined Variables Class Coefficients			Ability		
		r_{ij}	q_{ij}	p_{ij}	r_{ij}	q_{ij}	p_{ij}	r_{ij}	q_{ij}	p_{ij}
Parental ed. stress	X_3	−152	−146	−146	235	189	189	206	155	155
Taken for granted	X_4	−014	−007	−007	292	237	237	269	205	205
Curriculum gr. 9	X_5	−024	−019	−010	239	159	089	337	294	235
Peer col. int. gr. 9	X_6	−094	−087	−068	304	240	167	293	228	142
Educational ambition	X_7	−068	−058	−008	400	315	152	396	311	141
Curriculum gr. 10	X_8	−009	−002	029	291	196	048	406	353	154
Cnslr. enc. gr. 10	X_9	−065	−059	−014	274	172	009	420	374	130
Academic achvmt.	X_{10}	187	191	195	238	102	034	553	526	414
Peer col. int. gr. 12	X_{11}	045	052	060	283	232	148	256	194	059
Cnslr. enc. gr. 12	X_{12}	−062	−055	−086	309	209	073	423	367	062
Educational decision	X_{13}	−135	−126	−129	383	284	077	432	355	032
College entry	X_{14}	003	011	030	352	260	044	413	343	012

ardized (metric) path-regression coefficients to supplement the standardized path coefficients reported in earlier chapters when investigating the interaction effects of sex with other determinants of school outcomes.

Main Effects of Sex

Main effects of sex appear throughout the educational attainment process but form no simple, consistent pattern in size or direction. Table 8.2, based on data from the total sample, summarizes total effects and direct effects of sex, class, and ability on the endogenous variables in the causal model. Most of the effects of sex are negative, indicating a disadvantage for girls, but the largest effect of sex is the advantage for girls in grade-point average (X_{10}). This finding, consistent with prior research, shows that the direct effect of sex on grades of .20 is stronger than either its corresponding total effect or total association: negative indirect effects of sex on grades mediated by variables X_3 through X_9 tend to suppress the total effect. The direct effect of sex on grades is also larger than the corresponding effect of class on grades. Almost all the effect of class on grades is explained indirectly through its association with other school process variables, but the direct advantage to grades for girls remains unexplained by other variables in the model.

Just being a girl means that a student's class standing will be about one-fifth of a standard deviation higher than that of a boy with similar ability, class background, parental stress, and so on. We may interpret this effect as high school teachers' preference for girls or discrimination against boys, or alternatively try to account for it on the basis of some factor related to both sex and grades but not included in the model. The first explanation seems unlikely, especially in light of findings of widespread sexism against girls in the stories, projects, and problems chosen by teachers for classroom use.[7] The second explanation will appeal to most high school teachers, who admit that high grades are within the capabilities of most high school students if only those students, especially underachieving boys, would do their homework carefully and pay attention in class. Our guess, based on our own experience as teachers, is that girls' advantages in grades are earned by behaviors often referred to as "effort" or "cooperation" and unrelated to ability, class, educational plans, and the rest.

Girls' real advantage in grades does not result in their being more educationally ambitious than boys. Evidence from prior research overwhelmingly supports the finding repeated here that males are more educationally ambitious than females. Logan's[8] review of nineteen recent studies of educational ambition reporting results for both sexes shows that, with a single exception, males report higher educational ambition than females. The large national survey of Douvan and Adelson[9] done in the 1950s shows boys' educational plans consistently higher than girls'; and older high school girls' plans are less ambitious that those of girls under fourteen.

Judging from our data, twenty years have not altered this pattern. Although our students report plans for four or more years of college with greater frequency than did students in the 1950s, the differences between boys and girls remain about the same, and the gap between girls' and boys' educational goals increases through high school. Our data show a total effect of −.06 of sex on ninth-grade educational ambitions, and a total effect of −.13 of sex on twelfth-grade educational decisions, when 43 percent of the girls and 60 percent of the boys had made the decision to enter a four-year college.

These total effects of sex do not match those of class or ability on educational ambitions or decisions, but the direct effect of sex on twelfth-grade educational decisions is stronger than either of the direct effects from class or ability. In this case, just being a girl results in educational decisions about one-eighth of a standard deviation lower than those of a boy ($p_{13,\text{sex}} = -.13$) taking into account ability, class, significant others' influence, and other factors.

In this study, as in earlier work, educational goals reflect occupational goals more closely for boys than girls, and boys more often than girls aim for professional-level occupations. We find no evidence here for greater similarity of the sexes in educational plans, compared to earlier studies. In fact, the effect of sex on educational plans is stronger here compared to studies of high schoolers of the 1950s, and stronger than the effect of either class or ability.

A noteworthy result of the analysis in table 8.2 is the *non*-finding that the addition of sex as a third exogenous variable in the model does not help much in predicting post-high school educational activity. The favorable but trivially small main effect for girls on college entry indicates a change from earlier studies where males' educational attainment exceeds that of females. National statistics show three educational trends that are reflected in the equivalence of college entry for males and females in our sample. One trend shows that the long-standing female advantage in graduation from high school has just about disappeared;[10] for the 1970 class on which we have data, 4 percent of the women and 6 percent of the men did not graduate from high school by 1971. A second trend shows the narrowing gap between male and female enrollments in four-year colleges;[11] in our sample of individuals for whom a complete set of data is available, 35 percent of the men and 29 percent of the women were enrolled in four-year colleges one year following high school graduation. The third trend shows the enormous increase in both male and female enrollment in two-year colleges nationally since 1960;[12] 36 percent of the men and 40 percent of the women in our sample were enrolled in two-year colleges in 1971.

Where our data differ from national statistics is in the rates of enrollment by sex in two-year colleges. Nationally, males showed a 9-percentage-point advantage in 1970 in the proportion of high school graduates entering two-year colleges for the first time; our data show a 4-percentage-point advantage for women. And both men and women in our sample enroll in two-year colleges at much higher rates than in the U.S. generally. We attribute this to the long-term local presence of a public community college with an excellent reputation, an open-enrollment policy, and a successful record for transfer placement as well as vocational preparation.

Summary

The trivial total effect of sex on post-high school educational activity is a welcome finding, but not necessarily a cause for celebration of the arrival of sex equality in educational attainment. It remains to be seen if this relative equality is maintained when the class of 1970 has completed all formal education. In addition, the lack of a significant total effect of sex on college entry does not indicate that the schooling process works the same way for both sexes. The small sum of direct and indirect effects of sex on educational enrollment masks the balancing of positive and negative effects whose absolute sum is about .14. The two strongest indirect effects are a salutary effect for girls due to their higher grades (.04) and a benefit to boys explained by their more ambitious educational plans (−.04). The mediated effects of sex turn out to be about four times larger in absolute terms than the direct effect. Like class and ability, most effects of sex on enrollment are mediated by other variables in the model, but they cancel rather than reinforce one another to yield an insignificant total effect.

The main effects of sex in the schooling process are small but persistent and generally show a disadvantage for girls. Girls' direct advantage in grades is consistent with earlier studies of high school students, and the advantage shows no sign of weakening. The advantages for boys in parental and counselor encouragement also persist in strength compared to earlier studies. Boys' more ambitious educational plans are still apparent and loftier than ever. Girls appear to gain a slight advantage in curriculum location and peer influence as they progress through high school. Girls' advantage in educational enrollment one year after high school graduation is trivial and represents a reversal of the male advantage reported for earlier cohorts.

Although the males in our study, and nationwide in 1970, were still more likely than females to enter four-year colleges the year following high school graduation, the females were more likely to graduate from high school and more likely to enter two-year colleges. Controlling for ability and social class, the female advantage in grades and the male advantage in ambition offset each other and result in an educational stratification order very similar by sex one year after high school.

INTERACTION EFFECTS OF SEX WITH OTHER DETERMINANTS OF SCHOOL OUTCOMES

Examination of the main effects of sex on school outcomes permitted us to answer questions about the strength, direction, and persistence of the influence of sex in the schooling process. We were able to compare the class of 1970 with students from the 1950s and found that, although the effects of sex on college entry have almost disappeared, the effects of sex on grades, ambition, and encouragement from significant others persist. In some cases these effects appear stronger now than they were twenty years ago. In order to examine main sex effects we employed a causal model including sex as a third exogenous variable and estimated the effects from our total sample of males and females combined.

To examine interaction effects, we employ here models estimated separately for each sex, as in earlier chapters. The path coefficients displayed in earlier chapters permitted us to compare the relative size of effects within each sex group and answer questions about the relative importance for a given sex of class and ability as determinants of school outcomes. We showed that for the women of the class of 1970, in contrast to earlier female cohorts, ability outranks class as a determinant of educational plans and college entry. In order to answer questions about the relative importance of ability and class between sex groups, we must examine slopes in recognition of the differences in dispersion of the two groups on most variables. We retain trivial effects rather than setting them equal to zero as we did in the trimmed models of earlier chapters in order to facilitate comparisons between the sexes.[13]

We shall first focus on sex interaction effects on the two major outcomes, college entry (X_{14}) and educational decision in grade twelve (X_{13}). Our primary interest is to locate any noteworthy sex differences in the power of the school process variables on these two outcomes. Second, we examine sex-specific reduced-form models in order to assess interaction effects of sex with class and ability on each of the school process variables.

The differences in partial slopes for each causal variable in the prediction of educational plans are shown in table 8.3. Comparing slopes across rows of this table, we note that every school process factor varies by sex in its strength as a determinant of educational plans. A sensible yet precise verbal interpretation of slopes and their differences is not easy to compose for several of the variables here, but we may note that a negative sign of the difference indicates that the factor is a stronger determinant of educational decisions for boys compared to girls, controlling for all other variables in the model. Relative sizes of the differences are not comparable across variables in this unstandardized form and must be interpreted in terms of the metric of each variable, as described in chapter 2. For example, the 2.07 difference in slopes for academic achievement (X_{10}) indicates that each increase of a stanine-scale point in grade-point average returns to girls a benefit on the Hollingshead educational scale 2

TABLE 8.3. Sex Interactions in the Prediction of Educational Decisions in Twelfth Grade (X_{13})

Predictor Variable		Males	Females	Difference
		Partial Slopes[a]		
Social class	X_1	4.70	6.82	2.12
Scholastic ability	X_2	.73	−.21	−.94
Parental ed. stress	X_3	−.07	3.23	3.30
Taken for granted	X_4	10.37	−.81	−11.18
Curriculum gr. 9	X_5	5.94	−.34	−6.28
Peer col. int. gr. 9	X_6	3.11	1.50	−1.61
Educational ambition	X_7	27.42	20.27	−7.15
Curriculum gr. 10	X_8	3.45	9.95	6.50
Cnslr. enc. gr. 10	X_9	−.84	6.21	7.05
Academic achvmt.	X_{10}	7.32	9.39	2.07
Peer col. int. gr. 12	X_{11}	13.45	9.84	−3.61
Cnslr. enc. gr. 12	X_{12}	28.66	33.92	5.26
R		74.18	70.82	
R^2		.55	.50	

[a] Regression coefficients are multiplied by 10^2 for convenience of presentation.

percent of a point more than a similar academic achievement increase returns to boys, if all other factors in the model remain constant. Girls compared to boys get a minimally better payoff to plans from grades.

The largest sex difference is the 11 percent greater payoff to a boy if he perceives his parents as "taking it for granted" that he will go to college. Ninth-grade curriculum and early educational ambitions also have stronger impacts on boys' decisions than on girls'. The pattern that emerges from these simple interaction effects is that the influences on students' ambitions that occur early on, by ninth grade or sooner, are more effective for boys than for girls. Later influences are relatively more powerful for girls, especially counselor's encouragement. The relative power of counselor's encouragement is particularly noteworthy in view of the negative main sex effect on counselor's encouragement noted earlier. Other factors equal, being a girl means that counselors do *not* advise high educational goals; it also means that girls take the counselor's advice more seriously than boys in arriving at their educational decisions. Being a boy means that parents are much more likely to stress the importance of continued education beyond high school, but a boy is less likely than a girl to respond to that stress in making educational decisions.

Weak sex interactions are displayed for ability, peer influence, and class as well as grades, indicating that these variables operate with pretty much the same strength for both sexes. These aspects of the schooling process are obscured if we trim the model before inspecting interaction effects.

Overall, the model is a better predictor of boys' educational decisions than girls': factors related to sex but unrelated to the schooling process are more salient for girls' educational decisions than boys' (R^2 boys = .55; R^2 girls = .50). In predicting college entry, the reverse is true for our sample: in table 8.4 the variables in the model explain 51 percent of the variance of X_{14} for boys and 59 percent for girls. In contrast to earlier studies, these data show that in the transition from high school to college, outside influences related to sex but unrelated to schooling influences are more powerful for boys than for girls ($1 - R^2$ boys = .49; $1 - R^2$ girls = .41).

Since high school graduation became the statistical norm for Americans, gender-related influences have been important determinants of the attainment of higher education. In the past these influences were often related to marriage and fertility goals as well as occupational goals. We guess that occupationally relevant factors continue to operate in the transition from high school to college for the class of 1970, but family-related factors have declined in their influence on college enrollment. Early marriage, and especially early parenthood, influence the higher educational attainments of women more than men even today; but they are less noticeable in educational behavior one year out of high school than in plans for eventual educational attainment.

Several national trends converge to add support to these speculations. Since the 1950s, age at marriage and especially age at birth of first child have risen. In addition, many colleges and high schools no longer systematically exclude wives and mothers, as was common practice in the 1950s. Today's high school girls are more likely to aspire to a future that combines a career with parenthood; in the

TABLE 8.4.   Sex Interactions in the Prediction of College Entry (X_{14})

Predictor Variable		Partial Slopes[a]		
		Males	Females	Difference
Social class	X_1	6.95	5.47	−1.48
Scholastic ability	X_2	.27	−.62	.89
Parental ed. stress	X_3	2.76	−.66	−3.42
Taken for granted	X_4	13.28	4.77	−8.51
Curriculum gr. 9	X_5	−9.42	−.07	−9.35
Peer col. int. gr. 9	X_6	7.05	4.66	−2.39
Educational ambition	X_7	4.64	1.11	−3.53
Curriculum gr. 10	X_8	5.60	17.56	11.96
Cnslr. enc. gr. 10	X_9	8.51	−1.74	−10.25
Academic achvmt.	X_{10}	10.97	10.94	−.03
Peer col. int. gr. 12	X_{11}	7.93	13.12	5.19
Cnslr. enc. gr. 12	X_{12}	16.03	24.72	8.69
Educational decision	X_{13}	34.95	43.43	8.49
R		71.24	76.50	
R^2		.51	.59	

[a] Regression coefficients are multiplied by 10^2 for convenience of presentation.

1950s marriage and motherhood alone were the futures envisioned for themselves by a large majority of young women.

Continued study of the class of 1970 may reveal that eventual educational attainment is more highly related to senior-year educational decisions than it is to educational activity one year out of high school. However, our cohort of young people are reaching maturity at a time of hope for legal and social change in the relative statuses of the sexes. We optimistically predict that these hopes will be realized in narrower sex differences in their eventual educational and occupational attainments.

Our optimism is partly based on the sex interactions shown in table 8.4. Class, ability, and grades predict college entry with close to equal strength for men and women. The largest sex interactions show up in areas that are open to influence from educational decision makers: tenth-grade curriculum location and twelfth-grade counselor's encouragement. A year out of high school, both these factors influence girls' enrollment more than boys'. The stronger influence of tenth-grade curriculum location yields a benefit to girls as a group because its main effect is positive, but the stronger influence of twelfth-grade counselor's encouragement is not as beneficial to girls' enrollment—its main effect is negative. This is also the case with the effect of counselor's encouragement on educational decisions. A rise in educational ambition for girls results in a bigger payoff to college entry than it does for boys, but note that girls' decisions overall still tend to be lower than boys'.

The interaction effects show that the schooling process is indeed different for girls than for boys. A girl who rates the same as a boy on all other factors in the model has a slightly better chance of being in the college-preparatory curriculum in both ninth and tenth grades, and the effect of curriculum location is a stronger determinant of both her educational decisions and her post-high school entry into college. Other factors in the model equalized, a boy receives more encouraging educational advice from the counselor compared to girls, but he is less likely than a girl is to have the counselor's encouragement influence his educational decision or his entry into college.

When the school process variables are taken into account, class and ability show minimal interaction effects with sex. Class is slightly more powerful for girls than for boys in predicting educational decisions when we consider its effect on decisions not mediated by other variables. The reverse is true in predicting college entry. Ability actually shows a negative effect for girls on both decisions and entry when other variables are controlled. The effect of ability is stronger for girls in predicting college entry, but stronger for boys in predicting educational decisions.

When the school process variables are not included, we can estimate the total effects of class and ability for each sex. Table 8.5 displays the interaction of sex with class and sex with ability on each of the school outcomes. The predictive power of these reduced form models is of course much lower than the full models, indicating the power of intervening variables in explaining outcomes over and above the effects of ability and class. By comparing the sex interactions shown in the reduced-form estimates of table 8.5 with sex interactions in the full model, we may ascertain if the intervening

TABLE 8.5. Sex Interactions with Social Class and Scholastic Ability in Predicting School Outcomes, Reduced-Form Models[a]

	X_3	X_4	X_5	X_6	X_7	X_8	X_9	X_{10}	X_{11}	X_{12}	X_{13}	X_{14}
						School Outcomes (partial slopes $b_{ij,k}$)						
Social Class												
Boys	32.08	10.95	7.83	33.35	29.22	7.52	13.22	18.87	13.12	13.19	23.37	27.09
Girls	41.21	12.31	9.59	26.49	32.11	11.28	16.85	9.85	12.37	14.16	22.99	25.44
Difference	9.13	1.36	1.76	−6.86	2.89	3.76	3.63	−9.02	−.75	.97	−.38	−1.65
Ability												
Boys	2.35	−.86	1.04	2.56	2.56	1.32	2.67	9.06	1.54	2.39	3.24	3.58
Girls	2.79	1.00	1.63	2.68	2.10	1.82	3.19	9.79	2.16	2.97	2.95	3.17
Difference	.44	1.86	.59	.12	−.46	.50	.52	.73	.62	.58	−.29	−.41
R^2 Boys	.08	.13	.11	.29	.16	.15	.18	.32	.08	.20	.28	.25
R^2 Girls	.09	.15	.21	.25	.16	.27	.23	.33	.10	.23	.23	.22
Difference	.01	.12	.10	.04	.00	.12	.05	.01	.02	.03	.05	.03

[a] Reduced form models, estimated separately for each sex, are:

$X_3 = b_{13,2}X_1 + b_{23,1}X_2 + e_3$
$X_4 = b_{14,2}X_1 + b_{24,1}X_2 + e_4$
$X_5 = b_{15,2}X_1 + b_{25,1}X_2 + e_5$
$X_6 = b_{16,2}X_1 + b_{26,1}X_2 + e_6$
$X_7 = b_{17,2}X_1 + b_{27,1}X_2 + e_7$
$X_8 = b_{18,2}X_1 + b_{28,1}X_2 + e_8$
$X_9 = b_{19,2}X_1 + b_{29,1}X_2 + e_9$
$X_{10} = b_{1,10,2}X_1 + b_{2,10,1}X_2 + e_{10}$
$X_{11} = b_{1,11,2}X_1 + b_{2,11,1}X_2 + e_{11}$
$X_{12} = b_{1,12,2}X_1 + b_{2,12,1}X_2 + e_{12}$
$X_{13} = b_{1,13,2}X_1 + b_{2,13,1}X_2 + e_{13}$
$X_{14} = b_{1,14,2}X_1 + b_{2,14,1}X_2 + e_{14}$

school variables operate to neutralize or to intensify the interactions of sex with class and ability. We conclude that the sex-class interaction on college plans is intensified by the schooling process, and the sex-class interaction on enrollment remains about the same. Both sex-ability interactions are intensified by the schooling process. Three of these four comparisons show that the schooling process tends to produce outcomes more differentiated by sex than we would predict on the basis of just class and ability differences.

CLASS, ABILITY, AND SEX AS FACTORS IN EDUCATIONAL STRATIFICATION

The detection of persistent main and interaction effects of sex in the process of educational stratification weakens the argument that stratification is based on merit criteria. We found little evidence that sex effects in general are smaller now than in the past, but our data encourage the view that sex differences in college entry show signs of lessening.

For some school outcomes, sex is a more powerfully persistent factor than either class or ability. The schooling process as we have outlined it accounts for almost all the association of class and ability with educational decisions and college enrollment; the association of sex with school outcomes remains largely unexplained by these same schooling-process factors. Because some school-process factors operate to benefit boys and some to benefit girls, many sex differences in the schooling process are obscured by simple correlation coefficients. The variables we have studied in this short segment of individuals' socioeconomic careers tend to weaken the connection of class and ability with college entry and educational decisions; unless one translates class and ability advantages into higher grades, higher ambition, and the rest, these advantages disappear. The advantages that accrue to an individual by virtue of his or her sex are direct and for the most part intensified when we take into account the individual's high school experience. Counselor's educational encouragement and curriculum location are two factors that operate to intensify differences between boys and girls; they are also potentially susceptible to manipulation by educational policy makers.

Previous findings of a decline in the level of girls' educational goals relative to boys' as they progress through school were confirmed here, and were partly accounted for by the advice of the counselors and girls' responses to that advice. The major change noted for the class of 1970 compared to earlier cohorts was the elimination of large differences in college enrollment the year after high school. The same factors that account for the similar enrollment patterns by sex may tend to reduce lifetime educational attainment differences as well. One of these factors is the gain, compared to earlier studies, in the importance of ability over class background for women's college enrollment.

Earlier studies have shown women's educational attainment to be more dependent on class background than ability, the reverse of the pattern for men. We can only speculate about the lifetime educational attainment of the class of 1970, but we see that the pattern of class and ability effects on college entry has changed. In 1970, ability more than class determined women's college enrollment; but in total effects neither ability nor class predict college entry as strongly for women as for men.

Factors operating during the high school years, not those decided early on, are more important for women's than men's college decisions and college entry. Some of those factors tend to increase the likelihood of a decision for college entry, such as grades, curriculum location, and peer influence. Others, such as counselor's encouragement, tend to depress the level of decision and college entry for women.

Earlier studies, where women's college enrollment patterns were less well predicted by schooling factors, led researchers to hypothesize that latent influences outside the educational process but related to gender were most influential in the transition from high school to college. Our study does not confirm this hypothesis. We suspect that such factors, especially marriage and parenthood, may become manifest on educational attainment a few years later than was formerly the case. Changing admissions policies in higher education, the emerging importance of community colleges, women's greater ability to control fertility and their stronger desires for career involvement, all operate to increase the likelihood of close similarity in college entry rates for men and women. If these factors have a lasting influence, we look forward to seeing close similarity in the eventual educational attainments of the men and women of the class of 1970.

Only for grades does the total effect of sex exceed that of ability or class as a determinant of school outcomes. As for the direct effects of sex, they are so persistent that for six of the school outcomes they exceed the direct effects of class or ability. Controlling for other variables, the direct effect of sex is stronger than that of class as an influence on counselor's encouragement at tenth and twelfth grades, academic achievement, twelfth-grade educational decisions, and college entry. The direct effect of sex is stronger than that of ability on twelfth-grade peer influence, counselor's encouragement in twelfth grade, senior-year educational decisions, and post-high school college enrollment.

Since six of the twelve school outcomes measured here are more responsive to sex differences than to differences in ability or social-class background in terms of direct effects, we cannot dismiss the continuing influence of sex on the schooling process as trivial. Sex and social-class background are both ascribed criteria not encompassed in ideas about the importance of merit in educational stratification. Social-class background alone may not be as important a factor in the educational stratification process as merit criteria, such as scholastic ability. However, the combined effects of social-class background and sex are more powerful than ability as direct determinants of all but four of the school outcomes. Sex and social-class background combined have larger total effects than ability on six of the twelve outcomes. Ability ranks third to sex and social class as a direct determinant of twelfth-grade educational decisions, and ability ranks third also in its direct effect on college entry, following social class and sex.

When we include sex as a factor in the educational stratification process, our results show that an explanation of that process based on merit and class background as the major determinants of school outcomes must be modified. Ability certainly outweighs social-class background in total effects on educational decisions and college entry for both boys and girls; this was demonstrated in the two preceding chapters, where total effects were estimated separately for each sex. Also demonstrated in those chapters was the power of the schooling process as a mediator of class and ability effects. The total effects of sex on educational decisions and college entry are generally smaller than those of ability and class, but the result is a persistent direct effect of sex, often outweighing those of class and ability, throughout the educational stratification process.

NOTES

1. Oppenheimer's review of the sex segregation of jobs and Fuch's most recent analysis of wage differentials by sex are examples of studies that show large discrepancies in labor-force outcomes for men and women. Valerie Oppenheimer, *The Female Labor Force in the United States* (Berkeley: Institute of International Studies, University of California, 1970); Victor R. Fuchs, "Differences in Hourly Earnings Between Men and Women," *Monthly Labor Review* 94 (May 1971): 9–15.

2. See, for example, Gillespie's review essay of conjugal power studies, and the references cited therein. Dair L. Gillespie, "Who Has the Power? The Marital Struggle," *Journal of Marriage and the Family* 33 (August 1971): 445–66.

3. The most influential recent investigation of inequality in educational and occupational attainment, C. Jencks' et al., *Inequality: A Reassessment of the Effects of Family and Schooling in America* (New York: Basic Books, 1972), employs data for males only. A recent example of a mixed-sex population analyzed as if an identical process operates for boys and girls is Barbara Heynes' "Social Selection and Stratification Within Schools," *American Journal of Sociology* 79 (May 1974): 1434–51.

4. W. H. Sewell and V. P. Shah, "Socioeconomic Status, Intelligence, and the Attainment of Higher Education," *Sociology of Education* 40 (Winter 1967): 1–23; K. Alexander and B. K. Eckland, "Sex Differences in the Educational Attainment Process," *American Sociological Review* 39, no. 5 (1974): 668–82.

5. Sewell and Shah, p. 669.

6. Alexander and Eckland, "Sex Differences," 674–75. By main effects we refer to the total effects of sex ($q_{i,\text{sex}}$) and the direct effects of sex ($p_{i,\text{sex}}$) estimated from data for both sexes combined; sex is included as an additional exogenous or predetermined variable along with social class and scholastic ability.

7. Two of the many recent works documenting sex biases of school personnel are Judith Stacey and J. Daniels, *And Jill Came Tumbling*

After: Sexism in American Education (New York: Dell, 1974); and A. Fishel and J. Pottger, eds., *Sex Bias in the Schools: The Research Evidence* (Teaneck, N.J.: Fairleigh Dickinson University Press, 1975).

8.   Deana Logan, "Sex Differences in Adolescents' Goals and Expectations: Some Implications for Educators" (Paper presented at the 1975 annual meeting of the American Educational Research Association, Washington, D.C.).

9.   E. Douvan and J. Adelson, *The Adolescent Experience* (New York: Wiley, 1966).

10.   Dean Knudsen, "The Declining Status of Women: Popular Myths and the Failure of Functionalist Thought," *Social Forces* 48 (December 1969): 183–93.

11.   K. A. Simon and M. M. Frankel, *Projections of Educational Statistics to 1980–81,* 1971 edition (Washington, D.C.: U.S. Department of Health, Education, and Welfare, Office of Education, National Center for Educational Statistics, 1972.

12.   Ibid., p. 158.

13.   Suppose, for example, that a path coefficient less than .10 is deemed trivial, and the respective coefficients for boys and girls are .08 and .11. By deleting the trivial path of .08 and reestimating the trimmed model, we may erroneously assume a nontrivial interaction effect of .11 − .00 = .11 instead of the more accurate but unimportant effect of .11 − .08 = .03. In a study such as this one where the number of cases is large and represents in effect a case study of an entire population, not a probability sample, the nontriviality of effects is determined by substantive and theoretical considerations and not by statistical criteria. Therefore, our comparisons between sex groups are made on untrimmed models, and no tests of significance are reported.

9. Conclusions and Implications

From the beginning, the primary objective of our analysis has been to assess the empirical tenabilities of two contrasting theses of schooling in the United States: the revisionist and the meritocratic.

Inequalities in schooling, Samuel Bowles has written, "are part of the web of capitalist society," and are likely to persist as long as capitalism survives." [1] The origin of these inequalities in schooling lies "in the class structure of the larger society itself and in the class subcultures typical of capitalist societies." [2] Schools socialize successive generations of youth into an uncritical acceptance of inequality. And through their organizational structure and educational processes, schools distribute youth, generation after generation, into social positions in the class hierarchy roughly equivalent to those occupied by their parents. Elites in a capitalist society manage to ensure generational continuity of privilege through social inheritance, legitimated and certified by the school. Wealth, power, and privilege permit elites to define the rules of the schooling game, rules they have written so as to all but ensure the victory of their children, often at the expense of those less privileged and fortunate. Moreover, those of less privilege and fortune often accept their losses with equanimity because they have been beguiled into believing that the rules of the game are fair and just.

Within the schools, social-class origin is the primary axis along which youth are differentiated, or so argue the revisionists. Several mechanisms facilitate the differentiation of students along the lines of class origin. The existence of different curricula is one vehicle by which schools can perpetuate existing class distinctions. Students from middle- and upper-class homes receive preferential consideration for location in the academic program; students from working- and lower-class homes are shunted into the nonacademic program.

Guidance counseling is another vehicle that ensures the generational continuity of social class. Middle- and upper-class students are encouraged by their counselors to enter college; working- and lower-class students are encouraged to enter the labor market. Still another mechanism by which the schools help to perpetuate inequalities is through the procedure of testing and grading. Only in appearance is the academic evaluation procedure fair. In reality, argue the revisionists, standardized testing and teacher grading favor upper- and middle-class students at the expense of those from the working and lower classes. This is because decisions about testing and learning are made by members of the middle and upper classes. As members of boards of education, and as executives and professional personnel with the corporations that print textbooks and prepare the standardized examinations used in the schools, these individuals make decisions that create learning and testing environments that emphasize knowledge and skills possessed in greater quantity by students from privileged backgrounds. The result of this systematic process of class discrimination, assert the revisionists, is that social class becomes the most important variable in determining how far the individual will go in school. This has been the situation in the past; it is the situation in the present. And as long as capitalism survives, it will be the situation into the future. "The number of years of schooling attained by a child," writes Bowles, "depends upon the social-class standing of his father at least as much in the recent period as it did fifty years ago." [3]

Proponents of the meritocratic thesis are convinced by the results of their empirical research that scholastic ability, educational ambition, and academic achievement are at least as important as social class, if not more so, in the schooling process. Most of the proponents of this thesis are acutely aware of the presence of social-class bias in schooling; few, however, have argued that the roots of that bias are a permanent fixture of an exploitative capitalist system. Almost all the proponents of this thesis advocate programs and policies that would either reduce or eliminate social-class bias in the schools.

In their various inquiries into the schooling process, meritocratic social scientists have identified curriculum location, counselor (or teacher) educational encouragement, and academic achievement as important mechanisms by which the schools select and sort individuals in preparation for various postsecondary educational and occupational careers. Each of these mechanisms they have found to be affected by the social class of the student. Middle-class students have more of a chance than working-class students to be located in the academic program, but the class differential in curriculum location has not been found to be *strong*. Equally important is the fact that scholastic ability affects curriculum location at least as much as does social class. Similarly, educational encouragement to college by school guidance counselors and teachers has been found to be affected by the social class of the student. But it also has been found to be affected at least as much by scholastic ability, academic achievement, and student educational ambition. And, while academic achievement does vary with social origins, that variation is usually much weaker than are the variations in achievement that can be attributed to differences in scholastic ability and educational ambition. Finally, proponents of the meritocratic thesis agree with proponents of the revisionist thesis that graduation from high school and entry into a two- or four-year college is contingent upon social-class origin. Proponents of the meritocratic thesis do *not* agree, however, that social class is the most important determinant of how far the individual will go in school. At least as important as social class in the determination of ultimate educational attainment is scholastic ability, educational ambition, educational decision of the student, and academic performance.

RESULTS OF OUR INQUIRY

In our assessment of the empirical tenabilities of the revisionist and meritocratic theses, we have evaluated data from several thousand New York students surveyed at four different points in time beginning in ninth grade in 1967, followed by tenth grade in 1968, twelfth grade in 1970, and ending with a post-high school survey in in 1970–71.

In ninth grade our major interest was in the determinants of two outcomes related to the schooling process: *curriculum location* and *educational ambition*. Location in the academic program by the end of ninth grade for all our students depended more on superior scholastic ability than upon the privilege of social class. Moreover, for males, location in the academic program depended more on perceived parental educational influence that it did on social class. For girls, location in the academic program depended as much on perceived parental educational influence as it did upon social class. Educational ambition, an indicator of the student's motivation to use formal schooling as an instrument either to move up in the social-class hierarchy or to maintain an already privileged position in that hierarchy, was found to be dependent less on scholastic ability or on perceived parental educational influence than it was upon social-class origin. Evidence from ninth grade, then, is mixed: location in the college-preparatory program was determined more by merit than by class, but ambition to enter college was determined more by class than by merit.

In tenth grade, *curriculum location* was again an object of inquiry, but so was *perceived educational encouragement* from the guidance counselor. In tenth grade, as in ninth, location in the academic program depended more on ability than on class. In grade ten, however, curriculum location was most strongly determined by its temporal counterpart in grade nine. Continuity in either the academic or nonacademic programs over grades nine and ten was found to be very high. Such stability was more pronounced, however, for students who, as ninth graders, had been in the college-preparatory program. Among those ninth graders who had been in the non-college-preparatory program, there was some tendency to move "upward" into the college-preparatory program by the end of tenth grade. This tendency was most pronounced among those who had an educational ambition to a four-year college, a bit less pronounced among those with above-average scholastic ability, and least pronounced among those of the middle class. As it did with curriculum location in grade nine, perceived parental educational influence played a comparatively large role in curriculum location in grade ten, ranking above the effect of social class for males but below the effect of social class for females. Educational ambition also had an effect on curriculum location in grade ten. In fact, for males, an ambition to college measured at the end of ninth grade had more to do with being in the college-preparatory program at the end of tenth grade than did social class of origin.

Contrary to allegations by some revisionists, the encouragement of students by the guidance counselor to continue education beyond high school was found to be conditioned by scholastic ability to a far greater degree than by social class. In fact, we interpreted the lack of a direct class effect on perceived counselor educational encouragement as indicating a lack of overt class discrimination in the career counseling process. More important also than social class as a determinant of counselor educational encouragement in tenth grade was the educational ambition that the student had expressed at the end of ninth grade (and which, presumably, he had carried with him into tenth grade). Curriculum location also affected the educational encouragement attributed to the counselor by the student: location in the academic program increased the likelihood that the student would report being encouraged by the counselor to go to college, especially if the student were female. At least in terms of curriculum location and counselor educational encouragement, the evidence from tenth grade is more definitive than was that from ninth grade. Being in the college-preparatory program by the end of tenth grade and reporting that the school counselor had encouraged entry into college each depended more upon the merit of the student than upon his social class.

Academic achievement, measured as the student's cumulative grade-point average from the ninth to the eleventh year, was our next criterion. Achievement, we found, reflected much more of the student's scholastic ability and educational ambition than it did social class of origin. Achievement even reflected more of the educational encouragement the student reported receiving from the guidance counselor than it did the impact of social class. And what comparatively limited impact social class did have on achievement was indirect. No evidence, therefore, was found that would indicate that in the distribution of classroom grades, teachers overtly discriminate in favor of students from the middle class. Moreover, the lack of a direct effect from social class to academic achievement lends no support at all to the revisionist's contention that the form and content of the evaluation process is biased against students from less privileged social circumstances.

By the end of twelfth grade, the educational die is pretty well cast. Class, ability, parent and peer influence, curriculum location, counselor encouragement, educational ambition, and academic achievement each have had an influence on the *decision* of the student to seek entry into the labor force or into college. Most influential in that decision was scholastic ability. Indeed, ability was more influential in the decision to enter the labor force or college (measured toward the end of twelfth grade) than it was in the ambition to enter the labor force or college (measured toward the end of ninth grade), especially for males. Just as influential as ability in that decision for males, but a bit less so for females, was the motivational construct of educational ambition. Encouragement received from the guidance counselor in twelfth grade (itself largely free from the effects of social class) was, for females, just as important as an educational ambition for college in grade nine. And just below educational ambition fell academic achievement as a determinant of the decision a female will make about her postsecondary educational career. For males, then, the decision to enter college or the labor market depended more on scholastic ability and on educational ambition than it did on social class. For females, the decision to enter college or the labor market depended more on scholastic ability, educational ambition, twelfth-grade educational encouragement from the counselor, and academic achievement than it did on social class. In the final year of high school, merit more than class determined that most critical of decisions all seniors must make: whether to continue their formal education. Moreover, over the secondary school period, we noted an increase in the total effect that ability had on the educational goals of students. The total effect that scholastic ability had on the educational decisions of students by the end of twelfth grade was higher than that which it had on the educational ambition of students by the end of ninth grade. By contrast, over that same period of time, the total effect of social class declined.

Actual *entry into college* was the ultimate dependent variable of our inquiry. For parents, teachers, school administrators, many students, and often the community at large, going to college represents the consummation of the elementary and secondary schooling experiences. For the individual student, of course, entry into college may well be the beginning of a career that will be capped by a professional or executive occupation, a position from which control and authority can be exercised over the institutions of a modern industrial society.

Given the very high correlation between college entry and college completion, entry into college can be construed as a proxy for educational attainment. Under that assumption, we found almost no evidence to support the revisionist contention that the most important variable in predicting how far a person will go in school is social class. More important than social class in the determination of entry into college were the decision to enter college, academic achievement, and scholastic ability. In fact, social class played less of a role in actual entry into college after twelfth grade than it did in the student's ambition to enter college expressed at the end of ninth grade.

Within our sample of several thousand students, then, it was individual merit more than family social class that influenced progress from grade nine to grade twelve and subsequent entry into college or the labor market. We were able to find little empirical support for the propositions advanced by advocates of the revisionist thesis regarding social class and schooling in the United States.

BEYOND OUR STUDY

Specific though they may be to our sample of youth, restricted in both space and time, these findings constitute further evidence that merit is dominant over class as a determinant of progress within the educational system.

Within the secondary level studied in our analysis, it was merit more than class that determined curriculum location, counselor encouragement, academic achievement, and the decision to continue schooling beyond the twelfth grade. The implications of such findings have been expressed cogently by Hauser in his concluding remarks to his study of socioeconomic background and educational performance among Nashville youth:

> Our results present a picture of the relationship between family origin and educational performance quite different from that which sociologists sometimes draw. The contrast is one between a relatively loose process of stratification in which achievement is the primary mode of ascent or descent, and a rather tight process in which ascriptive treatment . . . perpetuates past inequalities. The present results appear to substantiate the view of the process of stratification as rather loose.[4]

Although we have little systematic evidence at our command that would enable us to infer whether, in point of fact, the role of social class *at the secondary level* has been declining since, say, the end of World War II, our suspicion is that it has. Class is not now overly important at the secondary level. This is primarily because the educational "center of gravity" has shifted upward from the secondary school to the college. Currently, among high-school-age youth, more than 90 percent are in high school; almost 80 percent complete high school, and among high school graduates, about 60 percent enter a degree-credit program in some college or university.[5] The virtual universality of a high school education, coupled with the substantial increase in college attendance, has diminished the importance of the high school as a sorter and allocator of individuals to the educational or occupational marketplace. In discussing the implications of this trend for social selection in the future, Karabel and Astin conjecture: "As more and more students enter higher education, the college-noncollege dichotomy will become increasingly anachronistic and the sorting of people *within* higher education will take on even greater importance." [6]

For the present, however, there are certain social scientists who will maintain that social selection *now* occurs at the time of college entry. They argue that upper-middle-class and middle-class students are considerably more likely to enter a high prestige university while working-class and lower-middle-class students populate the poorer-quality four-year institutions and two-year community colleges. Other social scientists extend this argument with the proposition that the probability of graduation from college favors students from upper- and middle-class families. Finally, those who argue that social class is stronger than individual merit in determining the quality of the college a student attends propose, as a corollary, that college quality is a major medium through which upper- and middle-class parents transmit their social and economic advantages to their offspring: the higher the social class of the family, the higher the quality of the college attended by the student; the higher the quality of the college attended by the student, the higher will be that individual's subsequent occupational status and earnings. Social selectivity by social class or by merit at the postsecondary level thus involves three questions: Is the quality of the college a student attends dependent more upon individual social class or on merit? Is the probability of college graduation dependent more on individual social class or on merit? And to what extent does the quality of the college attended serve as a medium through which the social class of the family is transmitted to the individual's subsequent occupational status and annual earnings?

With the singularly important exception of elite colleges where access still strongly favors students of privileged-class origins (but who comprise less than 3 percent of college students), Karabel and Astin have concluded that access to colleges of varying quality depends more on individual merit than on family social class. With data from 22,000 students representing 180 postsecondary institutions in 1966–67, and with college quality defined as selectivity (determined by the average academic aptitude of entering freshmen, "probably the best single measure of prestige in that it indicates a school's capacity to attract students of high ability"), Karabel and Astin were led to infer from their elaborate statistical analysis:

> Though the data show that the system of higher education is not purely meritocratic (i.e., SES has some independent relationship to quality of college attended) and that meritocratic standards themselves tend to favor the student of high social status, there is no gainsaying the predominantly meritocratic character of the process by which students are sorted into colleges of varying rank.[7]

Graduation from college also appears to depend somewhat more on individual merit than on family social class. With data from male Wisconsin high school seniors, class of 1957, who had attended college between 1957 and 1964, Wegner and Sewell found from their regression analyses that "rank in high school class clearly makes the greatest independent contribution to predicting graduation, followed by socioeconomic status, intelligence, and finally occupational aspiration."[8] Moreover, inspection of their published standardized regression coefficients reveals that the independent contribution of high school rank to college graduation is 2.6 times larger than that of social class. And, had Wegner and Sewell considered the indirect effect that intelligence has on graduation by way of high school rank, the total effect of IQ most likely would have exceeded that of social class.

Data from Sewell's Wisconsin sample of high school seniors, class of 1957, have been used by Alwin to address the question: "To what extent does choice of college represent a mechanism through which families pass on relative socioeconomic advantage to their offspring?"[9] By choice of college, Alwin means the prestige ranking of colleges attended by the men in the Wisconsin sample. As a prelude to a summary of his analyses, Alwin sounds a note of warning to those who would attribute large differences in occupational status or earnings to differences in the prestige ranking of colleges. Much of the variance in occupational status and in earnings, he notes, occurs among individuals *within* colleges, *not between* colleges rank-ordered on a dimension of prestige or selectivity. "We are cautioned by these results to be less than optimistic regarding the powerful role of college quality differences in the achievement process," says Alwin.[10] Thus forewarned, Alwin's conclusion is not surprising. Once appropriate statistical adjustments have been made for selection-recruitment differences among colleges of varying types, choice of college, that is, institutional prestige, is not a major mediator of parental socioeconimic status to the subsequent occupational status and annual earnings of the student.[11]

> With the possible exception of the earnings outcome, we believe that the analyses presented here provide a firm basis for a somewhat more skeptical view of the importance of college differences, especially college quality, on educational and socioeconomic achievements.[12]

On the specific issue of college selectivity as a vehicle by which parents might seek to transmit their economic advantages to their offspring, Alwin, along with Hauser and Sewell, again using the Wisconsin data, states bluntly:

> Less than ten percent of the effect of father's income on son's earnings could be attributed to the different colleges attended by sons of rich and poor families. Thus, "the old school tie" is not the connecting link between father's income and son's earnings.[13]

Several elaborate statistical inquiries into the relative effects of social class and merit at the high school and at the college level thus support the proposition that merit is the dominant determinant of student progress and access.

Within the context of the present, then, the evidence suggests that social class exercises a rather modest effect *within* the high school as well as at the *juncture* between high school and college and that college quality is *not* an efficient medium through which parents can transmit their social and economic advantages to their offspring.

In point of fact, when cast in a somewhat longer time perspective, our findings with respect to the modest role of social class in the contemporary schooling process appear to be a manifestation of a longer-term trend toward the diminution of social class in the entire schooling process. Evidence of this trend is most persuasive for the United States, largely because of the advanced state of survey design and analysis in this country, the method that produces much of the data on which the inference is predicated. We shall also see that the role of social class as a determinant of educational attainment has diminished in Europe since the end of World War II.

For the United States, initial indications of a drop in the degree to which class determines educational attainment were evident in a paper by Alexander and Eckland. With data from both Blau and Duncan's 1962 national probability sample of 20,000 U.S. males and from their own 1970 national probability sample of almost a thousand men who had been high school sophomores in 1955, Alexander and Eckland noted that the younger the cohort of men, the less the degree to which their educational attainment depended upon their social-class origins.[14]

More recently, Hauser and Featherman have examined the relationship between educational attainment and social background using national probability data from surveys conducted in 1962 and 1973. For each of nine five-year age cohorts of men, ranging from those born between 1907 and 1911 to those born during 1947 and 1951, they regressed educational attainment on eight social background variables, including occupation and education of father.[15] Among their conclusions:

1. Schooling is less dependent on social background in recent cohorts.
2. Inequality of schooling has declined among persons who are similar in respect to their social origins.
3. Thus, "both between and within significant social categories, inequality of access to schooling appears to have declined."[16]

From Europe, evidence of a decline in the dependence of educational attainment on class origin comes from the French social scientist Raymond Boudon and from a seminar on education, inequality, and life chances sponsored by the Organization for Economic Cooperation and Development. Defining the dependence of educational attainment on class origin as "inequality of educational opportunity" (IEO), Boudon writes that "strong empirical evidence suggests that [IEO] decreases over time in most industrial societies." [17] Equally succinct are the conclusions reached by Georg Busch of the OECD Secretariat. Updating earlier work by OECD on social selection in education, Busch concludes that while the ascribed attribute of social class still continues to affect access to education in all OECD countries, "inequality in access has been reduced everywhere. . . ." [18] However, in regard to that other ascriptive characteristic, sex, Busch cautions that "the limited evidence available by sex suggests that there is general discrimination against females in access to higher education." [19]

Virtually all the evidence we have reviewed, our own included, suggests that revisionist assertions regarding the strong and dominant role of social class in the progress of the individual through school and in the ultimate educational attainment of the individual are without empirical foundation. Indeed, those assertions are contrary to fact.

Empirically, then, the role of social class in the progress of the student through school is modest and probably declining, and the role of social class in the ultimate educational attainment of the individual is modest and definitely declining. Does this limited and diminishing effect of social class in the schooling system, and the stronger and increasing role of merit, imply that those who fail to win a coveted educational prize, such as entry to the university, will now accept their loss with greater equanimity? And does the apparently increasing role of merit within the schooling system signal a comparably increasing role of merit within the larger social system?

Psychologically, the gradual replacement of social class with merit as the more important determinant of progress within the educational system apparently does not ease the burden of individual failure. Indeed, it may be more injurious to the individual to accept a failure for which he believes no one but himself is responsible than to believe some system cause is the reason for his failure. Evidence on this issue is, to our knowledge, largely anecdotal. Informative, however, is the following remark attributed by a reporter for the *New York Times* to a Swedish university professor. Commenting on how students respond upon learning that they have failed to enter the highly merito-

cratic college and university system of that country, where achievement is almost the sole criterion for access, the professor observed:

> We have a situation in which two-thirds of young people feel they
> have failed. And they can't blame the social system, they can only
> feel inferior. This creates a far fiercer kind of alienation, a far harsher
> class system than the old divisions by wealth.[20]

Finally, does an increasingly meritocratic educational system imply
an increasingly meritocratic social system? If we would define the
larger social system as increasingly meritocratic the more income and
occupation come to depend upon educational attainment independently of social class, then the answer is in the affirmative. The
data are now all but compelling in support of the proposition that
occupational attainment has become increasingly dependent upon
educational attainment, independently of social class.[21] In a larger,
more theoretical sense, of course, Daniel Bell has argued that the
very nature of the modern postindustrial society thrusts it toward
being increasingly meritocratic.

> The post-industrial society, in its initial logic, is a meritocracy. Dif-
> ferential status and differential income are based on technical skills
> and higher education. Without those achievements one cannot fulfill
> the requirements of the new social division of labor which is a feature
> of that society.[22]

Bell is quick to recognize that as the total society becomes increasingly more meritocratic, ". . . the university, which once reflected the status system of the society, has now become the arbiter
of class position. As the gatekeeper, it has gained a quasi-monopoly
in determining the future stratification of the society." [23] The problem is, as Torsten Husén has noted, that "the educational system
in a modern society on the threshold of the post-industrial era, is
'one-dimensional' in the sense that one uniform, linear standard

(bright, average, slow student) is applied." [24] While we may quibble with Husén over the question of whether the educational system in a postindustrial society is "one" or "several" dimensional, the fact remains that among the most influential of those dimensions is scholastic ability. And ability, to a varying but not insignificant degree, is an ascribed characteristic of the individual, just as is social class.[25] Moreover, the other merit determinants of entry to the university, such as ambition, academic achievement, and the like, are at least partially social in origin and, with the environmental component of scholastic ability, thus are subject to the efforts of parents who themselves have achieved positions of power and influence in a meritocratic society to pass along the benefits of their privileged position through efforts at the effective socialization of their children. A meritocratic social system, then, does not eliminate social classes. It merely changes the criteria upon which class distinctions are based. Thus the question of the criteria upon which individuals are to be judged, sorted, and allocated into the social system is an issue that shall continue to confront the members of a truly meritocratic society. It is an issue, a problem, that the British economist, social philosopher, and advocate of things and systems small, E. F. Schumacher, would characterize as "divergent" rather than as "convergent." Divergent problems, contends Schumacher, are not amenable to solution through logical reasoning. They are not the problems of science and mathematics. By their very nature, divergent problems are those which "force man to strain himself to a level above himself; they demand, and thus provoke, the supply of, forces from a higher level, thus bringing love, beauty, goodness, and truth into our lives." [26] Divergent problems are, in the truest sense of the term, the real problems of education, which to cite Schumacher once again, is that complex set of processes involving "the transmission of ideas which enable man to choose between one thing and another." [27]

It is ironic, then, that a text that began with a scientifically tractable problem concerned more with schooling than with education ends with a problem that is amenable not to scientific but to moral and political resolution. The idea that we have sought to transmit is that social class is no longer the dominant force in schooling; merit has emerged as the larger determinant of the individual's progress through the school and of his or her ultimate schooling attainment. The choice with which we are left is whether, in a social system based primarily on merit, we ought, as J. R. Gass of OECD has in point of fact advocated,[28] seek to expand the range of talents, abilities, and attitudes used to select and allocate individuals in a way that will no longer prejudge what the system wants in a manner that serves the interests of existing elites.

NOTES

1. Samuel Bowles, "Unequal Education and the Reproduction of the Social Division of Labor," in *Schooling in a Corporate Society*, ed. Martin Carnoy (New York: McKay, 1972), p. 37.

2. Ibid.

3. Ibid., p. 52.

4. Robert Mason Hauser, *Socioeconomic Background and Educational Performance* (Washington, D.C.: Rose Monograph Series, American Sociological Association, 1971), p. 155.

5. Department of Health, Education, and Welfare, Office of Education, *Digest of Educational Statistics, 1971* (Washington, D.C.: Government Printing Office, 1971), pp. xi–xii.

6. Jerome Karabel and Alexander W. Astin, "Social Class, Academic Ability, and College 'Quality,'" *Social Forces* 53 (March 1975): 381.

7. Ibid., p. 394.

8. Eldon L. Wegner and William H. Sewell, "Selection and Context as Factors Affecting the Probability of Graduation from College," *American Journal of Sociology* 75 (January 1970): 671.

9. Duane F. Alwin, "Socioeconomic Background, Colleges, and Post-Collegiate Achievements," in *Schooling and Achievement in American Society*, ed. William H. Sewell, Robert M. Hauser, and David L. Featherman (New York: Academic Press, 1976), p. 346.

10. Ibid., p. 370.

11. Ibid.

12. Ibid.

13. Duane F. Alwin, Robert M. Hauser, and William H. Sewell, "Colleges," in William H. Sewell and Robert M. Hauser, *Education, Occupation, and Earnings: Achievement in the Early Career* (Madison: University of Wisconsin, Department of Sociology, 1974), p. 184.

14. Karl L. Alexander and Bruce K. Eckland, "Basic Attainment

Processes: A Replication and Extension," *Sociology of Education* 48 (Fall 1975): 457–95.

15. Robert M. Hauser and David L. Featherman, "Equality of Schooling: Trends and Prospects," *Sociology of Education* 49 (April 1976): 99–120. The eight social background variables are: (1) father's education, (2) father's occupation, (3) farm background, (4) number of siblings, (5) broken family, (6) southern origin, (7) Spanish origin, and (8) race. See p. 109.

16. Ibid., p. 108.

17. Raymond Boudon, *Education, Opportunity, and Social Inequality* (New York: Wiley, 1973), p. 110.

18. Georg Busch, "Inequality of Educational Opportunity by Social Origin in Higher Education," in Organization for Economic Cooperation and Development, *Education, Inequality, and Life Chances* (Paris: OECD, 1975), 1:163.

19. Ibid.

20. "Swedes, Flourishing, Feel Guilty About Their Wealth and Debate Obligations to Others," *New York Times*, 26 December 1974, p. 12.

21. See, for example, Alexander and Eckland, "Basic Attainment Processes"; see also Peter M. Blau and Otis Dudley Duncan, *The American Occupational Structure* (New York: Wiley, 1976), p. 180.

22. Daniel Bell, *The Coming of Post-Industrial Society* (New York: Basic Books, 1973), p. 409.

23. Ibid., p. 410.

24. Torsten Husén, "Strategies for Educational Quality," in OECD, *Education, Inequality, and Life Chances*, p. 319.

25. See, for example, Appendix A, "Estimating the Heritability of I.Q. Scores," in Christopher Jencks, et al., *Inequality* (New York: Basic Books, 1972), pp. 266–319.

26. E. F. Schumacher, *Small Is Beautiful* (New York: Harper & Row, 1973), p. 90. Schumacher attributes the distinction and

definition of these concepts to G. N. M. Tyrell but provides no citation.

27.   Ibid., p. 79.

28.   J. R. Gass, "The Equality Issue in Relation to Other OECD Work in the Social Field," in OECD, *Education, Inequality, and Life Chances*, p. 8.

APPENDIX A
Survey
Questionnaires

GRADE NINE: Spring 1967

(NUMERIC)

SURVEY OF CAREER PREFERENCES

(LAST NAME)

**PLEASE
PRINT**

(FULL NAME OF YOUR SCHOOL)

(FIRST NAME)

(NAME OF CITY OR TOWN)

PURPOSE OF THE RESEARCH

This study is being conducted in many high schools. The purpose of the study is to learn about the educational and occupational interests of students. These interests have important consequences not only for you as an individual but also for the society in which we live. In addition to learning about your own educational and occupational interests, the study seeks to learn some of the reasons why different people have different educational and occupational interests. If we can learn some of these reasons, then it may be possible to know several years ahead of time whether there are going to be too many or too few classrooms or whether in the future there is going to be a shortage of physicists, automobile mechanics, and telephone operators as there is in the country today. Of course, there are many and complicated reasons for people having different kinds of educational and occupational interests. This is why there are many different kinds of items in this questionnaire. By reading each item in the questionnaire carefully and by answering each item honestly, you can personally help to make this survey a true reflection of the interests of high school students.

THIS IS NOT A TEST. There are no right or wrong answers. There are only responses which are frank and honest. *No one in your school or your community will ever see your questionnaire or your responses.* Please answer each item to the best of your ability. Please answer each item frankly and honestly.

INSTRUCTIONS

I. A number of items use the terms "mother", "father", "sister", and "brother". If you are currently living with your natural mother and father and natural brother and sister, these terms should be taken to mean your natural parents and natural brothers and sisters. If you are not currently living with your natural mother or father, or with your natural brothers and sisters, then the terms should be taken to mean your *step*-mother, *step*-father, male guardian, or female guardian, *step*-brother, or *step*-sister.

II. READ ALL INSTRUCTIONS very carefully, especially those instructions on page 4.

III. A few items ask you to write several words. *Please write very clearly.*

IV. If you have a problem, raise your hand and a research worker will come to your place and assist you. *Please continue to answer the items with which you have no problem until the research worker comes to your place.* Otherwise, you will not finish on time.

V. GIRLS: In answering the items on occupations, you should think of "housewife" as an occupation.

〜

SAMPLE ITEM

Most of the items in the questionnaire can be answered by placing an (X) in the parenthesis to the left of the response choice which you select as your answer.

A sample item would be:

75. Which sport do you like best?

   1. ( ) Tennis   4. ( ) Hockey
   2. (X) Football   5. ( ) Golf
   3. ( ) Basketball   6. ( ) Baseball

The person responding to this item liked football best so he placed an (X) in the bracket to the left of the response choice which said "football."

Thank You: You May Now Turn To Page Two and Begin.

—1—

267

CARD ONE

16. **How old are you today?**
1. ( ) 13 years   5. ( ) 17 years
2. ( ) 14 years   6. ( ) 18 years
3. ( ) 15 years   7. ( ) 19 years
4. ( ) 16 years   8. ( ) 20 years or more

17. **What is your sex?**
1. ( ) Male
2. ( ) Female

Are your mother and father now living?
1. ( ) Both are living.
2. ( ) Only my father is living.
3. ( ) Only my mother is living.
4. ( ) Neither parent is living.

18-20. **What are the ages of EACH ONE of your brothers and sisters?** NOTE: If you have no brothers and/or no sisters, place a checkmark in the category "No brothers," or "No sisters."

Brothers   Sisters

_____   _____
_____   *Oldest*   _____
_____   *to*   _____
_____   *Youngest*   _____
_____   _____
_____   _____

No Brothers ( )   No Sisters ( )

21. **What kind of program are you taking in school?**
1. ( ) Academic or College Prep.
2. ( ) Science
3. ( ) General
4. ( ) Commercial or Business
5. ( ) Vocational Agriculture
6. ( ) Vocational Industrial Arts
7. ( ) Other (Specify: _____)

22. **How important is it for you to be an athlete in school?**
1. ( ) It is *not important* to me personally that I be an athlete in school
2. ( ) It is *somewhat important* to me personally that I be an athlete in school
3. ( ) It is *very important* to me personally that I be an athlete in school

23. **With whom do you live?**
1. ( ) With both my father and mother
2. ( ) With only my father
3. ( ) With only my mother
4. ( ) With my father and *step*-mother
5. ( ) With my mother and *step*-father

(Continued in next column)

6. ( ) With my aunt and/or uncle
7. ( ) With my grandparents
8. ( ) With other relatives or guardians
9. ( ) Other (Specify: _____)

24. **On the average, how much time do you spend doing homework outside of school,** like late in the afternoon, at night, etc.?
1. ( ) none, or almost none
2. ( ) less than ½ hour a day
3. ( ) about ½ to ¾ hours a day
4. ( ) about 1 hour a day
5. ( ) about 1½ to 1¾ hours a day
6. ( ) about 2 hours a day
7. ( ) about 3 or more hours a day

25-27. **How far did your father go in school?**
01. ( ) He has no formal schooling
02. ( ) He did not go any further than sixth grade in elementary school
03. ( ) He did not go any further than ninth grade in high school
04. ( ) He did not go any further than eleventh grade in high school
05. ( ) He finished high school
06. ( ) He went to trade or technical school but did not finish
07. ( ) He finished trade or technical school
08. ( ) He went to business school but did not finish
09. ( ) He finished business school
10. ( ) He went to college but did not finish
11. ( ) He finished college
12. ( ) He went to graduate or professional school but did not finish
13. ( ) He finished graduate professional school
14. ( ) Do not know

28-47. **Of all the boys in your grade, which boy:**
(You may name the same person more than once.)

	His First Name	His Last Name
1. Is the best athlete?	_____	_____
2. Is the best student?	_____	_____
3. Do the girls like the best?	_____	_____
4. Would you most like to be friends with?	_____	_____

48. **How often do you attend a worship service in a church, temple, or synagogue?**
1. ( ) Never
2. ( ) Seldom
3. ( ) Several times a year
4. ( ) About once a month
5. ( ) Two or three times a month
6. ( ) About once a week
7. ( ) More than once a week

49. **Generally, when your father makes decisions which concern you or when he makes rules for you to follow, does he explain to you the reasons for the decisions or for the rules?**
   1. ( ) He *almost never* explains his decisions or rules to me
   2. ( ) He *once in a while* explains his decisions or rules to me
   3. ( ) He *usually* explains his decisions or rules to me
   4. ( ) He *almost always* explains his decisions or rules to me

   What sort of things does it take to give a student importance, prestige, influence, etc., with other students in your school?, i.e., good grades, coming from the right family, being an athlete, etc. Try to name at least three, from first to third most important.

50. 1st most important: _____
51. 2nd most important: _____
52. 3rd most important: _____
53. 4th most important: _____

54-55. **What is the religious preference of your father?** NOTE: Please be as precise as possible in giving the specific religious preference of your father. Example: Baptist, Methodist, Roman Catholic, Reform Jewish, United Church of Christ, etc.

_____

Religious Preference of Father

56. **Regardless of what other students think, how do you personally feel about a good student being an athlete?**
   1. ( ) I don't think that a good student should be an athlete
   2. ( ) It doesn't make any difference to me whether a good student is an athlete
   3. ( ) I think it is somewhat important that a good student be an athlete
   4. ( ) I think it is very important that a good student be an athlete

57. **How often does your father attend a worship service in a church, temple, or synagogue?**
   1. ( ) Never
   2. ( ) Seldom
   3. ( ) Several times a year
   4. ( ) About once a month
   5. ( ) Two or three times a month
   6. ( ) About once a week
   7. ( ) More than once a week

58. **During the last few years or so, has your father wanted you to continue your education beyond high school,** that is, to go to a trade or business school, to college, etc.?
   1. ( ) Yes, he has stressed it a lot
   2. ( ) Yes, he has stressed it somewhat
   3. ( ) Yes, but he has seldom mentioned it
   4. ( ) He hasn't said one way or the other
   5. ( ) No, he would rather that I did not go beyond high school

59. **Generally, over the past 5 to 8 years or so, how often have your parents praised or rewarded you when you did something very well?**
   1. ( ) Hardly at all
   2. ( ) Sometimes
   3. ( ) Fairly often
   4. ( ) Very often
   5. ( ) Almost every time

60. **Generally, which one of the following statements best describes how students in your school feel about athletes being good students and good students being athletes?**
   1. ( ) They feel it doesn't matter if an athlete is a good student or if a good student is an athlete
   2. ( ) They feel a good student should be an athlete, but it doesn't matter if an athlete is a good student
   3. ( ) They feel an athlete should be a good student, but it doesn't matter if a good student is an athlete
   4. ( ) They feel that an athlete should be a good student and that a good student should be an athlete

Here are five statements about yourself. After you read each statement, indicate how strongly you agree or disagree with it by placing an "X" in the appropriate box.

61. **I feel that I have a number of good qualities.**
   1. ( ) Strongly disagree
   2. ( ) Disagree
   3. ( ) Agree
   4. ( ) Strongly agree

62. **On the whole, I am satisfied with myself.**
   1. ( ) Strongly disagree
   2. ( ) Disagree
   3. ( ) Agree
   4. ( ) Strongly agree

63. **All in all, I am inclined to feel that I am a failure.**
   1. ( ) Strongly agree
   2. ( ) Agree
   3. ( ) Disagree
   4. ( ) Strongly disagree

64. **I feel I do not have much to be proud of.**
   1. ( ) Strongly agree
   2. ( ) Agree
   3. ( ) Disagree
   4. ( ) Strongly disagree

65. **I wish I could have more respect for myself.**
   1. ( ) Strongly agree
   2. ( ) Agree
   3. ( ) Disagree
   4. ( ) Strongly disagree

66. When your <u>mother</u> disciplines or punishes you, how does she usually do it?

1. ( ) She usually spanks, slaps, or strikes me

2. ( ) She usually nags or makes fun of me

3. ( ) She usually takes away one or more of my privileges or things I like to do, such as not letting me use the car, go out at night or on weekends, not letting me watch TV, etc.

4. ( ) She usually tries to show me what it was I did wrong then talks with me so that I won't do it again

67. Generally, which <u>one</u> of the following statements best describes how <u>most</u> teachers feel about athletes and good students in your school?

1. ( ) They feel that an athlete should be a good student and that a good student should be an athlete

2. ( ) They feel an athlete should be a good student, but it doesn't matter if a good student is an athlete

3. ( ) They feel a good student should be an athlete, but it doesn't matter if an athlete is a good student

4. ( ) They feel it doesn't matter if an athlete is a good student or if a good student is an athlete

68. In general, how are most decisions between you and your father made?

1. ( ) My father usually doesn't care what I do.

2. ( ) I usually can do what I want regardless of what my father thinks

3. ( ) I usually can make my own decisions, but my father would like for me to consider his opinion

4. ( ) My opinions usually are as important as my father's in deciding what I should do

5. ( ) I have considerable opportunity to make my own decisions, but my father usually has the final word

6. ( ) My father listens to me, but usally he makes the decision

7. ( ) My father usually just tells me what to do.

CARD TWO

INSTRUCTIONS: The following few items are about your plans for a job and for an education. There are two types of questions. One type is called "LIKE TO" and the other type is called "EXPECT TO". There is a **very important difference** between the "LIKE TO" and the "EXPECT TO" types of questions.

    A "LIKE TO" question on jobs, for example, asks you to choose, from all the jobs you know about, the job you would *really* LIKE TO have when you finish your education. However, sometimes there is a difference between the job a person would *really* LIKE TO have and the job he *actually* EXPECTS TO have. For example, Bob may *really* LIKE TO become an aeronautical engineer. But, he knows that he cannot afford the college education which the job of aeronautical engineer requires. So, instead, he *actually* EXPECTS TO become an aircraft mechanic, a job with aircraft that does not require a college education.

    When you answer the questions below, please REMEMBER the *very important difference* between "LIKE TO" and "EXPECT TO" questions. Answer them to the best of your ability. Answer them frankly and honestly. Thank you.

16-23. SUPPOSING you could have the necessary abilities, education, grades, money, etc., what kind of work would you really LIKE TO do after you finish your education?, that is, after you get out of high school, technical, business, nursing school, or college. PLEASE BE VERY SPECIFIC. NOTE: If you would really LIKE TO go into the military, please specify the military rank you would really LIKE TO have.

_____

(SPECIFIC NAME OR TITLE OF job I would *really* LIKE TO have.)

24-31. CONSIDERING your abilities, grades, financial resources, chances for technical school, college, etc., what kind of work do you actually EXPECT TO do after you finish your education?; that is, after you get out of high school, technical, business, nursing school, or college? PLEASE BE VERY SPECIFIC. NOTE: If you actually EXPECT TO go into the military, please specify the military rank you actually EXPECT TO get.

_____

(SPECIFIC NAME OR TITLE OF job I *actually* EXPECT TO get.)

32-33. SUPPOSING you had the necessary abilities, grades, money, etc., how far would you <u>really</u> LIKE TO go in school?

1. ( ) 10th or 11th grade

2. ( ) Graduate from high school

3. ( ) Trade or technical school

4. ( ) Two-year business school

5. ( ) Nursing school

6. ( ) Two years of college

7. ( ) Four years of college

8. ( ) Graduate or professional school

34-35. CONSIDERING your abilities, grades, financial resources, etc., how far do you <u>actually</u> EXPECT TO go in school?

1. ( ) 10th or 11th grade

2. ( ) Graduate from high school

3. ( ) Trade or technical school

4. ( ) Two-year business school

5. ( ) Nursing school

6. ( ) Two years of college

7. ( ) Four years of college

8. ( ) Graduate or professional school

36. Generally, over the past 5 to 8 years or so, have your parents stressed or emphasized that you should take pride in things that you have done well?

1. ( ) Yes, they have stressed it a lot
2. ( ) Yes, they have stressed it somewhat

3. ( ) Yes, but they have seldom mentioned it
4. ( ) They haven't cared one way or the other
5. ( ) No, they would rather I not feel proud when I do something well

Generally, in talking with other people about what you are going to do after you get out of high school, how often do you talk with each of the following kinds of persons about whether or not you are going to continue your education after high school, such as whether or not you are going to trade school, college, etc.?

IBM	Type of Person	*How often I talk with each of these kinds of persons about whether or not I am going to continue my education after high school?*			
		Never	Sometimes	Often	Almost Constantly
37.	With my teachers				
38.	With my friends				
39.	With my father				
40.	With the guidance counselor				
41.	With the athletic coach				
42.	With my clergyman				
43.	With my mother				
44.	With my brothers or sisters				
45.	With a friend of the family				
46.	With friends of mine in college				

CARD THREE

In most schools there are usually one or two groups of students who have a lot of influence on student life around the school, i.e., the "in" group or the "leading crowd." What about in your school? **How many groups** of students are there that seem to be "in the middle of things" one way or another?

1. ( ) One group
2. ( ) Two groups
3. ( ) There are no such groups in this school

What is the best way to name and describe these one or two groups you had in mind when you answered the last question? Try to give the group or groups the name most students use in talking about it and describe the group or groups in terms of the interests and behaviors of its members.

Group A
Name:

Group B
Name:

Description: _____

Description: _____

Of the group or groups you just named, which one has has the **most influence** on student life?

1. ( ) Group A
2. ( ) Group B

What does it take to become a member of the group with the most influence, i.e., like coming from the right family, being a good student, an athlete, etc.?

_____ _____

_____ _____

Who are the students in the group with the most influence? Try to name the top five.

First Name Last Name   First Name Last Name

_____ _____   _____ _____

_____ _____   _____ _____

_____ _____   _____ _____

47. With regard to discipline and punishment, my **father** is:

1. ( ) Very easy
2. ( ) Fairly easy
3. ( ) Fairly strict
4. ( ) Very strict

48. During the last few years or so, has your mother wanted you to continue your education beyond high school, that is, to go to a trade or business school, to college, etc.?

1. ( ) Yes, she has stressed it a lot
2. ( ) Yes, she has stressed it somewhat
3. ( ) Yes, but she has seldom mentioned it
4. ( ) She hasn't said one way or the other
5. ( ) No, she would rather that I did not go beyond high school

The following two questions are about your father's job and his employer. If your father is not currently employed or if your father is deceased, please give the name of the employer your father LAST worked for and the kind of job he LAST had.

49-51. What is the full name of the company, business, or farm that your father works for? For example: General Motors Car Company. (If your father works for himself, write "self-employed" and give the name of your father's business.)

_____

(Name of company, business, or
farm which employs your father)

52-59. What KIND OF WORK does your father do? (PLEASE TRY TO GIVE THE SPECIFIC NAME OR TITLE OF HIS JOB, for example, "delivery truck driver", and DESCRIBE what he does. For example, "he drives a local delivery truck." ALSO: if your father is in the military, please GIVE HIS SPECIFIC MILITARY RANK.)

_____

(Specific name or title of
father's job or his military
rank)

_____

(Brief description of what he does)

_____

_____

60. Would you say that in your home it has been just about taken for granted that you will continue your education after you get out of high school?

1. ( ) Yes   2. ( ) No   3. ( ) Do not know

61. Generally, over the past 5 to 8 years, have your parents stressed or emphasized that you should try to come out on top in games, sports, and the like?

1. ( ) No, they would rather I not try to come out on top in games, sports, etc.
2. ( ) They haven't said one way or another
3. ( ) Yes, but they have seldom mentioned it
4. ( ) Yes, they have stressed it somewhat
5. ( ) Yes, they have stressed it a lot

62. How important is it to you personally that you be a good student?

1. ( ) It is _not important_ to me personally that I be a good student
2. ( ) It is _somewhat important_ to me personally that I be a good student
3. ( ) It is _very important_ to me personally that I be a good student

63. In general, how are most decisions between you and your mother made?

1. ( ) My mother usually just tells me what to do
2. ( ) My mother listens to me, but usually she makes the decision
3. ( ) I have considerable opportunity to make my own decisions, but my mother usually has the final word
4. ( ) My opinions usually are as important as my mother's in deciding what I should do
5. ( ) I usually can make my own decision, but my mother would like for me to consider her opinion
6. ( ) I usually can do what I want regardless of what my mother thinks
7. ( ) My mother usually doesn't care what I do

ASSUME FOR THE MOMENT that you are going to continue your education after high school and go on to technical school, college, etc. Below are some reasons why students want to continue their education after high school. Indicate how important each reason is to you personally if you were to go to technical school, college, etc.

		How Important To Me?		
IBM	Reason	VERY Important	SOMEWHAT Important	NOT AT ALL Important
64.	To get a better job or a higher income			
65.	To be better able to understand and appreciate ideas			
66.	To develop my ability to get along with different kinds of people			
67.	To develop my moral capacities, ethical standards and values			
68.	To prepare me for a happy marriage and family life			

CARD FOUR

16. **How much time, on the average, do you spend in practicing for, training for, or actually competing in interscholastic sports,** that is, in sports where your school competes against another school?

    1. ( ) None, or almost none
    2. ( ) about ½ hour a day
    3. ( ) about 1 hour a day
    4. ( ) about 1½ hours a day
    5. ( ) about 2 hours a day
    6. ( ) about 2½ hours a day
    7. ( ) about 3 hours a day
    8. ( ) more than 3 hours a day

17. **How often does your father give you praise, encouragement, or approval for what you do?**

    1. ( ) Almost never
    2. ( ) Very seldom
    3. ( ) Once in a while
    4. ( ) Frequently
    5. ( ) Very often

Here are some statements which students have opinions about. Please indicate how you personally feel about each statement by placing an "X" near "Strongly Agree" if you agree with it strongly, near "Agree" if you just agree with it, near "Disagree" if you just disagree with it, or near "Strongly Disagree" if you strongly disagree with it.

18. **When a person is born, the success he is going to have is already in the cards, so he might as well accept it and not fight against it.**

    1. ( ) Strongly agree
    2. ( ) Agree
    3. ( ) Disagree
    4. ( ) Strongly disagree

19. **A person's job should come first, even if it means spending less time in recreation and play.**

    1. ( ) Strongly disagree
    2. ( ) Disagree
    3. ( ) Agree
    4. ( ) Strongly agree

20. **The more education a person has, the better able is he to really enjoy and appreciate life.**

    1. ( ) Strongly agree
    2. ( ) Agree
    3. ( ) Disagree
    4. ( ) Strongly disagree

21. **A person should make plans for his life and not just accept what comes along.**

    1. ( ) Strongly disagree
    2. ( ) Disagree
    3. ( ) Agree
    4. ( ) Strongly agree

22. **When a person is making an important decision, he should consider the advice of his parents as more important than the advice of his friends.**

    1. ( ) Strongly agree
    2. ( ) Agree
    3. ( ) Disagree
    4. ( ) Strongly disagree

23. **A high school education is worth the time and effort it requires.**

    1. ( ) Strongly disagree
    2. ( ) Disagree
    3. ( ) Agree
    4. ( ) Strongly agree

24. **Whatever a person does, he should try to do it better than anyone else.**

    1. ( ) Strongly agree
    2. ( ) Agree
    3. ( ) Disagree
    4. ( ) Strongly disagree

25. **Generally, it is possible for a person to plan his future so that more things will come out right than wrong in the long run.**

    1. ( ) Strongly disagree
    2. ( ) Disagree
    3. ( ) Agree
    4. ( ) Strongly agree

26. **After a person is married, his (or her) main loyalty should continue to be to his (or her) parents.**

    1. ( ) Strongly agree
    2. ( ) Agree
    3. ( ) Disagree
    4. ( ) Strongly disagree

27. **A person should make serious efforts to overcome those obstacles put in his path by other people.**

    1. ( ) Strongly disagree
    2. ( ) Disagree
    3. ( ) Agree
    4. ( ) Strongly agree

28. **In business and industry, a person without a college education can get ahead just as rapidly as a person with a college education.**

    1. ( ) Strongly agree
    2. ( ) Agree
    3. ( ) Disagree
    4. ( ) Strongly disagree

29. **Other people have more control over a person's future than the person himself does.**

    1. ( ) Strongly disagree
    2. ( ) Disagree
    3. ( ) Agree
    4. ( ) Strongly agree

30. Which ONE of the following statements is most true about continuing your education after high school?

1. ( ) My father *never* urges me to continue my education
2. ( ) My father *sometimes* urges me to continue my education
3. ( ) My father *often* urges me to continue my education
4. ( ) My father *constantly* urges me to continue my education

31-33. How far did your mother go in school?

01. ( ) She has no formal schooling
02. ( ) She did not go any further than sixth grade in elementary school
03. ( ) She did not go any further than ninth grade in high school
04. ( ) She did not go any further than eleventh grade in high school
05. ( ) She finished high school
06. ( ) She went to technical or business school but did not finish
07. ( ) She finished technical or business school
08. ( ) She went to nursing school but did not finish
09. ( ) She finished nursing school
10. ( ) She went to college but did not finish
11. ( ) She finished college
12. ( ) She went to graduate or professional school but did not finish
13. ( ) She finished graduate or professional school
14. ( ) Do not know

34. If you could be remembered here at school for one of the six things below, which one would you like it to be?

1. ( ) For being a good student
2. ( ) For being a good athlete
3. ( ) For being popular
4. ( ) For being a good student and a good athlete
5. ( ) For being a good student and very popular
6. ( ) For being a good athlete and very popular

35. Generally, when your mother makes decisions which concern you or when she makes rules for you to follow, does she explain to you the reasons for the decisions or rules?

1. ( ) She *almost always* explains her decisions or rules to me
2. ( ) She *usually* explains her decisions or rules to me
3. ( ) She *sometimes* explains her decisions or rules to me
4. ( ) She *once in a while* explains her decisions or rules to me
5. ( ) She *almost never* explains her decisions or rules to me

36. How often does your mother give you praise, encouragement, or approval for what you do?

1. ( ) Very often
2. ( ) Frequently
3. ( ) Once in a while
4. ( ) Very seldom
5. ( ) Almost never

For each of the items below, check which ones you and your parents agree about, which ones you disagree about, or which ones you have not discussed with your parents.

IBM	The Items	Disagree	Agree	Have Not Discussed
37.	Whether I should or should not continue my education after high school			
38.	What course of study I should take if I do continue my education			
39.	What college, technical school, etc. I should go to if I continue my education			
40.	Whether I should live away from home if I continue my education			
41.	How much it will cost if I do continue my education			

42. With regard to discipline and punishment, my mother is:

1. ( ) Very strict
2. ( ) Fairly strict
3. ( ) Fairly easy
4. ( ) Very easy

43-44. If you were to continue your education after high school and go to trade school, college, etc., what subjects would you like most to study, i.e., liberal arts, business, science, etc.?

_____

(Name or names of subjects I would like most to study)

45. Regardless of what other students think, how do you personally feel about an athlete being a good student?

1. ( ) I don't think that an athlete should be a good student

2. ( ) It doesn't make any difference to me whether an athlete is a good student

3. ( ) I think it is somewhat important that an athlete be a good student

4. ( ) I think that it is very important that an athlete be a good student

46. Generally, over the past 5 to 8 years or so, have your parents stressed or emphasized that you should try to do things better than anyone else?

1. ( ) Yes, they have stressed it a lot

2. ( ) Yes, they have stressed it somewhat

3. ( ) Yes, but they have seldom mentioned it

4. ( ) They haven't said one way or the other

5. ( ) No, they would rather I not try to do things better than other people

47. Here are four statements which have been made about the Bible, and I'd like you to indicate which is closest to your own view.

1. ( ) The Bible is God's Word, and all it says is true

2. ( ) The Bible was written by men inspired by God, and its basic moral and religious teachings are true, but because the writers were men, it contains some human errors.

3. ( ) The Bible is a valuable book because it was written by wise and good men, but God had nothing to do with it.

4. ( ) The Bible was writen by men who lived so long ago that it is of little value today

Here are five statements about yourself. After you read each statement, indicate how strongly you agree or disagree with it by placing an "X" in the appropriate box.

48. I am able to do things as well as most other people.

1. ( ) Strongly agree

2. ( ) Agree

3. ( ) Disagree

4. ( ) Strongly disagree

49. At times I think I am no good at all.

1. ( ) Strongly disagree

2. ( ) Disagree

3. ( ) Agree

4. ( ) Strongly agree

50. I feel that I'm a person of worth, at least on an equal plane with others.

1. ( ) Strongly agree

2. ( ) Agree

3. ( ) Disagree

4. ( ) Strongly disagree

51. I take a positive attitude toward myself.

1. ( ) Strongly disagree

2. ( ) Disagree

3. ( ) Agree

4. ( ) Strongly agree

52. I certainly feel useless at times.

1. ( ) Strongly agree

2. ( ) Agree

3. ( ) Disagree

4. ( ) Strongly disagree

Generally, concerning your educational future, about how often have these people: (1) ENCOURAGED you or SUGGESTED to you that you should continue your education after high school, such as by going to a trade school, college, etc., (2) DISCOURAGED you or SUGGESTED that you should not continue your education after high school?

IBM	Type of Person	ENCOURAGED ME:				DISCOURAGED ME:			
		Never	Some-times	Often	Almost Con-stantly	Never	Some-times	Often	Almost Con-stantly
53.	Teachers								
54.	Neighbors								
55.	Brothers or sisters								
56.	Guidance counselors								
57.	School Principal								
58.	Athletic Coach								
59.	Clergyman								
60.	Relatives (other than parents)								
61.	Others (Please state type of person)								

CARD FIVE

16. **When your father disciplines or punishes you, how does he usually do it?**

1. ( ) He usually spanks, slaps, or strikes me
2. ( ) He usually nags or makes fun of me
3. ( ) He usually takes away one or more of my privileges or things I like to do, such as not letting me use the car, go out at night or on weekends, not letting me watch TV, etc.
4. ( ) He usually tries to show me what it was I did wrong and then talks with me so that I won't do it again

17. **What is your racial background?**

1. ( ) White   3. ( ) Oriental
2. ( ) Negro   4. ( ) Other (Specify:_____)

18. **In general, which one of the following best describes your own family?** PLEASE NOTE: The term "father" also includes "step-father", "guardian", etc. The term "mother" also includes "stepmother", "guardian", etc.

1. ( ) It is a family in which my mother is definite the head of the house and makes most of the important decisions herself without first talking things over with my father.
2. ( ) It is a family in which my mother is definitely the head of the house and makes most of the important decisions but usually talks things over first with my father.
3. ( ) It is a family in which both my father and my mother head the house together and they usually talks things over before both deciding what to do
4. ( ) It is a family in which my father is head of the house and makes most of the important decisions but usually talks things over first with my mother
5. ( ) It is a family in which my father is definitely the head of the house and makes most of the important decisions himself without first talking things over with my mother

19. **Which ONE of the following best describes the employment situation of your mother?**

1. ( ) Full-time housewife
2. ( ) Works part-time *at* her home (less than 30 hours)
3. ( ) Works part-time *outside* her home
4. ( ) Works full-time (30 hours a week or more) *at* her home doing something other than housework
5. ( ) Works full-time (30 hours a week or more) *outside* her home
6. ( ) Works sometime *at* her home
7. ( ) Works sometime *outside* her home
8. ( ) Other (Specify: _____)

20-27. (IF YOUR MOTHER WORKS PART OR FULL TIME AT HOME OR OUTSIDE THE HOME): **what KIND OF WORK does she do?** PLEASE TRY TO GIVE THE SPECIFIC NAME OR TITLE OF HER JOB AND DESCRIBE WHAT SHE DOES.

_____

(Specific name or title of mother's job)

_____

(Brief description of what she does)

_____

_____

The next few items are about sports and athletes in high school. The items are about interscholastic sports only, that is, sports where your school competes against another school.

28-30. **Have you taken part in any interscholastic sports this school year?**

1. ( ) No
2. ( ) Yes: IF YES—What are the names of the *interscholastic* sports in which you have taken part this year?

     1. _____   3. _____

     2. _____   4. _____

     5. _____

31-33. **Would you really LIKE TO go out for interscholastic sports next year?**

1. ( ) No
2. ( ) Yes: IF YES—What are the names of the *interscholastic* sports you would *really* LIKE TO go out for next year?

     1. _____   3. _____

     2. _____   4. _____

     5. _____

34-36. **IF YOU ANSWERED "YES" TO THE LAST ITEM: Which of these interscholastic sports you named in the last item do you actually EXPECT TO go out for next year?**

Names of the interscholastic sports I actually EXPECT TO go out for next year:

     1. _____   3. _____

     2. _____   4. _____

     5. _____

37. **IF YOU ACTUALLY EXPECT TO GO OUT FOR AN INTERSCHOLASTIC SPORT NEXT YEAR:**

Do you think you will actually make a varsity team before you get out of high school?

1. ( ) Definitely yes
2. ( ) Probably yes
3. ( ) Probably no
4. ( ) Definitely no

38. Do you think you will actually make a city, state, or regional all-star team before you get out of high school?

1. ( ) Definitely no
2. ( ) Probably no
3. ( ) Probably yes
4. ( ) Definitely yes

39. Do you have any brothers or sisters who were or who are now on an athletic team in high school?

1. ( ) Yes
2. ( ) No

40. Do your parents stress or emphasize your going out for an interscholastic sport in high school?

1. ( ) Yes, they stress it a lot
2. ( ) Yes, they stress it somewhat
3. ( ) Yes, but they seldom mention it
4. ( ) They don't care one way or the other
5. ( ) No, they would rather I not go out for an *interscholastic* sport

41. Check the one category below which comes closest to your feeling about yourself.

1. ( ) I don't like myself the way I am; I'd like to change myself completely
2. ( ) There are many things about myself I'd like to change, but not completely
3. ( ) I'd like to stay very much the same; there is very little about myself that I would change

42-43. If you have already decided on a specific field of study for when you go to trade school, college, etc., which field is it?, i.e., law, business, science, etc.?

_____

(Name of specific field of study
for trade school, college, etc.)

44. Generally, over the past 5 to 8 years, have your parents stressed or emphasized your being able to do things by yourself, like buying your own clothes, going places on your own, etc.?

1. ( ) They would rather I not try to do things by myself
2. ( ) They haven't said one way or the other
3. ( ) Yes, but they have seldom mentioned it
4. ( ) Yes, they have stressed it somewhat
5. ( ) Yes, they have stressed it a lot

45-47. What are the names of the three courses in which:
You get your better **48-50.** You get your poorer
or best grades. or poorest grades.

_____ _____
_____ _____
_____ _____

51-53. What are the names of the three courses which:
You like the most. **54-56.** You dislike the most.

_____ _____
_____ _____
_____ _____

57-59. What are the names of the three courses which:
You think are going **60-62.** You think are going to
to be the most use- be the least useful or
ful or important in important in your life's
your life's work. work.

_____ _____
_____ _____
_____ _____

63-64. What is the religious preference of your mother? NOTE: Please be as precise as possible in giving the specific religious preference of your mother.

_____

(Religious preference of Mother)

65. How often does your mother attend a worship service in a church, temple, or synagogue?

1. ( ) Never
2. ( ) Seldom
3. ( ) Several times a year
4. ( ) About once a month
5. ( ) Two or three times a month
6. ( ) About once a week
7. ( ) More than once a week

CARD SIX

Here are some more statements on which students differ in their opinions. Please indicate how you personally feel about each statement by placing an "X" next to that response category which best indicates your feelings.

16. A person should live as much for the future as for the present.

1. ( ) Strongly agree
2. ( ) Agree
3. ( ) Disagree
4. ( ) Strongly disagree

17. The most important qualities of a man are determination and driving ambition.

1. ( ) Strongly disagree
2. ( ) Disagree
3. ( ) Agree
4. ( ) Strongly agree

—11—

18.   Before a person is married, his (or her) main loyalty belongs to his (or her) parents.

1. ( ) Strongly agree

2. ( ) Agree

3. ( ) Disagree

4. ( ) Strongly disagree

19.   A person should make serious efforts to overcome the obstacles put in his path by nature and fate.

1. ( ) Strongly disagree

2. ( ) Disagree

3. ( ) Agree

4. ( ) Strongly agree

20.   Education tends to make a person more unhappy than happy.

1. ( ) Strongly agree

2. ( ) Agree

3. ( ) Disagree

4. ( ) Strongly disagree

21.   A person should live mainly for today and let tomorrow take care of itself.

1. ( ) Strongly disagree

2. ( ) Disagree

3. ( ) Agree

4. ( ) Strongly agree

22.   A man's job should come first, although it may require his spending less time with his wife and children.

1. ( ) Strongly agree

2. ( ) Agree

3. ( ) Disagree

4. ( ) Strongly disagree

23.   Generally, in making important decisions, a person should decide what is best for him even if it goes against what his parents and friends want him to do.

1. ( ) Strongly disagree

2. ( ) Disagree

3. ( ) Agree

4. ( ) Strongly agree

24.   A college education is worth the time and effort it requires.

1. ( ) Strongly agree

2. ( ) Agree

3. ( ) Disagree

4. ( ) Strongly disagree

25.   A person should use some of his time in the present to make plans for his future.

1. ( ) Strongly disagree

2. ( ) Disagree

3. ( ) Agree

4. ( ) Strongly agree

26.   When it comes time for a person to take a job, he should try to live near his parents, even if it means giving up the chances for a better job.

1. ( ) Strongly agree

2. ( ) Agree

3. ( ) Disagree

4. ( ) Strongly disagree

27.   Success in the occupational world depends more on luck than on ability and willingness to work.

1. ( ) Strongly disagree

2. ( ) Disagree

3. ( ) Agree

4. ( ) Strongly agree

28.   Except for growing old and the like, a person has more control over his own future than do the forces of nature or fate.

1. ( ) Strongly agree

2. ( ) Agree

3. ( ) Disagree

4. ( ) Strongly disagree

29.   Education helps a person use his leisure time to better advantage.

1. ( ) Strongly disagree

2. ( ) Disagree

3. ( ) Agree

4. ( ) Strongly agree

30.   It is more important to have friends than to be a success in one's job.

1. ( ) Strongly agree

2. ( ) Agree

3. ( ) Disagree

4. ( ) Strongly disagree

31.   Which ONE of the following statements is most true about continuing your education beyond high school?

1. ( ) My mother *never* urges me to continue my education

2. ( ) My mother *sometimes* urges me to continue my education

3. ( ) My mother *often* urges me to continue my education

4. ( ) My mother *constantly* urges me to continue my education

INSTRUCTIONS: THE FOLLOWING ITEMS ARE ABOUT YOUR THREE GOOD FRIENDS OF YOUR **OWN** SEX. The questions are not personal, so please try to answer them to the best of your ability and answer them frankly and honestly. NOTE: If one or more of your friends is not in high school, please try to recall the information asked for and then answer to the best of your ability. ALSO: GIRLS—since the question reads friends of your **OWN** sex, wherever you see a "he" in the questions on your three friends, change the "he" in your mind to a "she".

THESE QUESTIONS ARE ABOUT FRIEND **NUMBER ONE:**

32.   What kind of program is he (friend No. 1) taking in high school?

1. ( ) Academic or College Prep
2. ( ) Science
3. ( ) General
4. ( ) Commercial or business
5. ( ) Vocational Agriculture
6. ( ) Vocational Industrial Arts
7. ( ) Other (Specify: _____)

33.   How far does he (friend No. 1) actually EXPECT TO go in school?

1. ( ) 10th or 11th grade but not necessarily graduate
2. ( ) Graduate from high school
3. ( ) Trade or technical school
4. ( ) Two year business school
5. ( ) Nursing school
6. ( ) Two years of college
7. ( ) Four years of college
8. ( ) Graduate or professional school

34.   What is he (friend No. 1) doing currently?

1. ( ) In high school
2. ( ) Did not complete high school but is not currently working or in the service
3. ( ) Did not complete high school and is currently working or in the service
4. ( ) Finished high school but is neither currently working nor in the service, nor in technical school, college, etc.
5. ( ) Finished high school and is either currently working or in the service
6. ( ) Finished high school and is currently in technical, nursing, business school or college
7. ( ) FOR GIRLS ONLY: Is married and a housewife
8. ( ) Other (Specify: _____)

THESE QUESTIONS ARE ABOUT FRIEND **NUMBER TWO:**

35.   What kind of program is he (friend No. 2) taking in high school?

1. ( ) Academic or College Prep
2. ( ) Science
3. ( ) General
4. ( ) Commercial or business
5. ( ) Vocational Agriculture
6. ( ) Vocational Industrial Arts
7. ( ) Other (Specify: _____)

36.   How far does he (friend No. 2) actually EXPECT TO go in school?

1. ( ) 10th or 11th grade but not necessarily graduate
2. ( ) Graduate from high school
3. ( ) Trade or technical school
4. ( ) Two year business school
5. ( ) Nursing school
6. ( ) Two years of college
7. ( ) Four years of college
8. ( ) Graduate or professional school

37.   What is he (friend No. 2) doing currently?

1. ( ) In high school
2. ( ) Did not complete high school but is not currently working or in the service
3. ( ) Did not complete high school and is currently working or in the service
4. ( ) Finished high school but is neither currently working nor in the service, nor in technical school, college, etc.
5. ( ) Finished high school and is either currently working or in the service
6. ( ) Finished high school and is currently in technical, nursing, business school or college
7. ( ) FOR GIRLS ONLY: Is married and a housewife
8. ( ) Other (Specify: _____)

THESE QUESTIONS ARE ABOUT FRIEND **NUMBER THREE:**

38.   What kind of program is he (friend No. 3) taking in high school?

1. ( ) Academic or College Prep
2. ( ) Science
3. ( ) General
4. ( ) Commercial or business
5. ( ) Vocational Agriculture
6. ( ) Vocational Industrial Arts
7. ( ) Other (Specify: _____)

39.   How far does he (friend No. 3) actually EXPECT TO go in school?

1. ( ) 10th or 11th grade but not necessarily graduate
2. ( ) Graduate from high school
3. ( ) Trade or technical school
4. ( ) Two year business school
5. ( ) Nursing school
6. ( ) Two years of college
7. ( ) Four years of college
8. ( ) Graduate or professional school

CARD SEVEN

40. **What is he (friend No. 3) doing currently?**

1. ( ) In high school
2. ( ) Did not complete high school but is not currently working or in the service
3. ( ) Did not complete high school and is currently working or in the service
4. ( ) Finished high school but is neither currently working nor in the service, nor in technical school, college, etc.
5. ( ) Finished high school and is either currently working or in the service
6. ( ) Finished high school and is currently in technical, nursing, business school or college
7. ( ) FOR GIRLS ONLY: Is married and a housewife
8. ( ) Other (Specify: _____)

What are the names of your three friends?

41-45. Friend No. 1: _____ _____
(Last Name)   (First Name)

46-50. Friend No. 2: _____ _____
(Last Name)   (First Name)

51-55. Friend No. 3: _____ _____
(Last Name)   (First Name)

56. **Have you taken part in any school clubs, organizations, or activities this year?** For example: sports, music, newspaper, art, etc.

1. ( ) Yes
2. ( ) No

57-79. **IF YOU HAVE TAKEN PART IN SCHOOL CLUBS, ACTIVITIES, SPORTS, ETC.: What are they?** Name as many as you have participated in this year.

1. _____   6. _____
2. _____   7. _____
3. _____   8. _____
4. _____   9. _____
5. _____   10. _____

80. **How many offices have you held in the school clubs, organizations, or activities in which you have participated this year?**

1. ( ) I have not held any office
2. ( ) One office
3. ( ) Two offices
4. ( ) Three offices
5. ( ) Four offices
6. ( ) Five offices
7. ( ) Six offices
8. ( ) Seven or more offices

16-19. **If you DO NOT ACTUALLY EXPECT TO go on to technical school, business school, nursing school, or college: What are the four most important reasons why you do not expect to do so?** RANK these four reasons from 1 to 4. 1 for the first most important reason, 2 for the second most important, all the way through 4.

1. ( ) No desire to go
2. ( ) Costs too much
3. ( ) Low grades in school
4. ( ) Family responsibilities
5. ( ) Studies would be too hard
6. ( ) Have to work to help my family
7. ( ) Want to get a job of my own and make some money as soon as I get out of high school
8. ( ) I am tired of being a student
9. ( ) Other (Specify: _____)

20-23. **Where was your father born?** PLEASE TRY TO GIVE THE NAME OF THE COUNTRY IN WHICH HE WAS BORN. IF HE WAS BORN IN THE UNITED STATES, PLEASE TRY TO GIVE THE NAME OF THE STATE IN WHICH HE WAS BORN.

_____

(Name of Country and State in which
my *father* was born)

24-27. **Where was your mother born?** PLEASE TRY TO GIVE THE NAME OF THE COUNTRY IN WHICH SHE WAS BORN. IF SHE WAS BORN IN THE UNITED STATES, PLEASE TRY TO GIVE THE NAME OF THE STATE IN WHICH SHE WAS BORN.

_____

(Name of Country and State in which
my *mother* was born)

28-31. **If you are continuing your education after you get out of high school, what are the four most important reasons for deciding which school you will attend?** RANK these from 1 to 4. 1 for the first most important, 2 for the second most important, etc., all the way through 4.

1. ( ) Tuition costs
2. ( ) Closeness to home
3. ( ) The educational standards
4. ( ) Living costs
5. ( ) Courses of studies offered
6. ( ) Chances for financial aid
7. ( ) People I know who went or who are now going to the school
8. ( ) Chances for geting admitted

32-45. **IF YOU ARE GOING TO CONTINUE YOUR EDUCATION ON A FULL-TIME BASIS AFTER HIGH SCHOOL:**
What is the name of the school or college to which you will be going?

_____
(Full name of the school or college)

In what city and in what state is the school or college located?

_____   _____
(City)   (State)

46. Do you think that God is more pleased when people try to get ahead, or when people are satisfied with what they have and don't try to get ahead?

1. ( ) More pleased when people try to get ahead
2. ( ) More pleased when people are satisfied with what they have

47-50. What sort of reputation do most of the athletes in your school have, i.e., like "good students," "intelligent," "popular," "dumb," "troublemakers," etc.?

_____   _____

_____   _____

51. How often do you take part in any of the activities or organizations of your church, temple, or synagogue, other than attending worship services?

1. ( ) Often
2. ( ) Sometimes
3. ( ) Almost never

52. When you have decisions to make in your everyday life, how often do you ask yourself what God would want you to do?

1. ( ) Almost never
2. ( ) Sometimes
3. ( ) Often

53. What kind of a reputation do you have among your teachers as far as your school work goes?

1. ( ) Very good
2. ( ) Good
3. ( ) Fair
4. ( ) Poor
5. ( ) Very poor

54. About how many of your friends intend on going out for an athletic team in high school?

1. ( ) More than half
2. ( ) Just about half
3. ( ) Less than half
4. ( ) Almost none

55. What kind of a reputation do you have among your teachers as far as your behavior goes?

1. ( ) Very good
2. ( ) Good
3. ( ) Fair
4. ( ) Poor
5. ( ) Very poor

CARD EIGHT

Earlier, we asked you about the "in" group or the "leading crowd" in your school. Now we would like to ask you about the "out" groups, the groups which cause the greatest problems for the teachers and the principal. How many groups of students are there that seem to cause the greatest problems for the teachers and the principal?

1. ( ) One group
2. ( ) Two groups
3. ( ) There are no such groups in this school

What is the best way to describe these one or two groups? Try to give the group or groups the name most students use in talking about it and describe the group or groups in terms of the interests and behaviors of its members.

Group A   _Group B_
Name: Name:

Description: Description:

_____   _____

_____   _____

_____   _____

Of the group or groups that you just named, which one creates the most problems for the teachers and the principal?

1. ( ) Group A
2. ( ) Group B

What does it take to become a member of the group which creates the most problems in the school?

_____   _____

_____   _____

_____   _____

Thank you.

GRADE TEN: Spring 1968

CONFIDENTIAL

‾ ‾ ‾ ‾ ‾ ‾ ‾ ‾ ‾ ‾ ‾ ‾ ‾ ‾
(NUMERIC)

SCHOOL AND CAREER ATTITUDE SURVEY

(LAST NAME)		(FULL NAME OF YOUR SCHOOL)
PLEASE		
PRINT		
(FIRST NAME)		(NAME OF CITY OR TOWN)

OBJECTIVES OF THE SURVEY

This questionnaire is part of a continuing survey of high school students in a number of secondary schools. Its objectives are to gather information on: (1) what American high school students believe and feel about their school experiences; (2) the social characteristics of various groups in a high school, such as athletes, scholars, etc.; (3) student preferences for various kinds of occupational and educational careers; and (4) the many types of factors which influence different kinds of occupational and educational career interests.

In responding to the items in the questionnaire, there are several points we would like to emphasize:

1. *All* of your responses are *confidential*. Only trained and skilled research personnel see the questionnaires and then only for the purpose of transferring the questionnaire information onto data punch cards. No other person, whether in your school or your community, is ever permitted access to the research questionnaire.

2. Answer *all* of the items in the questionnaire. This improves the quality of the information considerably.

3. Try to answer each item as truthfully and as candidly as possible. Truthful and honest responses provide a more realistic picture of the high school, its faculty, and of the students.

INSTRUCTIONS

1. READ EACH QUESTION CAREFULLY. Answer candidly and to the best of your ability.

2. For the items about one or both parents, answer the item in terms of the person who is currently your parent, which may be your real father or mother, your step-father or step-mother, or your male or female guardian. If you are living with only one parent, then answer the questions about the other parent as though the other parent were still living with you.

3. Most items can be answered by placing an "X" in the box next to the answer you choose. For example:

Which one of the following things do you like best about the school you are currently attending?

1. ☐ The teachers
2. ☐ The courses
3. ☐ My fellow students
4. ☐ Student activities: sports, clubs, etc.
5. ☐ The school spirit
6. ☐ The counselors
7. ☐ The physical facilities: gym, library, etc.
8. ☐ None of the above

4. If you have a problem, raise your hand and a research worker will come to your place and assist you. *Please continue to answer the items with which you have no problem until the research worker comes to your place.* Otherwise, you will not finish on time.

THANK YOU! TURN TO PAGE TWO AND BEGIN

— 1 —

CARD ONE

16. **What kind of program are you taking in school?**
1. ☐ Academic or College Prep.
2. ☐ Science
3. ☐ General
4. ☐ Commercial or Business
5. ☐ Vocational Agriculture
6. ☐ Vocational Industrial Arts
7. ☐ Other (Specify): ....).

17. **During this school year, how much time, on the average, did you spend doing homework outside of school, like late in the afternoon, at night, etc.?**
1. ☐ None, or almost none
2. ☐ Less than ½ hour a day
3. ☐ About ½ to ¾ hours a day
4. ☐ About 1 hour a day
5. ☐ About 1½ to 1¾ hours a day
6. ☐ About 2 hours a day
7. ☐ About 3 or more hours a day

18. In making decisions about their careers, students often go to different kinds of people in their high school for advice about whether or not to continue their education beyond high school, that is, about whether or not to go to a trade school, a two year college, a four year college, etc. **Please rate your TEACHERS on their ability and their willingness to give you advice about continuing your education beyond high school.**
1. ☐ The TEACHERS are *able* and *willing* to give me such advice
2. ☐ The TEACHERS are *able* to give me advice, but they are not willing
3. ☐ The TEACHERS are *willing* to give me advice, but they are not able
4. ☐ The TEACHERS are neither able nor willing to give me such advice

19. **During your sophomore year, how often have you actually talked with your TEACHERS about whether or not to continue your education beyond high school?**
1. ☐ Several times a week or more
2. ☐ About once a week
3. ☐ Several times a month
4. ☐ About once a month
5. ☐ About once every two or three months
6. ☐ Several times this school year
7. ☐ Once or twice this school year
8. ☐ Not even once this school year

20. **When you talk with your TEACHERS, what do they usually suggest or encourage you to do?**
1. ☐ Go on to a four year college
2. ☐ Go on to a two year college
3. ☐ Go for technical or advanced job training
4. ☐ Go for business or commercial training
5. ☐ Go into the armed services
6. ☐ Get a job after I get out of high school
7. ☐ Other: ....

21. **How much formal education does or did your FATHER have?**
1. ☐ Less than sixth grade
2. ☐ Seventh, eighth, or ninth grade
3. ☐ Tenth or eleventh grade
4. ☐ High school graduate
5. ☐ Some college, trade, technical, or two year business school
6. ☐ College graduate
7. ☐ Graduate or professional school
8. ☐ Do not know

22. **If you could be remembered here at school for one of the six things below, which one would you like it to be?**
1. ☐ For being a *good student*
2. ☐ For being a *good athlete*
3. ☐ For being *popular*
4. ☐ For being a *good student* and a *good athlete*
5. ☐ For being a *good student* and *popular*
6. ☐ For being a *good athlete* and *popular*

23. **Would you say that in your home it has been taken for granted that you will continue your education after you get out of high school?**
1. ☐ Yes
2. ☐ No
3. ☐ Do not know

24. **During this past school year, how much time on the average, have you spent in practicing for, training for, or actually competing in interscholastic (varsity or junior varsity) sports, that is, in sports where your school competes against another school?**
1. ☐ None, or almost none
2. ☐ About ½ hour a day
3. ☐ About 1 hour a day
4. ☐ About 1½ hours a day
5. ☐ About 2 hours a day
6. ☐ About 2½ hours a day
7. ☐ About 3 hours a day
8. ☐ More than 3 hours a day

25. **How important is it to YOU personally that you be a good student?**
1. ☐ It is *not important* to me personally that I be a good student
2. ☐ It is *somewhat important* to me personally that I be a good student
3. ☐ It is *very important* to me personally that I be a good student

26. **In most high schools there are usually one or two groups of students who are referred to as the LEADING crowd or as the "IN" group. What about your school? How many LEADING crowds or "IN" groups are there in your school?**
1. ☐ One
2. ☐ Two
3. ☐ Three or more
4. ☐ None

How would you describe the sophomore, junior, or senior students who are members of the **most prominent or important** LEADING crowd or "IN" group? In the spaces provided next to each characteristic, indicate with an "X" the approximate proportion of the LEADING crowd or "IN" group in your school you believe are described by each of the following characteristics.

		Proportion of LEADING crowd or "IN" group described by each characteristic				
		More Than Half		About Half	Less Than Half	
	Characteristics	Almost All	Many		Some	Almost None
27	Upperclassmen: juniors and seniors					
28	Get along well with the teachers					
29	Really interested in school					
30	Active in many school activities *other than* sports					
31	Are considered in the TOP SCHOLAR group					
32	Friends of mine					
33	Get special privileges from the teachers					
34	Make trouble for the teachers					
35	In the academic or college preparatory curriculum					
36	Get in trouble with the police					
37	Come from families where the father has an important or prestigeful job					
38	Well liked by most of the students					
39	Try hard to make good grades					
40	Get special privileges from the principal					
41	Intelligent					
42	Intend to go to college					
43	Cause trouble for school officials					
44	Are INTERSCHOLASTIC (varsity or junior varsity) ATHLETES					

Which students, among all the sophomores in your school, are members of the most prominent or important LEADING crowd or "IN" group?

First Name	Last Name		First Name	Last Name	
		45–48.			57–61.
		49–52.			61–64.
		53–56.			65–68.

— 3 —

CARD TWO

Please indicate which, if any, of the following activities you have regularly participated in this year. Answer **all** items.

Activity	Have you regularly participated this school year?	
	No	Yes
16. Band or orchestra		
17. Chorus, choir		
18. Dramatics		
19. School paper, yearbook		
20. Debates		
21. Student government, (student council, class officer, etc.)		
22. Language clubs (French, German, Spanish, etc.)		
23. Hobby or interest clubs (auto, broadcasting, photography, rifle, etc.)		
24. School service activities (stage or projectionist crew, dance committees, Red Cross, etc.)		
25. Athletics: *inter*scholastic (varsity or junior varsity)		
26. Academic subject clubs (math., history, science, anatomy, etc.)		
27. Athletics: *intra*mural		
28. Academic honorary clubs or societies (National Honor Society, Key Club, etc.)		
29. Athletic support clubs (officials club, team manager, color guard, etc.)		
30. Career Clubs like Future Teachers of America, FNA, FFA, etc.		
31. Other: (Specify)		

32. How frequently does your FATHER encourage you to continue your education beyond high school, that is, to go on to technical school, college, etc.?

1. ☐ At least several times a week
2. ☐ About once a week
3. ☐ Several times a month
4. ☐ About once a month
5. ☐ About once every two or three months
6. ☐ Several times a year
7. ☐ Once or twice a year
8. ☐ Less than once a year

33. Generally, which one of the following statements best describes how most TEACHERS feel about athletes and good students in your school?

1. ☐ They feel that an *athlete* should be a *good student* and that a *good student* should be an *athlete*
2. ☐ They feel an *athlete* should be a *good student*, but it doesn't matter if a *good student* is an *athlete*
3. ☐ They feel a *good student* should be an *athlete*, but it doesn't matter if an *athlete* is a *good student*
4. ☐ They feel it doesn't matter if an *athlete* is a *good student* or if a good *student* is an *athlete*

34. Check the one category below which comes closest to your feeling about yourself.

1. ☐ I don't like myself the way I am; I'd like to change myself completely
2. ☐ There are many things about myself I'd like to change, but not completely
3. ☐ I'd like to stay very much the same; there is very little about myself that I would change

35. How much formal education does or did your MOTHER have?

1. ☐ Less than sixth grade
2. ☐ Seventh, eighth, or ninth grade
3. ☐ Tenth or eleventh grade
4. ☐ High school graduate
5. ☐ Some college, trade, technical, or two year business school
6. ☐ College graduate
7. ☐ Graduate or professional school
8. ☐ Do not know

— 4 —

Here are five statements about yourself. After you read each statement, indicate how strongly you agree or disagree with it by placing an "X" in the appropriate box.

36. I feel that I'm a person of worth, at least on an equal plane with others.
1. ☐ Strongly agree
2. ☐ Agree
3. ☐ Uncertain, but probably agree
4. ☐ Uncertain but probably disagree
5. ☐ Disagree
6. ☐ Strongly disagree

37. I certainly feel useless at times.
1. ☐ Strongly agree
2. ☐ Agree
3. ☐ Uncertain, but probably agree
4. ☐ Uncertain but probably disagree
5. ☐ Disagree
6. ☐ Strongly disagree

38. On the whole, I am satisfied with myself.
1. ☐ Strongly agree
2. ☐ Agree
3. ☐ Uncertain, but probably agree
4. ☐ Uncertain but probably disagree
5. ☐ Disagree
6. ☐ Strongly disagree

39. All in all, I am inclined to feel that I am a failure.
1. ☐ Strongly agree
2. ☐ Agree
3. ☐ Uncertain, but probably agree
4. ☐ Uncertain but probably disagree
5. ☐ Disagree
6. ☐ Strongly disagree

40. At times I think I am no good at all.
1. ☐ Strongly agree
2. ☐ Agree
3. ☐ Uncertain, but probably agree
4. ☐ Uncertain but probably disagree
5. ☐ Disagree
6. ☐ Strongly disagree

INSTRUCTIONS: The following few items are about your plans for a job and for an education. There are two types of questions. One type is called "LIKE TO" and the other type is called "EXPECT TO." There is a **very important difference** between the "LIKE TO" and the "EXPECT TO" types of questions.

A "LIKE TO" question on jobs, for example, asks you to choose, from all the jobs you know about, the job you would *really* LIKE TO have when you finish your education. However, sometimes there is a difference between the job a person would *really* LIKE TO have and the job he *actually* EXPECTS TO have. For example, Bob may *really* LIKE TO become an aeronautical engineer. But, he knows that he cannot afford the college education which the job of aeronautical engineer requires. So, instead, he *actually* EXPECTS TO become an aircraft mechanic, a job with aircraft that does not require a college education.

When you answer the questions below, please REMEMBER the *very important difference* between "LIKE TO" and "EXPECT TO" questions.

41–48. SUPPOSING you could have the necessary abilities, education, grades, money, etc., what kind of work would you really LIKE TO do after you finish your education?, that is, after you get out of high school, technical, business, nursing school, or college? PLEASE BE VERY SPECIFIC. NOTE: If you would really LIKE TO go into the military, please specify the military rank you would really LIKE TO have.

_____
(SPECIFIC NAME OR TITLE OF job
I would *really* LIKE TO have.)

49–56. CONSIDERING your abilities, grades, financial resources, chances for technical school, college, etc., what kind of work do you actually EXPECT TO do after you finish your education?, that is, after you get out of high school, technical, business, nursing school, or college? PLEASE BE VERY SPECIFIC. NOTE: If you actually EXPECT TO go into the military, please specify the military rank you actually EXPECT TO get.

_____
(SPECIFIC NAME OR TITLE OF job
I *actually* EXPECT TO get.)

57–58. SUPPOSING you could have the necessary abilities, grades, money, etc., how far would you really LIKE TO go in school?
1. ☐ 10th or 11th grade
2. ☐ Graduate from high school
3. ☐ Trade or technical school
4. ☐ Two-year business school
5. ☐ Nursing school
6. ☐ Two years of college
7. ☐ Four years of college
8. ☐ Graduate or professional school

59–60. CONSIDERING your abilities, grades, financial resources, etc., how far do you actually EXPECT TO go in school?
1. ☐ 10th or 11th grade
2. ☐ Graduate from high school
3. ☐ Trade or technical school
4. ☐ Two-year business school
5. ☐ Nursing school
6. ☐ Two years of college
7. ☐ Four years of college
8. ☐ Graduate or professional school

— 5 —

Please indicate by placing an "X" next to the answer which best describes how you personally feel about each of the following statements:

61. **When a person is born, the success he is going to have is already in the cards, so he might as well accept it and not fight against it.**
1. ☐ Strongly disagree
2. ☐ Disagree
3. ☐ Uncertain, but probably disagree
4. ☐ Uncertain, but probably agree
5. ☐ Agree
6. ☐ Strongly agree

62. **It is more important to have friends than to be a success in one's job.**
1. ☐ Strongly agree
2. ☐ Agree
3. ☐ Uncertain, but probably agree
4. ☐ Uncertain, but probably disagree
5. ☐ Disagree
6. ☐ Strongly disagree

63. **A person should make serious efforts to overcome those obstacles put in his path by other people.**
1. ☐ Strongly agree
2. ☐ Agree
3. ☐ Uncertain, but probably agree
4. ☐ Uncertain, but probably disagree
5. ☐ Disagree
6. ☐ Strongly disagree

64. **Education tends to make a person more unhappy than happy.**
1. ☐ Strongly disagree
2. ☐ Disagree
3. ☐ Uncertain, but probably disagree
4. ☐ Uncertain, but probably agree
5. ☐ Agree
6. ☐ Strongly agree

65. **A man's job should come first, although it may require his spending less time with his wife and children.**
1. ☐ Strongly agree
2. ☐ Agree
3. ☐ Uncertain, but probably agree
4. ☐ Uncertain, but probably disagree
5. ☐ Disagree
6. ☐ Strongly disagree

66. **A college education is worth the time and effort it requires.**
1. ☐ Strongly disagree
2. ☐ Disagree
3. ☐ Uncertain, but probably disagree
4. ☐ Uncertain, but probably agree
5. ☐ Agree
6. ☐ Strongly agree

67. **Whatever a person does, he should try to do it better than anyone else.**
1. ☐ Strongly agree
2. ☐ Agree
3. ☐ Uncertain, but probably agree
4. ☐ Uncertain, but probably disagree
5. ☐ Disagree
6. ☐ Strongly disagree

68. **After a person is married, his (or her) main loyalty should continue to be to his (or her) parents.**
1. ☐ Strongly disagree
2. ☐ Disagree
3. ☐ Uncertain, but probably disagree
4. ☐ Uncertain, but probably agree
5. ☐ Agree
6. ☐ Strongly agree

69. **Other people have more control over a person's future than the person himself does.**
1. ☐ Strongly agree
2. ☐ Agree
3. ☐ Uncertain, but probably agree
4. ☐ Uncertain, but probably disagree
5. ☐ Disagree
6. ☐ Strongly disagree

70. **Generally, in making important decisions, a person should decide what is best for him even if it goes against what his parents and friends want him to do.**
1. ☐ Strongly disagree
2. ☐ Disagree
3. ☐ Uncertain, but probably disagree
4. ☐ Uncertain, but probably agree
5. ☐ Agree
6. ☐ Strongly agree

71. **How frequently does your MOTHER encourage you to continue your education beyond high school, that is, to go on to technical school, college, etc.?**
1. ☐ At least several times a week
2. ☐ About once a week
3. ☐ Several times a month
4. ☐ About once a month
5. ☐ About once every two or three months
6. ☐ Several times a year
7. ☐ Once or twice a year
8. ☐ Less than once a year

CARD THREE

How would you describe the TOP SCHOLARS in your school, that is, those students among the sophomores, juniors and seniors who get the highest grades? In the spaces provided next to each characteristic, indicate with an "X" the approximate proportion of the TOP SCHOLARS in your school you believe are described by each of the following characteristics.

	Proportion of *TOP SCHOLARS* described by each characteristic				
	More Than Half		About Half	Less Than Half	
Characteristics	Almost All	Many		Some	Almost None
16. Get special privileges from teachers					
17. Friends of mine					
18. Are INTERSCHOLASTIC (varsity or junior varsity) ATHLETES					
19. Get along well with the teachers					
20. Popular with the girls					
21. Cause trouble for school officials					
22. Intend to go to college					
23. Try hard to make good grades					
24. Members of the LEADING or "IN" crowd					
25. Intelligent					
26. Make trouble for the teachers					
27. Get special privileges from principal					
28. Well liked by most of the students					
29. Come from families where the father has an important or prestigeful job					
30. Get in trouble with the police					
31. In the academic or college preparatory curriculum					
32. Active in many school activities other than athletics					

Which students, among all the sophomores in your school, are TOP SCHOLARS?

First Name	Last Name		First Name	Last Name	
_____	_____	— — — — 33–36.	_____	_____	— — — — 45–48.
_____	_____	— — — — 37–40.	_____	_____	— — — — 49–52.
_____	_____	— — — — 41–44.	_____	_____	— — — — 53–56.

The following two questions are about your FATHER'S job and his employer. If your FATHER is not currently employed or if your FATHER is deceased, please give the name of the employer your FATHER last worked for and the kind of job he LAST had.

57–64. What is the full name of the company, business, or farm that your FATHER works for? For example: General Motors Car Company. (If your FATHER works for himself, write "self-employed" and give the name of your FATHER's business).

_____

(Name of company, business, or farm which employs your FATHER)

What KIND OF WORK does your FATHER do? (PLEASE TRY TO GIVE THE SPECIFIC NAME OR TITLE OF HIS JOB, for example, "delivery truck driver", and DESCRIBE what he does. For example, "he drives a local delivery truck". ALSO: if your FATHER is in the military, please GIVE HIS SPECIFIC MILITARY RANK).

_____

(Specific name or title of FATHER'S job or his military rank)

_____

(Brief description of what he does)

_____
_____

65. Regardless of what other students think, how do YOU personally feel about a good student being an athlete?

1. ☐ I don't think that a *good student* should be an *athlete*
2. ☐ It doesn't make any difference to me whether a *good student* is an *athlete*
3. ☐ I think it is somewhat important that a *good student* be an *athlete*
4. ☐ I think it is very important that a *good student* be an *athlete*

CARD FOUR

The following statements can be used to describe your experiences in high school. Place an "X" next to the response category, e.g., Strongly agree, Disagree, etc., which best expresses how you personally feel about the statement.

16. I usually feel challenged in my school work; my potential ideas and skills are well used.
1. ☐ Strongly disagree
2. ☐ Disagree
3. ☐ Uncertain, but probably disagree
4. ☐ Uncertain, but probably agree
5. ☐ Agree
6. ☐ Strongly agree

17. In this school there is too much emphasis on surface performance rather than on real education; it's not important what you really know, just look alert and give the right answers.
1. ☐ Strongly agree
2. ☐ Agree
3. ☐ Uncertain, but probably agree
4. ☐ Uncertain, but probably disagree
5. ☐ Disagree
6. ☐ Strongly disagree

18. I believe that the teachers and administrators here are working for my best interests.
1. ☐ Strongly disagree
2. ☐ Disagree
3. ☐ Uncertain, but probably disagree
4. ☐ Uncertain, but probably agree
5. ☐ Agree
6. ☐ Strongly agree

19. There are high standards of justice here; grades are fair, punishments are justified; the student's side of each case is listened to, etc.
1. ☐ Strongly agree
2. ☐ Agree
3. ☐ Uncertain, but probably agree
4. ☐ Uncertain, but probably disagree
5. ☐ Disagree
6. ☐ Strongly disagree

20. What we do in high school is essentially preparation for what will come later; the pay-off will be in college or on the job.
1. ☐ Strongly disagree
2. ☐ Disagree
3. ☐ Uncertain, but probably disagree
4. ☐ Uncertain, but probably agree
5. ☐ Agree
6. ☐ Strongly agree

21. This school is very democratic; your standing is determined by what you do, not by what your family is.
1. ☐ Strongly agree
2. ☐ Agree
3. ☐ Uncertain, but probably agree
4. ☐ Uncertain, but probably disagree
5. ☐ Disagree
6. ☐ Strongly disagree

22. One of the problems in this school is finding enough time to do a good job. There is more emphasis on quantity than on quality.
1. ☐ Strongly disagree
2. ☐ Disagree
3. ☐ Uncertain, but probably disagree
4. ☐ Uncertain, but probably agree
5. ☐ Agree
6. ☐ Strongly agree

23. In making decisions about their careers, students often go to different people in their high school for advice about whether or not to continue their education after high school. **Please rate your GUIDANCE COUNSELORS on their ability and their willingness to give you advice about whether to go on to trade school, college, etc.**
    1. ☐ The COUNSELORS are *able* and *willing* to give me such advice
    2. ☐ The COUNSELORS are *able* to give me advice, but not willing
    3. ☐ The COUNSELORS are *willing* to give me advice, but not able
    4. ☐ The COUNSELORS are neither able nor willing to give me such advice

24. **During your sophomore year, how often have you actually talked with your GUIDANCE COUNSELOR about whether or not to continue your education after high school?**
    1. ☐ Several times a week or more
    2. ☐ About once a week
    3. ☐ Several times a month
    4. ☐ About once a month
    5. ☐ About once every two or three months
    6. ☐ Several times a year
    7. ☐ Once or twice a year
    8. ☐ Not even once a year

25. **When you talk with the GUIDANCE COUNSELOR, what does he suggest or encourage you to do?**
    1. ☐ Go on to a four year college
    2. ☐ Go on to a two year college
    3. ☐ Go for technical or advanced job training
    4. ☐ Go for business or commercial training
    5. ☐ Go into armed services
    6. ☐ Get a job after I get out of high school
    7. ☐ Other: ....

Here are five statements about yourself. Please indicate how strongly you agree or disagree with each statement by placing an "X" in the appropriate box.

26. **I am able to do things as well as most other people.**
    1. ☐ Strongly agree
    2. ☐ Agree
    3. ☐ Uncertain, but probably agree
    4. ☐ Uncertain, but probably disagree
    5. ☐ Disagree
    6. ☐ Strongly disagree

27. **I wish I could have more respect for myself.**
    1. ☐ Strongly agree
    2. ☐ Agree
    3. ☐ Uncertain, but probably agree
    4. ☐ Uncertain, but probably disagree
    5. ☐ Disagree
    6. ☐ Strongly disagree

28. **I feel that I have a number of good qualities.**
    1. ☐ Strongly agree
    2. ☐ Agree
    3. ☐ Uncertain, but probably agree
    4. ☐ Uncertain, but probably disagree
    5. ☐ Disagree
    6. ☐ Strongly disagree

29. **I feel I do not have much to be proud of.**
    1. ☐ Strongly agree
    2. ☐ Agree
    3. ☐ Uncertain, but probably agree
    4. ☐ Uncertain, but probably disagree
    5. ☐ Disagree
    6. ☐ Strongly disagree

30. **I take a positive attitude toward myself.**
    1. ☐ Strongly agree
    2. ☐ Agree
    3. ☐ Uncertain, but probably agree
    4. ☐ Uncertain, but probably disagree
    5. ☐ Disagree
    6. ☐ Strongly disagree

31. In making decisions about their careers, students often seek advice from their parents about whether or not to continue their education beyond high school. **Please rate your MOTHER on her ability and on her willingness to give you advice about continuing your education beyond high school.**
    1. ☐ My MOTHER is *able* and *willing* to give me such advice
    2. ☐ My MOTHER is *able* to give me advice, but she is not willing
    3. ☐ My MOTHER is *willing* to give me advice, but she is not able
    4. ☐ My MOTHER is neither able nor willing to give me such advice.

32. **During your sophomore year, how often have you actually talked with your MOTHER about whether or not to continue your education beyond high school?**
    1. ☐ Several times a week
    2. ☐ About once a week
    3. ☐ Several times a month
    4. ☐ About once a month
    5. ☐ About once every two or three months
    6. ☐ Several times this school year
    7. ☐ Once or twice this school year
    8. ☐ Not even once this school year

Here are some statements about which students have opinions. Please indicate how **you personally** feel about each statement.

33. **People like me don't have much of a chance to be successful in life.**
    1. ☐ Strongly disagree
    2. ☐ Disagree
    3. ☐ Uncertain, but probably disagree
    4. ☐ Uncertain, but probably agree
    5. ☐ Agree
    6. ☐ Strongly agree

34. **Every time I try to get ahead, something or someone stops me.**
    1. ☐ Strongly agree
    2. ☐ Agree
    3. ☐ Uncertain, but probably agree
    4. ☐ Uncertain, but probably disagree
    5. ☐ Disagree
    6. ☐ Strongly disagree

35. **The more education a person has, the better able he is to really enjoy and appreciate life.**
1. ☐ Strongly agree
2. ☐ Agree
3. ☐ Uncertain, but probably agree
4. ☐ Uncertain, but probably disagree
5. ☐ Disagree
6. ☐ Strongly disagree

36. **People who accept their condition in life are happier than those who try to change things.**
1. ☐ Strongly agree
2. ☐ Agree
3. ☐ Uncertain, but probably agree
4. ☐ Uncertain, but probably disagree
5. ☐ Disagree
6. ☐ Strongly disagree

37. **Education helps a person use his leisure time to better advantage.**
1. ☐ Strongly agree
2. ☐ Agree
3. ☐ Uncertain, but probably agree
4. ☐ Uncertain, but probably disagree
5. ☐ Disagree
6. ☐ Strongly disagree

38. **Generally, it is possible for a person to plan his future so that more things will come out right than wrong in the long run.**
1. ☐ Strongly disagree
2. ☐ Disagree
3. ☐ Uncertain, but probably disagree
4. ☐ Uncertain, but probably agree
5. ☐ Agree
6. ☐ Strongly agree

39. **When a person is making an important decision, he should consider the advice of his parents as more important than the advice of his friends.**
1. ☐ Strongly agree
2. ☐ Agree
3. ☐ Uncertain, but probably agree
4. ☐ Uncertain, but probably disagree
5. ☐ Disagree
6. ☐ Strongly disagree

40. **Good luck is more important than hard work for success.**
1. ☐ Strongly disagree
2. ☐ Disagree
3. ☐ Uncertain, but probably disagree
4. ☐ Uncertain, but probably agree
5. ☐ Agree
6. ☐ Strongly agree

41. **A high school education is worth the time and effort it requires.**
1. ☐ Strongly disagree
2. ☐ Disagree
3. ☐ Uncertain, but probably disagree
4. ☐ Uncertain, but probably agree
5. ☐ Agree
6. ☐ Strongly agree

42. **A person's job should come first, even if it means spending less time in recreation and play.**
1. ☐ Strongly agree
2. ☐ Agree
3. ☐ Uncertain, but probably agree
4. ☐ Uncertain, but probably disagree
5. ☐ Disagree
6. ☐ Strongly disagree

43. **Success in the occupational world depends more on luck than on ability and willingness to work.**
1. ☐ Strongly agree
2. ☐ Agree
3. ☐ Uncertain, but probably agree
4. ☐ Uncertain, but probably disagree
5. ☐ Disagree
6. ☐ Strongly disagree

44. **Except for growing old and the like, a person has more control over his own future than do the forces of nature or fate.**
1. ☐ Strongly disagree
2. ☐ Disagree
3. ☐ Uncertain, but probably disagree
4. ☐ Uncertain, but probably agree
5. ☐ Agree
6. ☐ Strongly agree

45. **Before a person is married, his (or her) main loyalty should belong to his (or her) parents.**
1. ☐ Strongly agree
2. ☐ Agree
3. ☐ Uncertain, but probably agree
4. ☐ Uncertain, but probably disagree
5. ☐ Disagree
6. ☐ Strongly disagree

46. **In business and industry, a person without a college education can get ahead just as rapidly as a person with a college education.**
1. ☐ Strongly agree
2. ☐ Agree
3. ☐ Uncertain, but probably agree
4. ☐ Uncertain, but probably disagree
5. ☐ Disagree
6. ☐ Strongly disagree

47. **A person should use some of his time in the present to make plans for his future.**
1. ☐ Strongly disagree
2. ☐ Disagree
3. ☐ Uncertain, but probably disagree
4. ☐ Uncertain, but probably agree
5. ☐ Agree
6. ☐ Strongly agree

48. **A person should live mainly for today and let tomorrow take care of itself.**
1. ☐ Strongly disagree
2. ☐ Disagree
3. ☐ Uncertain, but probably disagree
4. ☐ Uncertain, but probably agree
5. ☐ Agree
6. ☐ Strongly agree

49–62. IF YOU DO NOT ACTUALLY EXPECT TO go on to a four-year college after you get out of high school, what are the four most important reasons why you do **NOT** intend to go on to a four year college education? (Check the four reasons you consider most important).

1. ☐ I have no desire to go
2. ☐ Most of my friends are not going to a four year college
3. ☐ Costs too much
4. ☐ My teachers or guidance counselors did not encourage me to go
5. ☐ My grades are not good enough
6. ☐ I have to work to help my parents
7. ☐ I plan to get married soon after I get out of high school
8. ☐ I am tired of being a student

9. ☐ My parents do not want me to go to a four year college
10. ☐ I plan to attend business, trade-technical, or vocational school
11. ☐ I plan to attend a two year college like Broome Tech.
12. ☐ I plan to get a job after I get out of high school
13. ☐ I just don't like school
14. ☐ I plan to go into armed services and then go to college after discharge

CARD FIVE

16. **Regardless of what other students think, how do YOU personally feel about an athlete being a good student?**

1. ☐ I don't think that an *athlete* should be a *good student*
2. ☐ It doesn't make any difference to me whether an *athlete* is a *good student*

3. ☐ I think it is somewhat important that an *athlete* be a *good student*
4. ☐ I think that it is very important that an *athlete* be a *good student*

Here is a list of sports. Please read the questions very carefully and then answer each question.

Type of Sport	Did You Go Out For the Sport?		IF YOU DID GO OUT FOR THE SPORT:				
			Did You Play That Sport on?			Did You Complete the Season?	
	No	Yes	Varsity	Junior Varsity	Intra-mural	Yes	No
18–20. Football							
21–23. Basketball							
24–26. Baseball							
27–29. Soccer							
30–32. Softball							
33–35. Volleyball							
36–38. Track							
39–41. Cross-country							
42–44. Wrestling							
45–47. Swimming							
48–50. Gymnastics							
51–53. Golf							
54–56. Tennis							
57–59. Hockey							
60–62. Bowling							
63–65. Weightlifting							
66–68. Other: (Specify)							
69–71.							
72–74.							

75. **How good a student do you want to be in school?**
1. ☐ One of the best students in the sophomore class
2. ☐ Above the middle of the sophomore class
3. ☐ In the middle of the sophomore class
4. ☐ Just good enough to get by
5. ☐ I don't care

CARD SIX

16. **In general, how do you rate your own athletic ability?**
1. ☐ Not very good in *any* sport
2. ☐ Good, but not very outstanding in *one* sport
3. ☐ Good, but not very outstanding in *more than one* sport
4. ☐ Outstanding in *one* sport
5. ☐ Outstanding in *more than one* sport

Here is a second set of statements which can be used to describe your experiences in high school. Place an "X" next to the response category, e.g., Strongly agree, Disagree, etc., which best expresses how **you personally feel** about the statement.

17. **Too much of the work here is meaningless; much of it is "makework" with no particular point.**
1. ☐ Strongly agree
2. ☐ Agree
3. ☐ Uncertain, but probably agree
4. ☐ Uncertain, but probably disagree
5. ☐ Disagree
6. ☐ Strongly disagree

18. **I am proud to be a student here.**
1. ☐ Strongly disagree
2. ☐ Disagree
3. ☐ Uncertain, but probably disagree
4. ☐ Uncertain, but probably agree
5. ☐ Agree
6. ☐ Strongly agree

19. **Although I usually know what to do in school, I frequently don't know why I am supposed to do it.**
1. ☐ Strongly agree
2. ☐ Agree
3. ☐ Uncertain, but probably agree
4. ☐ Uncertain, but probably disagree
5. ☐ Disagree
6. ☐ Strongly disagree

20. **Personality, pull, and bluff get students through most of the courses here.**
1. ☐ Strongly disagree
2. ☐ Disagree
3. ☐ Uncertain, but probably disagree
4. ☐ Uncertain, but probably agree
5. ☐ Agree
6. ☐ Strongly agree

21. **What we do in school seems unreal; it has little to do with the important problems of living.**
1. ☐ Strongly agree
2. ☐ Agree
3. ☐ Uncertain, but probably agree
4. ☐ Uncertain, but probably disagree
5. ☐ Disagree
6. ☐ Strongly disagree

22. **There is too much emphasis here on grades and "success" rather than on true learning.**
1. ☐ Strongly disagree
2. ☐ Disagree
3. ☐ Uncertain, but probably disagree
4. ☐ Uncertain, but probably agree
5. ☐ Agree
6. ☐ Strongly agree

23 **The main reason for going to high school is to get the diploma; it is your passport to a good job or college.**
1. ☐ Strongly agree
2. ☐ Agree
3. ☐ Uncertain, but probably agree
4. ☐ Uncertain, but probably disagree
5. ☐ Disagree
6. ☐ Strongly disagree

24. **Please rate your FATHER on his ability and willingness to give you advice on whether or not to continue your education beyond high school.**
1. ☐ My FATHER is *able* and *willing* to give me such advice
2. ☐ My FATHER is *able* to give me advice, but he is not willing
3. ☐ My FATHER is *willing* to give me advice, but he is not able
4. ☐ My FATHER is neither able nor willing to give such advice

25. **During this past school year, how often have you actually talked with your FATHER about whether or not to continue your education beyond high school?**
1. ☐ Several times a week
2. ☐ About once a week
3. ☐ Several times a month
4. ☐ About once a month
5. ☐ About once every two or three months
6. ☐ Several times this school year
7. ☐ Once or twice this school year
8. ☐ Not even once this school year

How would you describe the INTERSCHOLASTIC ATHLETES in your school, that is, those students among the sophomores, juniors and seniors who regularly participate in junior varsity or varsity sports where your school competes against other schools? In the spaces provided next to each characteristic, indicate with an "X" the approximate proportion of INTERSCHOLASTIC ATHLETES in your school you believe are described by each of the following characteristics.

		Proportion of INTERSCHOLASTIC ATHLETES described by each characteristic				
		More Than Half		About Half	Less Than Half	
	Characteristics	Almost All	Many		Some	Almost None
26.	Active in many school activities in addition to athletics					
27.	Really interested in school					
28.	Get along well with the teachers					
29.	Popular with the girls					
30.	Cause trouble for school officials					
31.	Intend to go to college					
32.	Make trouble for the teachers					
33.	Try hard to make good grades					
34.	Members of the LEADING or "IN" crowd					
35.	Intelligent					
36.	Get special privileges from the principal					
37.	Well liked by most of the students					
38.	Come from families where the father has an important or prestigeful job					
39.	Get in trouble with the police					
40.	In the academic or college preparatory curriculum					
41.	Get special privileges from the teachers					
42.	Friends of mine					
43.	Are considered in the TOP SCHOLAR group					

Which students, among all the sophomores in your school, are INTERSCHOLASTIC ATHLETES?

First Name   Last Name   First Name   Last Name

_____ _____   ___ ___ ___   _____ _____   ___ ___ ___
                               44–47.   56–59.

_____ _____   ___ ___ ___   _____ _____   ___ ___ ___
                               48–51.   60–63.

_____ _____   ___ ___ ___   _____ _____   ___ ___ ___
                               52–55.   64–67.

68. Which one of the following statements best describes how STUDENTS in your school feel about athletes being good students and good students being athletes?

1. ☐ They feel it doesn't matter if an *athlete* is a *good student* or if a *good student* is an *athlete*

2. ☐ They feel a *good student* should be an *athlete*, but it doesn't matter if an *athlete* is a *good student*

3. ☐ They feel an *athlete* should be a *good student*, but it doesn't matter if a *good student* is an *athlete*

4. ☐ They feel that an *athlete* should be a *good student* and that a *good student* should be an *athlete*

69. How important is it for YOU to be an athlete in school?

1. ☐ It is *not important* to me personally that I be an athlete in school

2. ☐ It is *somewhat important* to me personally that I be an athlete in school

3. ☐ It is *very important* to me personally that I be an athlete in school

70. Do your parents stress or emphasize your going out for an interscholastic sport in high school?

1. ☐ Yes, they stress it a lot

2. ☐ Yes, they stress it somewhat

3. ☐ Yes, but they seldom mention it

4. ☐ They don't care one way or the other

5. ☐ No, they would rather I not go out for an interscholastic sport

CARD SEVEN

16. During this school year, did you ever stay away from school just because you didn't want to go?

1. ☐ No

2. ☐ Yes, for 1 or 2 days

3. ☐ Yes, for 3 to 6 days

4. ☐ Yes, for 7 to 15 days

5. ☐ Yes, for 16 or more days

17. Who is now acting as your mother? If you are adopted, consider your adoptive mother as your real mother.

1. ☐ My real mother, who is living at home

2. ☐ My real mother, who is not living at home

3. ☐ My stepmother

4. ☐ My foster mother

5. ☐ My grandmother

6. ☐ Another relative (aunt, etc.)

7. ☐ Another adult

8. ☐ No one

18. How bright or intelligent do you think you are in comparison with the other sophomore students in your school?

1. ☐ Among the brightest

2. ☐ Above average

3. ☐ Average

4. ☐ Below average

5. ☐ Among the lowest

19. Who is now acting as your father? If you are adopted consider your adoptive father as your real father.

1. ☐ My real father, who is living at home

2. ☐ My real father, who is not living at home

3. ☐ My stepfather

4. ☐ My foster father

5. ☐ My grandfather

6. ☐ Another relative (uncle, etc.)

7. ☐ Another adult

8. ☐ No one

20. How good a student do your parents want you to be in school.

1. ☐ One of the best students in the sophomore class

2. ☐ Above the middle of the sophomore class

3. ☐ In the middle of the sophomore class

4. ☐ Just good enough to get by

5. ☐ Do not know

21. What kind of reputation do you have among your teachers as far as your behavior goes?

1. ☐ Very good

2. ☐ Good

3. ☐ Fair

4. ☐ Poor

5. ☐ Very poor

In terms of the following characteristics, how would you describe **each** of your three BEST FRIENDS? In the spaces provided, indicate with an "X" whether the characteristic IS Descriptive or is NOT descriptive of Friend Number One, Friend Number Two, and Friend Number Three.

Characteristic	Friend Number One		Friend Number Two		Friend Number Three	
	IS Descriptive	NOT Descriptive	IS Descriptive	NOT Descriptive	IS Descriptive	NOT Descriptive
22. Active in many school activities *other than* sports						
23. Makes trouble for teachers						
24. Is a junior or senior in this school						
25. Tries hard to make good grades						
26. Well liked by most of the students						
27. Studies a lot						
28. Is a sophomore in this school						
29. Member of the LEADING or "IN" crowd						
30. Gets special privileges from the principal						
31. Is a student in another high school						
32. Intends to go to college						
33. Gets special privileges from the teachers						
34. Considered in the TOP SCHOLAR group						
35. Has dropped out of high school						
36. In the academic or college preparatory curriculum						
37. Causes trouble for school officials						
38. Is an INTERSCHOLASTIC (varsity or junior varsity) ATHLETE						
39. Comes from a family where the father has an important or prestigeful job						
40. Will probably drop out of school						
41. Really interested in school						
42. Gets in trouble with the police						
43. Dislikes school						
44. Gets along well with teachers						

What are the names of your THREE BEST OR CLOSE FRIENDS among all sophomores in this high school?

First Name   Last Name   First Name   Last Name

_____ _____   — — — —   _____ _____   — — — —
                                      45–48.   53–56.

_____ _____   — — — —   _____ _____   — — — —
                                      49–52.   57–60.

THE END. THANK YOU

— 15 —

CONFIDENTIAL   _ _ _ _ _ _ _ _ _ _ _ _ _
                                                                                    (NUMERIC)

SCHOOL AND CAREER ATTITUDE SURVEY

_____   _____
        (LAST NAME)   **PLEASE**   (FULL NAME OF YOUR SCHOOL)

                                             PRINT
_____   _____
        (FIRST NAME)   (NAME OF CITY OR TOWN)

OBJECTIVES OF THE SURVEY

Thirty percent of all students never complete high school. The social and economic implications of this loss of human resources are considerable. In a complex, technological society where education is a crucial institution, a more systematic and comprehensive understanding of the variables which influence educational goal decisions is required if enlightened programs are to be formulated to ensure that each person is accorded maximum opportunity to develop his potential. The variables which influence the educational goals of an individual are many in number and wide in scope, ranging from parental socialization practices, friendship patterns, to the social structure of the high school, including the characteristics of those who comprise the leading crowds, the top scholars, and the top athletes, as well as degree of participation in the various types of extra-curricular activities.

During the past four years we have asked your cooperation in our effort to assemble data on these various influences. Much has been learned from an analysis of that information. Now, in your senior year, we ask once again that you assist us in furthering an understanding of the complex processes of educational goal decesions. Some of the items in previous questionnaires are asked in this questionnaire. We do this because an understanding of the *dynamics* of educational goal decisions is crucial for formulating realistic policy recommendations.

Research findings from this study are published in the professional journals of sociology and education. They are also provided to each of the participating schools. And, a brief summary of the data is now available in your school library. We also invite you to visit the research office at the University by phoning 798-2600 for an appointment.
In responding to the items in the questionnaire, please:

1. Remember that *all* of your responses are *confidential*. Only trained research personnel are permitted to see the questionnaires and then only for the purpose of transferring the information to punch cards.

2. Answer *all* of the items in the questionnaire. This improves the quality of the data considerably.

3. Try to answer each item as truthfully and candidly as possible. Frank responses provide a more realistic picture of the school, its faculty, and the students.

INSTRUCTIONS

1. READ EACH QUESTION CAREFULLY: Answer each candidly and to the best of your ability.

2. For the items about one or both parents, answer the item in terms of the person who is currently your parent, which may be your real father or mother, your step-father or step-mother, or your male or female guardian. If you are living with only one parent, then answer the questions about the other parent as though the other parent were still living with you.

3. Most items can be answered by placing an "X" in the box next to the answer you choose. For example:

> **How relevant are most of your high school courses
> to contemporary society?**
>
> 1. ☐ Extremely relevant
> 2. ☐ Somewhat relevant
> 3. ☐ Not at all relevant

4. If you have a problem, raise your hand and a research worker will come to your place and assist you. Please *continue to answer the items with which you have no problem until the research worker comes to your place*. Otherwise, you will not finish on time.

THANK YOU! TURN TO PAGE TWO AND BEGIN

— 1 —

CARD ONE

16. What is your sex?
1. ☐ Male
2. ☐ Female

17. What kind of program are you taking in school?
1. ☐ Academic or College Prep.
2. ☐ Science
3. ☐ General
4. ☐ Commercial or Business
5. ☐ Vocational Agriculture
6. ☐ Vocational Industrial Arts
7. ☐ Other (Specify) : ....).

18. Generally, over the past 5 to 8 years or so, how often have your parents praised or rewarded you when you did something very well?
1. ☐ Hardly at all
2. ☐ Sometimes
3. ☐ Fairly often
4. ☐ Very often
5. ☐ Almost every time

Please indicate to what degree you **agree** or **disagree** with each of the following statements.

19. The American system of democracy can respond effectively to the needs of the people.
1. ☐ Strongly agree
2. ☐ Agree
3. ☐ Undecided, but probably agree
4. ☐ Undecided, but probably disagree
5. ☐ Disagree
6. ☐ Strongly disagree

20. There are legitimate channels for reform which should be used before attempting civil disobedience and disruption.
1. ☐ Strongly disagree
2. ☐ Disagree
3. ☐ Undecided, but probably disagree
4. ☐ Undecided, but probably agree
5. ☐ Agree
6. ☐ Strongly agree

21. The individual in today's society is isolated and cut off from meaningful relationships with others.
1. ☐ Strongly disagree
2. ☐ Disagree
3. ☐ Undecided, but probably disagree
4. ☐ Undecided, but probably agree
5. ☐ Agree
6. ☐ Strongly agree

22. Economic well-being and prosperity in this country is unjustly and unfairly distributed.
1. ☐ Strongly agree
2. ☐ Agree
3. ☐ Undecided, but probably agree
4. ☐ Undecided, but probably disagree
5. ☐ Disagree
6. ☐ Strongly disagree

23. There is too much concern with equality and too little concern with law and order in the country today.
1. ☐ Strongly disagree
2. ☐ Disagree
3. ☐ Undecided, but probably disagree
4. ☐ Undecided, but probably agree
5. ☐ Agree
6. ☐ Strongly agree

24. The whole social system ought to be replaced by an entirely new one; the existing structures are beyond reasonable hope of repair.
1. ☐ Strongly disagree
2. ☐ Disagree
3. ☐ Undecided, but probably disagree
4. ☐ Undecided, but probably agree
5. ☐ Agree
6. ☐ Strongly agree

25. Computers and other advanced technology are creating an inhuman and impersonal world.
1. ☐ Strongly agree
2. ☐ Agree
3. ☐ Undecided, but probably agree
4. ☐ Undecided, but probably disagree
5. ☐ Disagree
6. ☐ Strongly disagree

26. During your senior year, how often have you actually talked with your MOTHER about whether or not to continue your education beyond high school?
1. ☐ Several times a week
2. ☐ About once a week
3. ☐ Several times a month
4. ☐ About once a month
5. ☐ About once every two or three months
6. ☐ Several times this school year
7. ☐ Once or twice this school year
8. ☐ Not even once this school year

27. During your senior year, how frequently has your MOTHER encouraged you to continue your education beyond high school, that is, to go on to technical school, college, etc.?
1. ☐ At least several times a week
2. ☐ About once a week
3. ☐ Several times a month
4. ☐ About once a month
5. ☐ About once every two or three months
6. ☐ Several times a year
7. ☐ Once or twice a year
8. ☐ Less than once a year

28. During this school year, how much time, on the average, did you spend doing homework outside of school, like late in the afternoon, at night, etc.?
1. ☐ None, or almost none
2. ☐ Less than ½ hour a day
3. ☐ About ½ to ¾ hours a day
4. ☐ About 1 hour a day
5. ☐ About 1½ to 1¾ hours a day
6. ☐ About 2 hours a day
7. ☐ About 3 or more hours a day

29. How often does your FATHER give you praise, encouragement, or approval for what you do?
1. ☐ Almost never
2. ☐ Very seldom
3. ☐ Once in a while
4. ☐ Frequently
5. ☐ Very often

Here are some statements about which students have opinions. Please indicate how you personally feel about each statement.

30. People like me don't have much of a chance to be successful in life.
1. ☐ Strongly disagree
2. ☐ Disagree
3. ☐ Uncertain, but probably disagree
4. ☐ Uncertain, but probably agree
5. ☐ Agree
6. ☐ Strongly agree

31. Every time I try to get ahead, something or some-one stops me.
1. ☐ Strongly agree
2. ☐ Agree
3. ☐ Uncertain, but probably agree
4. ☐ Uncertain, but probably disagree
5. ☐ Disagree
6. ☐ Strongly disagree

32. A person should live mainly for today and let to-morrow take care of itself.
1. ☐ Strongly disagree
2. ☐ Disagree
3. ☐ Uncertain, but probably disagree
4. ☐ Uncertain, but probably agree
5. ☐ Agree
6. ☐ Strongly agree

33. The more education a person has, the better able he is to really enjoy and appreciate life.
1. ☐ Strongly agree
2. ☐ Agree
3. ☐ Uncertain, but probably agree
4. ☐ Uncertain, but probably disagree
5. ☐ Disagree
6. ☐ Strongly disagree

34. A person should make serious efforts to overcome those obstacles put in his path by other people.
1. ☐ Strongly agree
2. ☐ Agree
3. ☐ Uncertain, but probably agree
4. ☐ Uncertain, but probably disagree
5. ☐ Disagree
6. ☐ Strongly disagree

35. A person should live as much for the future as for the present.
1. ☐ Strongly disagree
2. ☐ Disagree
3. ☐ Uncertain, but probably disagree
4. ☐ Uncertain, but probably agree
5. ☐ Agree
6. ☐ Strongly agree

36. In business and industry, a person without a col-lege education can get ahead just as rapidly as a person with a college education.
1. ☐ Strongly agree
2. ☐ Agree
3. ☐ Uncertain, but probably agree
4. ☐ Uncertain, but probably disagree
5. ☐ Disagree
6. ☐ Strongly disagree

37. Whatever a person does, he should try to do it better than anyone else.
1. ☐ Strongly agree
2. ☐ Agree
3. ☐ Uncertain, but probably agree
4. ☐ Uncertain, but probably disagree
5. ☐ Disagree
6. ☐ Strongly disagree

38. A person should make serious efforts to overcome the obstacles put in his path by nature and fate.
1. ☐ Strongly agree
2. ☐ Agree
3. ☐ Uncertain, but probably agree
4. ☐ Uncertain, but probably disagree
5. ☐ Disagree
6. ☐ Strongly disagree

39. Which ONE of the following best describes the employment situation of your mother?
1. ☐ Full-time housewife
2. ☐ Works part-time at her home (less than 30 hours)
3. ☐ Works part-time outside her home.
4. ☐ Works full-time (30 hours a week or more) at her home doing something other than housework
5. ☐ Works full-time (30 hours a week or more) outside her home
6. ☐ Works sometime at her home
7. ☐ Works sometime outside her home
8. ☐ Other (Specify: ....)

40. **Good luck is more important than hard work for success.**
1. ☐ Strongly disagree
2. ☐ Disagree
3. ☐ Uncertain, but probably disagree
4. ☐ Uncertain, but probably agree
5. ☐ Agree
6. ☐ Strongly agree

41. **When a person is born, the success he is going to have is already in the cards, so he might as well accept it and not fight against it.**
1. ☐ Strongly disagree
2. ☐ Disagree
3. ☐ Uncertain, but probably disagree
4. ☐ Uncertain, but probably agree
5. ☐ Agree
6. ☐ Strongly agree

42. **The most important qualities of a man are determination and driving ambition.**
1. ☐ Strongly agree
2. ☐ Agree
3. ☐ Uncertain, but probably agree
4. ☐ Uncertain but probably disagree
5. ☐ Disagree
6. ☐ Strongly disagree

43. **Generally, over the past 5 to 8 years or so, have your parents stressed or emphasized that you should try to do things better than anyone else.**
1. ☐ Yes, they have stressed it a lot
2. ☐ Yes, they have stressed it somewhat
3. ☐ Yes, but they have seldom mentioned it
4. ☐ They haven't said one way or the other
5. ☐ No, they would rather I not try to do things better than other people

44. **If you could be remembered here at school for one of the six things below, which one would you like it to be?**
1. ☐ For being a *good student*
2. ☐ For being a *good athlete*
3. ☐ For being *popular*
4. ☐ For being a *good student* and a *good athlete*
5. ☐ For being a *good student* and *popular*
6. ☐ For being a *good athlete* and *popular*

45. **How often does your MOTHER give you praise, encouragement, or approval for what you do?**
1. ☐ Very often
2. ☐ Frequently
3. ☐ Once in a while
4. ☐ Very seldom
5. ☐ Almost never

46. **Would you say that in your home it has been taken for granted that you will continue your education after you get out of high school?**
1. ☐ Yes
2. ☐ No
3. ☐ Do not know

47. **Generally, when your FATHER makes decisions which concern you or when he makes rules for you to follow, does he explain to you the reasons for the decisions or for the rules?**
1. ☐ He *almost never* explains his decisions or rules to me
2. ☐ He *once in a while* explains his decisions or rules to me
3. ☐ He *usually* explains his decisions or rules to me
4. ☐ He *almost always* explains his decisions or rules to me

48. **For MALES AND FEMALES: What are your plans regarding marriage?**
1. ☐ I am married now
2. ☐ I plan to get married soon after I get out of high school
3. ☐ I plan to get married while in the service or while in trade school, business school, nursing school, or college
4. ☐ I plan to finish all my schooling and/or service obligations and then get married
5. ☐ I am undecided

49. **How much formal education does or did your FATHER have?**
1. ☐ Less than sixth grade
2. ☐ Seventh, eighth, or ninth grade
3. ☐ Tenth or eleventh grade
4. ☐ High school graduate
5. ☐ Some college, trade, technical, or two year business school
6. ☐ College graduate
7. ☐ Graduate or professional school
8. ☐ Do not know

50. **What kind of a reputation do you have among your TEACHERS as far as your SCHOOL WORK goes?**
1. ☐ Very good
2. ☐ Good
3. ☐ Fair
4. ☐ Poor
5. ☐ Very poor

51. **In most high schools there are usually one or two groups of students who are referred to as the LEADING crowd or as the "IN" group. What about your school? How many LEADING crowds or "IN" groups are there in your school?**
1. ☐ One
2. ☐ Two
3. ☐ Three or more
4. ☐ None

— 4 —

52. During your senior year, how often have you actually talked with your TEACHERS about whether or not to continue your education beyond high school?

1. ☐ Several times a week or more
2. ☐ About once a week
3. ☐ Several times a month
4. ☐ About once a month
5. ☐ About once every two or three months
6. ☐ Several times this school year
7. ☐ Once or twice this school year
8. ☐ Not even once this school year

53. When you talk with your TEACHERS, what do they usually suggest or encourage you to do?

1. ☐ Go on to a four year college
2. ☐ Go on to a two year college
3. ☐ Go for technical or advanced job training
4. ☐ Go for business or commercial training
5. ☐ Go into the armed services
6. ☐ Get a job after I get out of high school
7. ☐ Other: ....

How would you describe the sophomore, junior, or senior students who are members of the **most prominent or important** LEADING crowd or "IN" group? In the spaces provided next to each characteristic, indicate with an "X" the approximate proportion of the LEADING crowd or "IN" group in your school you believe are described by each of the following characteristics.

	Proportion of *LEADING* crowd or "IN" group described by each characteristic				
	More Than Half		About Half	Less Than Half	
.Characteristics	Almost All	Many		Some	Almost None
54. Get along well with the teachers					
55. Really interested in school					
56. Are considered in the TOP SCHOLAR group					
57. Get special privileges from the teachers					
58. Make trouble for the teachers					
59. Get in trouble with the police					
60. Come from families where the father has an important or prestigeful job					
61. Try hard to make good grades					
62. Get special privileges from the principal					
63. Intend to go to college					
64. Cause trouble for school officials					
65. Are INTERSCHOLASTIC (varsity or junior varsity) ATHLETES					

Which students, among all the seniors in your school, are members of the most prominent or important LEADING crowd or "IN" group? Please name three such students.

First Name   Last Name

_____ _____   — — — —
                                      66–69

_____ _____   — — — —
                                      70–73

_____ _____   — — — —
                                      74–77

CARD TWO

16. **Which one of the following statements comes closest to your own point of view?**

1. ☐ Resisting the draft is basically wrong—a citizen is obligated to serve his country regardless of his personal views about the justness of a war.

2. ☐ An individual should obey his conscience —if he feels that he is being drafted to fight in a war that is morally wrong, he should resist in any way he can.

Here are five statements about yourself. Please indicate how strongly you agree or disagree with each statement by placing an "X" in the appropriate box.

17. **I am able to do things as well as most other people.**
1. ☐ Strongly agree
2. ☐ Agree
3. ☐ Uncertain, but probably agree
4. ☐ Uncertain, but probably disagree
5. ☐ Disagree
6. ☐ Strongly disagree

18. **I wish I could have more respect for myself.**
1. ☐ Strongly agree
2. ☐ Agree
3. ☐ Uncertain, but probably agree
4. ☐ Uncertain, but probably disagree
5. ☐ Disagree
6. ☐ Strongly disagree

19. **I feel that I have a number of good qualities.**
1. ☐ Strongly agree
2. ☐ Agree
3. ☐ Uncertain, but probably agree
4. ☐ Uncertain, but probably disagree
5. ☐ Disagree
6. ☐ Strongly disagree

20. **I feel I do not have much to be proud of.**
1. ☐ Strongly agree
2. ☐ Agree
3. ☐ Uncertain, but probably agree
4. ☐ Uncertain, but probably disagree
5. ☐ Disagree
6. ☐ Strongly disagree

21. **I take a positive attitude toward myself.**
1. ☐ Strongly agree
2. ☐ Agree
3. ☐ Uncertain, but probably agree
4. ☐ Uncertain, but probably disagree
5. ☐ Disagree
6. ☐ Strongly disagree

22. **How important is it to YOU personally that you be a good student?**
1. ☐ It is *not important* to me personally that I be a good student
2. ☐ It is *somewhat important* to me personally that I be a good student
3. ☐ It is *very important* to me personally that I be a good student

23. **During your senior year, how often have you actually talked with your GUIDANCE COUNSELOR about whether or not to continue your education after high school?**
1. ☐ Several times a week or more
2. ☐ About once a week
3. ☐ Several times a month
4. ☐ About once a month
5. ☐ About once every two or three months
6. ☐ Several times a year
7. ☐ Once or twice a year
8. ☐ Not even once a year

24. **When you talk with the GUIDANCE COUNSELOR, what does he suggest or encourage you to do?**
1. ☐ Go on to a four year college
2. ☐ Go on to a two year college-
3. ☐ Go for technical or advanced job training
4. ☐ Go for business or commercial training
5. ☐ Go into armed services
6. ☐ Get a job after I get out of high school
7. ☐ Other: ....

25. **Check the one category below which comes closest to your feeling about yourself.**

1. ☐ I don't like myself the way I am; I'd like to change myself completely

2. ☐ There are many things about myself I'd like to change, but not completely

3. ☐ I'd like to stay very much the same; there is very little about myself that I would change

26. **Generally, when your MOTHER makes decisions which concern you or when she makes rules for you to follow, does she explain to you the reasons for the decisions or rules?**

1. ☐ She *almost always* explains her decisions or rules to me

2. ☐ She *usually* explains her decisions or rules to me

3. ☐ She *sometimes* explains her decisions or rules to me

4. ☐ She *once in a while* explains her decisions or rules to me

5. ☐ She *almost never* explains her decisions or rules to me

27. **Which one of the following views of American society and American life reflect your own feelings?**

1. ☐ The American way of life is superior to that of any other country

2. ☐ There are serious flaws in our society today, but the system is flexible enough to solve the flaws and problems

3. ☐ The American system is not flexible enough; radical change is needed

INSTRUCTIONS: The following few items are about your plans for a job and for an education. There are two types of questions. One type is called "LIKE TO" and the other type is called "EXPECT TO." There is a **very important difference** between the "LIKE TO" and the "EXPECT TO" types of questions.

A "LIKE TO" question on jobs, for example, asks you to choose, from all the jobs you know about, the job you would *really* LIKE TO have when you finish your education. However, sometimes there is a difference between the job a person would *really* LIKE TO have and the job he *actually* EXPECTS TO have. For example, Bob may *really* LIKE TO become an aeronautical engineer. But, he knows that he cannot afford the college education which the job of aeronautical engineer requires. So, instead, he *actually* EXPECTS TO become an aircraft mechanic, a job with aircraft that does not require a college education.

When you answer the questions below, please REMEMBER the *very important difference* between "LIKE TO" and "EXPECT TO" questions.

28. **SUPPOSING you could have the necessary abilities,**
— **education, grades, money, etc., what kind of work**
35. **would you really LIKE TO do after you finish your education?, that is, after you get out of high school, technical, business, nursing school, or college? PLEASE BE VERY SPECIFIC. NOTE: If you would really LIKE TO go into the military, please specify the military rank you would really LIKE TO have.**

(SPECIFIC NAME OR TITLE OF job
I would *really* LIKE TO have.)

36. **CONSIDERING your abilities, grades, financial re-**
— **sources, chances for technical school, college, etc.,**
43. **what kind of work do you actually EXPECT TO do after you finish your education?, that, is after you get out of high school, technical, business, nursing school, or college? PLEASE BE VERY SPECIFIC. NOTE: If you actually EXPECT TO go into the military, please specify the military rank you actually EXPECT TO get.**

(SPECIFIC NAME OR TITLE OF job
I *actually* EXPECT TO get.)

44. **SUPPOSING you could have the necessary abilities,**
— **grades, money, etc., how far would you really LIKE**
45. **TO go in school?**
1. ☐ Graduate from high school
2. ☐ Trade or technical school
3. ☐ Two-year business school
4. ☐ Nursing school
5. ☐ Two years of college
6. ☐ Four years of college
7. ☐ Graduate or professional school

46. **CONSIDERING your abilities, grades, financial re-**
— **sources, etc., how far do you actually EXPECT TO go**
47. **in school?**
1. ☐ Graduate from high school
2. ☐ Trade or technical school
3. ☐ Two-year business school
4. ☐ Nursing school
5. ☐ Two years of college
6. ☐ Four years of college
7. ☐ Graduate or professional school

IF YOU ACTUALLY EXPECT TO CONTINUE YOUR EDUCATION BEYOND HIGH SCHOOL: Please answer items 48-52. IF YOU DO NOT EXPECT TO CONTINUE YOUR EDUCATION BEYOND HIGH SCHOOL: Please answer items 53-64.

48. **CONTINUING YOUR EDUCATION BEYOND HIGH SCHOOL: How much do you think your first year of continued education will cost? Assume that you have to pay for everything in cash, e.g., tuition, room and board, books, etc.**
1. ☐ Under $500
2. ☐ $ 500—$ 999
3. ☐ $1000—$1999
4. ☐ $2000—$2499
5. ☐ $2500—$2999
6. ☐ $3000—$3499
7. ☐ $3500—$3999
8. ☐ $4000—$4499
9. ☐ $4500—or more

49–52. **About what percentage of your total costs for the first year of your continued education, including tuition, room and board, books, etc., do you think will be provided by: (1) your PARENTS AND OTHER RELATIVES, (2) SCHOLARSHIPS OR STUDENT LOANS, (3) money you will earn by WORKING YOUR WAY THROUGH, and (4) MONEY you have SAVED YOURSELF? For each source of funds listed in the middle column below, insert the percentage selected from the column on the right which best approximates the percentage of your FIRST YEAR CONTINUED EDUCATION COSTS which will come from that source. When you have made estimates for each of the four sources, add your percentages to ensure that they total 100.**

Percentage Estimate	Source	Percentages
		1. 0 = None
		2. 25 = A quarter
49. _____%	Parents and/or relatives	3. 33 = A third
50. _____%	Scholarships or student loan	4. 50 = A half
51. _____%	Working my way through	5. 67 = Two thirds
52. _____%	Money I have saved myself	6. 75 = Three fourths
TOTAL = 100%		7. 100 = About all

53–64. NOT CONTINUING YOUR EDUCATION BEYOND HIGH SCHOOL, what are the four most important reasons why you do NOT intend to continue your education beyond high school? (Check the four reasons you consider most important).

53. ☐ I have no desire to go
54. ☐ Most of my friends are not going to continue their education.
55. ☐ Costs too much
56. ☐ My teachers or guidance counselors did not encourage me to go
57. ☐ My grades are not good enough
58. ☐ I have to work to help my parents
59. ☐ I plan to get married soon after I get out of high school

60. ☐ I am tired of being a student
61. ☐ My parents do not want me to continue my education.
62. ☐ I plan to get a job after I get out of high school
63. ☐ I just don't like school
64. ☐ I plan to go into armed services and then go to college after discharge

65. A most perplexing problem for behavioral scientists has been the degree to which changes or consistency in the educational expectations of students from the freshman to the senior years of high school result from the influence of the student's friends and peers. We would be most appreciative if you would indicate which ONE of the following statements best describes your own situation from the freshman to the senior years with respect to your post-high school educational expectations.

1. ☐ My educational *expectations* as a senior *differ* from those I had as a freshman—a change due *not at all* to the influence of my friends
2. ☐ My educational *expectations* as a senior *differ* from those I had as a freshman—a change due *somewhat* to the influence of my friends
3. ☐ My educational *expectations* as a senior *differ* from those I had as a freshman—a change due *considerably* to the influence of my friends
4. ☐ My educational *expectations* as a senior *differ* from those I had as a freshman—a change due *almost entirely* to the influence of my friends
5. ☐ My educational *expectations* as a senior are the *same* as those I had as a freshman—a consistency due *almost entirely* to the influence of my friends
6. ☐ My educational *expectations* as a senior are the *same* as those I had as a freshman—a consistency due *considerably* to the influence of my friends
7. ☐ My educational *expectations* as a senior are the *same* as those I had as a freshman—a consistency due *somewhat* to the influence of my friends
8. ☐ My educational *expectations* as a senior are the *same* as those I had as a freshman—a consistency due *not at all* to the influence of my friends

66. FOR MALES ONLY: What do you plan to do about your military service?
1. ☐ Enlist after high school
2. ☐ Wait until I am drafted
3. ☐ Enlist after I finish trade school, business school, or college

4. ☐ Get an academic deferment
5. ☐ Get a deferment other than an academic deferment
6. ☐ Go to a military college or academy

Here are five statements about yourself. After you read each statement, indicate how strongly you agree or disagree with it by placing an "X" in the appropriate box.

67. I feel that I'm a person of worth, at least on an equal plane with others.
1. ☐ Strongly agree
2. ☐ Agree
3. ☐ Uncertain, but probably agree
4. ☐ Uncertain, but probably disagree
5. ☐ Disagree
6. ☐ Strongly disagree

68. I certainly feel useless at times.
1. ☐ Strongly agree
2. ☐ Agree
3. ☐ Uncertain, but probably agree
4. ☐ Uncertain but probably disagree
5. ☐ Disagree
6. ☐ Strongly disagree

69. On the whole, I am satisfied with myself.
1. ☐ Strongly agree
2. ☐ Agree
3. ☐ Uncertain, but probably agree
4. ☐ Uncertain but probably disagree
5. ☐ Disagree
6. ☐ Strongly disagree

70. All in all, I am inclined to feel that I am a failure.
1. ☐ Strongly agree
2. ☐ Agree
3. ☐ Uncertain, but probably agree
4. ☐ Uncertain but probably disagree
5. ☐ Disagree
6. ☐ Strongly disagree

71. At times I think I am no good at all.
1. ☐ Strongly agree
2. ☐ Agree
3. ☐ Uncertain, but probably agree
4. ☐ Uncertain but probably disagree
5. ☐ Disagree
6. ☐ Strongly disagree

CARD THREE

16. In general, how are most decisions between you and your FATHER made?

1. ☐ My father usually doesn't care what I do
2. ☐ I usually can do what I want regardless of what my father thinks
3. ☐ I usually can make my own decisions, but my father would like for me to consider his opinion
4. ☐ My opinions usually are as important as my father's in deciding what I should do
5. ☐ I have considerable opportunity to make my own decisions, but my father usually has the final word
6. ☐ My father listens to me, but usually he makes the decision
7. ☐ My father usually just tells me what to do

17. During this past school year, how much time on the average, have you spent in practicing for, training for, or actually competing in interscholastic (varsity or junior varsity) sports, that is, in sports where your school competes against another school?

1. ☐ None, or almost none
2. ☐ About ½ hour a day
3. ☐ About 1 hour a day
4. ☐ About 1½ hours a day
5. ☐ About 2 hours a day
6. ☐ About 2½ hours a day
7. ☐ About 3 hours a day
8. ☐ More than 3 hours a day

Please indicate by placing an "X" next to the answer which best describes how you personally feel about each of the following statements:

18. Success in the occupational world depends more on luck than on ability and willingness to work.

1. ☐ Strongly agree
2. ☐ Agree
3. ☐ Uncertain, but probably agree
4. ☐ Uncertain, but probably disagree
5. ☐ Disagree
6. ☐ Strongly disagree

19. A college education is worth the time and effort it requires.

1. ☐ Strongly disagree
2. ☐ Disagree
3. ☐ Uncertain, but probably disagree
4. ☐ Uncertain, but probably agree
5. ☐ Agree
6. ☐ Strongly agree

20. Except for growing old and the like, a person has more control over his own future than do the forces of nature or fate.

1. ☐ Strongly disagree
2. ☐ Disagree
3. ☐ Uncertain, but probably disagree
4. ☐ Uncertain, but probably agree
5. ☐ Agree
6. ☐ Strongly agree

21. Education helps a person use his leisure time to better advantage.

1. ☐ Strongly agree
2. ☐ Agree
3. ☐ Uncertain, but probably agree
4. ☐ Uncertain, but probably disagree
5. ☐ Disagree
6. ☐ Strongly disagree

22. Education tends to make a person more unhappy than happy.

1. ☐ Strongly disagree
2. ☐ Disagree
3. ☐ Uncertain, but probably disagree
4. ☐ Uncertain, but probably agree
5. ☐ Agree
6. ☐ Strongly agree

23. People who accept their condition in life are happier than those who try to change things.

1. ☐ Strongly agree
2. ☐ Agree
3. ☐ Uncertain, but probably agree
4. ☐ Uncertain, but probably disagree
5. ☐ Disagree
6. ☐ Strongly disagree

24. Other people have more control over a person's future than the person himself does.

1. ☐ Strongly agree
2. ☐ Agree
3. ☐ Uncertain, but probably agree
4. ☐ Uncertain, but probably disagree
5. ☐ Disagree
6. ☐ Strongly disagree

25. A person should use some of his time in the present to make plans for his future.

1. ☐ Strongly disagree
2. ☐ Disagree
3. ☐ Uncertain, but probably disagree
4. ☐ Uncertain, but probably agree
5. ☐ Agree
6. ☐ Strongly agree

— 9 —

Please indicate which, if any, of the following activities you have regularly participated in this year. Answer **all** items.

Activity	Have you regularly participated this school year?	
	No	Yes
26. Band or orchestra		
27 Chorus, choir		
28 Dramatics		
29 School paper, yearbook		
30 Debates		
31 Student government, (student council, class officer, etc.)		
32 Language clubs (French, German, Spanish, etc.)		
33 Hobby or interest clubs (auto, broadcasting, photography, rifle, etc.)		
34 School service activities (stage or projectionist crew, dance committees, Red Cross, etc.)		
35 Athletics: *inter*scholastic (varsity or junior varsity)		
36 Academic subject clubs (math., history, science, anatomy, etc.)		
37 Athletics: *intra*mural		
38 Academic honorary clubs or societies (National Honor Society, Key Club, etc.)		
39 Athletic support clubs (officials club, team manager, color guard, etc.)		
40 Career Clubs like Future Teachers of America, FNA. FFA, etc.		
41 Other: (Specify)		

Which of the following customs and norms of society and its institutions can you ACCEPT EASILY, which do you ACCEPT RELUCTANTLY, and which do you REJECT OUTRIGHT?

42. **Abiding by laws you do not agree with?**
1. ☐ Accept easily
2. ☐ Accept reluctantly
3. ☐ Reject outright

43. **Conforming in matters of personal clothing and grooming?**
1. ☐ Accept easily
2. ☐ Accept reluctantly
3. ☐ Reject outright

44. **The prohibition against marijuana?**
1. ☐ Accept easily
2. ☐ Accept reluctantly
3. ☐ Reject outright

45. **The prohibition against LSD?**
1. ☐ Accept easily
2. ☐ Accept reluctantly
3. ☐ Reject outright

46. **The prohibition against drugs such as heroin and cocaine?**
1. ☐ Accept easily
2. ☐ Accept reluctantly
3. ☐ Reject outright

47. **The power and authority of the police?**
1. ☐ Accept easily
2. ☐ Accept reluctantly
3. ☐ Reject outright

48. **The power and authority of your teachers and principal?**
1. ☐ Accept easily
2. ☐ Accept reluctantly
3. ☐ Reject outright

— 10 —

49. Have your parents stressed or emphasized your going out for an interscholastic sport in high school?

1. ☐ Yes, they have stressed it a lot

2. ☐ Yes, they have stressed it somewhat

3. ☐ Yes, but they seldom mention it

4. ☐ They don't care one way or the other

5. ☐ No, they would rather I not go out for an *interscholastic* sport

50. In general, how are most decisions between you and your MOTHER made?

1. ☐ My mother usually just tells me what to do
2. ☐ My mother listens to me, but usually she makes the decision
3. ☐ I have considerable opportunity to make my own decisions, but my mother usually has the final word
4. ☐ My opinions usually are as important as my mother's in deciding what I should do
5. ☐ I usually can make my own decision, but my mother would like for me to consider her opinion
6. ☐ I usually can do what I want regardless of what my mother thinks
7. ☐ My mother usually doesn't care what I do

During the senior year of high school, many students have made or plan to make application to schools, colleges, employers, or the military service. Below is a list of such places to which applications are usually made. The INSTRUCTIONS for answering this item are: Read over the entire list carefully; Then, Indicate (1) The number of applications you have made to each place in the column APPLIED; (2) The number of acceptances you have received from each place in the column ACCEPTED; (3) The number of replies you are awaiting from each place in the column AWAITING; (4) the number of rejections you have received from each place in the column REJECTED; (5) If you still plan to make applications, indicate the number of applications you plan to make to each place in the column PLAN TO.

FOR EXAMPLE: John applied to 4 four-year colleges and to 3 employers. He was accepted by 2 of the colleges, is awaiting a reply from 1, and was rejected by 1. Thus, on the line for "Four Year Colleges" he places a 4 in the column APPLIED, a 2 in the column ACCEPTED, a 1 in the column AWAITING, and a 1 in the column REJECTED. Of the 3 employers John applied to, 2 have accepted him and 1 has rejected him. Thus, on the line for "Employers" he places a 3 in the column APPLIED, a 2 in the column ACCEPTED, and a 1 in the column REJECTED.

IBM	Type of Place	NUMBER OF PLACES:				
		Applied	Accepted	Awaiting	Rejected	Plan To
51–55.	Trade or Technical Schools					
56–60.	Business or Nursing Schools					
61–65.	Two Year Community or Junior Colleges					
66–70.	Four Year Colleges					
71–75.	Employers					
76–80.	Military Services					

CARD FOUR (Part A: 16 — 52)

The following two questions are about your FATHER'S job and his employer. If your FATHER is not currently employed or if your FATHER is deceased, please give the name of the employer your FATHER last worked for and the kind of job he LAST had.

16–23. What is the full name of the company, business, or farm that your FATHER works for? For example: General Motors Car Company. (If your FATHER works for himself, write "self-employed" and give the name of your FATHER's business).

What KIND OF WORK does your FATHER do? (PLEASE TRY TO GIVE THE SPECIFIC NAME OR TITLE OF HIS JOB, for example, "delivery truck driver", and DESCRIBE what he does. For example, "he drives a local delivery truck". ALSO: if your FATHER is in the military, please GIVE HIS SPECIFIC MILITARY RANK).

_____

(Name of company, business, or farm which employs your FATHER)

_____

Specific name or title of FATHER'S job or his military rank)

_____

(Brief description of what he does)

_____

How would you describe the INTERSCHOLASTIC ATHLETES in your school, that is, those students among the sophomores, juniors and seniors who regularly participate in junior varsity or varsity sports where your school competes against other schools? In the spaces provided next to each characteristic, indicate with an ''X'' the approximate proportion of INTERSCHOLASTIC ATHLETES in your school you believe are described by each of the following characteristics.

		Proportion of *INTERSCHOLASTIC ATHLETES* described by each characteristic				
		More Than Half		About Half	Less Than Half	
	Characteristics	Almost All	Many		Some	Almost None
24.	Really interested in school					
25.	Get along well with the teachers					
26.	Cause trouble for school officials					
27.	Intend to go to college					
28.	Make trouble for the teachers					
29.	Try hard to make good grades					
30.	Members of the LEADING or "IN" crowd					
31.	Get special privileges from the principal					
32.	Come from families where the father has an important or prestigeful job					
33.	Get in trouble with the police					
34.	Get special privileges from the teachers					
35.	Are considered in the TOP SCHOLAR group					

Which students, among all the seniors in your school are INTERSCHOLASTIC ATHLETES? Please name three such.

First Name   Last Name

_____ _____   — — — —
                         36–39.

_____ _____   — — — —
                         40–43.

_____ _____   — — — —
                         44–47.

48. **Who is now acting as your father? If you are adopted consider your adoptive father as your real father.**

1. ☐ My real father, who is living at home
2. ☐ My real father, who is not living at home
3. ☐ My stepfather
4. ☐ My foster father
5. ☐ My grandfather
6. ☐ Another relative (uncle, etc.)
7. ☐ Another adult
8. ☐ No one

49. How bright or intelligent do you think you are in comparison with the other senior students in your school?

1. ☐ Among the brightest
2. ☐ Above average
3. ☐ Average
4. ☐ Below average
5. ☐ Among the lowest

50. During your senior year, how often have you actually talked with your FATHER about whether or not to continue your education beyond high school?

1. ☐ Several times a week
2. ☐ About once a week
3. ☐ Several times a month
4. ☐ About once a month
5. ☐ About once every two or three months
6. ☐ Several times this school year
7. ☐ Once or twice this school year
8. ☐ Not even once this school year

51. During your senior year, how frequently has your FATHER encouraged you to continue your education beyond high school, that is, to go on to technical school, college, etc?

1. ☐ At least several times a week
2. ☐ About once a week
3. ☐ Several times a month
4. ☐ About once a month
5. ☐ About once every two or three months
6. ☐ Several times a year
7. ☐ Once or twice a year
8. ☐ Less than once a year

52. With respect to your own personal role in seeking to bring about changes in your high school and/or in other institutions of our society, which ONE of the following statements best describes your own position?

1. ☐ I consider myself an activist
2. ☐ I am in sympathy with most of the activists' objectives, but not with all of their tactics
3. ☐ I am not emotionally involved, one way or the other
4. ☐ I am not sure that I approve of what the activists are trying to do, but I have no strong objection to letting them try
5. ☐ I am in total disagreement with the activists

CARD FIVE (Part A: 16 — 64)

Here is a list of sports. Please read the questions very carefully and then answer each question.

Type of Sport		As A Senior: Did You Go Out For the Sport?		IF YOU DID GO OUT FOR THE SPORT:				
				As A Senior: Did You Play That Sport on?			Did You Complete the Season?	
		No	Yes	Varsity	Junior Varsity	Intra-mural	Yes	No
16–18.	Football							
19–21.	Basketball							
22–25.	Baseball							
26–28.	Soccer							
29–31.	Softball							
32–34.	Volleyball							
35–37.	Track							
38–40.	Cross-country							
41–43.	Wrestling							
44–46.	Swimming							
47–49.	Gymnastics							
50–52.	Golf							
53–55.	Tennis							
56–58.	Hockey							
59–61.	Bowling							
62–64.	Weightlifting							

CARD FOUR (Part B: 53 — 78)

53. During the last few years or so, has your FATHER wanted you to continue your education beyond **high school,** that is, to go to a trade or business school, to college, etc.?

1. ☐ Yes, he has stressed it a lot
2. ☐ Yes, he has stressed it somewhat
3. ☐ Yes, but he has seldom mentioned it
4. ☐ He hasn't said one way or the other
5. ☐ No, he would rather that I did not go beyond high school

54. What kind of reputation do you have among your teachers as far as your behavior goes?

1. ☐ Very good
2. ☐ Good
3. ☐ Fair
4. ☐ Poor
5. ☐ Very poor

How would you describe the TOP SCHOLARS in your school, that is, those students among the sophomores, juniors and seniors who get the highest grades? In the spaces provided next to each characteristic, indicate with an "X" the approximate proportion of the TOP SCHOLARS in your school you believe are described by each of the following characteristics.

	Proportion of *TOP SCHOLARS* described by each characteristic				
	More Than Half		About Half	Less Than Half	
Characteristics	Almost All	Many		Some	Almost None
55. Get special privileges from teachers					
56. Are INTERSCHOLASTIC (varsity or junior varsity) ATHLETES					
57. Get along well with the teachers					
58. Cause trouble for school officials					
59. Intend to go to college					
60. Try hard to make good grades					
61. Members of the LEADING or "IN" crowd					
62. Make trouble for the teachers					
63. Get special privileges from principal					
64. Come from families where the father has an important or prestigeful job					
65. Get in trouble with the police					

Which students, among all the seniors in your school, are TOP SCHOLARS? Please name three such students.

First Name   Last Name

————————   ————————   — — — —
                                      66–69.

————————   ————————   — — — —
                                      70–73.

————————   ————————   — — — —
                                      74–77.

78. Who is now acting as your mother? If you are adopted, consider your adoptive mother as your real mother.

1. ☐ My real mother, who is living at home
2. ☐ My real mother, who is not living at home
3. ☐ My stepmother
4. ☐ My foster mother
5. ☐ My grandmother
6. ☐ Another relative (aunt, etc.)
7. ☐ Another adult
8. ☐ No one

— 14 —

CARD FIVE (Part B: 65 — 79)

65. **During the last few years or so, has your MOTHER wanted you to continue your education beyond high school, that is, to go to a trade or business school, to college, etc.?**
1. ☐ Yes, she has stressed it a lot
2. ☐ Yes, she has stressed it somewhat
3. ☐ Yes, but she has seldom mentioned it
4. ☐ She hasn't said one way or the other
5. ☐ No, she would rather that I did not go beyond high school

66. **In general, how do you rate your own athletic ability?**
1. ☐ Not very good in *any* sport
2. ☐ Good, but not very outstanding in *one* sport
3. ☐ Good, but not very outstanding in *more than one* sport
4. ☐ Outstanding in *one* sport
5. ☐ Outstanding in *more than one* sport

67. **How good a student do you want to be in school?**
1. ☐ One of the best students in the senior class
2. ☐ Above the middle of the senior class
3. ☐ In the middle of the senior class
4. ☐ Just good enough to get by
5. ☐ I don't care

68. **Generally, over the past 5 to 8 years, have your parents stressed or emphasized that you should try to come out on top in games, sports, and the like?**
1. ☐ No, they would rather I not try to come out on top in games, sports, etc.
2. ☐ They haven't said one way or another
3. ☐ Yes, but they have seldom mentioned it
4. ☐ Yes, they have stressed it somewhat
5. ☐ Yes, they have stressed it a lot

69–77. Which of the following have you been involved in, personally, during the past two years? FOR EACH ACTIVITY, place a check in the appropriate box.

Col.	INVOLVED PERSONALLY? Yes	No	ACTIVITY
69.			Marches in support of a cause
70.			Organization meetings to plan strategy for a cause
71.			Civil rights protests
72.			Membership in organizations like *Students for a Democratic Society, Young Americans for Freedom, United Student Movement,* etc.
73.			Strikes in support of a cause
74.			Sit ins in support of a cause
75.			Been arrested while demonstrating in support of a cause
76.			Political campaigns in the community for a person and/or for a cause, e.g., support or opposition to the Viet Nam war
77.			None of the above

78. **In high school, there are many reasons why one person chooses another person OF HIS OR HER OWN SEX as a friend. Behavioral scientists believe that one such reason may be that the persons have similar post-high school educational plans or expectations, e.g., a person who expects to go to a four-year college may be more likely to choose as a friend another person who expects to go to a four-year college; similarly, a person who expects to complete his education with the high school diploma may be more likely to choose as a friend another person who has a similar expectation. To what extent have you tended to choose as friends others who have similar educational expectations to yours?**
1. ☐ To almost no extent
2. ☐ To some extent
3. ☐ To a considerable extent
4. ☐ To a very great extent

79. **How important is it for YOU to be an athlete in school?**

1. ☐ It is *not important* to me personally that I be an athlete in school

2. ☐ It is *somewhat important* to me personally that I be an athlete in school

3. ☐ It is *very important* to me personally that I be an athlete in school

CARD SIX

In terms of the following characteristics, how would you describe **each** of your three BEST FRIENDS? In the spaces provided, indicate with an "X" whether the characteristic IS Descriptive or is NOT descriptive of Friend Number One, Friend Number Two, and Friend Number Three.

Characteristic	Friend Number One		Friend Number Two		Friend Number Three	
	IS Descriptive	NOT Descriptive	IS Descriptive	NOT Descriptive	IS Descriptive	NOT Descriptive
16. Active in many school activities *other than* sports						
17. Makes trouble for teachers						
18. Tries hard to make good grades						
19. Studies a lot						
20. Is a senior in this school						
21. Member of the LEADING or "IN" crowd						
22. Gets special privileges from the principal						
23. Is a student in another high school						
24. Intends to go to college						
25. Gets special privileges from the teachers						
26. Considered in the TOP SCHOLAR group						
27. Has dropped out of high school						
28. Causes trouble for school officials						
29. Is an INTERSCHOLASTIC (varsity or junior varsity) ATHLETE						
30. Comes from a family where the father has an important or prestigeful job						
31. Really interested in school						
32. Gets in trouble with the police						
33. Dislikes school						
34. Gets along well with teachers						

35. How much formal education does or did your MOTHER have?

1. ☐ Less than sixth grade
2. ☐ Seventh, eighth, or ninth grade
3. ☐ Tenth or eleventh grade
4. ☐ High school graduate
5. ☐ Some college, trade, technical, or two year business school
6. ☐ College graduate
7. ☐ Graduate or professional school
8. ☐ Do not know

36. During this school year, did you ever stay away from school just because you didn't want to go?

1. ☐ No
2. ☐ Yes, for 1 or 2 days
3. ☐ Yes, for 3 to 6 days
4. ☐ Yes, for 7 to 15 days
5. ☐ Yes, for 16 or more days

37–38. Among the SENIORS IN YOUR SCHOOL, who do you usually consider to be your closest or best friends?

First Name   Last Name   First Name   Last Name

_____ _____   ___ ___ ___ ___   _____ _____   ___ ___ ___ ___
                                 37–40.   45–48.

_____ _____   ___ ___ ___ ___
                                 41–44.

THE END. THANK YOU

SOUTHERN TIER HIGH SCHOOL STUDENT CENSUS QUESTIONNAIRE

Binghamton Public Schools, Catholic Central, Chenango Forks, Chenango Valley, Johnson City Schools, Maine-Endwell Schools, Seton Catholic, Susquehanna Valley, Union-Endicott, and Vestal Public Schools.

An important measure of a school's performance is the educational and occupational careers its students pursue. Your responses to the fourteen items in this questionnaire will help us assess our performance so that we may serve the community more effectively. Each question may be answered by placing a checkmark or an "X" in the box next to the category that best describes your current educational, occupational, marital, and (for males), military status. For those few questions which require a written response, please PRINT clearly. Read each and every question and answer all of those which apply to you. When you have completed the questionnaire, fold and seal it, and then place it in the mail. THANK YOU.

1. What is the highest grade you COMPLETED in high school?

1. ☐ Ninth grade   3. ☐ Eleventh grade
2. ☐ Tenth grade   4. ☐ Twelfth grade

IF YOU HAVE NOT GRADUATED FROM HIGH SCHOOL, PLEASE ANSWER QUESTIONS 2 and 3. IF YOU DID GRADUATE FROM HIGH SCHOOL, SKIP TO QUESTIONS 4–12.

2. Which ONE of the following best explains why you left high school before graduation?

1. ☐ Money problems
2. ☐ Medical reasons
3. ☐ Could do the school work O.K. but I didn't like school
4. ☐ Had trouble doing the school work and I didn't like school
5. ☐ Had trouble doing the school work even though I liked school
6. ☐ Felt that the school wanted to get rid of me

3. Do you think that you will get your high school diploma (or equivalency diploma) within the next two years?

1. ☐ Definitely no   3. ☐ Probably yes
2. ☐ Probably no   4. ☐ Definitely yes

13. What is your current occupational status? PLEASE READ CAREFULLY.

1. ☐ Employed full-time (30 hours a week or more)
2. ☐ Employed part-time (29 hours a week or less)
3. ☐ Part-time student and part-time employed
4. ☐ Part-time student and full-time employed
5. ☐☐☐☐☐ Full-time student and full-time employed
6. ☐ Full-time student and part-time employed
7. ☐ Full-time student and otherwise not employed
8. ☐ Housewife
9. ☐ Unemployed

IF YOU ARE EMPLOYED PART OR FULL-TIME:

14–21. What is the full name of the company employer for which you work?

_____

(Full Name of Company: Please Print)

22–24. What is the full name of your job or occupation with your employer or company?

_____

(Specific Job Name or Title: Print)

IF YOU HAVE GRADUATED FROM HIGH SCHOOL, PLEASE ANSWER QUESTIONS 4–12.

4. Are you currently a student in any type of educational institution or school?

1. ☐ NO: GO TO QUESTION 12
2. ☐ YES: a technical or trade school
3. ☐ YES: a business school
4. ☐ YES: a nursing school
5. ☐ YES: a two-year community college
6. ☐ YES: a four-year college
7. ☐ YES: any other type of educational institution or school

5–8. What is the full name of the school or college you now attend?

_____

(Full Name of School or College: Print)

9–11. In what field or subject are you now majoring or do you intend to major?

_____

(Name of Major Field or Subject: Print)

12. IF YOU ARE NOT NOW ENROLLED IN AN EDUCATIONAL INSTITUTION OR SCHOOL:

Do you think that you will enroll within the next two years or so?

1. ☐ No
2. ☐ Yes—probably in a trade or technical school
3. ☐ Yes—probably in a business school
4. ☐ Yes—probably in a nursing school
5. ☐ Yes—probably in a two-year community college
6. ☐ Yes—probably in a four-year college
7. ☐ Yes—probably in some type of school or college other than those cited in 2–6

25. Would you like to continue working in your present job for, say, two more years or so, or would you like to change jobs within the next two years?

1. ☐ I am not employed so this question doesn't apply
2. ☐ Definitely would like to continue in my present job
3. ☐ Probably would like to continue in my present job
4. ☐ Probably would like to change jobs
5. ☐ Definitely would like to change jobs

26. What is your present marital status?

1. ☐ Single and not expecting to get married within the coming year
2. ☐ Single and expecting to get married within the coming year
3. ☐ Married
4. ☐ Separated or divorced
5. ☐ Widowed

MILITARY STATUS: FOR MALES ONLY

27. What is your present military status?

1. ☐ In the Army or Marines
2. ☐ In the Air Force
3. ☐ In the Navy
4. ☐ In the Coast Guard
5. ☐ In the National Guard
6. ☐ Waiting to be drafted
7. ☐ Student deferment
8. ☐ Deferment for medical, dependency, occupational, or related reasons
9. ☐ Deferment because of C.O. status

28. IF YOU ARE IN A MILITARY SERVICE
Did you enlist or were you drafted?

1. ☐ Enlisted
2. ☐ Drafted

If you have a more recent address than the one on the questionnaire, would you kindly write it here?

_____ _____
Number   Street or Avenue

_____ _____
City   State

APPENDIX B
Distributions for the Variables
of the Model

TABLE B.1.   The Three Indicators of Social Class

$X1a.$ Occupation of Father: Frequency and Percentage Distribution

Occupation	Code	N	$\%$
Higher executive, major professional	1	308	11.0
Manager, lesser professional	2	299	10.7
Administrator, minor professional	3	342	12.3
Clerical and sales, technician	4	721	25.9
Skilled manual employee	5	615	22.1
Machine operator, semiskilled	6	368	13.2
Unskilled employee	7	135	4.8
TOTAL		2,788	100.0
No responses	0	94	3.4

Mean—unadjusted = 3.96; adjusted = 3.96
S.D.—unadjusted = 1.68; adjusted = 1.65

$X1b.c_6.$ Education of Parents: Frequency and Percentage Distributions

Education	Code	Father N	Father $\%$	Mother N	Mother $\%$
Graduate, professional school	1	165	5.9	71	2.5
Four years of college	2	443	15.9	237	8.5
Two years of college	3	318	11.4	436	15.6
High school graduate	4	1,244	44.6	1,518	54.4
Grades ten or eleven	5	266	9.5	259	9.3
Grades seven, eight, or nine	6	298	10.7	228	8.2
Grade six or less	7	54	1.9	39	1.4
TOTAL		2,788	99.9	2,788	99.9

No responses		0	306 11.0	229 8.2	
Means: unadjusted			3.73	3.89	
adjusted			3.76	3.90	
S.D.: unadusted			1.47	1.17	
adjusted			1.39	1.12	

TABLE B.2.   Index of Parental Educational Stress: Frequency and Percentage Distribution

Level and Code	N	$\%$
High = 1	974	34.9
2	497	17.8
3	487	17.5
4	291	10.4
5	258	9.3
6	113	4.1
7	133	4.8
8	26	.9
9	9	.3
Total	2,788	100.0
Mean = 2.79	S.D. = 1.87	

TABLE B.3.   Continued Education Beyond High School Taken for Granted. Frequency and Percentage Distribution

Level and Code	N	$\%$
Yes = 0	1,760	63.1
No = 1	1,028	36.9
Total	2,788	100.0
No Responses	130	4.7
Mean = .37	S.D. = .48	

TABLE B.4.   Ninth-grade Curriculum Location: Frequency and Percentage Distribution

Level and Code	N	$\%$
College-preparatory = 0	1,676	60.1
Noncollege prep. = 1	1,112	39.9
Total	2,788	100.0
No Responses	61	2.1
Mean = .39		
S.D. = .48		

TABLE B.5.   Number of Close Friends ("Peers") with College Intentions: Ninth Grade

Level and Code	N	$\%$
None = 0	877	31.5
One = 1	599	21.5
Two = 2	599	21.5
Three = 3	713	25.6
Total	2,788	100.0
Mean = 1.41		
S.D. = 1.18		

TABLE B.6. **Grade Nine: Educational Ambition Frequency and Percentage Distribution**

Level	Code	N	%
Graduate or professional school	1	284	10.2
Four-year college	2	1,056	37.9
Two-year college	3	886	31.8
High school graduate	4	535	19.2
Eleven years or less	5	27	1.0
TOTAL		2,788	100.1
No responses	0	23	.8

Mean: unadjusted = 2.63; adjusted = 2.63
S.D.: unadjusted = .94; adjusted = .94

TABLE B.7. **Grade Ten: Curriculum Location Frequency and Percentage Distribution**

Level and Code	N	%
College-preparatory = 0	1,700	63.1
Noncollege prep. = 1	995	36.9
TOTAL	2,695	100.0
No responses	22	.8

Mean: = .36
S.D.: = .48

TABLE B.8. Grade Ten: Reported Counselor Educational Encouragement Frequency and Percentage Distribution

Level	Code	Unadjusted		Adjusted	
		N	%	N	%
Four-year college	1	1,255	56	1,255	47
Two-year college	2	422	19	867	32
Technical, job training	3	188	8⎱	472	18
Business, commercial training	4	284	13⎰		
Armed services	5	21	1⎱	101	4
Get a job	6	80	4⎰		
No response	0	340			
Other	0	105			
Total		2,695	101	2,695	101

Mean: unadjusted = 1.95; adjusted = 1.78
S.D.: unadjusted = 1.34 adjusted = .86

TABLE B.9. Academic Achievement. Frequency and Percent Distribution

Stanine	N	%
1	145	5.9
2	182	7.4
3	248	10.1
4	345	14.1
5	482	19.7
6	485	19.8
7	367	15.0
8	165	6.7
9	28	1.1
TOTAL	2,447	99.8

Mean: adjusted = 4.94
S.D.: adjusted = 1.94

TABLE B.10. Close Friends Intending College: Grade Twelve. Frequency and Percent Distribution

Level and Code		N	%
None	= 0	178	7.3
One	= 1	264	10.8
Two	= 2	749	30.6
Three	= 3	1,256	51.3
TOTAL		2,447	100.0

Mean: unadjusted = 2.32
　　　adjusted = 2.26
S.D.: unadjusted = .95
　　　adjusted = .92

TABLE B.11. Grade Twelve: Counselor Encouragement. Frequency and Percentage Distribution

Level	Code	Unadjusted N	Unadjusted %	Adjusted N	Adjusted %
Four-year college	1	952	46	952	39
Two-year college	2	720	35	1,120	46
Tech., job training	3	90	4 ⎫	295	12
Bus., comm. training	4	205	10 ⎭		
Armed services	5	21	1 ⎫	80	3
Get a job	6	59	3 ⎭		
No response	0	78			
Other	0	322			
TOTAL		2,447	99	2,447	100

Mean: unadjusted = 1.93; adjusted = 1.80
S.D.: unadjusted = 1.21; adjusted = .77

TABLE B.12. Grade Twelve: Educational Decision. Frequency and Percentage Distribution

Level	Code	N	$\%$
Graduate or professional school	1	388	15.9
Four-year college	2	805	32.9
Two-year college	3	871	35.6
High school graduate	4	383	15.7
Eleven years or less	5	—	—
TOTAL		2,447	100.1
No response	0	52	2.1

Mean: unadjusted = 2.50; adjusted = 2.51
S.D.: unadjusted = .95; adjusted = .94

TABLE B.13. Postsecondary Enrollment Level. Frequency and Percentage Distribution

Level	Code	N	$\%$
Four-year college	2	731	29.7
Two-year college	3	807	32.8
High school graduate	4	707	28.7
Eleven years or less	5	218	8.9
TOTAL		2,463	100.0

Mean = 2.32
S.D. = 1.08

APPENDIX C

Gender - Specific Matrices of Correlation and Path Coefficients

TABLE C1. Correlations, Means, and Standard Deviations for Variables Used in the Analysis: *Males* (Constrained correlations above the diagonal, unconstrained below. Decimals omitted)

Variables	X_2	X_3	X_4	X_5	X_6	X_7	X_8	X_9	X_{10}	X_{11}	X_{12}	X_{13}	X_{14}	Mean	St. Dev.
Class Construct [a] (X_1)	245	243	304	241	327	455	251	260	238	209	283	375	359	3.235	1.118
Ability (X_2)		202	264	287	303	389	352	395	553	231	404	458	426	109.822	11.226
Par. Educ. Stress (X_3)	202		323	312	297	402	338	284	135	168	256	289	285	2.519	1.742
"Taken for Granted" (X_4)	255	315		237	302	483	270	328	256	242	328	399	376	.362	.481
Curriculum, Grade Nine (X_5)	276	305	229		315	421	569	328	238	229	325	363	289	.366	.482
Peer Educ. Infl. Gr. 9 (X_6)	303	297	297	308		513	317	347	244	250	287	396	385	1.517	1.214
Educational Ambition (X_7)	389	402	467	407	513		473	356	427	300	451	617	521	2.568	.974
Curriculum, Grade Ten (X_8)	350	337	266	554	313	467		478	327	257	383	410	371	.357	.479
Counselor Educ. Enc. 10 (X_9)	395	284	320	336	356	478	462		467	287	490	440	444	1.731	.851
Academic Achievement (X_{10})	553	135	243	226	244	427	324	401		259	491	516	522	5.281	1.934
Peer Educ. Infl. Gr. 12 (X_{11})	231	168	230	222	250	300	254	287	259		319	393	351	2.299	.904
Counselor Educ. Enc. 12 (X_{12})	404	256	311	317	287	451	380	490	491	319		569	516	1.752	.753
Educational Decision (X_{13})	458	289	389	352	396	617	406	440	516	393	569		629	2.391	.934
Postsec. Ed. Enroll. (X_{14})	426	285	367	278	385	521	365	444	522	351	516	629		3.235	1.118
Occupation of Father [b]	191	216	270	212	289	403	219	225	200	185	246	328	315	3.917	1.634
Education of Father	218	202	252	202	272	377	211	219	204	175	238	313	299	3.730	1.415
Education of Mother	234	164	205	165	221	306	175	182	174	143	197	258	246	3.881	1.096

[a] Following Hauser, 1972, the Class Construct has been assigned the mean and standard deviation of the last dependent variable in the model, i.e., of Postsecondary Educational Enrollment Level.

[b] Values for the three component elements of the social class construct are those of the constrained correlations.

TABLE C2. Partial Regression Coefficients in Standard Form for All Variables Used in the Analysis: *Males* (Decimals omitted)

Independent Variables	Dependent Variables											
	X_3 PES	X_4 TFG	X_5 CURR9	X_6 PCI9	X_7 AMB	X_8 CURR-10	X_9 CEA-10	X_{10} ACH	X_{11} PCI-12	X_{12} CEA-12	X_{13} DEC	X_{14} ENR
X_1 Class Construct	206	255	133	181	201	—[a]	—	—	062	045	057	069
X_2 Scholastic Ability	152	202	206	154	131	133	176	418	—	062	092	—
X_3 Par. Educ. Stress			238	132	127	100	—	-090	—	042	—	047
X_4 "Taken for Granted"			—	127	233		089		098	065	053	062
X_5 Curriculum, Grade Nine				156	162	413	—		061	—	—	—
X_6 Peer Educ. Influence, Gr. 9					249		093		094	084	044	084
X_7 Educational Ambition						208	197	213	—	—	297	050
X_8 Curriculum, Grade Ten							259	045	062	068	—	—
X_9 Counselor Educ. Enc. Gr. 10								139	108	219	—	—
X_{10} Academic Achievement									118	252	150	211
X_{11} Peer Educ. Influence, Gr. 12										102	133	068
X_{12} Counselor Educ. Enc. Gr. 12											236	125
X_{13} Educational Decision												295
Residual	959	932	914	876	707	766	808	787	921	777	671	704
Percentage of Variance Accounted for R^2	081	131	166	233	502	413	346	380	152	397	549	503

[a] No significant regression coefficient to this dependent variable from the independent variable. Other regression coefficients for this dependent variable are those from re-computations following the elimination of that particular independent variable from the set of regressors. See Chapter 2 for full discussion of this procedure.

TABLE C3. Correlations, Means, and Standard Deviations for Variables Used in the Analysis: *Females* (Constrained correlations above the diagonal, unconstrained below. Decimals omitted)

Variables	X_2	X_3	X_4	X_5	X_6	X_7	X_8	X_9	X_{10}	X_{11}	X_{12}	X_{13}	X_{14}	Mean	St. Dev.
Class Construct [a] (X_1)	291	262	326	306	353	399	358	312	216	208	299	355	349	3.228	1.032
Ability (X_2)		215	295	413	284	407	470	445	571	285	449	413	399	109.765	10.590
Par. Educ. Stress (X_3)	215		442	325	235	453	339	320	158	217	264	338	276	3.087	1.952
"Taken for Granted" (X_4)	285	442		393	301	472	406	336	233	197	271	324	311	.376	.484
Curriculum, Grade Nine (X_5)	406	318	384		322	482	649	479	339	232	422	398	391	.389	.488
Peer Educ. Infl. Gr. 9 (X_6)	284	235	296	315		442	341	342	259	261	297	338	353	1.297	1.122
Educational Ambition (X_7)	407	453	462	477	442		525	499	384	282	428	534	467	2.695	.892
Curriculum, Grade Ten (X_8)	466	336	391	636	339	520		635	400	293	481	474	480	.366	.482
Counselor Educ. Enc. 10 (X_9)	445	320	327	475	342	499	635		444	249	547	496	466	1.843	.872
Academic Achievement (X_{10})	571	158	222	330	259	384	394	444		270		500	541	4.557	1.867
Peer Educ. Infl. Gr. 12 (X_{11})	285	217	203	231	261	282	293	249	270		262	339	385	2.216	.934
Counselor Educ. Enc. 12 (X_{12})	449	264	267	417	297	428	477	547		262		586	589	1.848	.795
Educational Decision (X_{13})	413	338	326	398	338	534	474	496	500	339	586		690	2.646	.925
Postsec. Ed. Enroll. (X_{14})	399	276	307	391	353	467	480	466	541	385	589	690		3.228	1.032
Occupation of Father [b]	241	209	260	245	282	319	287	252	177	166	241	284	279	4.010	1.671
Education of Father	242	235	292	270	316	356	316	275	184	182	263	315	309	3.788	1.354
Education of Mother	223	188	234	222	253	288	260	228	163	150	218	256	253	3.912	1.152

[a] Following Hauser, 1972, the Class Construct has been assigned the mean and standard deviation of the last dependent variable in the model, i.e., of Postsecondary Educational Enrollment Level.

[b] Values for the three component elements of the social class construct are those of the constrained correlations.

TABLE C4. Partial Regression Coefficients in Standard Form for All Variables Used in the Analysis: *Females* (Decimals omitted)

Independent Variables		X_3 PES	X_4 TFG	X_5 CURR9	X_6 PCI9	X_7 AMB	X_8 CURR-10	X_9 CEA-10	X_{10} ACH	X_{11} PCI-12	X_{12} CEA-12	X_{13} DEC	X_{14} ENR
													Dependent Variables
Class Construct	X_1	218	262	118	225	121	079	—[a]			063	078	053
Scholastic Ability	X_2	152	219	287	114	144	172	142	441	105	085		-063
Par. Educ. Stress	X_3			141	055	210		053	-061	-105		070	
"Taken for Granted"	X_4			208	113	163	073						
Curriculum, Grade Nine	X_5				144	189	440						
Peer Educ. Influence, Gr. 9	X_6					199		070		138			053
Educational Ambition	X_7						177	152	132		079	205	
Curriculum, Grade Ten	X_8							447		117	097	070	081
Counselor Educ. Enc. Gr. 10	X_9								202		274		
Academic Achievement	X_{10}									111	235	187	198
Peer Educ. Influence, Gr. 12	X_{11}										043	099	119
Counselor Educ. Enc. Gr. 12	X_{12}											304	187
Educational Decision	X_{13}												390
Residual		954	922	847	892	736	695	732	786	920	764	708	644
Percentage of Variance Accounted for R^2		090	150	282	205	458	517	464	382	153	415	499	585

[a] No significant regression coefficient to this dependent variable from the independent variable. Other regression coefficients for this dependent variable are those from re-computations following the elimination of that particular independent variable from the set of regressors. See Chapter 2 for full discussion of this procedure.

Name Index

Acker, Joan, 70
Adelson, Joseph, 23, 247
Alexander, Karl, vii, 13, 25, 29–30, 42,
    68, 82, 174, 184, 188, 193–96, 201,
    203, 210, 212–14, 223–24, 226–27,
    229, 231, 246, 263–64
Alwin, Duane, vii, 256–57, 263
Anderson, C. Arnold, 113
Astin, Alexander W., 255–56, 263
Averch, Harvey A., 27

Bane, Mary Jo, 27
Bell, Daniel, 260, 264
Blalock, Hubert M., Jr., 60, 70, 113
Blau, Peter, vii, 170, 172, 194, 258, 264
Block, James H., 170
Boocock, Sarane Spence, 13, 29, 150, 170
Bordua, David, 69
Borgatta, Edgar F., 70, 113
Boudon, Raymond, viii, 258, 264
Bowles, Samuel, vii, 16, 19–20, 28, 30, 69,
    133, 147, 153–54, 170–72, 195, 263
Boyle, Richard P., 13, 29, 152, 164,
    170–71
Busch, Georg, 226, 259, 264

Carnoy, Martin, vii, 6, 18, 20, 28, 30, 133,
    141, 147, 155, 170, 195, 201–2, 227,
    263
Carter, Michael, vii
Charner, Ivan, ix
Cicourel, Aaron V., 13–14, 29–30, 75,
    113, 147
Clark, Kenneth B., 6, 28
Cohen, Michael, ix
Coleman, James, 80, 152, 165, 196
Conklin, Mary C., viii

Daniels, J., 246
Douglas, J. W. B., 80
Douvan, Elizabeth, 234, 247
Duncan, Beverly, 28, 194, 258, 264
Duncan, Otis Dudley, vii, 5, 10, 28, 70,
    170, 172

Eckland, Bruce K., vii, 13, 25, 29–30, 42,
    68, 82, 174, 184, 188, 193–96, 203,
    210, 212–14, 223–24, 226–27, 229,
    231, 246, 263–64
Eisenstadt, S. N., 90, 114
Erickson, Eric H., 113

Featherman, David L., vii, 28, 258,
    263–64
Fishel, Andrew, 247
Floud, Jean, 113
Frankel, Martin M., 247
Fuchs, Victor R., 246

Galtung, Johan, 27, 197, 225
Gass, J. R., 262
Gaumer, Judy, ix
Gillespie, Dair L., 246
Gintis, Herbert, vii, 17, 28, 30, 69, 150,
    170–71
Goffman, Erving, 114, 147
Goldberger, Arthur S., 67, 70
Goslin, David A., 5, 8, 10, 13–14, 28–30,
    154, 170
Granovetter, Mark, 50, 70, 194
Guilford, J. P., 69

Haller, Archibald O., vii, 195
Halsey, A. H., 113
Hargreaves, David H., 159, 161, 171

331

Subject Index

Academic achievement
  class bias in, 20
  college entry and, 219–21
  curriculum location and, 160–62
  defined, 49
  early educational expectations and, 148
  educational ambition and, 13
  educational decision and, 174–78,
    188–92
  income and, 152
  measurement of, 25
  meritocratic thesis and, 11, 21
  motivational component of, 11
  normative nature of, 151
  occupational achievement and, 152
  parent's influence and, 160–61
  peer influence and, 161
  revisionist thesis and, 17, 21
  scholastic ability and, 11, 19–20, 148
  sex differences in, 233
  social equity and, 153–54
  social class and, 19, 148, 165
  structure of, 150–51, 165
  teacher bias and, 252
  time-bound nature of, 151
Academic excellence, reward allocation
  and, 153
Academic performance. *See* Academic
  achievement
Academic success, contingencies of, 151
Affective learning, 15, 17–18
Ambition and schooling, 12–13. *See also*
  Educational ambition
Ascribed characteristics, success and, 154

Bivariate relationships, limitations of, 158
Blue-collar workers. *See* Working class
Bourgeoisie, urban, 155

Canadian high school youth, 105, 184
Capitalism and college access, 201–2
Capitalist society and school functions,
  155
Causal effects, definition of, 62
Causal model(ing), 23, 52–67
Class, social. *See* Social class
Cognitive ability. *See* Scholastic ability
College, decision to enter as symbol of
  ambition, 12
College enrollment as symbol of success of
  the high school, 12–13
College entry as proxy for educational
  attainment, 253
  curriculum location and, 213, 223
  educational decision and, 172–73
  interpersonal influence and, 203–9, 223
  merit criteria for, 199, 224
  sex differences in, 235, 244
  social class and, 199, 201, 224
Counselor educational advice
  academic achievement and, 161–62,
    164–65
  college entry and, 203–9
  curriculum location and, 132–33, 138
  definition of, 47, 49–50
  differential effects by sex, 238–39
  educational ambition and, 140–41
  educational decision and, 174–82
  intensifier of sex differences, 243
  location in causal model, 118, 134–38
  meritocratic thesis and, 21, 133–34
  revisionist thesis and, 17, 21, 133
  scholastic ability and, 141–43
  social class and, 17, 132–34, 143, 182
  tenth grade, 24–25, 144–54, 184, 208,
    251
  twelfth grade, 208–9

333